PROSECUTION

The Decision to Charge a Suspect with a Crime

PROSECUTION

The Decision to Charge a Suspect with a Crime

BY

FRANK W. MILLER

The Report of the American Bar Foundation's Survey of the Administration of Criminal Justice in the United States

* *

FRANK J. REMINGTON
Editor

LITTLE, BROWN AND COMPANY
BOSTON 1969 TORONTO

LIBRARY OF CONGRESS CATALOG CARD NO. 79-87781

SECOND PRINTING
(FIRST PAPERBACK PRINTING, 1974)

Published simultaneously in Canada
by Little, Brown & Company (Canada) Limited

PRINTED IN THE UNITED STATES OF AMERICA

WARD H. LEVI; WHITNEY NORTH SEYMOUR; ARTHUR H. SHERRY; JAMES V. BENNETT, *Special Adviser*

FORMER MEMBERS

ROBERT H. JACKSON (1953-1954), *Chairman*; WILLIAM J. DONOVAN (1954-1957), *Chairman*; GORDON DEAN (1953-1954); EDGAR N. EISENHOWER (1953-1954); JOHN D. M. HAMILTON (1959-1964); ALBERT J. HARNO (1955-1965); THEODORE KIENDL (1953-1954); WARREN OLNEY III (1953-1959); BOLITHA J. LAWS (1954-1958); HAROLD A. SMITH (1957-1965), *Chairman*; FLOYD E. THOMPSON (1954-1955); G. AARON YOUNGQUIST (1954-1955); EARL WARREN, *Adviser*

PROJECT STAFF

FRANK J. REMINGTON, *Director*
HARRY V. BALL
ROBERT O. DAWSON
WAYNE R. LAFAVE
DONALD M. MCINTYRE
FRANK W. MILLER
DONALD J. NEWMAN
DANIEL L. ROTENBERG
LAWRENCE P. TIFFANY

PILOT PROJECT STAFF

ARTHUR H. SHERRY, *Project Director*
JOHN A. PETTIS, JR., *Assistant Project Director*
FRANK J. REMINGTON, *Director of Field Research*
SANFORD BATES, *Consultant on Sentencing, Probation, and Parole*
EDMUND F. DEVINE, *Special Consultant*
FRED E. INBAU, *Consultant on Prosecution and Defense*
BENJAMIN A. MATTHEWS, *Consultant on Courts*
LLOYD E. OHLIN, *Consultant on Field Research*
O. W. WILSON, *Consultant on Police*

FIELD REPRESENTATIVES AND RESEARCH ASSOCIATES

ROBERT W. CASSIDY
HERMAN GOLDSTEIN
FRANK J. HODGES
WILLIAM L. HUNGATE
DONALD M. MCINTYRE
ROY C. MCLAREN
BRUCE T. OLSON
DONNELL M. PAPPENFORT
ARTHUR W. SCHUMACHER
LOUIS P. TRENT
JAMES D. TURNER
JOHN WARNER

DEDICATION

Dedicated to Walter P. Armstrong, Jr., who in 1952 as Chairman of the American Bar Association Commission on Organized Crime in Interstate Commerce, was largely responsible for the initiation of the present study of criminal justice administration. In addition, his service on the Project Advisory Committee for this study, first as Secretary and now as Chairman, makes clear his lifelong devotion to the improvement of the criminal law process through research.

> The interdisciplinary fact-finding approach represents a significant departure from traditional legal research. In the past, judging from most of the legal writing in the field lawyers have been more preoccupied with principles and precedent and with the facts of individual, isolated cases than with empirical analysis. However, it is abundantly clear that improvements cannot be based on legal concepts and case-by-case analysis alone. Account must also be taken of the viewpoints and needs of the police, correctional agencies and other nonlawyer functionaries and of the flow of cases through the system as a whole.

WALTER P. ARMSTRONG, JR.
Administration of Criminal
Justice: The American Bar
Foundation Project, 54 *American
Bar Association Journal* 261 (1968)

PREFACE

No one writes a book without encouragement. Nor does one do so without concrete help. Sometimes the encouragement and help take the form of simple expressions of confidence, and I have had those. Geoffrey Hazard and his predecessor administrators at the American Bar Foundation, and Dean Hiram H. Lesar of the Washington University School of Law, have all made clear their confidence and support in both tangible and intangible ways, and I am grateful to them.

No one who has had the pleasure of working with Professor Frank J. Remington, the general editor of this series, can fail to be affected by his incisive mind and great patience, by his imagination and his uncanny ability to get to the guts of a problem. I know that his influence on me has been great, and I am grateful to him.

But there is a special group of four former students to whom my obligations are exceptionally numerous. Each of them served as my research assistant early in his legal career, but each of them became much more as time passed. Each contributed far more than research memoranda on which this book is in part based. They reacted to my ideas, helpfully and critically. They, themselves, supplied ideas which are present in this book in a form little different from that in which they were presented to me. Had publication occurred sooner and in a slightly different form, it would not have been inappropriate to have called them collaborators or junior authors. They are now too mature, too far up the professional ladder for that any longer to be suitable. But my debt to Robert O. Dawson, James A. McCord, Kay Ellen Thurman, and Lawrence P. Tiffany will never be fully discharged. I like it that way and I hope they do too.

Publication of this volume by the American Bar Foundation signifies that the work is regarded as valuable and responsible. The analyses, conclusions, and opinions expressed are the author's and not those of the Foundation, its officers and directors, or others associated with its work.

SUMMARY OF CONTENTS

PART IV

TABLE OF CONTENTS

PART III

CHAPTER 7

PART IV

CHAPTER 8

CHAPTER 9

CHAPTER 10

CHAPTER 11

CHAPTER 12

CHAPTER 13

CHAPTER 14

CHAPTER 15

CHAPTER 16

CHAPTER 17

CHAPTER 18

CHAPTER 19

PROSECUTION

The Decision to Charge a Suspect with a Crime

INTRODUCTION

Charging in Current Criminal Justice Administration

How, why, and by whom the decision is made to charge a person with the commission of a crime is the concern of this volume. Necessarily included in an affirmative decision is the choice of charges; necessarily included in a negative decision is the further determination whether to release the suspect fully or to subject him to procedures which do not form part of the formal criminal justice administration system. Collectively, the decision to charge involves many of the same considerations that are important in making arrest and conviction decisions. For example, all three decisions require a judgment whether there is sufficient probability of guilt to justify subjecting the suspect to further stages in the criminal process and whether it would be in the community interest to do so. Despite these similarities, however, there are important differences as well. That responsibility for each decision is allocated to a separate agency brings different considerations into play at various stages in the process.

The charging decision has obviously serious implications for the individual involved. Not only does a decision to charge represent an affirmation of the need to condition the personal freedom of the accused on his ability to provide bail, it is also the decision that the accused should bear the economic and social costs of a trial. That he may avoid some of these costs by pleading guilty only enhances the impact of the decision. On the economic side, loss of earnings and the cost of preparing a defense may be considerable. On the social side, temporary loss of prestige and position are certain, and permanent damage to reputation not unlikely.

The decision to charge requires the resolution of three related, but independently important, issues:

1. There must be a determination of whether there is a sufficient probability of guilt to justify subjecting the suspect to a trial. Typically expressed in terms of the requirement that there be "probable cause" to believe the suspect guilty, a relatively detailed legal norm has been established with concomitantly detailed sanctions to enforce it. Furthermore, a judgment must be made whether a jury will be likely to acquit either (a) because they are unlikely to be convinced of the guilt of the suspect, or (b) because they will choose to exercise their power to acquit for reasons unrelated to the likelihood of guilt.

2. The prosecutor may conclude that prosecution is not in the community interest. In that event he must choose between release and pursuing some alternative other than criminal prosecution.

3. Finally, if a decision is made to prosecute, the specific crime or crimes with which the person is to be charged must be selected. This may be influenced by considerations of sentencing probabilities, ability to secure guilty pleas, and the prosecutor's conclusion about both the individual's and the community's interests.

IS THERE SUFFICIENT PROBABILITY OF GUILT TO WARRANT SUBJECTING THE PERSON TO A TRIAL?

Uncertainty about whether a suspect is guilty or innocent may be due to a lack of information about what in fact happened, or whether the suspect is the one who did the acts constituting the crime. On the other hand, it may be due to some ambiguity in the substantive law itself, or at least in the understanding of its meaning by one of the criminal law enforcement agencies.

The formal norm for insuring that innocent suspects do not become defendants is stated in substantially the same way as the formal norm for insuring that innocent persons are not arrested. In general, an arrest should not occur, nor should a formal charge be made, unless there is probable cause to believe that the suspected person has committed a crime. To what extent the specific delineation of these norms differs in the two situations is one of the questions under examination in this study.

Derived from the common law, some of the details of this norm have been filled out by the appellate judiciary in false imprisonment and malicious prosecution actions.

The first formal manifestation of the decision to charge is a complaint. In the states under consideration here, the complaint is followed by a warrant. The warrant should be issued only if there is probable cause to believe the person guilty of the crime set out in the complaint. Who decides whether a warrant should be issued receives a different statutory answer in each of the three states studied. In Michigan no warrant may be issued unless a finding of probable cause is concurred in by both the prosecutor and the magistrate. In Kansas the magistrate alone has authority to issue a warrant, and there is no formal requirement of concurrence by the prosecutor. In Wisconsin, at the time of the study, authority to issue a warrant could be exercised either by the prosecutor or by the magistrate, in each case without the concurrence of the other, although under current Wisconsin law, a prosecutor may not issue a warrant.

For serious offenses there is provision for judicial review of the initial decision to charge. The defendant is entitled to a preliminary examination at which the prosecution must present sufficient evidence to persuade the magistrate that there is probable cause to believe the defendant guilty of a crime. The accused may confront and cross-examine the state's witnesses and may call witnesses of his own.

There are other methods of review available in serious and less serious cases alike. An improper application of the probable cause norm in the charging process may result in acquittal or other discharge of the defendant later on and may, under some circumstances, give rise to tort liability.

ASSUMING SUFFICIENT PROBABILITY OF GUILT, SHOULD PROSECUTION NONETHELESS NOT FOLLOW?

The process of selecting which of the guilty are to be charged is perhaps the most important part of the decision to charge. Certainly it is the aspect of the problem about which least is known. The early crime surveys, by emphasizing "drop out points" and "drop out percentages," demonstrated statistically that factors other than probability of guilt influenced the decision to charge, but because of their nearly exclusive focus on system efficiency, they afforded inadequate insight into the basis for the decision not to prosecute.

That formal norms designed to guide the prosecutor in determining which of the guilty to charge can rarely be found either in statutes or in appellate judicial decisions leads to one of two tentative conclusions. Either it is assumed that all guilty persons will be charged, or it is assumed that selection will occur but that responsibility for making the selection resides in the nearly uncontrolled discretion of the prosecutor, except such control as inheres in the fact that the prosecutor is typically an elected official and thus responsive to community opinion.

It is common knowledge that not all guilty persons are, and

common belief that not all guilty persons should be, prosecuted for the crime they have committed. There are obvious reasons for this. An important one is that limits on our ability to formulate elaborate enough distinctions between offenses leads to identical rules for dissimilar offenders. To the extent that dissimilarities between offenders have significance from an ethical and moral, as well as from a practical and administrative, point of view, they lend an idealistic basis for the selection process.

Moreover, it is true that the underlying reason for a particular criminal statute can be found by asking what social objective the criminal sanction was intended to facilitate. For example, the non-support and desertion laws are designed not only to permit application of their sanctions to violators, they are also designed to compel heads of families to support their families. If some means short of charging accomplishes the same objective, for example, an advisory discussion with the prosecutor, resulting in the violator's agreement to support, it might be preferable not to use the stronger sanction. The same may be said of bad checks or certain other wrongful appropriation of property situations. If the objective of protecting individual property interests can be accomplished in a particular case by return of the property, perhaps that should end the matter. Again, if in assault situations of a not too serious nature, the assumption is made that the purpose is to protect against non-consensual interference with the person, it may be sound to say that uncoerced forgiveness by the victim ought to stop the criminal law machinery short of charging.

The assumption that it is possible to identify the guilty, and, in each case, to convince adjudicatory bodies of that guilt, is often true but sometimes it is not. The effect of evidentiary rules resulting in the exclusion of evidence for reasons not reflecting its inherent trustworthiness, and the knowledge that certain laws are so unpopular as to make conviction highly unlikely regardless of the state of the proof are illustrations of the distinction between a sound conclusion by the prosecutor that a suspect is guilty, and his ability necessarily to convince the trier of fact that it should concur in that conclusion. These are factors which do not relate directly to the fact of guilt or innocence, but they are factors which necessarily influence the selection among the guilty of who is to be charged.

A final and compelling reason for current practice is that the system could not be maintained without an increase of great magnitude in the number of personnel and the amount of money available if, in fact, all known perpetrators of crimes were charged.

SELECTION OF THE CRIME OR CRIMES FOR WHICH THE PERSON IS TO BE PROSECUTED

A single course of conduct may violate a large number of criminal statutes. Sometimes, this is because the same conduct has been declared criminal in more than one statute. Frequently, less serious crimes are integral parts of more serious crimes: for example, the crime of robbery cannot be committed without also committing the crime of larceny. When these situations occur, prosecutors select what seems to them to be the most appropriate single offense to charge.

Suspects frequently are apprehended who have committed a number of clearly separate criminal offenses, such as burglaries or forgeries. Again, prosecutors regularly charge fewer than all offenses that can be proved. Finally, often a suspect is charged who has previously been convicted and who is, therefore, liable for enhanced sentence under habitual offender laws. Not uncommonly, prosecutors decide not to make use of those laws.

Clearly, the perceived necessity for plea bargaining as a means of resource conservation explains many instances in which prosecutors have opted ultimately for the less serious charge, the lesser number of charges, or for noninvocation of habitual offender statutes. But in some instances, a sentence bargain would serve the purpose of inducing a guilty plea without recourse to charge bargaining, and, in any event, a prosecutor who contemplates a negotiation, leading to a plea of guilty, whether in return for a reduced charge or a reduced sentence, is not likely to make his *initial* charge less than he believes appropriate. Consequently, the selection of less than the most serious charge or less than the maximum number of charges at the complaint-warrant level must reflect something other than plea bargaining. And it does.

The factors reflected fall into two general classes: a desire to preserve resources, and a desire to avoid undue harm to the suspect. Resources are saved if the sentence ultimately imposed would be the same under either the more serious or the less serious charge and if conviction of the less serious offense involves a lesser expenditure of the time and efforts of the front-line enforcement agencies. Charging an offense whose label carries less social stigma than, for instance, "contributing to the delinquency of a minor," may be considered appropriate if the defendant is a man of repute in the community who is unlikely to present any serious further risk.

Even though there are limits on the precision and accuracy with which we can define the norms for selection in advance, the necessity for a selection process ought not to lead to the conclusion that the problem can be dismissed with the explanation that what is involved is the "prosecutor's discretion." Concern with such an approach has been expressed by Professor Wechsler in a statement relevant here:

> A society that holds, as we do, to belief in law cannot regard with unconcern the fact that prosecuting agencies can exercise so large an influence on dispositions that involve the penal sanction, without reference to any norms but those that they may create for themselves. Whatever one would hold as to the need for discretion of this order in a proper system or the wisdom of attempting regulation of its exercise, it is quite clear that its existence cannot be accepted as a substitute for a sufficient law. Indeed, one of the major consequences of the state of penal law today is that administration has so largely come to dominate the field without effective guidance from the law. This is to say that to a large extent we have, in this important sense, abandoned law — and this within an area where our fundamental teaching calls most strongly for its vigorous supremacy.[1]

The purpose of this volume, then, is to extract from the information available for the three jurisdictions investigated the answers to the following questions: (a) with whom does the prosecutor share responsibility for making the charging decision; (b) what criteria are used in fact; (c) have formal norms been stated to guide or control the decision; (d) are sanctions — either legal or informal — available to insure proper application of those norms?

1 Wechsler, The Challenge of a Model Penal Code, 65 Harv. L. Rev. 1097, 1102 (1952).

PART I

Responsibility for the Decision to Charge—Involvement of the Prosecutor

None of the surveys, however, searchingly faced, either in the gathering of fact data or in the discussion, this problem of whose function it should be to determine the instituting of prosecution and what should be the working methods and principles which govern its administration. Should the clerk of a court be the official in whom this function is placed, and using clerical methods, or the prosecuting attorney using methods appropriate to that office, or the magistrate using methods of a judicial nature?

BETTMAN, Criminal Justice Surveys Analysis in *Report on Prosecution,* No. 6, p. 88 of National Commission on Law Enforcement (1931).

The situation in Cook County is much different. Here the state's attorney is in the relatively unusual position of having, as a practical matter in most criminal cases, virtually no discretion in who is to be charged or what charge is to be filed.

OAKS and LEHMAN, The Criminal Process of Cook County and the Indigent Defendant, 1966 *University of Illinois Law Forum* 584, 608.

A problem of central significance in current criminal justice administration is who should have responsibility for making the initial charging decision. Professors Oaks and Lehman have described a practice in Cook County, Illinois, which leaves the initial decision in the hands of the police, a choice which closely resembles the traditional English practice. For the most part in this country, the decision rests with the prosecutor, a practice endorsed by the American Law Institute.[1] In behalf of the latter position it may be said that both fairness to the individual and system efficiency dictate that suspects who are either not convictable or whose conviction would not be in the community interest should be eliminated as quickly as possible; that the prosecutor whose responsibility it is to try cases or to seek pleas of guilty in appropriate cases is in the best position to make the former judgment, and that as an elected official, presumably more responsive to community attitudes, he is in a better position to make the latter decision as well. The principal counter-argument is that the prosecutor's office has been traditionally a stepping stone to higher office, at worst subject to misuse for political purposes or, more subtly, to assure a conviction record. Particularly in the case of decisions not to charge, greater visibility and presumably greater accountability result when cases are eliminated as the result of an appearance in open court.

Whatever the merits of that controversy, they have largely been obscured by statements which confuse the issue of who should bear responsibility for the decision with the issue of what methods should be used to make that decision. This has led to a preoccupation with form and a disregard of substance, such as whether a warrant or a complaint should serve as the charging document. That same preoccupation with form characterizes the practices described in Part I of this volume.

[1] American Law Institute, Model Code of Pre-Arraignment Procedure §602 and Comment (Tent. Draft No. 1, 1966).

CHAPTER 1

The Charging Process

The decision to charge, unlike the decision to arrest, is not a unitary decision made at a readily identifiable time by a specified individual. It is, instead, a process consisting of a series of interrelated decisions, and the steps in the process do not always occur in the same sequence. Most often the decision is made after a suspect has already been taken into custody. In some instances, the effective decision is made when the police decide not to ask the prosecutor to charge, but to release a suspect instead. Of greater significance are the decisions made by prosecutors, acting through their assistants, whether to charge suspects already in custody, in response to requests made by the police that they do so.

In Kansas, Michigan, and Wisconsin, the charging decision is evidenced by the issuance of a warrant in response to a complaint which seeks one. Despite the fact that most arrests are accomplished without a warrant, in practice the warrant is invariably issued if a subsequent decision to prosecute the suspect is made. Since the warrant is primarily conceived in law as an arrest-authorizing document,[1] the reasons for this practice are not immediately apparent. In most jurisdictions offenses triable by a justice of the peace may be tried, and a preliminary examination for serious offenses may be held, on a complaint alone.[2] There would seem to be no insurmountable reason why

[1] See, e.g., Draper v. United States, 358 U.S. 307, 314-325, 79 Sup. Ct. 329, 333-339, 3 L. Ed. 2d 327, 333-339 (1959) (dissent of Douglas, J.); Giordenello v. United States, 357 U.S. 480, 78 Sup. Ct. 1245, 2 L. Ed. 2d 1503 (1958).

[2] See, e.g., Ringer v. Municipal Court, 175 Cal. App. 2d 786, 346 P.2d 881 (1959); State ex rel. Schwanke v. Utecht, 233 Minn. 434, 47 N.W.2d 99 (1951); Nelson v. State, 115 Neb. 26, 211 N.W. 175 (1926); State v. Barreras, 64 N.M. 300, 328 P.2d 74 (1958); People v. Markowitz, 119 App. Div. 841, 104 N.Y.S. 872 (1907), *aff'd mem.*, 189 N.Y. 562, 82 N.E. 1130 (1907); Commonwealth ex rel. Di Dio v. Baldi, 176 Pa. Super. 119, 106 A.2d 910 (1954); State v. Ryan, 48 Wash. 2d 304, 293 P.2d 399 (1956); Pillsbury v. State, 31 Wis. 2d 87, 142 N.W.2d 187 (1966).

this could not be done everywhere.[3] The first point of inquiry, then, is the reasons for the practice.

Some officials charged with responsibility for administering the criminal law believe that the law requires that a warrant be issued even after a valid arrest without one. Other officials are simply uncertain. Of those who are certain that the warrant is required, some have no explanation; others give reasons ranging from statutory necessity[4] to custom,[5] including, in a few instances, justification of continued custody.[6] Yet all of them believe that whatever the necessity in law, in practice the warrant is the initial charging document in serious cases, and the only one used to charge minor offenses.

The need in law for a post-arrest warrant is far from clear, apart from circumstances in which it serves the purpose of justifying continuation of detention. One reason, and perhaps the most logical one, would be to provide an occasion for an early judicial determination that probable cause exists to condition the freedom of the defendant on his ability to provide bail. In none of the states studied was there any indication that a considered decision about probable cause was made by a judicial official at this stage. Other states which have considered the question of its necessity have nearly uniformly assumed that the complaint is the only necessary initial charging document.[7] Among the three states considered in detail here, only in Michigan have statutes been interpreted as requiring the use of the post-arrest warrant as a charging document.[8]

3 See Frisbie v. Collins, 342 U.S. 519 (1952).

4 For example, it might be argued that administration of the statute of limitations requires warrant issuance. See Model Penal Code §1.07, Comment (Tent. Draft No. 5, 1956). The same result might follow when a court construes statutes concerning warrants with reference to considerations of notifying an accused of the charges against him. See Town of Honea Path v. Wright, 194 S.C. 461, 9 S.E.2d 924 (1940).

5 See, e.g., People v. Losinger, 331 Mich. 490, 50 N.W.2d 137 (1951), *cert. denied,* 343 U.S. 911 (1952); Mooradian v. Davis, 302 Mich. 484, 5 N.W.2d 435 (1942) (recognizing uniform practice in Michigan of issuing post-arrest warrants).

6 See State v. Hollen, 22 Kan. 580, 584 (1879); State v. Beebe, 13 Kan. 589 (1874); State ex rel. City of Milwaukee v. Newman, 96 Wis. 258, 71 N.W. 438 (1897); but see City of Topeka v. Durein, 78 Kan. 661, 97 Pac. 967 (1908). And a 1949 statutory amendment derogates from the implication in the Wisconsin case that warrants are necessary: Wis. Laws 1949 c. 631 §181; Wis. Stat. Ann. §960.09 (1958) (defendant pleads to warrant or complaint).

7 See cases cited notes 2 and 3 *supra.*

8 A warrant is clearly required for offenses cognizable before a justice of the peace. People v. Lynch, 29 Mich. 274, 281 (1874) (dictum); see Sheldon v. Hill, 33 Mich. 171 (1876); Drennan v. People, 10 Mich. 169, 185 (1862). Its necessity in cases not cognizable by a justice of the peace is only indirectly supported. Mich.

It would be inaccurate, however, to assert that the issuance of a warrant inevitably reflects a decision to charge, for sometimes the decision to issue a warrant is made about suspects who are not yet in custody. When that happens the warrant clearly serves its traditional arrest-authorizing function, but it may or may not serve a charging function as well. Sometimes there is thought to be a need to secure custody under a warrant process before it is appropriate to decide whether to charge a suspect. When that happens, the warrant decision is not a charging decision. It

---

Stat. Ann. §28.1195 (1954) provides that no justice of the peace may issue warrants in any criminal case (with some minor exceptions not pertinent here) without the prior written approval of the prosecuting attorney. Although the two cases construing this section involve minor offenses, there is no reason to believe that the considerations underlying them would not also be applicable when the offense is not one cognizable by a justice of the peace. People v. Griswold, 64 Mich. 722, 31 N.W. 809 (1887) held that noncompliance with the statutory requirement did not deprive a justice of jurisdiction, but indicated that the policy was to assure that justices would inquire carefully into the circumstances of each case before initiating the criminal process. People v. Holbrook, 373 Mich. 94, 128 N.W.2d 484 (1964) specifically overruled Griswold on the jurisdictional point. Presumably, then, jurisdiction is now predicted on the issuance of a warrant agreed upon by prosecutor and justice in all criminal cases not covered by the minor exceptions set out in the statute. It has been argued that People v. Carter, 379 Mich. 24, 148 N.W.2d 860 (1967) implies a vacation of Holbrook and a return to Griswold on the jurisdictional points. This argument appears in the separate opinions of concurring judges in Carter — judges who had dissented in Holbrook — but the statement of the argument indicates that the majority judges in Carter did not agree that this was the import of the case. See also, Wheaton v. Beecher, 49 Mich. 348, 354, 13 N.W. 769, 771 (1882) (dissenting opinion).

A period of confusion at the trial court level occurred in Wisconsin subsequent to the field studies. The Wisconsin Supreme Court in State ex rel. White v. Simpson, 28 Wis. 2d 590, 137 N.W.2d 391 (1965) held that warrants authorizing arrests (or searches) could only be issued by a magistrate, not by a prosecutor as authorized by Wisconsin statutes. The Simpson decision was, of course, based on the constitutional requirements stated in Giordenello v. United States, 357 U.S. 480, 78 Sup. Ct. 1245, 2 L. Ed. 2d 1503 (1958) and Aguilar v. Texas, 378 U.S. 108, 84 Sup. Ct. 1509, 12 L. Ed. 2d 723 (1964). Although the warrant issued in Simpson was a pre-arrest warrant, and although the court expressly excluded any requirement of judicial participation in the issuance of a summons, Wisconsin trial judges in some instances applied the rule to post-arrest warrants which continued to be used, and indeed, in some instances held rather protracted hearings before issuing a post-arrest warrant. The sanction used was dismissal with leave to obtain a proper warrant, no doubt because the usual sanction of excluding evidence is not possible when the arrest and any incidental search are lawful. The whole matter was clarified in Pillsbury v. State, 31 Wis. 2d 87, 142 N.W.2d 187 (1966). The court there made it clear that no warrant need be issued to charge a suspect validly arrested without one, that jurisdiction is predicated on the suspect's appearance before a magistrate after his arrest and not on any particular document. Although the case does not authorize the use of post-arrest warrants issued by prosecutors, it dispenses with the need for post-arrest warrants and invites the use of a procedure common in other jurisdictions of treating the complaint as the charging document.

represents only an arrest decision, with the charging decision reserved until some later point in time. Most often, that later point in time cannot be established by reference to some clearly identifiable generic document.

On other occasions, a warrant issued prior to arrest represents both the arrest and the charging decisions: indeed, in such instances the two theoretically isolable decisions are telescoped into one. In some cases of less seriousness, there is no separate charging decision, since all persons arrested for certain offenses — with or without a warrant — are automatically charged. In those instances, too, the arrest and charging decisions may be characterized as a single decision.

Even when the prosecutor has concluded initially that prosecution is justified by the evidence and is in the community interest, that decision may later be changed. In some instances, the prosecutor changes his mind in the light of new facts brought to his attention. When this occurs, he terminates the prosecution by dismissing the warrant, or, if an information has already been filed, by entering a formal order dismissing the information.[9] The latter order is known as a nolle prosequi. In some instances, and at some stages of the process, he may dismiss the proceeding on his own initiative; in other jurisdictions, and particularly after an information has been filed, he may need the consent of the trial judge. But that consent, when required by law, is rarely withheld.

In still other instances, when the offense is a serious one and the suspect has insisted on his right to a preliminary examination, a magistrate may refuse to permit a prosecutor to file an information because he regards the evidence as insufficient to justify proceeding further.[10]

Even taking into account the congeries of exceptions and variations in the charging process, what emerges as the central conclusion is that the heart of the charging process is the decision to file a complaint and seek a warrant — conceived in law both historically and currently as a document issued by a judicial officer in response to a complaint and authorizing an arrest, but treated in current administration as a document most often issued after an arrest and representing, in a perfunctory sense, judicial approval of the decision to charge.

9 The law relating to dismissal of charges and practices of prosecutors and judges pertaining thereto are discussed in Chapter 20 *infra*.

10 Law and practice are discussed in Chapter 7 *infra*.

Although the law permits them to prevent charging by refusing to issue arrest warrants, magistrates rarely exercise that control.[11] The process may, therefore, be accurately conceived as one of self-limitation. Reasons are obvious why a prosecutor would find a situation intolerable in which a substantial number of persons were charged who later proved unconvictable. Not only would the ends of justice be disserved and limited resources dissipated to the detriment of efficient societal protection, but also the record of the prosecutor by which the public judges him — his success in obtaining convictions — would suffer.

These factors alone would provide an adequate incentive for establishing administrative controls to insure that his assistants, to whom are entrusted the daily routine decisions of the office, would charge only suspects against whom the evidence of guilt was clearly adequate to practically guarantee conviction. When this consideration is coupled with a desire to treat suspects uniformly — both to further widely held values of fairness and equality and to escape criticism for doing otherwise — a search for devices to insure that suspects are not charged on inadequate evidence is nearly inevitable.[12]

Three principal methods might be utilized to accomplish these ends. The most obvious one would be as complete as possible an examination and evaluation of evidence available at the time the charging decision must be made. A second would be the establishment of intra-office review procedures, and a third the development of specialists within the office or reliance on specialists in other departments.[13]

A. Investigation of Available Evidence

As a general proposition, a detailed consideration of the available evidence itself would be more likely to result in an accurate evaluation of its adequacy than would reliance on a police officer's oral or written summary of it. Perhaps in the interest of time

11 See Chapter 3 *infra*.

12 Obviously, other factors tend toward the same conclusion. Uniformity of treatment remains a desirable goal when considerations other than evidence sufficiency come into play, and procedures which assure that sensitive cases get full consideration are important to the politically minded prosecutor.

13 In practice the prosecutor sometimes takes advantage of specialization in other departments, e.g., police or welfare, but when that occurs reliance on the specialist is commonly so complete that there is no longer any decision by the prosecutor whether to charge, since the advice of the specialist is followed automatically.

preservation, a detailed consideration is not customary in any of the jurisdictions studied. In each of them, the source of information most often relied on is the police officer and his report or summary of the case that he brings with him when he requests a warrant. Occasionally witnesses or the suspect or the victim are also interviewed, but there is no readily discernible pattern. Indeed, it depends at least partially on whether the requesting police officer brings them with him, or whether the request is made by a private complainant rather than the police.[14] In some cases, but by no means routinely, reports of medical examiners, results of polygraph tests, physical evidence either of the crime or the condition of the victim are examined.[15] And occasionally, defense attorneys are permitted to present arguments about the sufficiency of the evidence and even to call the attention of the prosecutor to additional evidence.[16] It remains true, however, that in the usual case, maximum efforts to scrutinize each piece of evidence carefully are not made. Inevitably this must mean that screening on evidence-sufficiency grounds is not so complete as it might be.

B. Intra-Office Review Procedures

A quite highly regularized system of intra-office review was established in the Wayne County (Michigan) prosecutor's office, largely because of dissatisfaction over practices which had developed in the absence of such a system. Police officers, familiar — at least as they saw it — with the individual characteristics and reaction patterns of various assistants in that office, "shopped around" for the particular assistant who, they believed, would regard their requests for warrants most sympathetically.[17] To

14 In some cases, the police do not receive notice of the case until after the prosecutor's office has received the complaint. Primarily this occurs simply because the complainant decided to take that course of action rather than the more usual one of notifying the police first. When this occurs, it is obvious that the prosecutor will interview the complainant, even if a decision is not made at the time whether to charge, but the case is referred to the police. Often, in this type of case, the complainant will also bring witnesses to the prosecutor's office, and they will then also be interviewed.

15 Also commonly relied on is the prior record of the suspect, but in theory at least this would relate more directly to the general desirability of prosecution than to the sufficiency of evidence to warrant it.

16 The evidence which is perhaps adverted to most commonly by defense attorneys is the good character of the accused and his reputation in his neighborhood and on his job.

17 Several assistants in that office have attributed the initiation of this system to a period in the 1930's when the practice of "shopping around" was prevalent.

insure uniformity in charging both in its evidence-sufficiency and policy aspects, as well as to alert more experienced personnel to sensitive problem areas due to unusual community interest or political connotations, the prosecutor requires that the initial decisions of junior assistants be reviewed by one of two experienced senior assistants.[18] Although recommendations of warrants for felonies are thus normally reviewed,[19] review of recommendations for misdemeanor warrants is far from uniform. This is partly the result of misunderstanding among the assistants, and partly it reflects the fact that some misdemeanors are regarded as more important than others.[20] Whether denials of recommendations are similarly subject to review is also a matter of

---

Under the old system, all that was necessary to have a warrant typed up in the warrant clerk's office was a recommendation from one assistant prosecutor.

[18] At first the chief assistant prosecutor handled this review function, then one or two of the more experienced assistants were delegated that job, and today the bulk of such work is carried on by two men who are experienced prosecutors. Since there is generally no scheme for allocation of the review in any particular type of case to one or the other of the senior assistants, a very limited type of shopping is still possible on the review level. However, this was not observed in the actual functioning of the procedure.

[19] A general class of cases excepted from the review procedure is traffic offenses. One of the offices in the prosecutor's complex of offices is denominated "Traffic Warrant Division." A junior assistant is assigned to this office and his duty is to review all traffic cases throughout the county and either recommend or reject the issuance of a warrant. The same procedures are followed which generally prevail in other types of cases with the exception that no screening is done by senior members. This is apparently true whether the traffic offense charge is a felony or a misdemeanor.

[20] While generally the practice has developed that review is not sought in misdemeanor cases, there are discernible groups of cases constituting exceptions to that rule. One of these groups consists of accosting and soliciting cases. One of the two men primarily responsible for review stated that this exception arose in the 1930's as a result of a flood of such cases being sent to Recorder's Court and early sessions court, and that the judges objected because of the number of such cases. He continued, "Now it is up to us to screen these out before they get to court, and as a result of this about half of the accosting and soliciting cases which are brought before us are screened out, not particularly because there is or is not a defense of entrapment or any other defense, but principally because the Recorder's Court does not want to be bothered with this type of case any more than they have to."

A second group of misdemeanors — disputes arising between whites and Negroes — are sent for review despite any clear evidence-sufficiency question. This practice was attributed to the added public pressures caused by the National Association for the Advancement of Colored People. A third group of cases, those composed of sex crimes, which may or may not include misdemeanors, is subject to review. The purpose seems to be twofold: to keep track of sex offenders generally and to allow charges to be dropped against those charged with exposure who seem able to afford private treatment. If these are the only functions of review in this type of case, then it clearly does not serve evidence sufficiency purposes.

Other types of misdemeanors may also be subject to review, but the cases do

some disagreement in the office.[21] The result is that some assistants send the denials for review and others do not. Despite the fact that other goals are served as well, in actual operation the most significant effect of the system is to provide a review of the sufficiency of the evidence to nearly guarantee conviction.[22]

In Wayne County, the police officer seeking a warrant may still select his initial review assistant on any basis he wishes, and he conceivably would do so on the assumption that an initially favorable reaction would carry some weight with the final review assistant. Indeed, to the extent that negative decisions are not reviewed, it would be surprising if police officers did not continue to place importance on selection of the initial review as-

---

not fall into any discernible class other than that the officer seeking the warrant decided to take that course of action. In many of those cases, the police generally know that an offense has been committed but do not know exactly what offense to charge. Apart from these general practices, the senior assistants may get any type of case to review.

21 The predominant opinion of the assistants, both junior and senior, is that there is supposed to be review whether the decision by the junior assistant is affirmative or negative. The two points of view may be seen in the following exchange that took place between two junior assistant prosecutors: "All they [the senior assistants] are interested in is finding out what cases that you approve of. If you deny to recommend the issuance of a warrant, then it must be for some good reason, and they are not particularly interested in knowing what goes on." The other junior assistant disagreed, contending, ". . . when an assistant refuses a warrant recommendation he should send notice of this action to the final review assistants, because the purpose of the final review is to make sure that we are not taking the law into our own hands. It is even more important for those men to check up on the cases which we refuse because they do get to see the ones which we approve which are taken to them." The discrepancy between these two opinions may be attributed to the fact that there is no manual of procedure in the office, but those who contended that review was necessary even in case of a negative decision asserted that review in such cases had been the practice for many years prior to the exchange noted above.

22 The advisability of having such a system has not gone unchallenged by the prosecutors participating in it. A junior assistant strongly objected to the procedure: "Frankly, if I were organizing this office, I would eliminate that function. Most of us have been here as long as these two people who review the case, and although I have held that responsibility myself, I do not approve of it. Some say that two heads are better than one; my own feeling is that two heads are better than one if you do not want to get anything done. It is a little bit of an affront to have your judgment questioned and challenged, and in my own opinion I think this office should be eliminated." While this opinion does not seem to be generally shared by others in the office, some support was given it by another assistant who supposed that if the turnover in the prosecutor's office were less than it is, and "we didn't keep getting young, or comparatively new and inexperienced assistants" it would not be necessary to have this final review operation. The reporter in this office made another observation. He said he had the distinct impression that the assistant prosecutors on the other side of the floor, who originally review these cases, probably overcharge, and the principal function of people like one of the senior assistants is to sort of downgrade the offenses which are charged so that their likelihood of prosecution in court will be greater.

sistant. A similar result would be anticipated in the case of misdemeanors when they are not subject to review.

The same shopping-around practices existed in Milwaukee, but the response there differed from the Wayne County response. In Milwaukee, an investigator has been given the task of assigning police officers who come in with warrant requests to one of the assistant prosecutors. Since reference is made to whichever assistant happens to be free at that time, shopping around is effectively precluded. But there is no regularized review procedure as in Detroit. In Wichita, neither of the above techniques has been used. Police officers are free to select the assistant to whom they make their warrant requests, and the action of the assistant is not subject to any systematic review. Perhaps the much smaller size of the office in Wichita is a reason why the problem is not serious there. Of course, nothing precludes informal nonsystematic consultation among prosecutors in any of the offices.

C. Specialization

Another obvious way to insure charging of only those suspects against whom the evidence is adequate to make the likelihood of conviction extremely high is to leave the determination of charging to those with special knowledge of the proof requirements in particular classes of cases.[23] Specialization among the assistant prosecutors at the charging level is uncommon. Apparently the office in Wichita is completely unspecialized. There are some areas of specialization in Detroit; a single assistant handles all requests for warrants in traffic cases not handled as ordinance violations, and another handles all cases in which a proceeding under the sex psychopath statute is indicated. In addition the Felony Bureau of the prosecutor's office, a group of detectives assigned to the office conduct investigations in areas of white collar crime and make recommendations directly to one of the senior review assistants, thus bypassing the initial review stage. Similarly in Milwaukee, there are some areas of specialization within the prosecutor's office. For example, all cases of obscene literature are referred to a specific assistant, as are cases dealing with narcotics and automobile-financing problems. It is clear, however, that the percentage of cases which fall within any of these categories is relatively small, and that, for the most part, the warrant decision is not made by specialized assistants.

23 Obviously, if a specialist were required to pass on evidence sufficiency in certain classes of cases, shopping around would be impossible in those cases.

PART II

Separation of the Guilty from the Innocent—Evidence Required to Charge

> The first and most basic standard was the assistant's view of the accused's guilt of the crime to be charged. It was generally agreed that, regardless of the strength of the case, if the prosecutor did not actually believe in the guilt of the accused, he had no business prosecuting. . . . The great majority, if not all, of the assistants felt that it was morally wrong to prosecute a man unless one was personally convinced of his guilt.
>
> Assuming, then, as was generally assumed in the office, that the prosecutor believed the prospective defendant to be guilty, the next fundamental question to be asked was whether, in the light of the habits of judges and juries in the area, the case could be expected to result in a conviction. . . . Not only was the staff generally hard pressed to accommodate all of the cases which should have been brought to trial, but the assistants regarded the time and money spent on unsuccessful prosecution as completely wasted.
>
> KAPLAN, The Prosecutorial Discretion—A Comment, 60 *Northwestern University Law Review* 174, 178, 180 (1965).

The traditional legal position is that prosecution should be initiated only when there is reasonable basis for believing that a crime has been committed and that the suspect has committed it—in short the standard is "probable cause." That is the standard embodied in typical instructions to grand juries as well as the one used at the preliminary examination. And when prosecution is initiated by one who enjoys no immunity from a tort action for malicious prosecution, the absence of "probable cause" is a central element of the tort.

It is at least arguable that, whenever that standard is met, the prosecutor should file a complaint; that an honest and reasonable belief in the guilt of the accused should be an adequate basis for forwarding the suspect through the process, leaving further winnowing for the magistrate at the preliminary examination, or, when that institution is used, for the grand jury. Indeed, speaking in a different context, so eminent a jurist as Learned Hand, with the later approval of the Supreme Court of the United States, ruled that evidence not available for trial purposes but otherwise of clear probative value was adequate to support an indictment.[1] Obviously he did not believe it inappropriate to continue a probably guilty suspect in the process even without a preliminary showing that he could be convicted. And no one has suggested that the law should or does require proof beyond a reasonable doubt to justify either the initial or the final charging decisions.

On the other hand is the conclusion reached by Professor Kaplan. In general, a conviction standard obtained during his four years in the office of the United States Attorney for the Northern District of California clearly parallels the findings of the field research teams of the American Bar Foundation on which this study is based. It is not inaccurate to assert that an affirmative initial charging decision usually requires a belief on the part of the prosecutor that the suspect is guilty beyond a reasonable doubt.

Several factors tend to explain the use in practice of a convictability standard. In general, it is regarded as unfair to charge a man who obviously cannot be convicted. Limitations on resources are sufficiently stringent to make prosecutors keenly aware of the need for making the best possible use of them: if a suspect cannot be convicted either by plea or after trial, those resources are likely to be thought of as wasted. Although the research on which this study is based does not support it, Professor Kaplan and other former prosecutors emphasize the prosecutor's interest in a good conviction record.[2]

[1] Costello v. United States, 221 F.2d 668 (2d Cir. 1955), *aff'd*, 350 U.S. 359, 76 Sup. Ct. 406, 100 L. Ed. 397 (1956).

[2] See Seymour, Why Prosecutors Act Like Prosecutors, 11 Record of N.Y.C.B.A. 302, 304 (1956); Worgan and Paulsen, The Position of a Prosecutor in a Criminal Case — A Conversation with a Prosecuting Attorney, Prac. Law. 44, 51 (Nov. 1961).

The most difficult problems posed by the use of a convictability standard have a common thread — they all relate to whether trial rules of evidence should be taken into account in making the initial charging decision. The most dramatic, of course, are those rules which prevent the use of illegally obtained evidence at a trial. The choice not to charge when conviction is made unlikely by the probable application of exclusionary rules not based on trustworthiness may reflect no more than a particular application of the convictability standard: it may, however, also suggest that prosecutors sympathetic to the purpose of those rules have chosen voluntarily to implement them further by applying them when in law they are not required to do so.

But prosecutors also often apply other exclusionary rules, rules closely related to trustworthiness in the context of a jury trial. The typical assistant prosecutor does not ignore the effect of the hearsay rule or the corpus delicti rule requiring some proof, independent of any confession the suspect may have made, that a crime was committed by someone.

Although the data suggests the use of a somewhat lower level of proof when the likelihood of a plea of guilty is greater than usual, or when for a variety of reasons the desirability of a conviction is unusually great, there is no evidence that unconvictables are charged to coerce a guilty plea.

CHAPTER 2

The Warrant Standard

A. Relation to Standards for Arrest and Conviction

There seems to be a general assumption in law that the degree of probability of guilt necessary to subject a suspect to the next stage in the process increases through the various chronological stages.[1] Possibly beginning with the likelihood of guilt needed for field interrogation, certainly with the amount necessary for arrest, and progressing through charging and conviction, there is substantial basis for saying that more evidence is needed at each step.[2] There are, however, certain complexities in the sys-

[1] See generally LaFave, Arrest 300-318 (1965). Law bearing on this point in federal prosecutions is, however, ambiguous. In Mallory v. United States, 354 U.S. 449, 77 Sup. Ct. 1356, 1 L. Ed. 2d 1479 (1957), the Court held that federal officers had not complied with Rule 5(a), Fed. R. Crim. P., which directs them to take arrested suspects before a United States Commissioner for an initial presentment and a judicial determination of probable cause "without unnecessary delay." The suspect in this case had been detained for a period of time without a rule 5(a) appearance so that officers could investigate further. The confession which he gave during that period was held inadmissible in evidence at his subsequent trial. Justice Frankfurter said, "Presumably, whomever the police arrest they must arrest on 'probable cause.' It is not the function of the police to arrest, as it were, at large and to use an interrogating process at police headquarters in order to determine whom they should charge before a committing magistrate on 'probable cause.'" Id. at 456, 77 Sup. Ct. at 1360, 1 L. Ed. 2d at 1484. But see United States v. Vita, 294 F.2d 524, 532-533 (2d Cir. 1961), *cert. denied*, 369 U.S. 823 (1962); Goldsmith v. United States, 277 F.2d 335, 343 (D.C. Cir.), *cert. denied*, 364 U.S. 863 (1960) ("the quantum of evidence necessary to sustain an arrest is not, in all circumstances, the same quantum necessary to make out probable cause for charging a person with the crime").

[2] The states — either by statute or by case law — have generally permitted a delay between arrest and the time the charging decision must be made, during which the police may continue their investigation and accumulate more evidence against the suepect. Presumably the allowance of this period of time in which to investigate rests upon a need to satisfy a charging standard more stringent than the arrest standard. Those statutes and cases are discussed in LaFave, Detention for Investigation by the Police: An Analysis of Current Practices, 1962 Wash. U.L.Q.

tem which make that assumption an oversimplification. The first of these is that charging is recognized as a two-step process in serious cases. It is by no means clear that the probability standard for issuing a post-arrest warrant is identical to the probable cause standard applicable at the preliminary examination. In part this is because legislatures and courts have seldom addressed themselves to the problem of probability standards for post-arrest warrants.

Nor is the problem wholly solved simply by dividing warrants into two groups, those issued before and those issued after arrests. It has already been pointed out that in some circumstances — probably a majority of the instances in which pre-arrest warrants are used — the decision to issue a warrant for one not yet in custody represents both the decision to invoke the process and the decision to charge.[3] Under other circumstances, a pre-arrest warrant represents only a decision to take custody. Formal law sheds no light on whether the standard of probability of guilt is the same in the first situation as in the second.

When, as is the regular practice, warrants are issued after arrest, they can no longer be said to serve the arrest purpose. Although there is evidence that one purpose of the post-arrest warrant is to justify retention of custody, there can be no doubt that it also serves as the manifestation of the initial charging decision. Again, the formal law is not helpful on the question whether the standard of probability of guilt which must be met to justify issuance of a warrant after arrest is the same or different from the standard used when the warrant serves only the arrest purpose or when it serves both arrest and charging purposes.

Still disregarding the function served and standards applied in current administration, it is seldom that a court, when discussing the probable cause standard at the preliminary examination, sees the process as one in which the sufficiency of the evidence to issue a warrant is tested and reviewed at the pre-

331, 332-333. It also is clear that the law contemplates a higher standard for conviction than for either arrest or for charging, and this is evidenced by the different verbal formulae used at the different stages: there is no legal requirement that a person be charged only when there is available admissible evidence which establishes beyond a reasonable doubt that a crime has been committed and that the suspect committed it. This is, of course, the verbal formula for the conviction standard. The statutory standard for charging — whether manifested in a complaint, a post-arrest warrant as well as by a bindover order at the preliminary examination — is "probable cause," and for arrest it is either "reasonable grounds" or "probable cause."

[3] See the discussion in Chapter 1 *supra*.

liminary. For this reason, too, formal law statements about the probability standards for warrants used partially or exclusively as charging documents are lacking.

If one assumes that the standard at the preliminary is the same as the standard for warrants used as charging documents, it is quite accurate to confirm the earlier stated assumption that the probability of guilt needed to charge is higher than that needed to arrest in each of the three states. The *Arrest* volume has pointed out several particulars in which this is true.[4] Indeed, the very fact that, in each jurisdiction there may be found explicit statements that charging need not occur immediately after arrest but may be delayed for a reasonable time to permit in-custody investigation of the suspect, would seem to make clear that the standards are necessarily different in law.[5] Furthermore, since there is also recognition that charging occurs initially in a process in which the issuance of a post-arrest warrant immediately precedes the initial appearance, the recognition of the propriety of detention of properly arrested persons for a reasonable time prior to the initial appearance for further investigation also means that the standard for arrest is not so high as the standard for issuance of the post-arrest warrant. What is significant is that all of this is a matter of inference — though perhaps necessary inference — and is never expressly explained in the decisions. Furthermore, there continues to be no suggestion whether the post-arrest warrant standard is identical to the standard at the preliminary examination.

When one turns to current administrative practice, however, quite a different picture emerges. Police and prosecutors rely on formal law approval of the practice of detaining properly arrested suspects for a reasonable period of time while investigation continues. It is clear, then, that the charging standard as evidenced in the decision to issue a post-arrest warrant is higher than the standard for arrest. And there is considerable evidence that, when the warrant is issued prior to arrest but represents an affirmative charging as well as an invocation decision, the same higher standard is used by the prosecutor. What may be surprising, however, is that this higher standard for warrants representing exclusively or partly a decision to charge is considerably higher than the formal law standard for probable cause at the preliminary examination, which coincides generally with the

4 LaFave, Arrest 301-308 (1965).

5 LaFave, Detention for Investigation by the Police: An Analysis of Current Practices, 1962 Wash. U.L.Q. 331.

standard as applied in practice. While one cannot be certain, then, whether the formal law profile traced from investigation and arrest through charging — including both warrants, whose purpose is at least partially to charge, and preliminary examinations — through conviction is a constantly ascending one, it is certainly clear that in current administration such a profile would grossly distort the facts. In practice in each of the states — and it is suspected that the same would be true generally — the profile shows a giant step up from the pure arrest standard to the initial stage of charging followed by a step part way back toward the arrest standard, which marks the criterion used at the preliminary examination, followed in turn by another large step up to the "beyond a reasonable doubt" standard appropriate for conviction. The focal point of attention in this chapter is the standard used by prosecutors when they decide whether to issue a warrant whose purpose is at least partially to charge. The standard at the preliminary examination is considered in the following part.

Still another obstacle to clear analysis and exposition presents itself. Every effort has been made to isolate the question of likelihood of guilt from the questions of convictability and of discretion to refrain from proceeding against the probably guilty. The principal reason for sacrificing strict adherence to that division here is simple. It will be recalled that, in current practice, the step from arrest to warrant issuance is a giant one. Indeed so great is it that the warrant standard is higher than the bindover standard, and it is wholly accurate to refer to the warrant standard as one of "convictability." It is not enough that the prosecutor is convinced of the suspect's guilt, or even that he is confident that he can surmount the preliminary examination. Almost without exception, a warrant will not be issued for charging purposes unless the prosecutor is convinced that a conviction, either as the result of a trial or of a guilty plea, is nearly certain to follow. It is just because the standard for issuance of the warrant to charge so far exceeds any formal law requirement of probable cause that probability of guilt cannot be completely separated from some of the other factors which control the warrant decision.

Four problem situations are identifiable. In the first of them, either the evidence is insufficient to convince the prosecutor that the suspect is guilty, or to convince him that a jury would think so. In all of the other situations, the prosecutor is convinced that the suspect is guilty. In the second situation, the prosecutor realizes that he cannot surmount the preliminary examination, or that the case will fail at trial, because the evidence on which he bases his conclusion of guilt is not available to him at the preliminary examination or at the trial. In this situation, even though there is no question of guilt in the mind of the prosecutor, he will ordinarily decline to prosecute for reasons which in the aggregate can fairly be called evidence-sufficiency reasons. It is important, however, that the evidence available is not inadequate to induce a firm belief in the guilt of the suspect — indeed, in some cases involving confessions or physical evidence illegally seized, it is overwhelming. This is the explanation for the great importance attached here to the fact that the standard for determining evidence sufficiency is probability of conviction in addition to probability of guilt. Both of these problem situations are considered in detail in this chapter devoted to evidence sufficiency.

The third problem situation also posits evidence available to convince the prosecutor of the suspect's guilt. It differs from the second, however, in that the prosecutor has no reason to doubt that the jury will also believe that the suspect engaged in the criminal conduct of which he is accused. But, in some situations juries, or even judges, will not convict despite a belief in the guilt of the suspect, for reasons of policy wholly unrelated to guilt. The law has long recognized the function of the jury to ameliorate the harshness of the law, and so have prosecutors. Ordinarily prosecutors will not charge under these circumstances either.

The final problem situation involves the traditional discretion of the prosecutor. Even though he is convinced of the guilt of the suspect, even though he knows he can surmount the preliminary, even though he is confident he can persuade a jury of the guilt of the suspect, even though he is aware of no pattern of acquittals for extra-official reasons, a prosecutor will decline to charge when he believes that prosecution is not in the community's interest.[6] These latter two problem situations are different not merely in degree from the earlier two. In the latter two, the decision not to charge is based on factors unrelated to the ability of the prosecutor to convince the judge or jury of the fact that the suspect did the acts complained of and that those acts amounted to a crime technically. It is based either on a belief that he will be unable to convince a judge or jury that

[6] For detailed discussion of this problem see Chapter 8 *infra.*

prosecution of this particular obviously guilty man is socially desirable, or on a belief of his own that prosecution of this particular guilty man is socially undesirable. For this reason, these two problem situations form the subject matter of Part IV of this volume, "Discretion and the Charging Decision."

Because the construction of the four classes of problem situations involves the exercise of judgment inherent in any classification process, it is in a sense arbitrary. Certainly it is not so perfect as to permit automatic classification of every problem. One problem which does not clearly fit within any of the categories arises in cases in which the victim or principal witness indicates to the prosecutor a lack of willingness to aid in the prosecution of the case. While it is perfectly clear that the private citizen could be compelled by legal process to participate in the trial by testifying against the suspect, in practice this is not done, especially in cases involving offenses which the police and prosecutors view as relatively minor infractions.

This problem is difficult to classify under the construct used here for analysis because the fact that charges are not made in those cases may be explained in various ways. On the one hand, when the victim or witness makes known to the prosecutor his reluctance to testify against a person, it is clear that his reticence may have an adverse effect on the probability of successful prosecution because the jury will be influenced by his attitude. And if prosecution is attempted without the aid of the complainant, there may be insufficient evidence apart from his testimony to allow a conviction. In this sense, the problem is perhaps classifiable as one in which there simply will be insufficient evidence to convict.

On the other hand, instances are frequently observed in which it is clear that a prosecution would be successful despite the reluctance of the victim to testify. Still, in most of those cases the prosecutor will not charge. In these instances it is clear that the refusal to issue a warrant is not predicated on any prosecutorial perception of an evidence-sufficiency problem. Rather, the decision may be based on any one of several policy considerations unrelated to evidence sufficiency.

The following illustration is typical:

Illustration No. 1: A mother complained to the police that a man had had intercourse with her minor daughter, as a result of which the daughter had become pregnant. The daughter was contacted by the prosecutor. She stated that she had in fact had intercourse with the suspect, but that

> she had since married another man, that she wanted nothing to do with her former boyfriend, and that she would not sign a complaint or aid in prosecution of the case by testifying against him. The prosecutor did not issue a warrant.

Here it is clear that the prosecutor could insist that she testify and, if necessary, compel her to. However, even if one assumes that it is highly probable that the suspect would be convicted, the reasons for not taking that possible alternative are clear. The embarrassment caused to the victim and the possibility of jeopardizing her subsequent marriage combine with the fact that she obviously considered her own interests were best served by not prosecuting and result in a situation in which it would be highly undesirable to invoke the criminal process. Thus, the problem primarily raised by the reluctant victim is one normally unrelated to the probable guilt of the suspect. Because the factors resulting in a failure to prosecute in these cases are predominantly nonevidence-sufficiency considerations, the problem is not discussed in detail in this section.[7]

B. Doubt About Whether Suspect Is Guilty

The initial task of the prosecutor facing a request for a warrant is to determine whether the suspect is guilty and whether a judge and jury will concur in his belief in the suspect's guilt. It is those determinations which the law assumes to be the primary function of the prosecutor,[8] and the range of evidence upon which they must be predicated is great.

The task may be difficult because analytically separable factors rarely occur in isolation in life. Still, it is important to try to distinguish the factors likely to persuade the trier of fact that the suspect indeed performed the act complained of from other factors which make judges or juries reluctant to convict even the clearly guilty.

[7] In another type of case, it is not possible to separate completely evidence-sufficiency problems from those arising out of the reluctance of juries to convict for reasons not related to evidence sufficiency. When the chief witness for the state is a person who will be considered by the jury to be immoral, or who has engaged in some illegal activities himself, there is a reluctance on the part of juries to convict. It is not clear in many of these cases whether the reticence of the jury to convict is based on their own concepts of what constitutes those classes of cases in which it is socially desirable to convict, or whether it is because the status of the complainant renders him incredible. To the extent possible, these cases have been treated separately in their most probable categories, either in this chapter or in Part IV.

[8] This is discussed more extensively in Chapter 8 *infra*.

Two gross categories of situations are identifiable. In the first category are the many instances which confront prosecutors every day in which there is doubt whether the suspect did the act complained of; in the second are situations in which no doubt about the facts exist, but there is uncertainty about the legal consequences of the known course of action.

1. *Doubt about the law.*

> *Illustration No. 2:* A police officer assigned to a special detail in the prosecutor's office received a telephone call from an oil company which had delivered oil to the wrong house. The home-owner had refused either to pay for the oil or to permit the company to retrieve it. After consulting with an assistant prosecutor, the police officer informed the oil company that there was a basis for complaint, but he also expressed the hope that the matter could be resolved by conference between the parties in his office.

Certainly one of the most common situations in which prosecutors are faced with a charging decision when it is doubtful whether a crime was committed occurs when the uncertainty is not about the facts but about the legal consequences of a course of action. This very absence of doubt about the facts explains two characteristics of the cases which fall within this category: most often, because there is no need for police investigation, the prosecutor is called upon to decide without a request from the police; further, there is so rarely any need for immediate custody that ordinarily the charging decision is made prior to arrest. Thus, in Illustration No. 2, no purpose would be served either by investigation or by an arrest made independently of the charging decision. What was in doubt was whether the suspect's actions did constitute a crime. Although it is not known positively, it is assumed that the suspect was not aware of the mistaken delivery until after it was completed. It is, of course, this factor which makes it doubtful that a crime was committed and which caused the assistant prosecutor to prefer a course of negotiation and settlement, although he was willing that his office be used to encourage that result.

Similar cases of borderline criminality are not infrequent. Many species of fraud crimes cause the same difficulty in determining whether, on a given set of facts, the conduct complained of is criminal,[9] and so do a number of other nonviolent property

[9] Frequently the problem presented is the sufficiency of the evidence to establish the requisite intent in fraud cases. In one case, the suspect had sold cheap sewing machines for three times their value. He had promised to refund to each purchaser

crimes. In general, perhaps because these offenses are in some sense regarded as civil rather than criminal in character, there is a reluctance to charge whenever the prosecutor has doubts about the law.

> *Illustration No. 3:* A young man and a girl were returning from a party in an automobile driven by the man, who had been drinking. When he realized too late that he was approaching an intersection, he braked hard, throwing the car into a skid. When the car crashed into a pole, the girl was killed. The request of the investigating officer for a negligent homicide warrant was refused.

Automobile homicide cases constitute a second category in which the facts are usually clear but the law is not. The difficulty which inheres in these cases is that of determining in advance of trial the legal standard to be applied to known conduct. The formal law standard for determining guilt in a negligent homicide case or an involuntary manslaughter case is an objective one couched in terms of the degree of care to be exercised in operating the vehicle. The standard presents what is called a "mixed question of law and fact," which is left to the jury to particularize in the light of the facts before it. Such a vague standard — as well as the procedures for particularizing it — affords the prosecutor little guidance in determining whether a crime has been committed. He is therefore reluctant to issue warrants in close cases and utilizes the coroner's report to protect himself in a decision not to charge.[10] When the same problem arises in indictment jurisdictions, the issue is commonly given to the grand jury to test lay reaction.

$20 for each new customer that she referred to the suspect. Some refunds were made, but additional suspicious circumstances were present, including the fact that some of his checks were returned for insufficient funds. The problems presented to the assistant prosecutor were two-fold: first, did the suspect intend to keep his promises about refunding? Here the evidence was probably insufficient in the minds of the prosecuting staff. Second, would mere intention not to keep a promise meet the misrepresentation requirement for obtaining property by false pretences? On this point, the assistant prosecutors were uncertain. The final decision was not to recommend issuance of a warrant.

10 In Wisconsin, not all cases of suspected homicide are referred for inquest by the prosecutor as literally required by Wis. Stat. Ann. §966.01 (1958). Cases which are referred to the medical examiner are primarily those involving negligent homicide resulting from the operation of a motor vehicle. Prosecutors there have stated that the function of referring the case to the medical examiner is two-fold: (1) obtaining the testimony of witnesses under oath gives a clear statement of the facts and makes possible a charging decision; and (2) in cases of doubtful criminality, responsibility for the decision is shared, thus giving added assurance to the public in the decision-making process.

The automobile homicide cases differ in some particulars from the borderline property crime cases. Not infrequently some investigation by the police is necessary to resolve the factual questions; thus it is less unusual that the prosecutor makes the decision on the basis of a request from the police for a warrant. As in the borderline property crime cases, however, the warrant, when issued, represents both the arrest and charging decisions, since the need for immediate custody is lacking, either to prevent escape or to permit in-custody investigation.

> *Illustration No. 4:* A person was found with an athletic starting gun with a solid barrel. A regular barrel could be interchanged for the solid barrel, but no regular barrel was found in the person's possession. A request for a warrant charging carrying a dangerous weapon was refused.

Concealed weapons cases comprise a third category in which there is doubt whether the admitted facts constitute a crime. Typically, an instrument which could under some circumstances be used as a weapon is found in the possession of a suspect. The problem arises because it is not clear whether the weapon is "dangerous" within the meaning of that term in the applicable statute.[11] To indicate the closeness of the case and the difficulty of the problem, the prosecutor in Illustration No. 4 said he would have recommended a warrant if a regular barrel had been found in the suspect's possession, even though it was not integrated with the stock of the gun. As in the previous categories, no facts are in dispute in this class of cases. Unlike them, how-

---

The Wayne County medical examiner, as well as those of other counties in Michigan that have abolished the office of coroner under an act adopted by the legislature in 1953, Mich. Stat. Ann. §§5.953(1) to 5.953(2) (1961), are required to make a medical investigation of all deaths over which the coroner formerly had jurisdiction but are neither required nor authorized to make the full investigation connoted by a coroner's inquest. Lipiec v. Zawadzki, 346 Mich. 197, 77 N.W.2d 763 (1956). Before the 1953 enactment, the coroner conducted many inquests, and one prosecutor, adverting to the change in practice this enactment had occasioned, said, "There were many cases in which it was extremely hard for the prosecutor to decide whether or not to issue a warrant. There were many cases in which the defendant seemed to be technically guilty, but the surrounding circumstances of the case had a tendency to balance the scales in favor of not issuing a warrant It is in this situation that the inquest took the prosecutor off the hook. The responsibility was placed upon the shoulders of the coroner's jury, if one was ordered, and their decisions were followed by the prosecutor without fear of criticism."

Thus, in Wisconsin, and until 1953 in Michigan, the inquest served the purpose of providing support for the prosecutor in refusing a warrant in negligent homicide cases, and provided a buffer between him and public opinion.

[11] E.g., Kan. Stat. Ann. §21-2411 (1964) ("any pistol, bowie knife, dirk, sling shot, knucks, or any other deadly weapon . . .").

ever, the decision whether to charge is a response to a request for a warrant by a police officer who has already taken the defendant into custody. Therefore, warrants issued in this class of cases — when they are issued — are post-arrest warrants and reflect only the charging decision.

2. *Doubt about the facts.* Because the next step in the charging process in serious cases is the preliminary examination, it might be expected that prosecutors would permit borderline cases in which there is some doubt about the guilt of the suspect to be resolved there.[12] If they were to follow that tack, they would apply the preliminary examination standard — probable cause to believe the suspect guilty. Both in law and in current administration, that standard has often been equated with the test for determining whether the evidence would permit submission of the case to a jury at trial.[13] The most significant fact which emerges from the observed practice, however, is that prosecutors impose on themselves a much higher standard of probability. There is no evidence to suggest that prosecutors ever recommend warrants charging persons whom they do not believe to be clearly guilty. Beyond this, they will not recommend warrants unless they are convinced that a judge and jury are very likely to concur in their belief about the suspect's guilt. Thus the standard for warrant issuance far exceeds that required to be met at the preliminary examination — either in law or in current administration.

The problem is one of degree in the sense that the quantum of evidence as well as its probative value must be considered and evaluated in every case. The variation in fact patterns also leads to case by case decision-making. When this is added to the fact that, in many offices a number of assistant prosecutors make individual decisions, the conclusions to be drawn must be more general than would be ideal. Unusually difficult problems recur in two areas — situations in which circumstantial evidence predominates and those in which substantial questions arise about the credibility of witnesses, particularly the complainant.

12 The distinct significance of the preliminary as a current screening device in some parts of Illinois is noted by Oaks and Lehman, The Criminal Process of Cook County and the Indigent Defendant, 1966 U. Ill. L. Forum 584, 618-628. The significance of the considerable number of prosecutions discontinued at the preliminary stage in the state was noted earlier by Knight, The Prosecutor (Outside of Chicago) in Felony Cases, in Illinois Crime Survey at 258-260 (1929); Healy, The Prosecutor (in Chicago) in Felony Cases, id. at 296-298. In Missouri the significance of the preliminary was found to be more questionable. Lashley, Preparation and Presentation of the State's Case, in Missouri Crime Survey at 128-131 (1926).

13 See the discussion in Chapter 5 *infra.*

a. *Circumstantial evidence problems.*

Illustration No. 5: A and B were in A's bedroom when A put a wallet containing $300 in a drawer B then asked to use A's phone which was located in the hall. B returned from the phone, and told A that a woman wanted to talk to A on the phone. A went to the phone leaving B alone in the bedroom. When A returned, B left. When A went to get his wallet from the drawer, it was missing. A accused B of stealing his wallet. A similar complaint had been made against B at an earlier time. A warrant was refused.

One of the most difficult tasks a prosecutor faces in making the charging decision is determining the weight which should be given to circumstantial evidence. Certainly in Illustration No. 5 there is a probability of guilt sufficient to meet the probable cause norm at the preliminary examination. Yet the refusal to recommend a warrant is typical in this kind of case. The obvious inference is that prosecutors are not willing to devote resources to charging merely because the law would permit them to do so. Instead they insist that the evidence be of a nature that conviction is very likely to follow.[14]

b. *Witness credibility problems.*

Illustration No. 6: Two prostitutes complained to the police that a pair of men whom they had solicited for intercourse had on more than one occasion threatened them with a knife and had, on the most recent occasion, not only accomplished intercourse by threatening to kill the girls, but had robbed them as well. An armed robbery warrant was refused.

In a substantial number of instances, warrants are refused not

[14] Another class of cases commonly arises which is difficult to classify. Prosecutors regularly refuse to charge when the only evidence that a suspect has been driving under the influence of alcohol is the result of an alcometer test. To convict, some evidence such as the fact that the officer observed the person staggering, smelling of alcohol, or slurring his speech would be necessary in addition to the evidence obtained by use of the alcometer, despite the obvious fact that such evidence would be merely cumulative. The difficulty in classification results because it is not known whether the jury's refusal to convict in those cases is based on a belief in the inherent untrustworthiness of the administered test, a belief that a conviction is unwarranted unless the person also showed signs that the alcohol actually affected his motor responses, or an expression of disapproval of the test, despite its trustworthiness. When the case is not entirely circumstantial, a prosecutor may charge if the eye-witness or other testimony is sufficient to bolster what circumstantial evidence is available, but he will not charge if the eye-witness evidence is also weak. In one case, an undercover officer entered a disorderly house and was offered an opportunity to have intercourse with one of the three daughters of the proprietress. The prosecutor determined that the officer was unsure which of the three daughters was involved. A warrant was denied. In this type of case the fact that a crime was committed is clear but the identity of the perpetrator is not.

because the prosecutor does not believe the complainant's story but because he thinks that a jury is unlikely to believe it. Once again, a pattern is identified in which charging does not occur despite the fact that the preliminary examination apparently poses no substantial obstacle. The same inference mentioned in connection with the circumstantial evidence cases is reinforced here. Prosecutors do not charge unless they are practically certain that a jury will also believe in the guilt of the suspect.[15]

C. Law Precludes Consideration of Evidence Pointing Clearly to Guilt

In other situations, evidence is also available to a prosecutor which leaves no doubt that the suspect is guilty. Equally clear is that the evidence would not be admissible at a trial — perhaps not admissible at a preliminary examination — because the rules of evidence applicable to those proceedings would forbid its in-

15 Prosecutors have learned through experience that one of the most reliable indicia of a lack of veracity on the part of a complainant is improper motive in instituting the prosecution. If it is clear to the prosecutor that the reason for making complaint is other than to bring a person to justice, then it is likely that defense counsel could make the same point before the jury. In one case, a woman accused a grocer of molesting her daughter in his store in the mother's presence. It was later discovered that the woman had had a dispute with the grocer for some time because of her neglect in paying her bills, and that the grocer had told her to take her business elsewhere. In this case the warrant was issued because the fact of bad motive was not determined until later judicial proceedings. When the judge discovered the complainant's motive the case was dismissed. The prosecutor stated that the issuance of that warrant was a mistake.

The polygraph test is commonly used by prosecutors to determine guilt or innocence. This occurs in two types of situations. In the first, if a woman complains to police that she has been forcibly raped, the prosecutor insists upon administration of a polygraph test to the victim and will not charge unless the results indicate that she is telling the truth. Here the prosecutors may be motivated by a fear that a conviction could be obtained whether or not the person accused by the woman was in fact guilty, because of the danger of jury prejudice aroused by the nature of the crime involved. They are apparently reinforced in their belief in the necessity for this practice by the number of cases in which rape is reported when there has been no crime committed at all. These cases clearly indicate that prosecutors use a guilt standard in addition to a conviction standard.

The polygraph is also used in another situation. Prosecutors often insist on corroboration not only of the complainant's statement but also of exculpatory statements of suspects. Thus, as an investigative device, polygraph tests are often used when the investigation of a suspected crime requires the interviewing and screening of a large number of suspects, who may or may not have been arrested. The test is, of course, voluntary, but is offered to the suspect as a quick way to clear himself of suspicion. When the suspect's guilt is put in doubt by the test — i.e., when the test indicates he is telling the truth — no charge is placed against him. Again, this clearly indicates that the prosecutors use a guilt standard as well as a conviction standard.

troduction. Some of these rules of exclusion are based ultimately on an evaluation of the inherent trustworthiness of certain kinds of evidence, others reflect policies totally unrelated to trustworthiness.

Whether the exclusionary rules of evidence are directly applicable at the warrant-issuing stage is ambiguous. No law has been found in any of the three states suggesting their applicability to the warrant stage of the charging decision. Of greater importance, however, is that these rules are considered by prosecutors faced with the charging decision. The reason is clear: because prosecutors use a criterion of probable *conviction,* in addition to probable *guilt,* they necessarily place themselves in the position of the person who must present the case in court without the benefit of evidence which the evidence rules exclude. In brief, only evidence which is admissible at the trial is considered in making the charging decision, although there is some indication that the likelihood of a guilty plea may temper this practice in some instances. Again because of the use of a probable conviction standard, it is not important at this stage whether the trial rules of evidence also apply at the preliminary examination.

1. *Hearsay.* It may appear to be a contradiction but warrants are commonly issued on hearsay. Particularly in Michigan, when the evidence actually scrutinized by the assistant prosecutor consists of the statements contained in the police report — obviously hearsay in most instances — the warrant recommendation is based on evidence not admissible in that form at the trial. But in the course of his scrutiny, the assistant assures himself that the witnesses who will testify at the trial and whose statements are summarized in that police report have nonhearsay knowledge. It is in this sense that the prosecutor considers the hearsay rule. In many instances, the same sequence occurs in the other states. When the only evidence which could be offered at the trial on any essential element of the case is hearsay, a warrant is refused.

2. *Corpus Delicti.*

Illustration No. 7: A woman reported to the police that she had been raped the evening before. On close questioning the woman admitted that she had not been raped but had made the false felony report to explain her absence to her husband and that he had then insisted she contact the police. The woman was not charged.

Illustration No. 8: A young man was stopped by police for speeding and admitted to them that he knew that the large number of cigarettes in his car were stolen. A report had been filed with the police several days before that a large number of cigarettes had been stolen. A warrant was issued for receiving stolen property.

Illustration No. 9: The police discovered a man sitting in another's car. A strip of tinfoil which could be used to start the car without a key was found lying on the floor of the car underneath the ignition switch. The man admitted that he did not know to whom the car belonged, and that he was attempting to steal it. A warrant was issued charging attempted larceny of an automobile.

The corpus delicti rule forbids admission into evidence of out-of-court confessions or admissions unless there is proof independent of the confession or admission tending to show that the crime confessed to was in fact committed by someone, or tending to corroborate the details of the confession. This means that the fact that a crime was committed by the subject cannot be proved by his uncorroborated confession alone. While the rule is not applied by prosecutors with the strictness that is required on trial, it nevertheless is taken into consideration by them in the decision whether to charge. If it is clear that the corpus delicti cannot be proved, there generally will be no charge.

Illustration No. 7 presents perhaps the most common case where the rule is encountered and is one in which the corpus delicti is the most difficult to prove. The state at trial would have had to prove, independent of the confession of the woman, that she was not in fact raped on that evening. The difficulties of proving such a negative proposition are obvious, and the woman in this case was not charged. The prosecutor who denied the warrant pointed out that he might have charged her with making a false felony report if she had gone so far as to pick a particular person out of a line-up. The more particular the report made by the woman, the easier it is to negate.

The difficulty faced in Illustration No. 8 is proving that the cigarettes in the possession of the man were in fact stolen, and this must be shown independently of his own statements concerning them. If the goods are not specifically identifiable, this presents a formidable obstacle to prosecution and hence to charging. The prosecutor in that case admitted those difficulties, but a warrant was issued charging receiving and concealing stolen property. A warrant charging attempted larceny of an automobile was issued in Illustration No. 9, although there too the prosecutor admitted that the corpus delicti probably could not be proved on trial.

While it is clear that the rule is considered in the charging decision, it is not entirely clear why charges are made in the face of admissions by prosecutors that a conviction at trial probably is not possible in the particular case, or that the state probably could not even get a bindover order at the preliminary examination. There are three possible explanations. In Illustrations Nos. 8 and 9, the prosecutors may feel that, on a more thorough investigation of the case, the corpus delicti may be proved, or they may be inclined to expose a clearly guilty person to as much of the criminal justice process as possible. The most probable explanation is that, since the suspect has admitted his guilt, he will be likely to plead guilty and thus remove the obstacle to conviction.

In one sense this represents a deviation from the usual probable conviction standard, but in another sense it does not. Ordinarily the probable conviction standard is assumed to mean likelihood of conviction of one who pleads not guilty and who must be tried before a jury or a judge sitting as a trier of fact. But when the likelihood of a guilty plea is unusually great, the probability of conviction is also great, though this time by the guilty plea method of adjudication instead of through the trial process. It is in that sense that the standard remains one of probable conviction. In any event, when the adverse publicity which may result from failure to charge a confessed criminal is considered, the reason for the practice becomes clearer.

Illustration No. 10: A police officer saw a woman at a distance with yellow slips of paper in her hand. Suspecting on the basis of prior experience that they were bet slips, the officer approached the woman. When she saw him the woman put the slips of paper in her blouse. She was arrested for engaging in an illegal occupation and taken to headquarters where a search of her person revealed that the yellow slips were in fact bet slips. The prosecutor refused to recommend a warrant.

Illustration No. 11: A police officer saw a man he suspected of being a gambler talking to another man on the street. He then watched them through binoculars and saw money and policy slips exchanged, but he could not have seen this without the aid of the binoculars. He arrested the suspect for engaging in an illegal occupation, searched him, and found the policy slips on his person. The prosecutor recommended that a warrant be issued.

A number of rules forbidding the use of particular kinds of evidence at the trial are not based on notions about the inherent trustworthiness of that evidence. For the most part, the rules relating to privileges are of this class, and, to some extent, the rule forbidding the use of coerced confessions exists independently of trustworthiness considerations. Of particular importance in current administration is the rule which forbids the use at trial of illegally seized evidence. The rule that illegally seized evidence is not admissible at a trial has long been in force in Wisconsin,[16] and, subject to a limited number of exceptions, in Michigan.[17] Until the Supreme Court of the United States imposed the exclusionary rule on the states in 1961,[18] Kansas law permitted the use of illegally seized evidence in its courts.[19]

Almost invariably, illegally seized evidence is of great probative value. Because of that fact, it is obvious that, when the police obtain evidence illegally, a situation usually arises in which there is no doubt about the guilt of the suspect. It is clear, then, that the uniform practice in Michigan and Wisconsin of refusing to charge whenever there is not sufficient untainted evidence shows clearly that the standard is not only one of probable guilt, but of probable conviction as well. Thus in Illustration No. 10, the prosecutor believed that the prior experience of the police, which related the color of the pieces of paper to their use as bet slips, was not sufficient to supply the reasonable grounds necessary to make a valid arrest without a warrant. Because the arrest was thought to be illegal, so was the subsequent search, thus rendering the evidence inadmissible at trial. It is significant that the prosecutor was unwilling to put to the test of adjudication whether the officer's prior experience would be enough to justify the arrest.

When, however, the prosecutor believes that a court might uphold the validity of the arrest and so of the search, despite the presence of some doubt, he frequently recommends issuance of a warrant. Thus in Illustration No. 11, the basis on which the arrest and search could be said to be unauthorized was so tenuous that the prosecutor showed little concern for the possibility and little hesitancy in recommending a warrant.

16 Since Hoyer v. State, 180 Wis. 407, 193 N.W. 89 (1923).

17 After Michigan adopted the rule in People v. Marxhausen, 204 Mich. 559, 171 N.W. 557 (1919), and reaffirmed in People v. Stein, 265 Mich. 610, 251 N.W. 788 (1933), a state constitutional amendment was passed making the rule inapplicable to non-dwelling searches for weapons or narcotics. See LaFave, Arrest 430 and n.89 (1965) for a detailed discussion.

18 Mapp v. Ohio, 367 U.S. 643, 81 Sup. Ct. 1684, 6 L. Ed. 2d 1081 (1961).

19 The exclusionary rule was rejected in State v. Johnson, 116 Kan. 58, 226 Pac. 245 (1924).

No reason is readily apparent why the same attitude which prevails in cases involving the corpus delicti rule is not prevalent when the question is one of charging on evidence made inadmissible for reasons unrelated to trustworthiness. Indeed, in a sense one might expect that the rules based on trustworthiness would be more rather than less stringently applied at this stage. And despite Judge Danaher's admonition,[20] there is no direct sanction against prosecutors who charge on the basis of evidence inadmissible at the trial.

Two reasons may be advanced to explain the difference in practice in the two situations. In the corpus delicti situations encountered, the suspect has confessed. The likelihood of a guilty plea is, therefore, substantial, thus eliminating the obstacle to conviction. Further, prosecutors may feel a stronger compulsion to enforce the exclusionary rule at the charging stage than the corpus delicti rule because of the official illegality inherent in the one and not present in the other. The judicial attitude toward official lawlessness which is at the root of the exclusionary rule may be shared by some prosecutors to a greater extent than is generally assumed.

In Kansas, trials were observed in which illegally seized evidence was used. Even there, however, there was some indication that prosecutors were in some instances reluctant to rely too heavily on illegally seized evidence because skilled defense attorneys built arguments thought to be effective with juries on the fact of police illegality.[21]

[20] "The rules as to searches of private dwellings without a search warrant are so clear and have so often been stated, it would seem to be nothing short of astonishing that we should continue to receive cases presenting the point involved here. . . And so it would seem, and yet these cases reach us. If, perchance, the police are not familiar with the rules, the prosecutor is, or is presumed to be. The opinions referred to have cited many other cases which he should recognize. It is the duty of the prosecutor to know not only whom to prosecute, but *when*. Thus, in the course of preparation of his case for trial, absent 'exceptional circumstances,' seldom found, the prosecutor should appraise the available evidence and should apply the rules. Unhesitatingly he should refuse to go forward with the presentation of evidence which has been obtained by illegal police invasion of a private home. If his case *depends* upon such evidence, he should dismiss the prosecution. If he can present a case without the use of evidence illegally procured, it should not be offered. But if notwithstanding, he insists upon introducing evidence illegally gained through improper invasion of the sanctity of a dwelling, we should tell him once again and for all, we will reverse a conviction, as we now do." Williams v. United States, 263 F.2d 487, 491 (D.C. Cir. 1959), *cert. denied*, 365 U.S. 856 (1961) (concurring opinion of Danaher, J.).

[21] Although no instances were observed in which witness competency presented a problem in practice, rules relating to who may testify present, as a logical possibility, a situation in which the law would preclude jury consideration of evidence

D. Summary

The conclusion to be reached from this analysis is that evidence which would only satisfy the probable cause standard used at the preliminary examination is not enough to cause prosecutors to issue warrants. Warrants are issued only if prosecutors are convinced of the guilt of the suspect and are convinced that a jury or judge will share that belief on the basis of the same evidence and if the judge and jury will not be prevented from considering that evidence by rules of trial evidence whether related to trustworthiness or not. It thus becomes accurate to describe the standard of probability utilized in administering the warrant decision as a dual one: there must not only be a very strong probability of guilt, there must also be a strong probability of conviction.

The exceptions to that pattern of conduct are few. It will be recalled that, in cases involving confessions when the prosecutor understandably believes that the person is guilty and is likely to

---

which might convince the prosecutor of the guilt of the suspect. Thus, e.g., the only witness to an alleged crime might be a person so mentally immature or defective, that it is clear he would not be allowed to testify on trial. E.g., if the story of a very young child convinced the prosecutor of the guilt of the suspect, another situation could exist in which the prosecutor was satisfied as to the guilt of the suspect, but he probably would not charge because the evidence needed to convict would not be available to the jury.

Appellate cases in both Michigan and Wisconsin present another possibility. Suppose, e.g., a mother accuses her husband of having sexual intercourse with their daughter, claiming that she is an eye-witness to the offense. Cases similar to this have arisen in Michigan. In People v. Westbrook, 94 Mich. 629, 54 N.W. 486 (1893), the complaint was signed by the defendant's wife and she was allowed to testify against him on a charge of indecent assault of their daughter. The conviction was reversed because the wife was not competent to testify against the husband in this class of offenses. The applicable statute was subsequently amended, Mich. Stat. Ann. §27A. 2162 (1962), to provide another exception to the rule that one spouse may not testify against the other. That exception apparently was intended to prevent the necessity of reversals in cases like Westbrook, since it provided that a spouse could testify "in cases of prosecution for a crime committed against the children of either or both." That problem was again presented in People v. Clarke, 366 Mich. 209, 114 N.W.2d 338 (1962). Defendant was charged with indecent liberties with a minor girl who lived with defendant and his wife. The wife had signed the complaint and had testified against him at trial. On trial it was shown that the child did not belong to either parent. Again, a conviction was reversed because the wife was not competent to testify against the defendant or to sign the complaint. Despite the fact that illustrations of this problem were derived not from practice but from appellate cases, the latter would seem to be ample evidence that some problem does exist in practice when the state's chief witness is not competent to testify on trial. See also People v. Werner, 225 Mich. 18, 195 N.W. 697 (1923); People v. Trine, 164 Mich. 1, 129 N.W. 3 (1910); Goodwin v. State, 114 Wis. 318, 90 N.W. 170 (1902). Spouses are not incompetent to testify against each other in criminal cases in Kansas. Kan. Stat. Ann. §62-1420 (1964).

plead guilty, suspects are sometimes charged despite serious doubt in the mind of the prosecutor — because of the corpus delicti rule — whether the case would result in a conviction by trial.

This pattern of behavior results in a system in which it is unlikely that a person will be charged unless it is evident that the final result will be conviction. It is even more unlikely that the end result would be conviction of any but guilty persons. There is little doubt, however, that many persons who are obviously guilty are not charged at all. To the extent that guilty persons are not charged because of perceived problems in the sufficiency of the evidence to convince the trier of fact of guilt, it is difficult to attribute the cause for this pattern of behavior to the prosecutor alone. Almost invariably the charging pattern is related to a play-back effect of past trials on similar charges under similar circumstances from which prosecutors have derived experience enough to realize that to charge would be a futile gesture, at most resulting in a dismissal or not-guilty verdict at trial. Prosecutors do not view the charging system as a species of punishment; they do not take it on themselves to charge for the purpose of causing inconvenience to one they believe to be guilty who otherwise would be immediately released without further exposure to criminal procedural processes. The reason for what might be an exception to this — cases involving confessions — is not entirely clear. It is likely, however, that charging in those cases may result from an understandable prosecutorial belief that the case will actually result in a conviction because of a high probability that a person who has previously confessed to the crime will also plead guilty.

Thus, on the one hand the probability that an innocent person will be charged is at best remote, and on the other hand, those cases in which obviously guilty persons are not charged because of lack of sufficient evidence are attributable to predictions as to judge and jury reactions to the case. Although there is no evidence that those predictions are inaccurate, it is clear that the line is drawn in a sufficiently cautious manner to leave it unclear whether a substantial number of them might not be convicted, either at trial or by guilty plea.

PART III

Judicial Involvement in and Review of the Decision to Charge—Evidentiary Sufficiency

The object or purpose of the preliminary investigation is to prevent hasty, malicious, improvident, and oppressive prosecutions, to protect the person charged from open and public accusations of crime, to avoid both for the defendant and the public the expense of a public trial, and to save the defendant from the humiliation and anxiety involved in public prosecution, and to discover whether or not there are substantial grounds upon which a prosecution may be based.

JUSTICE ROSENBERRY, in *Thies v. State,* 178 Wis. 98, 103, 189 N.W. 539, 541 (1922).

In many other cases, however, the advantages [of a preliminary examination] are illusory, while the disadvantages may be real. Consider the following: (1) The publicity may be vastly increased, by getting morbid details in the hands of the press, so that it is harder to get a jury. (2) A witness may be important to the prosecution, yet if he does not testify in a hearing, subject to cross-examination, his testimony is not perpetuated. Thus if he dies or disappears before trial, his testimony may not be read and the case may fall. (3) A witness may have a change of heart after the lapse of time. A victim of an assault may mellow when his scars heal; the victim of a bad check may relent when the check is later made good. If he has not committed himself in sworn testimony at the hearing, his testimony at the trial may be somewhat more favorable than might otherwise be the case. (4) Once you have cross-examined a witness in court, he is more likely to identify himself with the prosecutor's side and resist any interviews. He is more likely to throw himself enthusiastically into the opposition's camp.

Harris B. Steinberg in Steinberg and Paulsen, A Conversation with Defense Counsel on Problems of a Criminal Defense, 7 *The Practical Lawyer* 25, 30 (No. 5, 1961).

It is commonly asserted that judicial participation in charging is desirable. In practice, this ideal is only partially realized. There is only formal judicial participation in the issuance of post-arrest warrants. Although judges conduct initial appearances, those proceedings are not used to test the appropriateness of charging decisions. Similarly, habeas corpus proceedings are not used to challenge the charging decision. It is only at the preliminary examination that the judiciary participates even perfunctorily in the charging decision.

The preliminary examination is designed to perform a valuable function by assuring, through the objective judgment of a member of the judiciary, that sufficient evidence of guilt exists to justify imposing on the defendant the obvious burdens and risks of the adjudication decision. In current practice, however, it is apparent that this goal, stated by Justice Rosenberry, is not often realized. There are a number of reasons for this, including (1) the unavailability in some places of counsel for the indigent at the preliminary, (2) the objective of each party to minimize disclosure of his case, (3) the reluctance of magistrates to scrutinize carefully the evidence at the preliminary in deference to the judgment of the prosecutor and in reliance on the availability of the trial to correct charging errors, and (4) the considerations, discussed by Mr. Steinberg, an experienced defense counsel, which often make the preliminary examination a disadvantage to the defendant. The issue is raised, therefore, whether the preliminary examination is or can be made a sufficiently valuable evidence-sufficiency screen to justify its retention as a separate step in charging.

CHAPTER 3

Judicial Involvement in the Charging Decision Prior to the Preliminary Examination

In some jurisdictions, the initial charging decision is reflected in a complaint filed by a citizen, policeman, or prosecutor.[1] If the suspect named in that document has not yet been taken into custody, the complaint ordinarily serves as a request for the issuance of an arrest warrant by a judicial official.[2] Constitutional imperatives embodied in the Fourth and Fourteenth Amendments require that the judicial official make his decision on the basis of evidentiary facts brought to his attention in such a manner that he may reach an independent judgment whether there are reasonable grounds to believe the suspect guilty.[3] If there has been a valid arrest without a warrant, and a warrant is not

1 For a discussion of the procedure in one state, see Golde, Interviewing Clients: Initial Steps, in California Criminal Law Practice at §349.55 (Calif. Practice Handbook No. 23, 1964).

2 See People v. Krumery, 74 Ill. App. 2d 298, 220 N.E.2d 241 (1966).

3 The need for a deliberate, impartial judgment about the propriety of either an arrest or search warrant, made by a judicial officer to be interposed between the citizen and the police, is emphasized in Wong Sun v. United States, 371 U.S. 471, 481-482, 83 Sup. Ct. 407, 414, 9 L. Ed. 2d 441, 451-452 (1962); see United States v. Ventresca, 380 U.S. 102, 85 Sup. Ct. 741, 13 L. Ed. 2d 684 (1965); Aguilar v. Texas, 378 U.S. 108, 84 Sup. Ct. 1509, 12 L. Ed. 2d 723 (1964); Lopez v. United States, 370 F.2d 8 (5th Cir. 1966). Judicial concern over assuring an independent judgment, in the sense that basic facts are to be presented to the magistrate from which he may draw his own inferences about whether there is probable cause to believe a particular suspect guilty as opposed to magisterial reliance upon inferences already drawn from undisclosed basic facts by those who are applying for a warrant, can be traced to Johnson v. United States, 333 U.S. 10, 13-14, 68 Sup. Ct. 367, 369, 92 L. Ed. 436, 440 (1948), and, arguably, to Nathanson v. United States, 290 U.S. 41, 54 Sup. Ct. 11, 78 L. Ed. 159 (1933). See generally Tiffany, McIntyre and Rotenberg, Detection of Crime 99-120 (1967).

needed for any other purpose in the jurisdiction, these issues do not arise.

When, as in Kansas, Michigan and Wisconsin at the time of the survey, the complaint serves as a warrant request, even after a valid arrest without one, the warrant may or may not serve as an arrest-authorizing document. When it does, it is certainly subject to the same constitutional requirements as are arrest-authorizing warrants in any other jurisdiction. When it does not, however, a question arises whether the choice of the post-arrest warrant as the initial charging document carries with it a requirement of the same kind of judicial participation as is needed to validate pre-arrest warrants, or, indeed, whether judicial participation of any kind is required.[4]

[4] As indicated in Chapter 1, notes 1-8 *supra* and accompanying text, there is little agreement among the states about whether warrants must be issued in certain situations even after valid arrests without them. Within a single state, whether a warrant is required may depend on the nature of the case and the type of function other than arrest authorization it is to serve in the case. Warrants might serve nonarrest functions ranging from justifying detention to representing the initial charging step in prosecution. The difficulty is that the Fourth Amendment, upon which the authorities cited in note 3 *supra* are based, relates to arrest and not to these other functions including charging. The courts typically do not trace the ramifications of this distinction which is, however, noted in the dissent of Rives, J., in Giordenello v. United States, 241 F.2d 575, 581-586 (5th Cir. 1957), *rev'd,* 357 U.S. 480, 78 Sup. Ct. 1245, 2 L. Ed. 2d 1503 (1958). Judge Rives objects to the majority's conclusion that a warrant can be stated in the words of the statute defining the substantive offense in question because an indictment can be worded in that way. He points out that the cases sanctioning this form of indictment were construing it as a pleading, or charging, document, and were not concerned about the validity of an arrest predicated thereon. Thus, a charge phrased in the language of the statute alleged to have been violated will satisfy the Sixth Amendment but not the Fourth. "The 'probable cause' requirement of the Fourth Amendment as a prerequisite to the issuance of a warrant is different and in some ways more stringent than the pleading or notice requirements of the Sixth Amendment." Id. at 581. That the courts either do not notice the distinction, or make ambiguous statements about its significance, is revealed by Jaben v. United States, 381 U.S. 214, 85 Sup. Ct. 1365, 14 L. Ed. 2d 345 (1965). In Jaben a complaint charging income tax evasion was filed shortly before the lapse of time permitted by the applicable statute of limitations for return of a valid indictment. No arrest warrant was issued pursuant to this complaint. Instead, a summons was issued directing the defendant to appear at a preliminary hearing. The statute of limitations provided a nine-month extension of the time within which an indictment could be returned, in the event that a valid complaint was filed within the statutory period. An indictment was returned within nine months but after the lapse of the primary period. The issue was, therefore, whether the complaint was valid. The majority held that it was a valid complaint and that prosecution upon the indictment was not barred. The interesting point, alluded to in the dissent of Goldberg, J., was that the complaint was not being reviewed in connection with a question about the validity of arrest but served a pleading or charging function.

"While it is not necessary, under my view of the case, to determine whether the complaint showed probable cause, since the Court reaches that issue, I believe it appropriate to express my disagreement with its conclusion. If the Court means

Although the necessity for extensive and independent judicial participation in the warrant issuing process arose after the field survey was completed, subsequent developments in Wisconsin are of particular relevance. It will be recalled that, at the time of the survey, an arrest warrant could be issued either by a magistrate or by a prosecutor in Wisconsin.[5] Although in practice, prosecutors did not regularly exercise this statutory power, they did on some occasions. That occasional practice was challenged in Wisconsin after the Supreme Court of the United States ruled that judicial participation in the issuance of arrest warrants was mandated by the Fourth Amendment's search and seizure provision[6] and made applicable to the states through the Fourteenth Amendment's due process of law clause.[7]

The response in Wisconsin was a holding that arrest warrants issued by prosecutors were invalid.[8] The Wisconsin Court did

---

that the standard of probable cause required for the issuance of a summons directing the defendant to appear at a preliminary hearing is the same as the standard required for issuance of a search warrant or an arrest warrant, which will place the defendant under immediate physical restraint, the complaint before us fails to demonstrate probable cause . . . ." Id. at 230, 85 Sup. Ct. at 1373, 14 L. Ed. 2d at 356 (dissenting opinion of Goldberg, J.). The distinction also has significance in State v. Howe, 219 A.2d 116 (Me. 1966); Crouse v. State, 384 P.2d 321 (Wyo. 1963).

[5] See Chapter 1, note 8 *supra* and accompanying text. The former situation in Wisconsin is also discussed in Miller and Tiffany, Prosecutor Dominance of the Warrant Decision: A Study of Current Practices, 1964 Wash. U.L.Q. 1, 6.

[6] Giordenello v. United States, 357 U.S. 480, 78 Sup. Ct. 1245, 2 L. Ed. 2d 1503 (1958).

[7] Aguilar v. Texas, 378 U.S. 108, 84 Sup. Ct. 1509, 12 L. Ed. 2d 723 (1964). The Fourth Amendment had been made generally applicable to the states by Mapp v. Ohio, 367 U.S. 643, 81 Sup. Ct. 1684, 6 L. Ed. 2d 1081 (1961). It is clear that the Fourth Amendment applies both to arrest and search warrants. State v. Licari, 153 Conn. 127, 214 A.2d 900 (1965).

[8] State ex rel. White v. Simpson, 28 Wis. 2d 590, 137 N.W.2d 391 (1965); accord, State v. Matthews, 270 N.C. 35, 153 S.E.2d 791 (1967); see Bush v. Wilcox, 223 Ga. 89, 153 S.E.2d 701 (1967). But see State v. Coolidge, 106 N.H. 186, 208 A.2d 322 (1965), in which search warrants issued by a state prosecutor, possessing the title of attorney general, were upheld. This case does not in form contravene the proposition that search and arrest warrants can be issued only by judicial officials, because in this case the prosecutor was also an acting justice of the peace. However, a departure from the substance of Aguilar may appear because this dual official nevertheless retained his role as advocate for the state. A greater departure in form, but perhaps a lesser one in substance, appears in Commonwealth v. Penta, 225 N.E.2d 58 (Mass. 1967), in which search warrants issued by clerks of court were held to be valid. It might be argued that these clerks, as adjuncts of the judicial office, shared some of its presumptive impartiality.

State ex rel. Sahley v. Thompson, 151 S.E.2d 870 (W. Va. 1966) presents a more complicated possible departure from Aguilar. The case validated certain warrants issued by a city police lieutenant and also upheld city charter provisions allowing city clerks and police officers to issue warrants generally (without specifying which

not confront the issue whether the ruling was applicable to post-arrest warrants, but the issuance of post-arrest warrants by prosecutors was discontinued. A second problem soon developed. The same line of federal cases required, in addition to formal participation by a judicial official, that the latter make an independent decision about whether probable cause existed, based on evidentiary facts presented to him which were adequate to enable him to do so.[9] Some Wisconsin trial judges interpreted the Wisconsin response to be that all warrants — whether search or arrest, whether pre- or post-arrest — must meet the quantitative and qualitative requirements clearly applicable to pre-arrest warrants. In some instances protracted hearings on the issue were held. Finally, the Wisconsin Supreme Court invited the use of a complaint procedure for charging, dispensing with the need for warrants whenever the arrest in question was valid without one.[10] Thus, without any direct determination whether the requirements for judicial participation in issuing arrest warrants applied to post-arrest warrants, the Wisconsin Court in effect authorized a return to the substance, though not the form, of the initial charging decision used in Wisconsin — indeed in all three states — at the time of the field studies.

It is, perhaps, obvious that judges might participate in the charging decision prior to the holding of a preliminary examination in a serious case, prior to trial in a minor one, on any of three different occasions. The first of these occasions is at the issuance of a warrant, the second is at the initial appearance, and the third at a habeas corpus hearing between the time of the

---

kinds of warrants). Close reading of the case reveals, however, that the particular warrants in question had probably been issued after arrest and were, at any rate, being used as charging documents. Aguilar does not unequivocally apply to post-arrest warrants as it does to pre-arrest and search warrants, and it is therefore not directly contravened by the validation of warrants in Thompson. If, however, the general upholding of the charter is taken to mean that clerks and policemen can issue pre-arrest and search warrants as well, a more certain basis appears for designating the case to be out of line with federal constitutional requirements. In connection with the latter observation, it is noteworthy that, while the West Virginia court ignored Aguilar, it quoted at length from Ocampo v. United States, 234 U.S. 91, 34 Sup. Ct. 712, 58 L. Ed. 1231 (1914). Insofar as this latter case characterizes the finding of probable cause for arrest as a "quasi-judicial" function which need not be performed by a strictly judicial officer, it appears to have been overruled by Aguilar. The West Virginia court also relied, among other older authorities, upon State v. Van Brocklin, 194 Wis. 441, 217 N.W. 277 (1927), (search warrants issued by clerk of court), which appears to have been superseded by the Simpson case, *supra*.

9 See authorities cited note 3 *supra*.

10 Pillsbury v. State, 31 Wis. 2d 87, 142 N.W.2d 187 (1966).

initial appearance and the preliminary examination or trial when there is no preliminary examination. This chapter examines the relevant practice in the three states.

A. Judicial Participation in the Warrant Decision

During the time of the field studies, there was no apparent reason to establish one set of practices for issuing warrants which were to serve as arrest documents and another set for those which were to serve only as charging documents. *Giordenello v. United States*[11] and its progeny had not been decided, so it was not even clear that judicial participation in issuing pre-arrest warrants was constitutionally mandated for federal officers.[12] Certainly the form that participation had to take was not clear.[13] And it was

[11] 357 U.S. 480, 78 Sup. Ct. 1245, 2 L. Ed. 2d 1503 (1958).

[12] See Ocampo v. United States, 234 U.S. 91, 34 Sup. Ct. 712, 58 L. Ed. 1231 (1914).

[13] The basic question has been to what extent the judge is permitted to rely upon information presented to him by the applicants for a warrant — usually police officers or prosecutors but sometimes private complainants — as opposed to conducting some sort of independent investigation on his own. The facts surrounding criminal activity will come to the attention of the applicants or complainants first, and they will convey the information to the issuing judge. The latter is not expected to conduct an independent investigation in the sense of leaving his courtroom and searching out facts other than those presented to him by officers, prosecutors, and complainants. What is contemplated is that he will perform an independent investigatory function in assuring, basically, (1) that the information presented to him is reliable, and (2) that it is presented to him in a detailed and explicit enough form to facilitate an independent judgment on his part about the existence or nonexistence of probable cause.

Under the first of these two concerns, there is emphasis on the need for the applicant to support his allegations by oath or affirmation. See State v. Licari, 153 Conn. 127, 214 A.2d 900 (1965). It has been held that, in addition to signing a sworn complaint to serve as an application for a warrant, the complainant when available must appear in court to be interrogated by the judge. People v. Krumery, 74 Ill. App. 2d 298, 220 N.E.2d 241 (1966). The first concern also appears in the typical situation in which the applicant or complainant has acquired his information in second-hand fashion and is able to swear to the facts only "on information and belief," as opposed to having perceived the occurrences himself in which case he could swear to his "direct knowledge." The courts generally approve the issuance of warrants on the basis of hearsay testimony, but the issuing judge must ferret out that portion of the information which is hearsay and assure himself that the applicant's informants were reliable. See United States v. Ventresca, 380 U.S. 102, 85 Sup. Ct. 741, 13 L. Ed. 2d 684 (1965); Aguilar v. Texas, 378 U.S. 108, 84 Sup. Ct. 1509, 12 L. Ed. 2d 723 (1964); Giordenello v. United States, 357 U.S. 480, 78 Sup. Ct. 1245, 2 L. Ed. 2d 1503 (1958); see also Draper v. United States, 358 U.S. 307, 79 Sup. Ct. 329, 3 L. Ed. 2d 327 (1959); see generally Tiffany, McIntyre and Rotenberg, Detection of Crime 99-120 (1967).

The second of the two basic concerns dovetails with a judgment that the basic facts surrounding criminal activity, as opposed to inferences already drawn by

not until *Aguilar v. Texas*[14] was decided in 1964 that the requirements of the *Giordenello* line of cases were applied to the states as well.[15] In any event no differences in the extent of judicial participation in pre- and post-arrest warrant issuance were observed. Of course, the practices in effect in all of the states presumably have changed in pre-arrest warrant situations, but because so few arrests are made pursuant to a warrant, the importance of the field data is not substantially diminished.

The three states have allocated the power to issue warrants in three different ways. Nonetheless, it is readily apparent from a study of current practice that in each of those states the prosecutor alone makes the effective warrant decision. Of primary interest is that the formal law in each state provides in varying degree for judicial intervention in the warrant process, which could serve as a limitation on the power of the prosecutor. However, magistrates vested with power to so control prosecutors have not exercised the power.

In Michigan, statutes confine the power to issue warrants to magistrates both in cases which are cognizable before them and

---

applicants from facts which are not disclosed to the issuing judge, should be presented to him. See note 3 *supra*. But see In re Davis, 224 A.2d 905 (Vt. 1966). This conclusion is clear from the Aguilar and Giordenello cases. However, the Supreme Court has addressed itself only to cases involving second-hand information presented to the issuing judge as "information and belief." This has caused some state courts to require less specification of fact when the applicant is able to testify to his "direct knowledge." See State v. Taylor, 391 S.W.2d 929 (Mo. 1965); State ex rel. White v. Simpson, 28 Wis. 2d 590, 596-597, 137 N.W.2d 391, 394 (1965). The apparent syllogism is that, if the information has not filtered down from informants other than the instant applicant, the latter is in a favorable position to interpret the facts which he has directly perceived. The issuing judge should, therefore, be allowed to rely upon inferences drawn by the applicant from basic facts rather than drawing them himself.

Another issue which falls within the purview of the second basic concern is whether all the facts adjudged necessary to satisfy the requirements relating to presentation of information to the issuing judge must appear on the face of the complaint. The present Federal Rules of Criminal Procedure do not explicitly sanction the practice of judicially interrogating applicants, or any witnesses they might have brought to court with them, in order to supply the information needed to remedy a complaint which is otherwise defective on its face for lack of specificity. However, an amendment proposed by the current Reporter for the Advisory Committee on the Federal Rules of Criminal Procedure to Fed. R. Crim. P. 3 does explicitly recognize the practice, as does Lopez v. United States, 370 F.2d 8 (5th Cir. 1966); see Ex parte Krusiewiez, 263 Mich. 74, 248 N.W. 554 (1933); Curnow v. Kessler, 110 Mich. 10, 67 N.W. 982 (1896).

[14] See note 7 *supra*.

[15] It is noteworthy, however, that a few cases cited in note 8 *supra* indicate reluctance to accept the obvious requirement of judicial participation exacted by Aguilar.

in cases which are not.[16] Warrants may not be issued except on probable cause, and prior approval of the prosecutor is required.[17] The observed practice does not reflect this formal allocation of power and responsibility. Typically, after the prosecutor's office has issued to the complainant or to the police officer an official recommendation for a warrant, the police officer and the complainant then go to the Recorder's Court warrant clerk's office. In this office complaint forms are kept which contain the required language for twenty-six of the most common misdemeanors and forty-seven felonies and high misdemeanors. The blank spaces in the printed forms are filled in with information taken from the prosecutor's recommendation, and, if further information is needed, it may be obtained from the investigating officer's write-up, or from the complainant or the officer orally. The complaint is then signed. The signed complaint and the warrant are taken to a judge of Recorder's Court who has been given responsibility for signing warrants. This judge is responsible as well for conducting initial appearances and preliminary examinations.

While one or the other of those proceedings is in progress, the police officer and the complainant approach the clerk, who administers the oath to the complainant, and then take the warrant to the bench for the judge's signature. At most, the judge cursorily scans the warrant before signing; frequently he signs without examining the contents at all. Obviously, whatever the reasons, it is clear that magistrates do not exercise any real control over the issuance of warrants, and the effective decision is made by the prosecutor.[18]

The Kansas statute also confines the power to issue warrants to magistrates, but, unlike the Michigan statute, does not require the concurrence of the prosecutor in the decision.[19] Thus, the

16 Mich. Stat. Ann. §§28.860 to 28.1195 (1954).

17 A significant rift has developed in the Michigan Supreme Court in regard to the significance of this requirement of prosecutor approval. See note 29 *infra*. For present purposes suffice it to say that the provision distinguishes Michigan from the other two states surveyed which authorize only magistrates to issue warrants and impose no requirement of prior prosecutorial approval.

18 One judge responsible for the signing of warrants stated that he, being a former prosecutor himself, placed much faith in the ability of the present prosecutor to screen cases. Consequently, he did little more than scan the information contained in the warrant before signing it. Another judge was observed signing his name to warrants while listening to the testimony of witnesses in other matters. Still another was stopped before entering an elevator and asked to sign a warrant, which he did without completely unfolding the document to ascertain the charge.

19 Kan. Stat. Ann. §§62-601 to 62-602, 63-201 (1964).

formal law gives the magistrate exclusive authority to make the determination of probable cause prerequisite to the issuance of arrest warrants; observation of the practice, however, makes it clear that the magistrate plays virtually no role in the warrant decision. In Wichita, the complaint and warrant are both prepared by the county attorney's office and are then delivered to the office of the clerk of the Court of Common Pleas, where the complaint is signed before a deputy clerk of that court, who then issues the warrant. That there is considerable doubt expressed by personnel of the county attorney's office about the validity of warrants so issued does not inhibit the practice, except if extradition may be involved. Then, because of the increased probability that the warrant might be challenged as improperly issued, the judge is usually requested to sign it.

Either the magistrate or the prosecutor could issue arrest warrants in Wisconsin without the concurrence of the other.[20] Despite this express authority, the prosecutor seldom signed warrants himself. Typically, the complaint was prepared by the prosecutor's office but was taken to the clerk of court who prepared and signed the warrant. One judge authorized to issue warrants told a field reporter that he had never refused a warrant, that he seldom knew anything about its being issued, and that he regarded it as a ministerial function of the clerk. What purpose was then thought to be served by insisting that magistrates, or their clerks, perform this step is unclear. Perhaps some notion of freedom from responsibility, or even from civil liability, induced it.

In short, while the details vary considerably from state to state, and even among different courts of a state, there is virtually no judicial inquiry into the existence of probable cause for the issuance of arrest warrants. And this is true despite the variety of formal schemes for the allocation of this function. In each of the three states the determination whether a warrant should be issued is made by the office of the prosecuting attorney.

Although researchers have not dealt thoroughly with the subject,[21] enough work has been done to make clear that the present dominant position of the prosecutor over the warrant decision did not derive from English common law.[22] The public prosecu-

[20] This remained true until the court in State ex rel. White v. Simpson, 28 Wis. 2d 590, 137 N.W.2d 391 (1965) held that only magistrates could issue them.

[21] See Moley, Politics and Criminal Prosecution 48 (1929); Note, The District Attorney — A Historical Puzzle, 1952 Wis. L. Rev. 125, 138.

[22] The very institution of public prosecution is largely an American invention.

tor, as that institution is known in this country, plays a comparatively small role in the administration of criminal justice in England today;[23] that role was an even smaller one at the time the American institutions developed.[24] Various explanations have been offered why the English practice of leaving control over prosecutions for the most part in private (and police) hands was not adopted here.[25] But, whatever explanation is accepted, earlier observers of the system agreed that the prosecutor is the most important figure in the administrative process.[26] Moley underscored a major premise of his work:

> I have attempted to indicate the very great importance of the public prosecutor, a fact which is particularly American. The sheriff and the coroner, the grand jury, and finally the petit jury, products of a long historical evolution, have quite faded into insignificance. Likewise, both the examining magistrate and the trial judge in state courts partially through their own lack of capacity, partly through legal limitations upon their powers, and largely because they have no means for knowing what they should know about the cases before them, perform no dominant role. In the midst of the decay and impotence of his official associates, the prosecutor rises to a definite mastery. To a considerable extent he is police, prosecutor, magistrate, grand jury, petit jury, and judge in one.[27]

When the prosecutor's de facto control over prosecutions generally is combined with the observed practice of using the arrest warrant primarily as a charging document rather than to perform its historical arrest-authorizing function, it is inevitable that the prosecutor should assume control over its issuance. It is nonetheless true, however, that the law, while liberally recognizing that the prosecutor has great discretion in controlling prosecutions,[28] still conceives of the arrest warrant as performing its historical function, and, for the most part, still vests in the judiciary the

---

The development of this institution and the controls that have been maintained over it by other officials and private citizens are discussed in Chapter 20 *infra*.

[23] See generally Williams, The Power to Prosecute, 1955 Crim. L. Rev. 596

[24] See generally Moley, *supra* note 21, at 193-198.

[25] See, e.g., National Commn. on Law Observance and Enforcement, Report on Prosecution 7 (1931).

[26] Moley, *supra* note 21, at vii; see Healy, The Prosecutor (In Chicago) in Felony Cases, in Illinois Crime Survey 285 (1929); Hurst, The Growth of American Law: The Law Makers 174 (1950); Lashly, Preparation and Presentation of the State's Case, in Missouri Crime Survey 113 (1926).

[27] Moley, *supra* note 21, at vii

[28] This point is covered extensively in Chapter 8 *infra*.

power to determine the sufficiency of the evidence to justify arrest. Magistrates, in fulfilling this role, would theoretically be determining whether the available evidence was sufficient to justify an arrest, while the prosecutor's principal concern would be with the existence of adequate evidence to charge, along with his estimate of the social desirability of commencing or preventing prosecution for other reasons than probability of guilt.

Why this contemplated distribution of function is not realized in current administration is not entirely clear. What is clear is that some pragmatic considerations enter the picture. If magistrates were to issue arrest warrants against the wishes of the prosecutor — or even issue them frequently without prior consultation — many initial arrests or further detentions of persons suspected of crime who have already been screened out by the prosecutor would occur. That screening may have been on technical evidence-sufficiency grounds, on a stiffer standard of probable convictability, or on nonevidence-sufficiency grounds. Whatever the grounds, it will have occurred. To issue a warrant under those circumstances would entail the following: (1) a belief on the part of the magistrate that his judgment is superior to that of the prosecutor; (2) a belief, at least in some instances, that the nonevidence-sufficiency basis utilized by the prosecutor is inappropriate; or (3) a willingness to take what would, in all likelihood, be a futile step, since the power of the prosecutor to nolle prosequi the case would almost certainly be exercised to prevent prosecution. The refusal to issue a warrant without prior prosecutor approval, then, is not mysterious.[29]

[29] The pragmatic considerations cited in the text can be identified without an empirical survey of current administration to the extent that they receive recognition in the formal law pertaining to the allocation of power to control prosecutions. The prosecutor is typically designated as the official who is, by virtue of his active role in law enforcement and his intimate connection with the circumstances of individual cases, best qualified to decide as a matter of routine whether the lodging of criminal charges or their subsequent withdrawal would serve the community interest. See, e.g., Pugach v. Klein, 193 F. Supp. 630, 635 (S.D.N.Y. 1961); State ex rel. Griffin v. Smith, 363 Mo. 1235, 1239-1240, 258 S.W.2d 590, 593 (1953). The pertinent cases and statutes are canvassed more exhaustively in Chapter 8 *infra*. It appears to be contemplated in law that, as long as his charging decisions fall within a flexible standard of expectability, the prosecutor will be allocated principal control of prosecutions as a matter of routine. Judicial displacement of the prosecutor's discretion in charging is reserved for the atypical situation in which the latter's activities do not meet that standard because they reflect either bad faith or corruption on his part. This is the principal basis for the interpretation of formal law developed in Chapter 20 *infra*.

The warrant decision becomes a kaleidoscope for the pragmatic considerations insofar as it relates to charging. Michigan law provides a prime example; the state has long followed the policy of advising magistrates (or justices of the peace)

Why magistrates perfunctorily issue warrants requested by prosecutors is less clear and depends to a substantial extent on different considerations. Ordinarily, a prosecutor would be effectively stymied by the refusal of a magistrate to issue a warrant, because he cannot proceed without the technical approval of a magistrate. Of course, outside the large metropolitan centers, the

---

to consult prosecutors about the wisdom of charging before prosecutions are initiated by warrants. See Beecher v. Anderson, 45 Mich. 543, 548, 8 N.W. 539, 541 (1881). The policy is codified in Mich. Stat. Ann. §28.1195 (1954), which provides that a justice of the peace cannot issue warrants, except in some specified kinds of minor offenses, without first securing the written approval of the prosecutor. "The object sought to be accomplished by that statute was to guard against the indiscretion, frequently indulged in by magistrates, in permitting legal proceedings to be instituted against parties for crime without any previous inquiry into the circumstances." People v. Griswold, 64 Mich. 722, 723, 31 N.W. 809, 810 (1887). Griswold held, nevertheless, that noncompliance with the statutory requirement did not deprive a justice of jurisdiction over the person charged by a warrant issued without prosecutor approval. Even this jurisdictional reservation to the policy has now been overruled by People v. Holbrook, 373 Mich. 94, 128 N.W.2d 484 (1964), in which the court stated: "The policy behind the statute would appear to be to insure orderly procedure by, in the main, funnelling all law enforcement through the prosecuting attorney, the chief law enforcement officer of a county." Id. at 97, 128 N.W.2d at 486. The state supreme court was divided on the jurisdictional point and the aftermath is People v. Carter, 379 Mich. 24, 148 N.W.2d 860 (1967). There the prosecutor had not signed an order specifically authorizing the magistrate to issue a warrant. However, he had prepared and signed a complaint. The court, noting that the statute did not designate any particular form for his written approval, held the complaint to be sufficient approval to validate the subsequently issued warrant and establish jurisdiction. In separate opinions, some of the dissenting judges in Holbrook were quick to assert that Carter implied a return to the Griswold position. It is noteworthy that their objections to Holbrook extended only to its particular jurisdictional position — under the view that it had, by encouraging collateral attacks on convictions, introduced an unnecessary administrative complication — and not to the basic statutory policy enunciated in both Griswold and Holbrook.

The difficulty with this policy, of course, is that it has not been reconciled with the distinct constitutional considerations which relate to the arrest-authorizing functions of a warrant. When these considerations are drawn, a shift in conceptual focus is necessary. The magistrate becomes the pre-eminent figure in the warrant process. Actually, however, the prosecutor dominates the concrete fact of warrant issuance and this magisterial role is only a hypothetical one called for by articulations in law relating solely to arrest. The fact is conceptually divided into distinct arrest and charging considerations and articulations of these are attached synthetically back to the gross occurrence. The considerations have not been reconciled with one another. See note 4 *supra*. The active, adversary role of the prosecutor in law enforcement is said to furnish the very reason for his competence to dominate the charging function, whereas reference is made to this same role when preference is expressed for control of the arrest function by an impartial judicial official. Articulated considerations about charging reflect with reasonable accuracy what actually occurs but those about arrest do not. It is natural enough, when prescriptions concerning the dominant figure in a single process entertain contradictory presuppositions, that the position least compatible with the realities of practice would receive the lesser realization.

prosecutor could "shop around," and present his request to a series of magistrates until he found an acquiescent one. And it may be that, under the old fee system, fear of retaliation by the prosecutor with a consequent loss of fees was a factor in magisterial relinquishment of control. But the same reluctance to oppose the wishes of the prosecutor is found in large metropolitan centers with unitary multi-branch courts which effectively prevent "shopping around."

Another possible explanation is that magistrates realize that their offices have certain inherent limitations to which a prosecutor is not subject. Traditionally magistrates have been laymen who might feel a certain diffidence in disputing the essentially legal conclusions reached by law-trained persons.[30] Whether lawyers or laymen, magistrates do not have the investigational facilities available to prosecutors. These may be overriding reasons for deferring to the prosecutor's judgment in so many cases that automatic issuance has become the accepted practice, with the power to refuse effectively lost by disuse. Then too, in serious cases, magistrates may feel that their control over the process can be exercised more effectively at the preliminary examination stage. In short, the complete dominance of the prosecutor over the warrant decision is partly a concomitant of his general power to control prosecutions, and partly a recognition of his greater capacity to make the initial decision correctly.

B. Judicial Participation in the Charging Decision at the Initial Appearance

Immediately after a post-arrest warrant has been issued, the suspect is brought before a judicial official for what is variously called an initial appearance or an arraignment on the warrant. In practice the initial appearance serves two functions: an occasion for setting bail and for determining whether the suspect wishes a preliminary examination. Extensively in Michigan, to a lesser extent in Kansas, and scarcely at all in Wisconsin, the latter determination was made by asking the defendant to plead guilty or not guilty. A plea of guilty was interpreted as a waiver of the preliminary examination.[31] When the plea system is not used, or

30 It is arguable that this factor relates to the "indiscretion" of certain justices referred to in the quote from People v. Griswold, note 29 *supra*.

31 Waiver of the preliminary and the utilization of this pleading device to

if the plea is not guilty, the defendant is simply asked whether he desires a preliminary examination. His answer in general determines whether he will have a preliminary examination, although the absence of an attorney may be an important factor in some courts in the decision whether to permit him to make such a waiver.

Of greatest significance here is that, if he makes any protest of innocence, or attempts to offer any explanation for his conduct, he is simply told that it is the purpose of the preliminary examination, and not of the initial appearance, to determine whether there is adequate evidence of his guilt to justify holding him for trial. It is thus clear that, in practice, the initial appearance is not an occasion for judicial supervision over or review of the charging decision.

---

determine waiver are discussed more extensively in Chapter 6 *infra*. The observed Michigan practice was to require defendants to plead at the initial appearance as a matter of routine. In Sedgwick County, Kansas, only those defendants who either appeared with counsel, or stated that they wanted none, were asked to plead. Defendants requesting counsel were not asked to plead and preliminary hearings were set for them without asking whether the latter were desired. Wisconsin has a statute specifying that defendants shall not be required to plead in cases not triable by the magistrate, Wis. Stat. Ann. §954.04 (1958), but a few instances were observed in which voluntarily offered pleas were accepted as waivers.

Asking defendants who are not represented by counsel to plead at initial proceedings has given rise to several problems concerning the consequences of uttering a guilty plea at this stage. In some states the practice was followed of admitting these admissions of guilt into evidence if the defendant ultimately asserted his innocence and went to trial. This gave rise to the "critical-stage" rationale of White v. Maryland, 373 U.S. 59, 83 Sup. Ct. 1050, 10 L. Ed. 2d 193 (1963) and Hamilton v. Alabama, 368 U.S. 52, 82 Sup. Ct. 157, 7 L. Ed. 2d 114 (1961). If the indigent defendant is required at this early stage to do anything that might substantially prejudice his case, counsel must be appointed to advise him about the possible consequences. Since the practice of admitting guilty pleas taken at this stage into evidence at the trial was not observed in the three states under consideration, this particular problem did not present itself. There remains concern, however, over how fair it is in Michigan to involve the unrepresented accused in a procedural routine which might have the unexpected effect of waiving his preliminary hearing. The Supreme Court has never ruled that the loss of a preliminary is prejudicial enough per se — as is entry of a guilty plea into evidence — to render the initial appearance a "critical stage" because of the possibility of waiver at that point. Guthrie v. Boles, 261 F. Supp. 852 (N.D.W. Va. 1967). Nevertheless, Michigan now has a remand procedure designed to assure that defendants unrepresented by counsel do not lose any defense advantages because they are unaware of the significance of waiving the preliminary at the initial appearance. Convictions can be overturned by trial courts and cases can be remanded for preliminary hearings when waiver has been accomplished without benefit of counsel. The state appellate judiciary has made it clear that the trial courts are expected to administer this remand procedure liberally. People v. Wiggins, 6 Mich. App. 340, 149 N.W.2d 261 (1967).

C. Availability of Habeas Corpus to Test the Evidentiary Basis for the Charging Decision Prior to the Preliminary Examination or Summary Trial

Even though judicial participation in the charging decision is perfunctory, at the end of the initial appearance there will be some kind of judicial direction which authorizes continued custody — or the conditioning of freedom on bail or personal recognizance — though there will not often have been any meaningful judicial finding of probable cause to believe the suspect guilty.[32] The law obviously contemplates that in serious cases the question whether sufficient evidence exists to justify charging will be answered at the preliminary examination, if one is held.[33] Further, in minor cases, with no provision for a preliminary examination or if one is waived in serious cases, it assumes that no regular part of the process would serve as the necessarily appropriate or exclusive occasion for determining whether the evidence justified the initial charging decision. The issue then is the extent to which the charging decision, evidenced by the filing of a complaint, issuance of a warrant, and the holding of an initial appearance, is subject to attack for lack of evidence at this stage of the proceedings.

The procedures which might arguably be used to test the sufficiency of the evidence to charge at this stage are the motion to quash the warrant and habeas corpus.[34] Because these procedural devices raise substantially the same questions, only incidental attention is given to differences between them. Under some circumstances, the complaint-warrant complex or other commitment orders are subject to attack. In Kansas, for example, an improperly verified warrant may be quashed, with the consequent necessity for amendment or re-issue.[35] The same result is reached

[32] See Whalen v. Cristell, 161 Kan. 747, 173 P.2d 252 (1946); State v. Beebe, 13 Kan. 589 (1874); State ex rel. City of Milwaukee v. Newman, 96 Wis. 258, 71 N.W. 438 (1897); In re Eldred, 46 Wis. 530 (1879).

[33] See Anderson v. State, 240 Ala. 169, 198 So. 169 (1940); In re De Mello, 18 Cal. App. 2d 407, 63 P.2d 1157 (1937); In re Peoples, 47 Mich. 626, 14 N.W. 112 (1882); Ex parte McCorkle, 29 Tex. App. 20, 13 S.W. 991 (1890); In re Eldred, note 32 *supra*, at 530.

[34] These remedies are discussed in greater detail in Chapter 7 *infra* relating to reviewability of the bindover order handed down at the end of the preliminary. Since they are not generally available for review of the sufficiency of evidence supporting the initial charge, they are only mentioned at this point.

[35] See State v. Gleason, 32 Kan. 245, 4 Pac. 363 (1884). The Kansas court was willing to uphold a certain form of verification of an information filed by the prosecutor directly in the court of general trial jurisdiction only when the in-

when there is an inadequate statement of the offense.[36] Inquiry by habeas corpus is available only if the process which authorizes commitment is defective in form or invalid on its face.[37]

---

formation — which the court analogized to a complaint under the circumstances at hand — was not to serve as the basis for an arrest warrant. The inquiry into the form of verification of an initial charging document — whether an information filed directly in the court of general trial jurisdiction or a complaint filed with a magistrate — reflects concern only over the validity of the arrest process and not the sufficiency of evidence to support the initial charge. See State v. Bjorkland, 34 Kan. 377, 8 Pac. 391 (1885).

[36] The standard for the degree of detail that must be included in a complaint in describing the offense is uncertain in all three states. In Kansas, it is usually sufficient to state the complaint in terms of the statute alleged to have been violated, State v. Armell, 8 Kan. 288 (1871), but beyond that statement the standard is uncertain. It is clear, however, that the degree of detail or the accuracy of the detail need not be as great as is required for informations. In State v. Smith, 13 Kan. 274 (1874), the complaint-warrant charged defendant generally with embezzling money from funds belonging to the county and the information following preliminary alleged different funds. The court on appeal affirmed the conviction "with some hesitation." The court took judicial notice that most justices were unlearned in the technicalities of the law so that the standard for setting out the offense in the complaint should be less than the requirement for the information. See also State v. Richardson, 137 Kan. 58, 19 P.2d 735 (1933); State v. Oliver, 129 Kan. 719, 284 Pac. 357 (1930); State v. Stoffel, 48 Kan. 364, 29 Pac. 685 (1892); Wagstaff v. Shippel, 27 Kan. 450 (1882). Little authority has been found on the sufficiency of the detail of the information filed for a misdemeanor, but it appears that the standards may be the same as for complaints. For example, in State v. Grewell, 19 Kan. 193 (1877), involving an attack on the sufficiency of an information, the court relied for its general rule on State v. Armell, *supra*, where the attack was on the sufficiency of a complaint. See also State v. Farmer's Union Cooperative Assn., 170 Kan. 171, 223 P.2d 747 (1950).

In Wisconsin, the standard for the sufficiency of detail for a complaint is apparently also the same for misdemeanors, State v. Larson, 231 Wis. 207, 234 N.W. 21 (1939), as for felonies, Butler v. State, 102 Wis. 364, 78 N.W. 590 (1899). See also Heckman v. Swarts, 64 Wis. 48, 24 N.W. 473 (1885). The verbal formula for that standard is "a substantial statement of some offense." See State v. Huegin, 110 Wis. 189, 85 N.W. 1046 (1901). Stating the charge in the language of the statute alleged to have been violated satisfies that minimum standard, Butler v. State, *supra*. The complaint-warrant might be reviewed under habeas corpus for the sufficiency of its statement of an offense, but it is fairly certain that there can be no inquiry into the underlying evidentiary base for the charge prior to the preliminary. See Wolke v. Fleming, 24 Wis. 2d 606, 129 N.W.2d 841 (1964).

The question is largely unlitigated in Michigan. The reason complaints in felony cases are not challenged in these terms may be explained when it is recalled that the complaint may be oral, and there is no requirement for reduction to writing. However, it is not clear why warrants, which must be in writing in all cases, and complaints which must be written in cases triable before a magistrate, are not challenged on grounds of insufficiency of the charge as they are in Kansas and Wisconsin. The only case located in which such a challenge was made — unsuccessfully — is People v. Whitemore, 102 Mich. 519, 61 N.W. 15 (1894).

[37] See Whalen v. Cristell, 161 Kan. 747, 749, 173 P.2d 252, 254 (1946): ". . . court can and should always inquire into and determine questions pertaining to the validity and sufficiency of the commitment on its face to justify the detention and

In no case, however, has a court sustained a motion to quash or granted a writ of habeas corpus on the ground that the evidence was insufficient to support the initial charge decision. Courts consider the probable cause question in serious cases to be one for the magistrate to determine at the preliminary examination. They refuse to inquire into it on habeas corpus, believing the determination to be premature, although habeas corpus may be granted if the preliminary examination is inexcusably delayed or refused.[38]

The attitude of the courts in felony cases is summed up in the following quotation from an Alabama case:

> The rule seems to be well settled that when an affidavit is made before a committing magistrate, charging the defendant with the commission of an offense as to which such magistrate has only the jurisdiction to hold a preliminary trial, the defendant remains within the jurisdiction of such magistrate until after the preliminary trial is held. If the magistrate refused to grant a preliminary trial, he can be compelled to do so by a writ of mandamus; but the petition for a writ of habeas corpus cannot be filed, praying for the discharge of such a defendant, until after the preliminary trial is had. . . .
>
> After preliminary trial and before indictment, the legality of the defendant's commitment can always be inquired into upon a petition for a writ of habeas corpus; and if the facts of his case show that there is no probable cause for believing him guilty of the offense with which he is charged he is entitled to discharge from said prosecution.[39]

It was earlier noted that not all courts relegate suspects whose preliminaries are unreasonably delayed to an action to compel prompt examination. Habeas corpus is, under those special cir-

---

the jurisdiction of the court issuing that process." It is significant that, although habeas corpus might lie to challenge detention under a currently defective commitment process, it no longer lies to correct an earlier defect after judgment of conviction and sentencing by the court of general trial jurisdiction, which had acquired jurisdiction by the filing of an information stating a public offense. McGee v. Crouse, 190 Kan. 615, 376 P.2d 792 (1962). Compare Wolke v. Fleming, 24 Wis. 2d 606, 129 N.W.2d 841 (1964). Defects in the form of the complaint-warrant process can also be waived by the defendant — even before the case is before the court of general trial jurisdiction. See State v. Barry, 183 Kan. 792, 332 P.2d 549 (1958). The holding might be different, at least in the latter situation, if no complaint at all — as distinguished from one which is defective in form — has been filed. See Dodge City v. Day, 195 Kan. 305, 403 P.2d 1004 (1965).

38 See generally LaFave, Arrest 407-410 (1965) for discussion of the possibilities of challenging detention prior to the preliminary.

39 Ex parte Simpson, 3 Ala. App. 222, 229, 57 So. 518, 520 (1912).

cumstances, available to secure release from detention. Despite which remedy is made available, no inquiry is made whether the evidence is sufficient to charge.[40]

The rule appears to be the same in cases triable by magistrates without a preliminary examination. The legality of the detention may be tested only as to its form, not as to its underlying evidentiary basis.[41] The explanation for this rule may be related to the reasons set forth in the following quotation from a Georgia case:

> This is a misdemeanor case. It cannot be questioned that the defendant could have and may have been immediately released on small bail, as well when he was arrested as after the trial on habeas corpus. If the applicant . . . can ignore the criminal prosecution in the court in which it is pending, choose his own remedy and own forum in such a case as this, any person charged with the infraction of any law or municipal ordinance may do likewise. In the most trivial case, where any person is arraigned in a recorder's court, if the present proceeding is permitted, he may ignore the court in which the prosecution is pending, and institute habeas corpus in the superior court, the effect of which would be the overburdening of the most important trial court, where litigation is expensive, and where the adjudication of important cases would be delayed by a flood of petty litigation which should and could be ended in the courts where it originated.[42]

Thus, the attitude of the courts seems to be that the preliminary examination is the exclusive means of testing the probability question in serious cases, and there is no practical need in misdemeanor cases to test it prior to the summary trial at all.[43]

That the field studies revealed no attempts to challenge the charging decision at this stage is consistent with the rationale of the cases: the accused should not be able to select his own mode of procedure to determine whether the charge was justified. In serious cases, legislatures have provided for the preliminary examination for that very purpose. When summary trial procedures are provided for in less serious cases, there simply is no real need for a determination of probable cause to charge prior to the trial itself, which normally follows soon after the charge is made.

40 See Ex parte Leib, 255 Mich. 601, 238 N.W. 473 (1931); In re Peoples, 47 Mich. 626, 14 N.W. 112 (1882).

41 See People v. France, 370 Mich. 156, 121 N.W.2d 476 (1963); State v. Green, 251 N.C. 40, 110 S.E.2d 609 (1959).

42 Jackson v. Lowry, 170 Ga. 755, 154 S.E. 228 (1930).

43 See People ex rel. Conway v. Warden, 180 App. Div. 336, 337-338, 167 N.Y.S. 220, 221 (1917).

CHAPTER 4

The Preliminary Examination as an Adversary Proceeding

An examining magistrate's decision to dismiss a suspect or to hold him for trial is rarely based on all the evidence available to the prosecutor and the defendant.[1] This conclusion, based on a study of current administration, does not reflect the formal law view of the preliminary examination:[2] indeed, it is in marked contrast to the preliminary apparently contemplated by the draftsmen of the relevant statutes. Statutes, which typically contain elaborate provisions regulating the conduct of the preliminary, give the impression that the preliminary is, in effect, a nonjury trial in miniature with all the formal characteristics of the trial itself. The Wisconsin statute is representative:

> As soon as may be, the magistrate shall swear and examine or permit the district attorney to examine the witnesses for the state, in the presence of the defendant, in relation to the crime charged in the complaint; and they may be cross-examined. Then the witnesses for the defendant shall be sworn and examined and may be cross-examined. The defendant may be assisted by counsel.[3]

If the full implications of such statutes were realized in current administration, prosecutors would offer all the evidence at their disposal; defense counsel would subject prosecution witnesses to rigorous cross-examination and would offer all the evidence at

[1] See the description of typical preliminaries in text at notes 4-5 *infra* this chapter.

[2] Although many changes in criminal law administration have occurred since the Crime Surveys, Moley, Our Criminal Courts 20-36 (1930), contains an interesting discussion of the contrast between the preliminary as it appeared (and to a large extent still does appear) in the formal law and in contemporaneous practice.

[3] Wis. Stat. Ann. §954.08(1) (1958). See Kan. Stat. Ann. §§ 62-614 to 62-615 (1964); Mich. Stat. Ann. §§28.922 to 28.930 (1954); ALI, Code of Criminal Procedure §§46, 49, Comment at 287-289, 293-297 (1931).

their disposal; prosecutors would cross-examine defense witnesses carefully; and magistrates would make careful determinations only after extended argument by counsel. In short, the preliminary examination would be clearly an adversary proceeding, with extensive participation by both prosecutor and defense counsel.

The preliminary examinations observed, however more closely approximated an ex parte proceeding, for although the defendant was present,[4] he rarely participated. Typically, the prosecutor put on one or two of his witnesses; the defendant, even when represented by counsel, did little cross-examining and put on no evidence of his own; and the bindover decision was made without the benefit of extensive argument by counsel. Thus, the adversary proceeding contemplated in the statutes has not materialized, and the result is that determinations are made on considerably less than all of the available evidence.

The failure of the preliminary to insure that bindover decisions will be made on the basis of all the facts is marked by three specific characteristics: (1) minimum disclosure by prosecutors, (2) inadequate cross-examination of prosecution witnesses, and (3) no disclosure by the defendant. Each of these ways in which the preliminary fails to compel full disclosure of the facts is discussed separately. The *typical* preliminary examination, at least in the three jurisdictions under study here,[5] is described. That discussion is followed by a summary, in which an attempt is made to discover why most preliminary examinations follow this typical pattern, and, more importantly, why some preliminaries deviate from it.

A. Disclosure by the Prosecutor

In each of the three states, statutes provide, in substance, that the magistrate shall examine "the complainant and the witnesses to support the prosecution."[6] Case law interpretation makes it

[4] Statutes in each of the three states require the defendant's presence. See note 3 *supra*. The defendant is invariably present for his preliminary examination, even though he may waive his right to confrontation. See State v. Justus, 86 Kan. 848, 122 Pac. 877 (1912); 2 Op. Wis. Att'y Gen. 345 (1913). The confrontation requirement precludes the use of affidavits at preliminary examinations. Seyfer v. Bloomer, 132 Kan. 877, 297 Pac. 681 (1931). In People v. Asta, 337 Mich. 590, 60 N.W.2d 472 (1953), the court said that the confrontation requirement precluded the use of hearsay evidence at a preliminary examination.

[5] For an indication that the preliminary examination typically follows this same pattern in other jurisdictions, see Moreland, Modern Criminal Procedure 152-158 (1959); Note, 106 U. Pa. L. Rev. 589 (1958); see also note 2 *supra*.

[6] Kan. Stat. Ann. §62-614 (1964); Mich. Stat. Ann. §28.922 (1954); Wis. Stat. Ann.

clear that this language does not require the prosecutor to use all the available witnesses.[7] Indeed, formal law does not even require the complainant to testify,[8] provided, of course, that probable cause can be shown without his testimony. No case can be conceived, however, in which it would not be necessary to use at least one witness in order to show probable cause.[9] Although the issue is unlitigated, apparently formal law does not require the prosecutor to produce at the preliminary any relevant documents which he may have in his possession.[10]

---

§954.08(1) (1958) ("the witnesses for the state") See ALI, Code of Criminal Procedure §§40, 42, 46 (1931).

7 "It is claimed by the plaintiffs in error that this statute [presently Wis. Stat. Ann. §954.08(1) (1958)] is mandatory, and that, unless the complaining witness and all the witnesses known to the state are examined, no legal preliminary examination is had. It is sufficient to say that we cannot agree with this contention. We regard the statute as directory only. A sufficient number of witnesses were examined to amply justify the magistrate in binding over [the defendant] for trial, and this must be held to satisfy the statute." Emery v. State, 92 Wis. 146, 155, 65 N.W. 848, 851 (1896). At the time of Emery, the language of the statute was identical with the present Kansas and Michigan provisions. Wis. Rev. Stat. §4786 (1878). See note 6 *supra* and accompanying text.

8 Lundstrum v. State, 140 Wis. 141, 121 N.W. 883 (1909). Holding the same way in People v. Curtis, 95 Mich. 212, 54 N.W. 767 (1893), the court said, "We think this statute is directory as to the quantity of testimony to be taken. If it be given too literal a construction, then, in any case where there are no witnesses other than the complainant, the respondent cannot be held; so, if the complainant should die after the complaint, the proceedings must abate. What is intended by the language quoted is that the justice shall receive such testimony from the complainant and his witnesses as may be offered, and act upon it." Id. at 215, 54 N.W. at 767.

9 The defendant's right to confrontation prevents the use of affidavits at the preliminary examination. See note 4 *supra*.

10 The state may be required to produce documents or permit their inspection by the defendant under discovery laws. Although formal law is lacking, it is likely that the issuance of a complaint or a warrant (or both) is necessary in order to give jurisdiction to the magistrate to hold a preliminary examination. In current administration, both documents are invariably issued prior to the preliminary. See Chapter 1.

Again, although formal law is lacking, in current administration the defendant rarely sees even the complaint or warrant. The contents of these documents are read to the defendant, or he is informed generally of the charge against him, at the initial appearance. Of course, formal law requires notice of the charge prior to trial; in practice formal notice is given at the arraignment on the information. At the preliminary examination, however, it is common for the assistant prosecutor to make his opening statement by reading the complaint, by paraphrasing it, or by simply handing the magistrate a copy of that document.

In addition to the complaint and warrant, an assistant prosecutor's case file at the preliminary examination stage normally contains a prior conviction report and a police summarization of expected testimony. No case was observed in which the defendant was given access to these latter two documents. Of course, if a determination of probable cause cannot be made without a given document, the prosecutor will have to introduce it into evidence. If the defendant has made a confession and it has been reduced to writing, the assistant prosecutor's case file will contain

Given this freedom by the formal law, assistant prosecutors who represent the state at preliminary examinations normally follow a policy of revealing no more evidence than is necessary to obtain a bindover.[11] Although this policy could be implemented by a limited questioning of most of the witnesses available to him, an assistant prosecutor in the typical case, probably from considerations of convenience and the possibility of cross-examination, attempts to secure a bindover by a relatively complete questioning of only one or two of his witnesses.[12] His purpose, of course, is to limit discovery by the defendant as much as possible.[13] The witness most likely to be called is the arresting

---

that document. One Kansas case was observed in which, although there was a written confession by the defendant, it was not introduced into evidence or even referred to at the preliminary examination.

11 A Milwaukee County district judge said that assistant prosecutors in his county have made it a policy to put on as little evidence as possible to secure a bindover at the preliminary examination. An assistant prosecutor in Detroit said it is the policy of the prosecutor's office to reveal just enough of its evidence at the preliminary to obtain a bindover. In outstate Michigan, an assistant prosecutor, commenting on a preliminary he had just completed, said, "On examination, we do not usually use so many witnesses. However, I thought that the case started out to be an assault and battery, and as I got into it deep I found out that there was something more involved so I decided to hear all of the witnesses."

An assistant prosecutor in Kansas City who handles part of the department's trials said that it is usual for the assistant prosecutor handling the preliminary to use all the witnesses available. He said that, if the case is cut and dried, if it is a capital offense, or a very serious felony, only some of the witnesses may be used. One of the reasons for this practice is that the transcript of the testimony of the witnesses at the preliminary is valuable in preparing for the trial. For an indication that the assistant prosecutors in Kansas City do not use all their witnesses, see note 17 *infra*. Generally, assistant prosecutors in Kansas used more witnesses at the preliminary than were used in Michigan and Wisconsin.

12 An assistant district attorney in Milwaukee told of a preliminary in which he intended to use only a police officer and one other witness. However, in conversation with the officer, he was doubtful, as was the police officer, whether more witnesses might be required. He finally told the officer to have the other witnesses in the hall outside the courtroom for his use in case they were needed. The assistant prosecutor used the police officer and rested his case. Then the defense attorney called each of the state's other witnesses who were in the hall and placed them under direct examination.

In Michigan, only seven preliminaries were observed in which the number of witnesses testifying is known; in four of them only one witness testified, and in three of them two witnesses testified. An assistant prosecutor in Detroit said that most judges require only one witness for proof of probable cause. A few judges, however, want it well established that the witness seeing the defendant committing the crime was able to make a reasonably certain identification. Once the defendant is identified as the person who was seen committing the crime or who confessed to it, most judges are willing to hold him for trial without requiring any more evidence.

13 The function of the preliminary examination as a discovery tool is discussed in Newman, Conviction: The Determination of Guilt or Innocence Without Trial (1966).

officer, probably because, for the assistant prosecutor, he is the most convenient witness available as well as the most experienced at testifying. If necessary, the arresting officer's testimony is followed by medical or eye-witness testimony. In any event, the effort is to keep the number of witnesses to a minimum.

In addition, it is likely that fullest use is not normally made of those witnesses who are called, because assistant prosecutors conduct the state's case with a minimum of preparation, at least in the larger cities. The case load, in all probability, prevents assistant prosecutors from conducting the type of preparation prior to the preliminary which the trial assistants conduct prior to the trial of a case.[14] In the typical case, they do not interview any of the witnesses, with the possible exception of an arresting officer, prior to the preliminary examination. Instead, they rely almost exclusively upon the prosecution report prepared by the police. This is a summary of the information which each witness has given to the police. The lack of opportunity for extensive preparation is probably the reason why magistrates occasionally find it necessary to interrupt direct examination by the assistant prosecutor and to ask several questions in order to establish necessary facts.[15]

The consequences of a prosecutor's failure to disclose all evidence available to him at the preliminary examination are, to a large extent, not discoverable.[16] Field observations show, however, that, at least on occasion, dismissals result unnecessarily from this policy.[17] Furthermore, magistrates bind over in some

[14] A deputy county attorney in Kansas City explained that he often does a certain amount of investigation when he is preparing his case for trial, but that he does almost no investigation or interrogation of witnesses prior to the preliminary examination. In preparing for trial, he stated that he examines the documents in the case file, interrogates all the witnesses, visits the scene of the crime, and makes a diagram of the physical layout of that place.

[15] In a preliminary examination on a first degree murder charge, when causation between a gunshot wound and the victim's death was placed in doubt, the examining magistrate interrupted the direct examination of first the victim's doctor and then a pathologist to make direct inquiry as to the cause of death.

At quite the opposite extreme, a magistrate will occasionally interrupt direct examination to round off the testimony and establish an essential element, such as venue, when he becomes convinced that probable cause has been proved.

[16] The consequences of inadequate disclosure on the bindover standard are discussed in Chapter 5 *infra*.

[17] A Wisconsin judge recalled one preliminary for second degree murder which he dismissed because the defendant had put much of the state's evidence in doubt. After the preliminary, the district attorney indicated that he did not know the defense was going to put on so much evidence and go into so much detail, and that he might have done better if he had known. A Kansas judge told a field re-

clearly borderline situations with considerable misgivings, because of this same policy.[18]

When the charge is statutory rape, preliminary examinations present a major exception to the policy of minimum disclosure of proceeding with minimum preparation. Statutory rape victims, young girls, are reluctant to testify and do so only with great embarrassment. Yet prosecutors believe that the nature of the offense makes it necessary that most of the evidence come from the lips of the victim. They think it essential that she testify in great detail to the circumstances surrounding the commission of the offense to insure that there is some evidence on each of the necessary elements. For these reasons prosecutors proceed more carefully and with less concern about concealing the facts from the defendant. In this endeavor they are sometimes aided by the magistrate who permits leading questions and on occasion excludes the public to save the witness embarrassment.[19]

---

porter of one case in which the defendant was dismissed because the prosecutor, in his efforts not to disclose all of his evidence at the preliminary examination, had failed to prove probable cause. When the case was refiled, the assistant county attorney, according to the judge, saw fit to produce a great deal more evidence, which easily proved probable cause.

18 In one preliminary in Wisconsin on a charge of negligent homicide, a motion to dismiss was made on the grounds that there was no proof of intoxication or that the defendant was driving the automobile which killed the victim. The judge remarked that he remembered no evidence of intoxication. The assistant district attorney replied, "No, your honor, we haven't introduced that. We intended merely to introduce enough evidence to get the bindover to Circuit Court." The judge, in binding the defendant over for trial, said: "The Court has dismissed many cases in the past because of lack of evidence showing the essential features of what constituted the basis for the complaint. Now, I again repeat that the defense counsel is certainly correct in his contention that there was no proof offered that the defendant was driving the car, nor that he was under the influence of liquor at the time he was driving and that his driving caused the death of the defendant. However, the Court is of the opinion that there has been enough evidence produced to show that there was an accident, that the defendant was involved to some extent in it, to what extent I certainly will not determine; and if this were a trial, of course, certainly the state, I hope, would produce more evidence than they have produced today to justify the court in determining that an offense has been committed, otherwise the Court would dismiss the case; and I think it is really asking a great deal of the court to surmise that the defendant was driving the car and that he was under the influence of liquor, or that he was guilty of any offense." The same judge was observed to complain of the inadequacy of the state's evidence on two other occasions, although defendant was bound over on both occasions.

19 In one Kansas case observed, the complainant, seventeen years old, was having a great deal of difficulty answering the assistant county attorney's questions. The judge tried to comfort her twice and then cleared the courtroom of spectators. He questioned the girl himself for about fifteen minutes and then permitted the assistant county attorney to resume direct examination by asking leading questions.

B. Cross-Examination of Prosecution Witnesses

Statutes in each of the three states provide that witnesses testifying at a preliminary examination are subject to cross-examination.[20] Although in two of the states the statutes are worded in terms of each party's right to cross-examine the other party's witnesses, in current administration, the prosecution seldom has an opportunity to cross-examine.[21] Redirect and recross-examination rarely occur in a preliminary examination;[22] and in light of the difficulties in assuring adequate cross-examination, the issue whether further examination is authorized by the statutes is not of significance in current administration.[23]

The manner in which the defendant's right to cross-examine is utilized is important in terms of compelling full disclosure of the facts as a basis for the probable cause determination. Because the prosecutor ordinarily calls only one or two witnesses,[24] full development of the facts can be aided only by a careful examination of those witnesses. In addition, since lack of time for preparation inhibits full development of the evidence on direct examination,[25] it is even more important that the cross-examination be thorough. For both of these reasons, the use made of the defen-

[20] Kan. Stat. Ann. §62-615 (1964); Mich. Stat. Ann. §28.930 (1954); Wis. Stat. Ann. §954.08(1) (1958).

[21] This is because the defendant seldom puts witnesses of his own on the stand. See discussion in section C *infra*. The Kansas statute, note 20 *supra*, is unusual in that it speaks only of cross-examination by the defendant. Since no attempts to cross-examine defense witnesses were observed in any of the three states, the practical construction of this provision is unknown.

[22] Redirect examination was observed in only one or two instances; no instances of recross-examination were observed.

[23] There was a great deal of confusion by Kansas officials over whether the defendant has the right to cross-examine and offer evidence in bastardy hearings. Kan. Stat. Ann. §62-2304 (1964) provides for a pretrial hearing in a bastardy case similar to the preliminary examination provided for in felony cases, but it speaks only of the testimony of the mother being taken at that hearing. An assistant prosecutor in Sedgwick County said there was a great deal of variation among the judges in conducting these bastardy hearings. He said one of the judges of the Common Pleas Court allows direct examination of only the complaining witness and does not permit the defendant's attorney to cross-examine her or to introduce other evidence or testimony on behalf of the defendant; that another judge has the same policy with the additional ruling that the defendant's attorney is permitted to cross-examine the witness; that the third judge permits the defendant's attorney to cross-examine the witness and introduce his own evidence on the defendant's behalf. The judges, on the other hand, said that none of them permits the defendant in a bastardy hearing to offer evidence and that all of them permit him to cross-examine the complaining witness.

[24] See note 12 *supra* and accompanying text.

[25] See notes 14 and 15 *supra* and accompanying text.

dant's right to cross-examine bears directly on whether the probable cause decision will be made on all of the facts available.

The right to cross-examine at the preliminary examination has not been the subject of separate appellate court consideration in any of the three states, although it was necessarily involved in the cases treating the right to confrontation.[26] In the practice, magistrates were generally careful to preserve the defendant's right to cross-examine.[27] Officials responsible for conducting the preliminary examination apparently believe that rudimentary standards of fairness require them to inform unrepresented defendants of their right to cross-examine: indeed, there was evidence of such a policy of officials in Michigan and parts of Kansas.[28]

26 See note 4 *supra*.

27 Only one practice was observed which fairly clearly prevented a defendant's exercise of his right to cross-examination. It was the practice of a Michigan judge, once he had become convinced that the state had established probable cause, to interrupt the prosecutor in his direct examination of a witness and to bind the defendant over for trial immediately after asking the witness several questions to establish essential facts, such as venue. In such a case the defendant, of course, has no opportunity to cross-examine the last witness on the stand.

28 Since defendants were represented by counsel in all the preliminaries observed in Wisconsin, whether notice of the right to cross-examine would be given to an unrepresented defendant is uncertain. The problem does not arise in Sedgwick County, Kansas, because virtually all defendants were represented by counsel at their preliminary examinations.

Note 53 *infra* discusses some recent United States Supreme Court decisions which apparently have had the effect of increasing the number of defendants who are represented by counsel at the preliminary since the survey was made. The court has never held categorically that all defendants have a constitutional right to be represented at all preliminaries and that counsel must be appointed for them if they are indigent, but it has required appointment when special procedural occurrences at some preliminaries render them "critical stages" in the sense that unrepresented defendants might prejudice their overall defense strategy by uneducated responses to these occurrences. White v. Maryland, 373 U.S. 59, 83 Sup. Ct. 1050, 10 L. Ed. 2d 193 (1963). The field survey makes clear that the assistance of counsel, or the lack of it, is a significant factor in determining whether state's witnesses will be effectively cross-examined. This factor proved to have a constitutional dimension, relating to the right to confront witnesses guaranteed by the Sixth Amendment, in Pointer v. Texas, 380 U.S. 400, 85 Sup. Ct. 1065, 13 L. Ed. 2d 923 (1965). The defendant, lacking counsel, was said to have been unable to effectively cross-examine the state's witnesses at the preliminary. The defendant subsequently went to trial where he had counsel. One of the witnesses who had testified at the preliminary was unavailable for the trial and the state had the transcript of his testimony at the preliminary admitted, over objection by defense counsel, into evidence at the trial. In reversing the conviction, the Supreme Court held that the defendant had been denied the right to confront this witness at the trial — that his only opportunity to cross-examine the witness had been at the preliminary where he could not avail himself of the opportunity without counsel. Of course this falls short of holding that there is a right to counsel as a blanket rule in every preliminary or even that there is a right to a preliminary. And only the unique circumstance of the witness's unavailability brought the importance of counsel into focus in this particular preliminary which, in retrospect, proved thereby to have

Scope and length of cross-examination present occasional problems in current administration. Usually the defense is given considerable latitude in the scope of its cross-examination, although objections pertaining to scope are sometimes sustained.[29] Cross-examination of the complaining witness in a statutory rape preliminary is sometimes a series of harsh questions by defense counsel concerning the witness's resistance and sensations at the time of intercourse. Although such questions are probably irrelevant, they are usually permitted on the theory that the defense has the right to examine all the circumstances surrounding the commission of the act. Latitude in scope of cross-examination is particularly great when the right is exercised by a defendant unrepresented by counsel.[30]

Magistrates occasionally impose limits on the length of cross-examination. Although cross-examination by unrepresented defendants, even when it occurs, usually takes the form of a question or two, cross-examination by defense counsel is apt to be longer. Magistrates sometimes interrupt a lengthy cross-examination with a reminder that other preliminaries are scheduled for that day. In Detroit, after it has been reasonably established that probable cause exists, magistrates often interrupt defense counsel, tell him that he is not permitted to go on a "fishing expedition," and decline to permit further questioning.[31] A controlling factor in this practice is that only a short time is allotted to each preliminary scheduled, and extensive questioning would interfere

been a "critical stage." But the case does indicate respects in which states can avoid reversals of convictions by voluntarily following the policy of providing counsel at the preliminary as a matter of routine. The Michigan and Wisconsin policies in this regard are discussed in note 53 *infra*.

29 Usually, these objections would also be sustained at trial. In a Kansas preliminary for assault with intent to do great bodily harm, the defense attorney cross-examined the victim about his general reputation as a trouble maker. Objections to these questions were sustained. In another Kansas preliminary, the defense attorney cross-examined the coroner in detail about the spots of blood that were surrounding the body nearby on the highway. The prosecutor objected that this was beyond the scope of cross-examination, and the objection was sustained. The defense attorney then cross-examined in great detail on the dress of the deceased, and another objection was sustained. The defense attorney then moved the court to allow him to make the coroner his own witness.

30 One judge of Detroit's Recorder's Court said that scope of cross-examination gives him a great deal of difficulty when the defendant is not represented by counsel. He said that usually he gives such defendants great latitude when they choose to cross-examine, so at least they can feel that they have had their "day in court."

31 An assistant prosecutor in Detroit said that eight of the ten judges of Recorder's Court do not permit cross-examination of witnesses to any degree once it has been reasonably established that the defendant should be held for trial.

with the schedule. No comparable practices were observed in Wisconsin or Kansas.

In general, then, in current administration, the responsible officials — the magistrate and the assistant prosecutor — create optimum conditions for effective cross-examination. Notice of the right to cross-examine is given when necessary; examination scope and length are generous. The opportunity to test the sufficiency of the evidence by cross-examination is available to any defendant who is able to use it.[32] Although cross-examination is unlikely if the defendant is unrepresented, it occurs sporadically.[33] When an unrepresented defendant chooses to cross-examine, however, he is inevitably ineffective,[34] occasionally destructive of his own interests.[35] Because the right to cross-

[32] This, of course, is not true when the magistrate permits no cross-examination by interrupting the prosecution's direct examination and binding the defendant over for trial. See note 27 *supra.* But even then it might be argued that the evidence-sufficiency function of cross-examination is not imperiled since the magistrate interrupts the prosecution only when he has become convinced that probable cause has already been proved. Similarly, when the magistrate interrupts the defendant's cross-examination, it is likely that no evidence-sufficiency functions are being performed, and that the cross-examination is directed solely to discovery of the state's case. Thus, counsel is told that he is not permitted to go on a "fishing expedition."

[33] An assistant prosecutor in Detroit told a field reporter that, on some days, unrepresented defendants are content to listen to the testimony and not cross-examine; on other days, however, five or six defendants take an extremely active part in cross-examining. The assistant prosecutor offered the explanation that it only takes one defendant who considers himself a jailhouse lawyer to discuss with the prisoners in the bullpen the advantages of cross-examining witnesses and possibly proving to the court that there is no probable cause. The prisoners listen with awe and come into court fully convinced that they will be able to have the case dismissed as a result of their deft cross-examination.

[34] One defendant cross-examined a police officer by saying, "I made a statement at the prosecuting attorney's office and, at that time, stated that I was innocent." The officer replied that he knew nothing of the statement. Another defendant, accused of larceny from a store, cross-examined the clerk in this way, "Do you know what perjury is, young lady?' The witness replied that she did. "You have just committed perjury in case you are interested. You did not see me in your store because I have never been there. What you have just done is told a lie." The prosecutor interrupted the defendant and advised him that he was privileged only to ask questions and not to accuse the witness. In one Michigan preliminary when the accused was pointed out by the witness, the prosecutor stated to him, "Is there anything you want to ask this man?" The accused stated, "Man, I want an attorney." The prosecutor stated, ' No attorneys at this stage."

Only one instance of anything which approached effective cross-examination by an unrepresented defendant was observed. A witness testified that he saw the defendant swinging a knife during the night in question. The defendant cross-examined the witness simply by asking him if he could really testify that he had seen anything because of the darkness.

[35] In one Michigan preliminary observed, the defendant, accused of larceny from an auto and unlawful taking, cross-examined the arresting officer, who had testified that he found the defendant in the auto with two suits on his lap: "When you found me in the car the two suits were not in my lap. They were laying beside

examine is rarely utilized by unrepresented defendants, and never effectively, its overall value as an evidence-sufficiency device is dependent on whether counsel is present.

When defendant is represented by counsel at the preliminary, the right to cross-examine is potentially important, and is often actually so, although not exclusively for evidence-sufficiency reasons. Unlike the defendant, counsel is capable of conducting effective cross-examination to test the sufficiency of the evidence; however, based on observed preliminaries, he is most likely to cross-examine for reasons other than assuring that the evidence is sufficient to establish probable cause. Typically, the major purpose of cross-examination is discovery of the state's case.[36] In addition, in statutory rape cases he is likely to cross-examine the prosecutrix solely to discourage her from testifying at the trial.[37] Despite these generalizations, however, defense counsel do, at times, conduct extensive cross-examinations which are visibly aimed at testing the sufficiency of the evidence.[38]

---

me like the suitcase." The patrolman did not bother to reply. In a Kansas City preliminary, the complainant testified he stopped the defendant leaving his clothing store with a large bundle under his arm and, upon opening it, discovered that it contained three suits and other things. The magistrate told the defendant that he had a right to cross-examine. The defendant said, "I don't want to cross-examine this witness but I do want to tell you that there were only two suits in the bundle instead of three." The magistrate fought back a grin, and informed the defendant that he could take the witness stand and testify in his own behalf if he wished.

In a talk with a field reporter, the examining magistrate who conducted the Kansas City preliminary said that it was quite obvious the defendant was guilty of larceny when he said, "It wasn't three suits only two," and that such a statement merely embarrassed the court somewhat, rather than influencing its decision. The magistrate said that this was a problem that he very frequently encountered when a defendant did not have access to counsel. He felt that the system was inadequate but offered no theories or suggestions as to how it could be improved.

[36] A Milwaukee County district court judge said that typically the preliminary is used by the defense attorney to see what is in the prosecution's case. To accomplish this, he would need no witness. Indeed, he would make no serious effort to get off at this stage.

[37] See text accompanying note 30 *supra*. An examining magistrate asked a defense attorney during a recess of a preliminary examination on statutory rape why he was going into so much detail in his cross-examination of the complaining witness when it was obvious that the case would have to be bound over, since the only facts that needed to be proved were that the girl was under seventeen and that the defendant had intercourse with her. The defense attorney stated that, since the statute allows so little defense for one accused of this crime, it was imperative that he make it known to the complaining witness what she would have to face at a trial and to make her unwilling to do so.

[38] In a preliminary on a first degree murder charge observed in Kansas the state used eight witnesses. The first three, all eye-witnesses, were cross-examined extensively (cross-examination of the first witness lasted for thirty minutes) on whether the gun could have been fired accidentally. The fourth witness, the victim's physician, was not cross-examined. The fifth witness, a pathologist, was subjected to

C. Disclosure by the Defendant

Statutes in each of the three states, in almost identical language, provide: "After the testimony to support the prosecution, the witnesses for the prisoner, if he have any, shall be sworn and examined . . . ."[39] Although there are no appellate cases interpreting these provisions, apparently "witnesses for the prisoner" is regarded in the practice as encompassing the defendant.[40] Presumably the defendant has a right to offer documents into evidence.

On several observed occasions an examining magistrate informed an unrepresented defendant of his right to take the stand to testify in his own behalf,[41] although this practice apparently occurs with less regularity than that of informing unrepresented defendants of their right to cross-examine the state's witnesses.[42] No case was observed in which a defense request to offer evidence was refused, although the practice by one Michigan judge of binding the defendant over in the middle of the prosecution's direct examination clearly precludes offering evidence.[43] Several preliminaries were observed in Michigan in which the magistrate bound an unrepresented defendant over for trial without informing him of his right to offer evidence. In one Michigan preliminary, after defense counsel finished cross-examining a witness for the state, the assistant prosecutor moved that the defendant be held for trial. The court quickly sustained the

---

extensive cross-examination on his veracity. The last three witnesses, a police detective, a police laboratory technician, and a patrolman, were not cross-examined.

39 Kan. Stat. Ann. §62-615 (1964); Mich. Stat. Ann. §28.930 (1954); Wis. Stat. Ann. §954.08(1) (1958).

40 ALI, Code of Criminal Procedure §§47, 49 (1931) provides for both the defendant testifying and making an unsworn statement as well as offering other witnesses in his own behalf. Section 47 provides, "When the examination of the witnesses for the State . . . is closed, the magistrate shall inform the defendant that he may make a statement, not under oath, regarding the charge against him; that he is accorded this right in order to enable him, if he sees fit, to answer the charge and to explain the facts appearing against him; that he may refuse to make any statement, and that such refusal may not be used against him at the trial, but that if he makes such statement, whatever he says therein may be given in evidence against him at the trial." A number of states have similar provisions. See ALI, Code of Criminal Procedure, Comment at 389-393 (1931).

41 On each occasion, the magistrate took care to explain to the defendant that he did not have to testify but could do so if he wished.

42 See note 28 *supra* and accompanying text. Perhaps this is because the right to offer evidence is used less frequently than the right to cross-examine.

43 See note 27 *supra*. There is no indication what this judge's response would be to a defense request to offer evidence made while he was winding up the prosecution's direct examination and before he bound the defendant over for trial.

motion. If defense counsel's motion to dismiss were overruled,[44] the magistrate would normally bind the defendant over immediately, apparently on the assumption that the defense desired to offer no evidence.

Defendants, whether or not represented by counsel, rarely offer evidence in their own behalf.[45] Of eleven preliminaries observed in Michigan, the defense offered evidence in only one.[46] Preliminaries are so frequently utilized by defense counsel for the sole purpose of discovering the state's case that it would be surprising if counsel often presented defense witnesses. Indeed, serious efforts to secure a dismissal are rare because the cases have been so thoroughly screened by the prosecutor prior to preliminary examination.

Because the defense offers evidence so infrequently, it is difficult to assess the effect of such evidence in terms of its importance in securing dismissals or reductions in charges.[47] To some extent the assessment depends on whether the particular examining magistrate limits his consideration of defense evidence

44 See text accompanying note 51 *infra*.

45 In a Kansas City preliminary observed, the magistrate told the unrepresented defendant that he could take the stand and testify if he wished, adding: "It is ordinarily the practice for defendants while going through a preliminary hearing not to take the witness stand. You can do whatever you like." In spite of the fact that defendants testify infrequently, or put other witnesses on the stand even more infrequently, continuances are automatically granted when requested by defense counsel on the grounds of the absense of a material defense witness.

46 In that case the defendant was not represented by counsel. After all the witnesses had testified, the judge told the defendant the purpose of the testimony and that he had an opportunity to testify, but that he did not have to. The defendant took the stand and stated that he had been hit first by the complainant, that the complainant had come at him with a knife, that in self-protection he drew his own knife and cut the complainant. The defendant was bound over for trial.

47 The possibility of charge reduction becomes particularly troublesome in murder cases. A judge of the Court of Common Pleas in Sedgwick County said that he had been greatly bothered in a few murder cases as to whether to reduce the charge for which the defendant would be bound over. He said that this discretion gives him somewhat the feeling of God in that he could prevent the possibility of a jury finding the man guilty of first degree murder and a District Court judge condemning the man to death. In a Michigan preliminary observed on a second degree murder charge, the defense moved that the defendant be dismissed because there was no evidence of the elements necessary to prove murder in the second degree. The judge interrupted defense counsel and stated, "I am going to hold this defendant to answer to a manslaughter charge, but I could not sleep at night were I to hold this young man on a murder charge. The elements of murder in the second degree require all the elements of murder in the first degree, with the exception of premeditation. In this case it is apparent that there was no intent to murder."

to impeachment or gives it a substantive effect. In two observed instances — one in Kansas[48] and one in Wisconsin[49] — it is fairly clear that cases were dismissed at the preliminary on the basis of evidence produced by the defense. In contrast, statements by other examining magistrates indicate that defense evidence has no influence on their decisions.[50]

If the defendant is represented by counsel, a motion to dismiss will invariably be made at the close of the state's case. Most frequently the motion is accompanied by a brief explanation of the grounds, usually in terms of failure to prove a specific element of the offense charged. Sometimes the motion is immediately overruled and the defendant is bound over for trial. At other times, however, the judge will call for relatively extensive argument by the prosecutor and defense counsel and then make his ruling. Most defense counsel visibly regard the motion to dismiss as a formality, holding no hope, in the typical case, for a favorable ruling.[51] Accordingly, they do not make extensive argument unless the judge indicates that he wishes them to do so, apparently because they are reluctant to reveal the theory of their defense to the prosecution.

48 In Kansas City the state had just finished its case and arguments on a motion to dismiss were made. The charge was first degree murder The judge carefully read the various sections of the code dealing with homicide and stated that there was still some doubt in his mind whether the state had produced sufficient evidence to bind the defendant over to district court. He stated, however, that it did appear that the question would probably be best resolved by the jury since the defendant had not taken the witness stand in her own behalf to explain her side of the story. The judge then looked directly at the defendant's attorney and inquired if he planned to offer any evidence. The defendant took the stand and testified; there was cross- and redirect-examination. The judge then reviewed the facts of the case for a few minutes. He said that he felt in his own mind that the testimony had established that the defendant was acting in self defense and that "it would hardly be worth while to refer the case to a jury for a determination of guilt or innocence." The case was dismissed.

49 A judge in outstate Wisconsin recalled a case on a charge of second degree murder which he had dismissed because the defense had made a strong showing. He said that afterwards the district attorney indicated that he did not know the defense was going to put on so much evidence and go into so much detail and that he might have made a better showing.

50 A justice of the peace in Wayne County, Michigan, stated that in determining probable cause he considers only the state's evidence. The defendant might cross-examine or impeach, but any evidence offered by the defendant would not be considered by him in the real sense of defense evidence.

51 At the close of the state's case in a Kansas preliminary on statutory rape, the defense attorney announced to the court that he was going to move that the case be dismissed. He also informed the court, before the judge had a chance to make his ruling, that he realized his motion would be overruled but that he wanted his motion for dismissal to be made part of the record.

D. Summary

Because of excellent police and prosecutor screening, there is little need for further evidence-sufficiency screening by the time most cases reach the preliminary examination stage. Occasionally, of course, an evidence-sufficiency problem remains. This problem is capable of solution by virtue of the examining magistrate's power to dismiss the case or reduce the charge, assuming his attention is directed to it. A hearing would seem necessary; the type of hearing, ex parte or inter partes, is another question. The grand jury, performing a comparable screening function under the indictment method of prosecution, operates on an ex parte basis. On the other hand, preliminary examinations have historically been inter partes or adversary proceedings, and the preliminary in the three states under observation is no exception. Thus, a defendant is given the right to confront the state's witnesses, to cross-examine them, to offer evidence in his own behalf, and to be assisted by counsel. These rights seem designed to insure that the magistrate's attention is directed to any evidence-sufficiency problems which exist, by compelling a relatively full disclosure of the facts in the case. The assumption of the formal law seems to be that an adversary procedure is more likely to assure full disclosure than is an ex parte proceeding.

To a large extent, the formal law assumes that the defendant is in fact represented by counsel at the preliminary examination.[52] If he has no counsel, it is unlikely that he will perceive any evidence-sufficiency problems, which may in fact exist in his case; and if he does perceive them, there is little he can do about it. If counsel is present, it is likely that whatever determination the examining magistrate makes will be based on a more complete knowledge of the facts than if counsel is not present.

In terms of their performances as fact-disclosing devices, preliminary examinations can be segregated into four categories: (1) defendant has no counsel and an evidence-sufficiency problem is not perceived by anyone; (2) defendant has no counsel and an evidence-sufficiency problem is perceived by someone; (3) defendant has counsel and an evidence-sufficiency problem is not perceived by anyone; and (4) defendant has counsel and an evidence-

[52] In each of the three states, a defendant has a statutory right to be represented by counsel at his own expense at the preliminary. Kan. Stat. Ann. §62-615 (1964); Mich. Stat. Ann. §28.930 (1954); Wis. Stat. Ann. §954.08(1) (1958). As discussed in note 53 *infra*, however, only one of the states now has an unequivocal statutory requirement for the appointment of counsel as a matter of routine in every preliminary for defendants financially unable to retain their own counsel.

sufficiency problem is perceived by someone. There are really four preliminary examinations, not the unitary preliminary assumed by the formal law, conforming to these four categories.

1. *Defendant has no counsel and no evidence-sufficiency problem is perceived.* This may be termed the "perfunctory preliminary." A bindover is, by definition, a certainty in this situation; a charge reduction is very unlikely. It is likely that here, as in most preliminaries, the prosecutor fails to perceive an evidence-sufficiency problem because he does almost no preparation of the case prior to the preliminary. He will put only one or two witnesses on the stand and rest his case. The defendant will fail to cross-examine, and, if he does, it will not be effective because he sees no specific evidence-sufficiency problem to direct his cross-examination toward. He will sometimes be asked if he wishes to take the stand and testify in his own behalf; typically, he will refuse. The magistrate will bind him over for trial with no argument by the prosecutor and little apparent deliberation. The total time consumed will be considerably less than an hour. A large percentage of preliminaries in Michigan and Wisconsin fall into this pattern.

2. *Defendant has no counsel and an evidence-sufficiency problem is perceived.* A bindover is less certain; a charge reduction is within possibility, especially if the charge is murder. If the prosecutor perceives the evidence-sufficiency problem, he will use more than the one or two witnesses which he normally uses. He will attempt to explore the problem more fully on direct examination, in an attempt to discover his own case. No instances of voluntary dismissals by the prosecutor were observed. The magistrate may, if he perceives a problem, question some of the state's witnesses himself, which may encourage the prosecutor to put more of his witnesses on the stand. If the defendant perceives the problem, he will probably attempt cross-examination; normally this is ineffective. He may take the stand to testify for himself, sometimes at the gentle urging of the magistrate Occasionally, the magistrate may discuss the case with the prosecutor.

3. *Defendant has counsel and no evidence-sufficiency problem is perceived.* This may be termed the "discovery-aimed preliminary." Because counsel is present, the prosecutor will be especially careful to limit the number of witnesses he uses in order to prevent more discovery by the defense than is absolutely necessary. Defense counsel is likely to cross-examine these witnesses. The cross-examination is not likely to be heated or extensive, because he is simply trying to discover any facts which the wit-

ness might know but did not disclose on direct examination. No attempt to attack the witness's credibility is made. Defense counsel will not present any evidence, in order to keep discovery by the state to a minimum. After perfunctory argument by each side, the defendant will be bound over for trial. Preliminaries in Sedgwick County typically follow this pattern.

4. *Defendant has counsel and an evidence-sufficiency problem is perceived.* This may be termed the "evidence-sufficiency preliminary." If the problem is perceived by the prosecutor, he will follow the pattern detailed in (2) above. If the problem is perceived by the magistrate, he will call for extensive argument after the close of the preliminary and may interrupt the examination of witnesses in order to bring out obscure details. A continuance is not unlikely in order to give him time to deliberate. If the problem is perceived by defense counsel, whether as a result of his initial perception or indirectly through the perception of either the prosecutor or the magistrate, he will cross-examine extensively, similarly to the cross-examination normally done at trial. He might put the defendant and, though less likely, other defense witnesses on the stand. He will argue extensively before the court the absence of proof on an element of the offense. A dismissal is not unlikely; neither, of course, is a charge reduction.

The form which a preliminary examination will take, then, depends on the absence or presence of counsel and whether any of the persons involved perceives what he thinks is an evidence-sufficiency problem. A magistrate's determination made after a preliminary of type (1) is based on a minimum of facts; type (3) produces only a few more facts; type (2) produces still more facts; and type (4) produces the most facts, comparable, in some instances, to a trial.

The primary difficulty with the preliminary examination as observed in current administration is the failure of the states to provide counsel for indigent defendants in order to represent them at the preliminary examination.[53] Without counsel, an

53 This problem, which is brought into focus by the survey, has been the recurrent concern of the United States Supreme Court in the years following the survey. The basic case is Gideon v. Wainwright, 372 U.S. 335, 83 Sup. Ct. 792, 9 L. Ed. 2d 799 (1963), in which the Sixth Amendment was applied through the Fourteenth to the states which were required to appoint counsel for indigent defendants, in cases involving serious offenses, as early as the arraignment on the information or indictment. The requirement of appointment at earlier stages than this has been conditioned on a finding that special circumstances at those stages call for the skilled assistance of counsel. Thus, appointment of counsel is required

evidence-sufficiency problem must be perceived by the prosecutor, the magistrate, or the defendant. The probabilities of these persons perceiving such a problem are not great. It must be assumed that some preliminaries are "perfunctory" simply because

---

— unless waived by the suspect — when the police interrogate him in custody immediately following arrest. Miranda v. Arizona, 384 U.S. 436, 86 Sup. Ct. 1602, 16 L. Ed. 2d 694 (1965); see Escobedo v. Illinois, 378 U.S. 478, 84 Sup. Ct. 1758, 12 L. Ed. 2d 977 (1964). Appointment is required at the initial appearance or preliminary if it can be characterized as a "critical stage" when certain practices, such as requiring a plea of guilty or not guilty and later admitting a response of "guilty" into evidence at the trial, are followed. The principle is that the defendant must have the assistance of counsel at these early stages if he is to avoid prejudicing his overall defense strategy. White v. Maryland, 373 U.S. 59, 83 Sup. Ct. 1050, 10 L. Ed. 2d 193 (1963); Hamilton v. Alabama, 368 U.S. 52, 82 Sup. Ct. 157, 7 L. Ed. 2d 114 (1961). Although the Texas preliminary in Pointer v. Texas, 380 U.S. 400, 85 Sup. Ct. 1065, 13 L. Ed. 2d 923 (1965) did not feature any of these procedural peculiarities that would demand its blanket classification as a "critical stage," a particular circumstance did arise which reflected the need for counsel to conduct cross-examination at this stage. See the discussion of the case in note 28 *supra*. As discussed below, this line of cases concerning the right to counsel appears to have affected practices since the survey. But the survey is nonetheless a valuable indicator of the kind of problems that led the Court into its position on right to counsel. Description of former practices can facilitate evaluation of any changes in practice that have resulted. It can also aid judgments about further changes that need to be made in light of particular considerations voiced by the Court in response to problems arising from the former practices.

The changes in law and practice appear to be considerable. A recent survey of practices and statutes in all fifty states relating to appointment of counsel is reported in Silverstein, The Defense of the Poor, App. D (1965). Among the three states under consideration, the changes appear to be greatest in Michigan and Wisconsin. As indicated in note 52 *supra*, the statutes in existence at the time of the survey did not require appointment of counsel for the preliminary, although they allowed a defendant to retain his own if he could afford it. It remains true at the present in Kansas that appointment for indigents earlier than the arraignment on the formal charge is not mandated. Kan. Stat. Ann §62-1302 (1964) conforms to the minimum constitutional mandate established in Gideon by requiring appointment for indigents only at that stage. In Sedgwick County, the practice of appointing counsel for indigents in time for the preliminary was observed in the survey despite the absense of a statutory requirement. In Kansas City, however, appointments for the preliminary were made only occasionally — usually in serious cases attracting a great deal of publicity. At present there appears to be neither a statutory nor constitutional requirement that counsel be appointed for indigents in time for the preliminary in all parts of Kansas as a matter of routine. See State v. Bloomer, 197 Kan. 668, 421 P.2d 58 (1966); State v. Richardson, 194 Kan. 471, 399 P.2d 799 (1965). The present practice in the state, therefore, is a matter of conjecture. In none of the three states was the practice observed of admitting pleas of guilty made at early stages into evidence at subsequent trials. Thus the regular preliminary held in each state would not be classified as a "critical stage" under the direct holding in White v. Maryland, *supra*. Nevertheless, Michigan has taken the initiative of requiring appointments as a matter of course in time for preliminaries. Mich. Stat. Ann. §28.1253 (1954), as amended, Mich. Pub. Acts, No. 256 (1957). There is, however, no requirement that appointments be made in time to assist the defendant in deciding at the initial appearance whether he

defense counsel was not present to perceive the problems.

---

wishes to waive the preliminary. Thus an indigent accused might miss the benefits of having counsel at the preliminary by waiving it altogether. The response in Michigan has been liberal administration of a statute, Mich. Stat. Ann. §28.982 (1954), as amended, Mich. Pub. Acts, No. 38 (1957), which entitles a defendant who has waived preliminary without counsel to a remand for a preliminary under some circumstances after counsel has been appointed for him. See People v. Wiggins, 6 Mich. App. 340, 149 N.W.2d 261 (1967). The Wisconsin statute has now been amended to require appointment not only in time for the arraignment on the formal charge but also for any earlier stage of the proceedings in which it is "constitutionally required." Wis. Stat. Ann. §957.26 (1958), as amended (Supp. 1967).

The amendment was apparently drafted in light of the Supreme Court decisions requiring early appointment when special circumstances or procedural occurrences demand this. The Wisconsin Supreme Court has stated that neither this statute nor the federal and state constitutions demand appointment as a matter of routine for the typical preliminary held in the state. (Of course an even earlier appointment might be necessitated by in-custody police interrogation.) In the absence of these "special circumstances," the statute still does not, in terms, require appointment before the arraignment on the formal charge. Wolke v. Rudd, 32 Wis. 2d 516, 145 N.W.2d 786 (1967). The latter case does indicate — and the court approves this — that the statute has been interpreted throughout the state as calling for a voluntary policy of appointing counsel for indigents in time for the preliminary, and a rather elaborate procedure has been established in Milwaukee County for accomplishing this. As in Michigan, however, the possibility remains that an unrepresented defendant might waive the preliminary altogether, and similar to Michigan, there is a statute providing for remand when this occurs. Wis. Stat. Ann. §955.18 (1958). There is some indication that a less liberal administration of the statute is expected than that which is demanded by the Michigan appellate judiciary. See Whitty v. State, 34 Wis. 2d 278, 149 N.W.2d 557 (1967).

CHAPTER 5

The Bindover Standard

The criterion for the examining magistrate's bindover decision is "probable cause." One explanation for the relatively low percentage of cases dismissed at the preliminary examination may be that the probable cause requirement is a minimum one which screens out only the extremely weak cases. There is considerable proof, however, that the reason for the relatively low dismissal rate is the extensive evidence-sufficiency screening which the prosecutor requires as a condition to permitting a case to proceed along the pretrial process toward the preliminary examination.[1] The prosecutor and police do the bulk of pretrial evidence-sufficiency screening in current administration, both in terms of the number of cases screened[2] and the number of cases dismissed.[3]

In Wisconsin, less than 10 per cent of the defendants given preliminary examinations are dismissed. In Kansas, a comparable dismissal rate prevails. In Michigan, statistics from Recorder's Court indicate that 17 per cent are dismissed,[4] but personnel in

[1] This screening is manifested by the prosecutor's approval of, or refusal to approve, issuance of a post-arrest warrant. Pre-warrant issuance screening reflects factors which clearly relate to the sufficiency of the evidence to convict and other factors which clearly do not so relate, as well as a number of factors which are difficult to categorize. This part of the volume focuses primarily on evidence-sufficiency screening. The factors not clearly related to evidence sufficiency are discussed in Part 4 of this volume.

[2] Many cases are screened by the prosecutor and do not reach the preliminary examination even when prosecution is approved by him. Thus, prosecutors screen a number of minor offenses which do not require preliminary examinations under current formal law. In addition, the preliminary examination is waived in a number of cases in which the formal law permits it to be given. See Chapter 6 *infra*. In each of these categories, the prosecutor does all the pre-trial evidence-sufficiency screening, as well as screening those cases which are processed through the preliminary examination for additional screening.

[3] Although no statistics relating to warrant refusals are available, there is considerable evidence that a higher percentage of warrants is refused than defendants dismissed at the preliminary examination. See Chapter 4 *supra*.

[4] 1956 Ann. Rep. for the Recorder's Court of the City of Detroit, Michigan, 11.

the Detroit prosecutor's office believe that 5 per cent is a more accurate figure. In each of the three states, then, a very small percentage of defendants given preliminaries is dismissed.

The dismissal rate at the preliminary drops even lower when waivers are considered.[5] Thus, in Kansas, 66 per cent of the defendants eligible for preliminaries waive them; in Wisconsin statistics indicate, with some doubt surrounding them,[6] that 90 per cent waive;[7] in Michigan, 72 per cent waive.[8] When dismissals are considered in relation to all cases in which preliminaries are authorized by law, the dismissal rate in Kansas drops to 3 per cent, in Michigan to 1.4 or 4.75 per cent (depending upon which dismissal rate figures are used), and in Wisconsin to 1 per cent. An average dismissal rate of 2 per cent of all persons entitled to preliminaries is probably a substantially accurate reflection of current practice.[9]

A. Probable Cause — The Verbal Formula

In those jurisdictions which allocate formal responsibility for pretrial evidence-sufficiency screening to the preliminary examination,[10] the screening standard is invariably provided by a

5 For a detailed discussion of the role of waiver of preliminary examination in current administration, see Chapter 6 *infra*.

6 The doubt arises because it is uncertain whether the statistics include those defendants who waive preliminary examination but are given one later under the remand statute, Wis. Stat. Ann. §955.18(2) (1958). If this is the case, the waiver rate is considerably lower than 90 per cent because the remand statute has seen substantial usage. See Chapter 6.

7 This figure is an average of the waiver rates for each of the years between January 1, 1958, and July 1, 1961, as computed by the Wisconsin Judicial Council. See Wisconsin Judicial Council, Biennial Rep. J-153-58 (1959); Wisconsin Judicial Council, Judicial Statistics B-109-13 (1959); Wisconsin Judicial Council, Biennial Rep. 1-108-13 (1961); Wisconsin Judicial Council, Judicial Statistics B-108-13 (1961).

8 1956 Ann. Rep. for the Recorder's Court of the City of Detroit, Michigan, 11.

9 Emphasis here should be placed on the word "current." Although comparison is difficult, apparently some thirty or more years ago a much higher proportion of cases was dismissed at the preliminary. Raymond Moley has said: "The faulty administration of preliminary hearings would not be so serious if so many cases were not finally disposed of at that stage of procedure. But it constitutes a shifting process of very great importance. In some of the large cities a majority of felony cases do not get beyond the preliminary hearings; in all of them, a large proportion die there." Moley, Our Criminal Courts 25-26 (1930).

10 Use of the preliminary examination as the only formal law pretrial evidence-sufficiency screening device has accompanied the shift from indictments to informations as methods of prosecution in serious cases. There has been no recent survey to determine the extent of use of information vis-à-vis indictments. Even in the twenties, however, a large number of states permitted prosecutions of serious offenders by information, and there is no indication of a reverse trend. See Orfield, Criminal Procedure from Arrest to Appeal 209-212 (1947).

statutory formula. The language of the Michigan statute is typical of that found in many jurisdictions:

> If it shall appear to the magistrate upon the examination of the whole matter, *either that no offense has ben committed or that there is not probable cause for charging the defendant therewith*, he shall discharge such defendant. If it shall appear to the magistrate upon the examination of the whole matter, *that an offense not cognizable by a justice of the peace has been committed and there is probable cause for charging the defendant therewith*, said magistrate shall forthwith bind such defendant to appear before the circuit court of such county or any court having jurisdiction of said cause, for trial.[11]

The statutory language divides the probable cause standard in two. First, the requirement that the corpus delicti be proved is a requirement that an offense be shown to have been committed by someone. Second, the identity element requires evidence that the defendant was the person who committed the offense. A literal reading of the Michigan statute indicates that the commission of the crime must be proved with more certainty than the defendant's participation. Although the usual interpretation of similar statutes imputes to the legislature no intent to differentiate between the degrees of proof necessary to establish each of these elements,[12] the Michigan Supreme Court has interpreted the statute literally.[13] On the other hand, a 1949 amend-

[11] Mich. Stat. Ann. §28.931 (1954) (emphasis added). The comparable Kansas provisions are cast in virtually identical language. Kan. Stat. Ann. §§62-618 to 62-619 (1964). The language of the Wisconsin provisions differs slightly. Wis. Stat. Ann. §§954.12 to 954.13 (1958).

ALI, Code of Criminal Procedure §§54, 55 (1931) contains language virtually identical to the Michigan provisions. For a collection of the types of statutory formulations in the various states, see Code at 308-316. For a discussion of the semantic difficulties encountered in statutory formulations, see Moley, *supra* note 9, at 23.

[12] See, e.g., State v. Howland, 153 Kan. 352, 359, 110 P.2d 801, 806 (1941).

[13] People v. Asta, 337 Mich. 590, 609-610, 60 N.W.2d 472, 482-483 (1953). Prior to this case the Michigan courts did not uniformly predicate this distinction between degrees of proof on the statutory language. See People v. Wilkin, 276 Mich. 679, 268 N.W. 779 (1936) ("probable cause for believing that the defendants were guilty as charged" and "good reason to believe that defendants were guilty of the crime charged"); but see People v. Matthews, 289 Mich. 440, 286 N.W. 675 (1939).

Several Michigan cases prior to Asta have indicated that the corpus delicti portion does not have to be proved with more certainty than the identity portion. See People v. White, 276 Mich. 29, 267 N.W. 777 (1936) ("probable cause that the crime of either larceny or conspiracy to steal has been committed by anyone"); People v. Southwick, 272 Mich. 258, 261 N.W. 320 (1935) ("probable cause that a crime was committed"); People v. Lee, 231 Mich. 607, 204 N.W. 742 (1925) ("a probability that the fire was caused by human intervention"). See also State v. Hastings, 263 Minn. 261, 116 N.W.2d 548 (1962) ("probable cause for believing the defendant guilty");

ment to the Wisconsin statute indicates clearly that the same degree of proof obtains for both the fact of commission and the identity elements.[14] Under either formulation difficulty in particularizing the degree of proof necessary to establish the elements remains.

A statement repeatedly found in appellate opinions discussing the preliminary examination is that the bindover standard can be satisfied by less than proof beyond a reasonable doubt.[15] While it is clear that the bindover standard is lower than the standard required for conviction, it is somewhat less clear that it is higher than that required for arrest. Logic and practicality seem to dictate that the arrest standard be lower.[16] On this assumption, the degree of certainty of guilt required ascends from the "reasonable grounds" needed for arrest, through the "probable cause" at the preliminary, to the "proof beyond a reasonable doubt" at trial. Doubt is inserted into this scheme, however, for two reasons: first, there is little explicit formal law statement differentiating between the arrest and preliminary examination standards;[17] and, second, it is not clear that the position of the

---

Orfield, Criminal Procedure from Arrest to Appeal 49 (1947) ("there is normally a preliminary examination by the magistrate to determine whether there is probable cause for maintaining a criminal proceeding"); 4 Wharton, Criminal Law and Procedure 518 (1957) ("probable guilt").

14 Prior to 1949 the probable cause requirement was cast in language substantially identical to the Michigan provision. Wis. Stat. §361.18 (1947) provided: "If it shall appear that an offense has been committed and that there is probable cause to believe the prisoner guilty. . . ." The 1949 amendment, however, stated: "If it appears *probable* that a crime has been committed . . . and that the defendant is probably guilty, he shall be committed to await trial." Wis. Laws c. 631, §47 (1949), now Wis. Stat. Ann. §954.13 (1958) (emphasis added). Even before the amendment, the Wisconsin courts apparently did not distinguish between degrees of proof on the basis of the language in the pre-amendment statute. See State v. Whatley, 210 Wis. 157, 245 N.W. 93 (1932) ("probable cause to believe that the accused is guilty of the crime charged").

15 See, e.g., In re Gates, 152 Kan. 616, 106 P.2d 650 (1940); People v. Davis, 343 Mich. 348, 72 N.W.2d 269 (1955); State v. Hastings, 363 Minn. 261, 116 N.W.2d 548 (1962); State ex rel. Wojtycski v. Hanley, 248 Wis. 108, 20 N.W.2d 719 (1945). See also Orfield, Criminal Procedure from Arrest to Appeal 68 (1947).

16 See United States v. Vita, 294 F.2d 524, 532-533 (2d Cir. 1961), *cert. denied,* 369 U.S. 823 (1962); Goldsmith v. United States, 277 F.2d 335, 343 (D.C. Cir.), *cert. denied,* 364 U.S. 863 (1960). Current police practices indicate a need to arrest on evidence insufficient for charging in order to permit interrogation of the arrestee and other investigation. Certainly, these investigatory methods would be unwarranted if the arrest standard were as high as that required for bindover at the preliminary. See generally LaFave, Arrest 300-318 (1965). It is possible, however, to read Mallory v. United States, 354 U.S. 449, 77 Sup. Ct. 1356, 1 L. Ed. 2d 1479 (1957) as a denial of these observations and as an equating of the arrest and charging standards.

17 The federal cases cited in note 16 *supra* address themselves only to the relation-

formal law on the relation between the arrest and preliminary examination standards is significant in view of the interjection in current administration between arrest and the preliminary of the prosecutor's decision to issue a post-arrest warrant, based in virtually every case on proof sufficient nearly to assure conviction.[18]

One of the reasons for the paucity of formal law on the relation between the arrest and preliminary examination standards is that the preliminary has always been regarded either as an independent step in the administrative process or as a device for predicting the jury verdict at trial, but rarely as a device to review the arrest or other preliminary decisions. The failure of the formal law to inquire into the relationship between the standard at the preliminary and the standards used for decisions prior to the preliminary prevents a comparison which might be useful in understanding the evidence-sufficiency standard at the preliminary. Most appellate cases, further, fail to state the evidence-sufficiency norm applicable at the preliminary, beyond simply reciting the statutory formula or briefly paraphrasing it.[19] Those cases which attempt to analyze the probable cause concept fall into two categories: those which discuss the concept without reference to other stages in the administrative process and those which discuss it in relation to the trial. In either event, the discussion is invariably brief.

The first approach is illustrated by a well-known excerpt from a Kansas case:

> It [probable cause] has been said to be a term difficult to define, but signifying about the same in law as in common parlance . . . and in Bouvier's Law Dictionary . . . it is thus defined: "A reasonable ground of suspicion, supported by circumstances sufficiently

---

ship between the amount of evidence needed for arrest and that needed to support the charge presented at the initial appearance in federal prosecutions. Mallory v. United States, 354 U.S. 449, 77 Sup. Ct. 1356, 1 L. Ed. 2d 1479 (1957) can be read as equating the two. If so, it remains unclear whether the Court requires federal officers to have gathered enough evidence by the time of the initial appearance to satisfy the degree of proof needed to show probable cause at the preliminary. Even if this requirement can be read into the case, there is no reason for asserting, in addition, that federal officers cannot investigate, in the interim between the initial appearance and the preliminary, to strengthen their case against the defendant.

18 This matter is discussed in greater detail in Chapter 2 *supra*. Examination of practices analyzed there suggests that commonly in current administration a giant step is taken from the standard for arrest to that for initial charging, followed by a regression to the probable cause standard at preliminaries, which is less rigorous than that employed at the second step.

19 See notes 12-14 *supra* and accompanying text and cases cited.

strong in themselves to warrant a cautious man in the belief that a person accused is guilty of the offense with which he is charged."[20]

The second approach is simply to fix the meaning of probable cause in terms of the amount of proof needed in a trial to get the case to the jury — the so-called "prima facie case" test.[21] Under this test, there exists probable cause only if, on the facts presented at the preliminary, a trial judge would overrule a motion to dismiss for failure to make a submissible case. This test is commonly used by examining magistrates in current administration; thus, it is not unusual for a magistrate to overrule a motion to dismiss at the end of a preliminary on the ground that the prosecution has presented enough evidence on the disputed point to "let the jury decide the issue."

The prima facie test brings to light some administrative problems concerning the interpretation of "probable cause." For one thing the intensity of magisterial involvement in charging at the preliminary examination stage is influenced by what sorts of inquiries he is permitted to make in order to establish the degree of proof denoted by that term. Can he, for example, pass on the credibility of witnesses appearing at the preliminary? A strict application of the prima facie test would dictate that the magis-

[20] State v. Howland, 153 Kan. 352, 359, 110 P.2d 801, 806 (1941). See People v. Karcher, 322 Mich. 158, 33 N.W.2d 744 (1948); People v. Dellabonda, 265 Mich. 486, 251 N.W. 594 (1933); State v. Hastings, 263 Minn. 261, 116 N.W.2d 548 (1962); State ex rel. Wojtycski v. Hanley, 248 Wis. 108, 20 N.W.2d 719 (1945).

[21] See, e.g., People v. Medley, 339 Mich. 486, 64 N.W. 2d 708 (1954), in which the trial judge sustained a motion to quash the information on the grounds that "the evidence introduced at the examination does not make a prima facie case, and there has been a clear abuse of discretion"; People v. Weiden, 239 Mich. 169, 214 N.W. 120 (1927), in which the Supreme Court characterized the issue as "was there any evidence from which a jury might reasonably find that Stephen Weiden was murdered?" and concluded that "it is for a jury to say whether such injuries were received in a fall from the basement stairs or feloniously inflicted by some person"; State v. McGinley, 153 Wis. 5, 140 N.W. 332 (1913) in which the Supreme Court reversed an order sustaining a plea in abatement, noting that the trial judge did not give due latitude to the magistrate's discretion: "If, in deciding that the evidence was insufficient to make out a prima facie case, the judge viewed such evidence from the standpoint of a trial court, grievous error was committed."

In People v. Dellabonda, 265 Mich. 486, 251 N.W. 594 (1933) the court said: "To authorize the examining magistrate to bind appellant over for trial there must have been good reason to believe appellant guilty of the crime charged. Some cases hold a prima facie case against the accused must be made out. This court has not defined what contitutes probable cause, leaving each case to be determined upon its facts." Id. at 490.

Finally, it has been noted that "in most states a defendant has the right to insist on a preliminary hearing before an examining magistrate. At this hearing the prosecution must give prima facie evidence that the defendant is guilty of a crime. . . ." ALI, A Survey and Statement of the Defects in Criminal Justice 21-22 (1925).

trate not dismiss a defendant because he doubts the credibility of a witness. As long as a witness testifies to enough facts, which on their face establish the commission of an offense by the defendant, the case — in theory at least — must be sent to the jury who must decide whether the witness was telling the truth. Yet, there are statements which give the magistrate authority to decide the issue of credibility at the preliminary.[22] If the law of a jurisdiction grants this authority and also adopts the prima facie test, at least a surface inconsistency appears.[23] Authoritative reconciliation of the two positions is not likely to be found.[24] Thus, magistrates have no clear indication of how intensive their

22 See People v. Karcher, 322 Mich. 158, 33 N.W.2d 744 (1948). Compare State ex rel. Tessler v. Kubiak, 257 Wis. 159, 42 N.W.2d 496 (1950). In the latter case, the court held that the magistrate could, in passing on a motion to suppress evidence made by the defendant at the preliminary, consider the credibility of the police officers who denied the facts alleged concerning their seizure of the evidence in question.

23 Statements authorizing the examining magistrate to pass upon witness credibility have been found only in Michigan and Wisconsin. See note 22 *supra*. In the formal law in none of the three states can it be said that the prima facie case test has been firmly adopted, and the test has apparently been rejected by at least one case in Michigan. See note 21 *supra*. Further, the cases authorizing the magistrate to pass upon witness credibility have all been cases in which the result of the preliminary was a bindover. Indeed, the almost total absence of review rights in the prosecution necessitates such a situation. See Chapter 7 *infra*. Thus, confining the the statements to the facts of the cases, the courts have simply said that it was not erroneous for the magistrate to believe the prosecution's witnesses. The result — a bindover — would not differ if the magistrate had simply refused to pass on credibility on the ground that the issue was one for jury determination under the prima facie case test. Thus, on the facts of the cases, the pronouncements are not inconsistent with an application by the magistrate of the prima facie case test.

24 The issue probably has not been raised enough in the past to call for clarification because of the general non-use of cross-examination and defense evidence and the relatively infrequent participation by defense counsel. See Chapter 4 *supra*. An extreme picture of failure to recognize the problem is presented by the Michigan case of People v. Karcher, 322 Mich. 158, 33 N.W.2d 744 (1948). Prior to a prosecution for abortion, the complainant and her husband attempted to extort $4000 from the defendant, threatening to expose him to the authorities if he refused to pay. When he failed to pay, prosecution was instituted. The defendant was bound over for trial in a preliminary in which all these facts were developed. The trial court dismissed the information subsequently filed with it and the supreme court, on appeal by the state, reversed. The court first adverted to a definition of probable cause which does not incorporate the notion of a prima facie case. But it indicated that the facts at the preliminary presented a jury case — the prima facie test — and further noted that the magistrate was authorized to pass on the credibility of the complainant: "Complainant's admitted attempt to obtain money from defendant and other aspects of her testimony stressed by defendant go to her credibility, are proper subjects of inquiry and of argument by counsel on trial, to be considered by the jury in determining the weight to be accorded her testimony. . . . Testimony as to these matters affecting the complainant's credibility having been received into evidence before the magistrate, it was no abuse of discretion for him, nevertheless, to believe her testimony which established probable cause. It is, therefore, not the function of the circuit court or this Court to substitute its judgment for that of the magistrate in that regard." Id. at 164, 33 N.W.2d at 746.

participation in charging is to be in this respect. Some magistrates have based bindover orders on the grounds that the prosecution has presented a jury case. Other magistrates have said that they consider the defendant's evidence as it bears on the credibility of prosecution witnesses.

The question whether witness credibility is part of the concept of probable cause, then, has been raised and remains unsolved. Whether the approach to defining probable cause is the prima facie case approach or not, two additional problems remain unsolved. The first is whether a dismissal at the preliminary may be based on proof of an affirmative defense. An illustration is helpful.

> *Illustration No. 1:* In a preliminary examination on a charge of first degree murder, the prosecution produced seven witnesses to a tavern brawl leading to the death of a customer, allegedly through the fault of the defendant-bartender. The defendant did not testify, but three defense witnesses testified to facts which tended to prove that the defendant shot the deceased when the latter was lunging toward him with a knife, after the defendant had kicked him in an attempt to break up the fight. The defendant was dismissed.

In most jurisdictions, the state at trial has the ultimate burden of proving no self-defense, but it need not introduce evidence on the issue until after the defendant has introduced some evidence of self-defense — the state enjoys a rebuttable presumption of no self-defense.[25] If probable cause is regarded as testing only the state's initial burden of introducing evidence, then evidence of self-defense is no part of the case at the preliminary. If, on the other hand, the state's presumption is rebuttable at the preliminary, then a dismissal may be based on proof of the affirmative defense.

Partly because formal law is largely lacking,[26] magistrates in

[25] See 1 Wharton, Criminal Evidence 245 (1955); 9 Wigmore, Evidence §2512 (1940).

[26] No general discussion has been found in the formal law. In State ex rel. Kowaleski v. Kubiak, 256 Wis. 518, 41 N.W.2d 605 (1950) the court said, "Appellant contends that the circumstances under which he was arrested constitute an unlawful entrapment. . . . Since unlawful entrapment is a matter of defense and evidence thereof is admissible upon a trial we refrain from reciting the testimony which convinces us that, for the purposes of the preliminary examination, there was no unlawful entrapment. . . . The record discloses that the magistrate was warranted in concluding that an intent to commit an offense originated in appellant's mind and that he had done every act essential to the completion of an offense." Id. at 520-521, 41 N.W.2d at 607. In State v. Hastings, 263 Minn. 261, 116 N.W.2d 548 (1962) the court said, "We think that these facts meet the test of probable cause in

current administration are not in agreement on this basic question. Some magistrates take the position that affirmative defenses are not part of the proof in a preliminary. Other magistrates contend that there is no probable cause if uncontradicted evidence of an affirmative defense is introduced. In Illustration No. 1, the judge remarked that he was dismissing the defendant because he obviously had a valid defense of self-defense and an acquittal at trial would be extremely likely.

On the one hand, it seems futile to bind a defendant over for trial when it is evident that he will be acquitted because he has a valid affirmative defense. On the other hand, such a decision could be a dangerous one because typically all the facts of the case are not developed at the preliminary.[27] In addition, such a decision certainly requires a more refined judgment than would be necessary if no dismissals were permitted because of affirmative defenses. Again, the problem is raised and remains unsolved.

The importance of the problems about magisterial consideration of witness credibility and affirmative defenses can be expected to assume greater importance as the trend of affording counsel for more defendants at preliminaries continues.[28] If the law of a jurisdiction allows these factors to be considered — or does not clearly preclude them — defense counsel would be more likely to bring them to the attention of the magistrate than would an unrepresented defendant. Cross-examination of prosecution witnesses might produce doubts about their credibility that would not otherwise appear. Moreover, counsel would be most likely to perceive the possibility of an affirmative defense and call this to the attention of the magistrate. Clearer articulation of the extent of magisterial inquiry contemplated by law at the preliminary combined with greater participation by defense counsel can be expected to have an impact on the number of dismissals which occur at this stage, always assuming constancy in the prosecution's screening standard.

---

that they establish a reasonable probability of the defendant's present intention or knowledge of the fact that the check was worthless and would not be honored. The defendant's contention that the transaction involved no more than an ordinary credit arrangement is a matter of defense which may be asserted at the trial." Id at 267, 116 N.W.2d at 552. See 1912 Wis. Ops. Att'y Gen. 265, in which the opinion is expressed that a plea of insanity should not be tried in a preliminary examination.

27 See Chapter 4 *supra*.

28 See notes 54-55 *infra* and accompanying text. The discussion in Chapter 4 *supra* suggests that the preliminary is often a perfunctory proceeding because in the absence of defense counsel possible insufficiencies in the evidence are not perceived.

This impact on administration is likely to be weaker in the three states under consideration than in jurisdictions where pre-preliminary screening is less intensive. A recent study[29] has demonstrated that in Cook County, Illinois, the screening function tends to be delayed until the preliminary; it is apparently anticipated that the magistrate will play an active role in that function. In the three states, on the other hand, only a residue of cases that might present issues about the extent of magisterial considerations are likely to reach the preliminary. There remains, however, the possibility that resolution of the issue in the law of the three states, combined with greater participation by defense counsel in the residue of cases, might have an additional impact on administration by influencing the pre-preliminary screening policies of the prosecutor. For example, a prosecutor may decide to postpone charging in some cases, simply because evidence tending to support an affirmative defense would be brought out if it were clear that it could properly be considered by the magistrate, and if defense counsel's availability would make it likely that the evidence would be presented.

Another problem exists in understanding the concept of probable cause. May a dismissal be based only on improbability of guilt, or may it be based on factors which are not related to likelihood of guilt, but which bear on jury convictability?

> *Illustration No. 2:* In a preliminary examination on a charge of concealing mortgaged property, the evidence was that the defendant, an illiterate, had driven a car across the state line not knowing he was violating a statute. After the last witness testified, the judge called the attorneys into his office and suggested that the case be dismissed. The assistant prosecutor urged a bindover because he had been harassed by the complainant — a used car company — to prosecute for some time. The defendant was bound over.

In Illustration No. 2 all the elements of the offense charged were proved. There were no difficulties with affirmative defenses, and there was clearly enough evidence to support a jury verdict of guilty. The judge bound the defendant over for trial but recommended a dismissal on the grounds that, practically, a jury conviction was impossible in that case because the defendant was morally innocent and the complainant — a used car company

[29] Oaks and Lehman, The Criminal Process of Cook County and the Indigent Defendant, 1966 U. Ill. L.F. 584, 623-630. The study did reveal, however, that pre-preliminary screening is more intensive in some downstate counties of Illinois than it is in Cook County (Chicago).

— was unpopular with the local populace. It might be added that convictability can also be expected to assume greater importance as more defendants are represented at the preliminary by counsel who is likely to call the magistrate's attention to convictability factors.

The problem created by the technical violation is that, while there is enough evidence to support a jury verdict, a guilty verdict is improbable in light of the nonevidence-sufficiency factors in the case.[30] Again, the law does not speak directly to the point.[31] In current administration, three positions are discernible. Per-

[30] Discussion of the preliminary in this part is structured in such a way as not to challenge the usual assumption that the preliminary's screening function is restricted to consideration of evidence-sufficiency factors. There is no explicit denial, however, that nonevidence-sufficiency considerations may be intertwined in practice with evidence-sufficiency ones, or may even be dominant, in a magistrate's decision to have prosecution discontinued at the preliminary. The central concept which is taken in this series of volumes to be relevant to the play of nonevidence-sufficiency factors is official discretion not to charge or to acquit persons against whom the evidence is sufficient to show probable guilt. This form of discretion receives the focus of attention in Part 4 *infra,* and it is there attributed primarily to the prosecutor. Its exercise by judges at various stages, including the preliminary, is treated extensively in Newman, Conviction 131-173 (1966). Formal law generally denies this form of discretion to judges but it nevertheless exists because of limitations imposed by formal law on the ability of the prosecution or anyone else to seek review and reversal of a judicial acquittal or dismissal based on nonevidence-sufficiency considerations. Id. at 131-133. Review procedures are such that magistrates or other judges are not forced to articulate precisely the considerations that dominated their decisions. Thus, while discussion of the magisterial role can proceed for purposes of conceptualization and organization in the present part on the assumption that only evidence sufficiency is considered, that assumption might be found to distort what actually occurs in practice in at least a few cases.

[31] As suggested in note 30 *supra,* the failure of formal law explicitly to grant or deny magisterial discretion to acquit the probably guilty is correlated with the unavailability of review procedures to restrict the magistrate to evidence-sufficiency considerations. Yet there are indirect suggestions that he cannot go beyond evidence sufficiency in making his decision. Statutes in each of the three states authorize him to dismiss if he finds, in the words of the Michigan statute, "either that no offense has been committed or that there is not probable cause for charging the defendant therewith." Mich. Stat. Ann. §28.931 (1954). See notes 11-14 *supra* and accompanying text. Impliedly, he may not dismiss except in one or the other of the specified situations. It would be entirely consistent to permit him to dismiss upon a finding of no probable guilt, or of no probable convictability and yet not permit him to dismiss when a conviction seems extremely unlikely because of a lack of jury appeal inherent in the facts of the case. This position has been asserted. See Miller and Remington, Procedures Before Trial, 339 Annals 111, 122 (1962). Further, it has been held that a trial judge has no right to acquit one as to whom the evidence of guilt is sufficient. State v. Evjue, 254 Wis. 581, 37 N.W.2d 50 (1949).

In addition no formal law has been found which authorizes the magistrate to take nonevidence-sufficiency factors into consideration when he makes his bindover determination. There is an indication that it was the practice of some magistrates to take such factors into account, at least that was the practice as revealed by the Crime Surveys. See Moley, Our Criminal Courts 23 (1930).

haps most magistrates would simply bind the defendant over for trial on the grounds that their function is solely to test the sufficiency of the evidence as it bears on probability of guilt and that to dismiss a technical violator is to invade the province of the jury or the prosecutor. A second group would dismiss the case on the grounds that the function of the preliminary is to screen out unconvictables, whether they were probably guilty or not. Another group takes a middle ground and binds the defendant over for trial but, as in Illustration No. 2, recommends that the prosecutor dismiss the case.

B. Probable Cause — The Rules of Evidence

The probable cause requirement might be interpreted to mean either that enough evidence must be presented to convince the magistrate that the defendant is probably guilty of an offense, or that, even though sufficient facts could be presented to show guilt, the defendant must be dismissed at the preliminary when it is unlikely that he could be convicted at trial. It might be possible to present enough evidence to convince the magistrate that a defendant is guilty, but he might, nevertheless, be unconvictable because this evidence is in a form which would not be admissible at trial.[32] More frequent participation by defense counsel, likely to call attention to these evidentiary problems, could be expected to apply pressure for clarification of what evidentiary rules obtain for the preliminary as well as for the trial. The more of these rules that are applied to the preliminary — and thus the closer the probable cause standard approaches convictability rather than probability of guilt — the greater is the possibility of an increase in the dismissal rate for preliminaries. If these possibilities become realities, it is also likely that the importance of the preliminary will increase, that this increased importance will be recognized, that it will become a "crucial stage" in the constitutional sense, and that counsel will be required for all preliminaries as a matter of constitutional mandate.[33]

32 This reason for unconvictability is generally included under the conceptual format of this volume as an evidence-sufficiency factor, as opposed to the nonevidence-sufficiency factors discussed at the end of the preceding subsection and emphasized in Part 4 *infra*.

33 At present, appointment of counsel for indigent defendants is required only when extraordinary practices or occurrences at the preliminary make that step a critical one from the standpoint of overall defense strategy. See White v. Maryland, 373 U.S. 59, 83 Sup. Ct. 1050, 10 L. Ed. 2d 193 (1963). The possibilities of

Formal law in the three states is not in agreement on whether the rules of evidence used in criminal jury trials must be followed in preliminary examinations. General statements in Kansas indicate that the jury trial rules need not be followed in that jurisdiction.[34] While no general statements have been found in the other two states, cases in Michigan[35] and Wisconsin[36] indi-

---

characterizing the preliminary as a critical step because of the far-reaching advantages which a defendant might receive as a result of his having counsel to deal with problems of evidence presentation as a matter of routine at regular preliminaries are as yet generally unrecognized, although unusual circumstances did bring them into focus in Pointer v. Texas, 380 U.S. 400, 85 Sup. Ct. 1065, 13 L. Ed. 2d 923 (1965). See Chapter 4, notes 28 and 54 *supra* and accompanying text.

[34] In McIntyre v. Sands, 128 Kan. 921, 278 Pac. 761 (1929) the only evidence at the preliminary examination to connect the defendant with the alleged arson was a fire marshal's statement of an accusation made against the defendant by his co-defendant. Defendant's application for an original writ of habeas corpus alleging the admission of this evidence as error was denied. The court said "Probably this testimony would have been stricken if it had been given upon the final trial of the defendant in the district court. Proceedings in a preliminary examination are not expected nor required to be as regular and formal as in a final trial. The same strictness as to the admissibility of evidence is not as necessary where probability of guilt is at issue as when actual guilt is the matter on trial.' Id. at 523, 278 Pac. at 762. Accord, State v. Earley, 192 Kan. 167, 386 P.2d 189 (1963); cf. State v. Bailey, 32 Kan. 83, 3 Pac. 769 (1884). But see Seyfer v. Bloomer, 132 Kan. 877, 297 Pac. 681 (1931), holding that the defendant's right to confrontation precludes the unnecessary use of affidavit evidence at the preliminary examination.

[35] Mich. Stat. Ann. §28.1045 (1954) provides: "The rules of evidence in civil actions, insofar as the same are applicable, shall govern in all criminal and quasi criminal proceedings except as otherwise provided by law." Although the preliminary examination is arguably at least a "quasi criminal" proceeding, no cases have been found which have considered the applicability of this statute to it. See Turner v. People, 33 Mich. 363 (1876) for a general statement that since the preliminary does not result in a final decision, it should be conducted with more informality than the trial, but no mention was made specifically of the rules of evidence.

The following cases have held that the corpus delicti confession rule must be followed in preliminaries: People v. Asta, 337 Mich. 590, 60 N.W.2d 472 (1953); People v. Lee, 307 Mich. 743, 12 N.W.2d 418 (1943); People v. Campbell, 301 Mich. 670, 4 N.W.2d 51 (1942); People v. White, 276 Mich. 29, 267 N.W. 777 (1936); Peterson v. Oceana Circuit Judge, 243 Mich. 215, 219 N.W. 934 (1928); People v. Lee, 231 Mich. 607, 204 N.W. 742 (1925).

In People v. Rice, 206 Mich. 644, 173 N.W. 495 (1919) a general rule was arguably pronounced: "The principal grounds upon which defendant sought an order quashing the information and here urged as basis of assignments of error upon the refusal to grant such order are that the examining magistrate received improper testimony and that the testimony produced before him did not establish the commission of the offense and probable cause. The objected testimony consisted of portions of the examination of the defendant before the referee in bankruptcy in proceedings in which he was adjudged a bankrupt. It is not claimed by the prosecution that such testimony was admissible and it was not offered upon the trial. An information will not be quashed because of the admission of incompetent evidence where there is sufficient competent evidence to establish the commission of the offense by the defendant." Id. at 648-649, 173 N.W. at 496.

[36] While no general statements on the necessity for following jury trial rules of

cate, in the aggregate, that a substantial number of the jury trial rules must be followed in preliminary examinations in those jurisdictions. Despite the uncertainty of the formal law position in some instances, and despite statements indicating a contrary practice,[37] it is clear that the jury trial rules of evidence are followed in preliminary examinations in all three states. Objections to the admission of evidence are made and sustained or overruled on the basis of those trial rules. At least some magistrates believe that they are under legal compulsion to follow those rules.[38]

Against this background of law and practice, two problems require attention. The first is raised by the United States Supreme Court opinion in *Costello v. United States*[39] in which the Court held that an indictment returned by a federal grand jury

---

evidence in preliminary examinations appear in the Wisconsin cases, a number of specific rules have been discussed and accepted or rejected by the court. See State ex rel. Wojtycski v. Hanley, 248 Wis. 108, 20 N.W.2d 719 (1945), holding the rule excluding illegally seized evidence applies; State v. Baltes, 183 Wis. 545, 198 N.W. 282 (1924); State v. Faull, 178 Wis. 66, 189 N.W. 274 (1922), holding the trial rule of relevancy must be followed. But see State ex rel. Brill v. Spieker, 271 Wis. 237, 72 N.W.2d 906 (1955), holding that the best evidence rule does not apply at the preliminary. In the following cases, specific rules of evidence were discussed by the court, but it is difficult to determine whether they must be followed at the preliminary: State v. Goodchild, 272 Wis. 181, 74 N.W.2d 624 (1956), *cert. denied*, 351 U.S. 958, corpus delicti — confession; Lundstrum v. State, 140 Wis. 141, 121 N.W. 883 (1909), same; State ex rel. Wojtycski v. Hanley, 248 Wis. 108, 20 N.W.2d 719 (1945), hearsay rule; State v. Shatley, 210 Wis. 157, 245 N.W. 93 (1932), same.

The closest to a general statement on the question found in Wisconsin appears in Hancock v. Hallmann, 229 Wis. 127, 281 N.W. 703 (1938), where the court said: "It is well established that one who is charged with crime may be held for trial only when the evidence establishing substantial grounds for such action is competent. . . . It follows that when the action of the magistrate in holding a defendant for trial rests solely upon the testimony of an incompetent witness, he acts without jurisdiction, and the defendant is entitled to be released on habeas corpus." Id. at 131, 281 N.W. at 705.

37 See Orfield, Criminal Procedure from Arrest to Appeal 88 (1947): "The same strict rules of evidence applied in the trial of a criminal case are not applied to the preliminary hearing. The finding of the Illinois Crime Survey is that the 'rules of evidence are dispensed with to such an extent that proceedings are marked by hearsay and other incompetent forms of testimony.' In practice hearsay evidence is considered, leading questions are permitted, and insufficient opportunity is given for cross-examination."

38 In a Kansas preliminary examination on a forgery charge, the defendant's attorney, a young man who had just recently passed the bar examination, objected to practically every question asked by the assistant prosecutor. The judge was careful to explain to the young attorney the reason for overruling the objection on each occasion. Finally, the assistant prosecutor expressed exasperation and desperation at his opponent's performance. At that point, the judge carefully pointed out to the prosecutor that the defendant's attorney certainly had a right to object to a question whenever he deemed it advisable and in the best interest of his client.

39 350 U.S. 359, 76 Sup. Ct. 406, 100 L. Ed. 397 (1956).

is not invalid simply because all the evidence presented to the grand jury would have been inadmissible had the proceeding been a criminal jury trial. The second problem is raised by the Michigan Supreme Court opinion in *People v. Asta*[40] in which the court held that the statute granting a defendant the right to confrontation at he preliminary examination precludes the use of hearsay evidence in that proceeding.

The *Costello* case[41] points up sharply the position of the Supreme Court of the United States that indictments may rest wholly on evidence inadmissible at the trial[42] and contains a dictum that the same result would follow when the preliminary examination information process is used.[43] The Supreme Court of Michigan has taken the opposite position with respect to preliminary examinations.[44] The writer of a recent note[45] suggests that the difference may lie in a divergence of attitude toward the meaning of probable cause — is the requirement to be inter-

40 337 Mich. 590, 60 N.W.2d 472 (1953).

41 Costello v. United States, 350 U.S. 359, 76 Sup. Ct. 406, 100 L. Ed. 397 (1956), *rehearing denied,* 351 U.S. 904 (1956), *aff'g* 221 F.2d 668 (2d Cir. 1955), which affirmed a conviction by a United States District Court (no reported opinion). Frank Costello was indicted for willfully attempting to evade payment of federal income taxes. A pre-trial motion to dismiss the indictment was denied. At the trial, the government offered evidence designed to show increases in the defendant's net worth as proof that he received more income during the years in question than he had reported. Defense counsel questioned each of the 144 government witnesses to determine which ones had testified before the grand jury; only three investigating officers had. At the close of the government's case, another motion for dismissal of the indictment was made on the ground that the sole evidence before the grand jury was hearsay, since the three officers had no firsthand knowledge of the transactions upon which their computations were based. This motion was denied and defendant was convicted.

42 When the Supreme Court decided the Costello case in 1956 it had available a long line of federal cases, beginning with Holt v. United States, 218 U.S. 245, 31 Sup. Ct. 2, 54 L. Ed. 1021 (1910), holding that an indictment is not invalid because the grand jury heard (and probably considered) inadmissible evidence, if it heard, in addition, some admissible evidence, no matter how little. There were, however, cases in the 8th Circuit holding that an indictment is invalid when *all* the evidence presented to the grand jury would be inadmissible at trial. Brady v. United States 24 F.2d 405 (8th Cir. 1928); Nanfito v. United States, 20 F.2d 376 (8th Cir. 1927) State court opinions on grand jury proceedings and preliminary examinations were in conflict on this point. See note 45 *infra.* There was apparently no precedent on this point concerning the federal preliminary examination.

43 Mr. Justice Black, speaking for the majority, said: "An indictment returned by a legally constituted and unbiased grand jury, like an information drawn by the prosecutor, if valid on its face, is enough to call for trial of the charge on the merits." Costello v. United States, 350 U.S. 359, 363, 76 Sup. Ct. 406, 410, 100 L. Ed. 397, 402 (1956).

44 See note 40 *supra.*

45 Note, The Rules of Evidence as a Factor in Probable Cause in Grand Jury Proceedings and Preliminary Examinations, 1963 Wash. U.L.Q. 102.

preted as meaning that the accused is probably guilty or that he is also probably convictable? He goes on to point out that, in an illegally-seized evidence situation in which the evidence seized is contraband, there can be no doubt the suspect is guilty of possession of the contraband. It would be quite common, however, in the light of cases like *Mapp*[46] and *Wong Sun*[47] that such a suspect could never be convicted. If the requirement of probable cause means likelihood of guilt, he should be bound over at a preliminary examination, but if it means likelihood of conviction, he should be dismissed. In general, judicial utterances seem most often to assume that likelihood of guilt is the standard,[48] but in current administration likelihood of conviction is the criterion both at the warrant issuing level,[49] where there is no formal structure for administering such rules, and at the preliminary examination.[50] What is clear is that the decision whether to apply the trial rules at preliminary examinations should be influenced largely by whichever meaning is given to the probable cause requirement.[51] Obviously, probability of con-

[46] Mapp v. Ohio, 367 U.S. 643, 81 Sup. Ct. 1684, 6 L. Ed. 2d 1081 (1961).

[47] Wong Sun v. United States, 371 U.S. 471, 83 Sup. Ct. 407, 9 L. Ed. 2d 441 (1963).

[48] When Costello was before the Second Circuit, Judge Hand, in the majority opinion, assumed that probable cause meant probability of guilt, not probability of conviction: "[Exclusionary rules] apply to evidence that is relevant rationally, but that courts will not accept, not because it does not prove the issue, but it is thought unjust to the opposite party to use it against him, or because it is within some privilege to suppress the truth. We should be the first to agree that, if it appeared that no evidence had been offered that rationally established the facts, the indictment ought to be quashed." United States v. Costello, 221 F.2d 668, 677 (2d Cir. 1955). Judge Frank's opinion, in which he "reluctantly" concurred with Judge Hand, proceeds from a different concept of probable cause: "I have very serious misgivings about concurring in a conclusion that a grand jury may indict solely on the basis of evidence that would not support a verdict after trial." Id. at 679.

It is clear that the Brady and Nanfito cases, note 42 *supra,* holding, prior to Costello, that an indictment may not rest entirely upon inadmissible evidence, assume that probability of conviction is the meaning of probable cause. The Court in Nanfito said the rule that probable cause may not rest entirely upon inadmissible evidence is necessary so that "the time of the trial courts may not be consumed in disposing of matters incapable of proof by competent evidence." On the other hand, the court in McIntyre v. Sands, 128 Kan. 521, 278 Pac. 761 (1929) assumed that probability of guilt was the proper interpretation. See note 34 *supra.*

[49] See Chapter 2 *supra.*

[50] See text accompanying notes 37 and 38 *supra.*

[51] The author of the student note referred to in note 45 *supra* quotes an excerpt from Professor Davis's treatise on administrative law on the point that the trend in that area is to relax generally the jury trial rules of evidence, and notes that the Davis conclusion is supported, in part, by a reference to Judge Hand's opinion in Costello. He continues to note, however, that convictability should control: "If probable cause is regarded as indicating probability of conviction, then there is a

viction cannot be assessed without regard to the rules of evidence which will apply at the trial.[52]

At the preliminary examination in *People v. Asta*,[53] an investi-

---

need to apply the trial rules of evidence to the preliminary examination and grand jury proceeding. If probable cause is conceptualized in that way, the grand jury proceeding and the preliminary examination do not function as independent proceedings (as does an administrative hearing, for example) but rather as *proceedings ancillary to the criminal jury trial.* It is not the purpose of these proceedings to make a final determination, but rather to predict the determination which will be made at the trial. If the rules of evidence regulate the proof on the basis of which conviction at the trial must rest, and if the purpose of the grand jury proceeding and preliminary examination is to predict the probability of such a conviction, then a prediction which does not take into account those rules of evidence is not a prediction at all, but an independent determination of probable guilt." Note, The Rules of Evidence as a Factor in Probable Cause in Grand Jury Proceedings and Preliminary Examinations, 1963 Wash. U.L.Q. 102, 128 (italics in original).

52 In Note, Exclusion of Incompetent Evidence from Federal Grand Jury Proceedings, 72 Yale L.J. 590 (1963), there appears a discussion of the problem raised by Costello, but it is limited to federal grand juries. The note is concerned primarily with the practical problem of applying the rules of evidence in the ex parte grand jury proceedings, and it concludes with a recommendation for use of motions to suppress and presiding masters in order to enforce the rules of admissibility. At one point in this discussion, the conclusion is reached that the rules of evidence ought to apply because of the likelihood-of-conviction notion, but this conclusion is reached in a peculiar fashion: "Because of the presumption of innocence, 'guilt' within the criminal process can be defined only in terms of conviction and thus can be applied only after the fact of conviction; 'innocence,' on the other hand, unless an individual has been acquitted, represents a state that may at any time turn into guilt. Thus, when sanctions are inflicted at preconviction stages they are necessarily borne by *innocent* people. The justification for the infliction of sanctions against persons presumptively innocent is the need for an efficacious and fair procedure leading to conviction. But the presumption of innocence requires that the imposition of preconviction sanctions be kept at a minimum consistent with allowing the process to run its course.

"If preconviction sanctions are to be kept within a process leading to conviction, the evidence considered at pretrial stages should, to the extent feasible, be limited to that evidence which would be admissible at trial. . . . Because variations between evidentiary standards used at trial and at grand jury proceedings may distort the relationship between indictment and the likelihood of conviction at trial, an examination of the feasibility of imposing trial-type evidentiary standards on federal grand juries seems warranted." Id. at 590-591 (italics in original).

It could be asserted that, in addition to considerations of fairness to unconvictable persons, considerations of efficiency in administration suggest carrying prosecutions of these persons no further than the preliminary examination. Whatever the reasons, cases of this kind could be discontinued at the preliminary by invoking evidentiary restrictions which would be applicable at trial. It is noteworthy that the reporter for the Advisory Committee for the Federal Rules of Criminal Procedure has proposed an amendment to Fed. R. Crim. P. 5.1(b)(2) to the effect that: "Objections to evidence because improperly acquired which do not cast doubt upon the trustworthiness of the evidence must be deferred until the case reaches the United States District Court." Other prominent figures in debates regarding this proposal are concerned about providing some means by which the legality of evidence could be tested before prosecutions reach the court of general trial jurisdiction.

53 337 Mich. 590, 60 N.W.2d 472 (1953). Defendants were prosecuted for con-

gating officer testified to what an informer told him. This was objected to as violating the rule against hearsay, but the objection was overruled. On appeal, the court commented:

> On the preliminary examination . . . the defendants were, under the statute, entitled to have the witnesses examined in their presence. . . . In view of the nature and purpose of the proceeding, the fact that the crime charged had been committed could not be established by hearsay testimony.[54]

The statute cited by the court provides: "The magistrate . . . shall examine the complainant and the witnesses in support of the prosecution, on oath *in the presence of the prisoner. . . .*"[55]

The major purpose of confrontation provisions, such as the statute cited in *Asta,* is, in the words of Wigmore, "to secure for the opponent the opportunity of cross-examination."[56] Does the confrontation requirement, a standard provision in statutes governing the conduct of preliminary examinations,[57] constitute a statutory mandate that the magistrate follow the hearsay rule, as the court in *Asta* indicates?

It is difficult to understand what the court intended in the quoted material. One interpretation is that it intended to prohibit the use of any hearsay evidence in the preliminary examination. This interpretation is unlikely because the typical interpretation of confrontation provisions in statutes and constitutions does not preclude the use of evidence admissible under the various exceptions to the hearsay rule. This interpretation is explained by McCormick:

---

spiracy to violate the Michigan cigarette tax act by transporting cigarettes into Michigan for sale within that state. The Michigan police were told by an informer, whose name they refused to disclose, that the defendants would be transporting a truckful of cigarettes from St. Louis to Michigan on a certain day. The Michigan police followed the truck from a place in Indiana and arrested the defendants just after they crossed the Michigan border. Defendants were bound over for trial at the preliminary examination in spite of their contention that there was no proof of their intent to sell the cigarettes in Michigan — that their behavior was consistent with a purpose to transport the cigarettes through Michigan into another state for distribution. A motion to quash the information on the same ground was upheld. The state appealed and the trial court's action was affirmed.

54 People v. Asta, 337 Mich. 590, 612, 60 N.W.2d 472, 482 (1953). Compare Pointer v. Texas, 380 U.S. 400, 85 Sup. Ct. 1065, 13 L. Ed. 2d 923 (1965).

55 Mich. Stat. Ann. §28.922 (1954) (emphasis added).

56 5 Wigmore, Evidence 123 (3d ed. 1940). See Chapter 4, note 28 *supra* and accompanying text for further discussion of the relationship between confrontation and cross-examination.

57 See Kan. Stat. Ann. §62-614 (1964); Wis. Stat. Ann. §954.08(1) (1958). See also ALI, Code of Criminal Procedure §46, Comment at 287-289 (1931).

> Do the confrontation provisions in state and Federal constitutions limit the use for the prosecution of hearsay declarations falling within the exceptions to the hearsay rule? This was once a matter of doubt but it has now been established for a hundred years that those exceptions which were accepted when these provisions were included in the earliest American constitutions were not intended to be abrogated. Most if not all of the common-law exceptions were so accepted by the 1780's. . . . There seems no reason to doubt that the other traditional exceptions as developed and liberalized by judicial decisions should be similarly treated. New statutory liberalizations of the hearsay exceptions should likewise, it seems, meet with no obstacle from these provisions. . . .[58]

This interpretation of the confrontation requirement is consistent with the language of the *Asta* case.[59] The statement of the informer would probably be excluded under the hearsay rule because it does not meet any generally recognized exception to the rule.[60] Thus, the court probably did not intend to state that all hearsay evidence is inadmissible at the preliminary. On the other hand, it probably intended to say that the hearsay rule with its exceptions must be applied at the preliminary examination. It is clear in all three states that the hearsay rule as it is applied at trial with its exceptions is followed in preliminary examinations.[61]

C. Probable Cause — Problem Areas in Practice

Thus far, discussion of probable cause has served to block out large, basic problems in the administration of that concept. It seems clear — *Asta* notwithstanding — that the corpus delicti does not have to be proved to a greater degree of certainty than the defendant's participation.[62] Further, it is clear that in current administration the probable cause requirement serves to screen cases on the basis of probability of conviction, not just probability

58 McCormick, Evidence 486 (1954). Wigmore said, "it follows equally that the constitutional provision [on confrontation] does not exclude evidence admissible by way of *exception to the Hearsay rule.*" 5 Wigmore, Evidence 141 (3d ed. 1940) (italics in original).

59 See text accompanying note 54 *supra*.

60 The confrontation requirement has been held to preclude the use of affidavits at preliminary examinations. Seyfer v. Bloomer, 132 Kan. 877, 297 Pac. 681 (1931). But see McIntyre v. Sands, 128 Kan. 521, 278 Pac. 761 (1929). See also notes 35 and 36 *supra*.

61 See text accompanying notes 37 and 38 *supra*.

62 See notes 12-14 *supra* and accompanying text.

of guilt, although the formal law is uncertain on the proposition.[63]

It is far from certain — either in formal law or current administration — whether a finding of no probability of conviction may be based on evidence tending to prove a probability of acquittal because of an affirmative defense.[64] It is also not clear whether probability of conviction should be assessed by taking into account doubts as to witness credibility.[65] Finally, it is uncertain whether probability of conviction should be taken so literally as to permit a dismissal on the strong likelihood that a trial jury would acquit for policy reasons.[66]

Even if all these basic questions in the administration of the probable cause requirement were raised and answered, there would still remain the problem of deciding for each case, within the framework created by the answers to the basic questions, whether the evidence is sufficient to prove the "guilt" of the defendant to the required degree of certainty.[67] Perhaps the most fruitful approach to this last problem is to isolate specific situations which cause difficulty in daily administration. Four problem areas have been isolated. The first two — uncertain eye-witness identification and reluctance of the victim to testify — have given the prosecutor's office in Detroit particular difficulty and together account for by far the largest number of cases dismissed at the preliminary examination. Difficult issues arise more frequently in the third problem area — circumstantial evidence — but probably fewer dismissals result. The identity of the offender, the fact that a crime was committed, and the element of intent present particularly difficult problems of proof by circumstantial evidence. The final problem area is created by vague statutory proscriptions.

63 See notes 41-52 *supra* and accompanying text.

64 See notes 25-27 *supra* and accompanying text.

65 See notes 22-24 *supra* and accompanying text.

66 See notes 30-31 *supra* and accompanying text. The problem raised by the technical violation — whether the preliminary examination may include a review of the nonevidence-sufficiency factors which are active in the prosecutor's decision to charge — is basic to the organization of this entire volume. Thus, it has been assumed for purposes of organization, that the preliminary examination is limited to evidence-sufficiency review even though in an isolated case or two nonevidence-sufficiency considerations are clearly important to the magistrate's decision. The availability of review of the nonevidence-sufficiency factors in the decision to charge is discussed in Chapter 20, while the preliminary examination is discussed exclusively in the evidence-sufficiency portion of the volume.

67 It will be recalled that, when the standard of certainty is expressed in formal law without use of the statutory language or a close paraphrase of it, either language indicating proof by a probability or proof sufficient to make out a prima facie case is used. See notes 15-21 *supra* and accompanying text.

In Chapter 4 the difficulties which magistrates encounter in administering the probable cause requirement in the face of partial disclosure of the facts of the case were discussed. These difficulties are not solvable in terms of compelling a fuller disclosure of the facts, for example, by securing a fuller participation in the hearing by the defendant. Indeed, most of the problems described here are disclosed or augmented by the participation of the defendant. Thus, some problems of uncertain eye-witness identification and reluctance of the victim to testify are magnified by abnormally complete cross-examination. These problem areas constitute the limiting cases in the administration of the probable cause requirement. Other problem areas exist, such as the difficulty of proof of a conspiracy by circumstantial evidence, but the areas isolated point out by and large the difficult cases. It is these cases which receive the benefit of whatever screening efficacy the preliminary possesses.

As pointed out earlier, only a residue of cases in the three states under consideration would be touched by an increase in the screening efficacy of the preliminary. This is true because pre-preliminary screening by the prosecutor is especially intensive in those states and only a few in which the propriety of charging is questionable reach the preliminary. As indicated by at least one recent study,[68] however, the preliminary does perform a routine screening function in some jurisdictions; therefore the factors discussed below, which are significant for only the unusual case in the three states, could be expected to assume importance more often in other jurisdictions. The factors can be expected to assume greater importance everywhere, but especially in those jurisdictions with an increase in the number of defendants who are represented by counsel at the preliminary; counsel would be likely to perceive possibilities of dismissal because of inadequacies in the evidence and call them to the attention of the magistrate.

No attempt has been made to isolate statistically the factors which account for dismissals. The problems have two things in common which lead one to believe that they are the major causes of dismissals: each recurs with some regularity and each creates more doubt as to the sufficiency of the evidence than is normal. The doubt created sometimes is sufficient to result in a dismissal; at other times it might be sufficient only to interject an element of deliberation into an otherwise routine bindover decision. In

[68] Oaks and Lehman, The Criminal Process of Cook County and the Indigent Defendant, 1966 U. Ill. L.F. 584.

any event, it is clear that the large bulk of cases pass through the preliminary without the difficulties created by these problem areas.

1. *Uncertain eye-witness identification.*

Illustration No. 3: In a line-up, Witness A had identified defendant as the offender. At the preliminary examination he expressed doubt concerning his previous identification. The defendant was dismissed.

Illustration No. 4: At the preliminary examination, the complaining witness testified he saw the defendants removing a window fan from a tavern at four a.m. Long and heated cross-examination on the accuracy of his vision in the early morning light failed to weaken this witness's testimony. The defendant was bound over.

A frequently recurring evidence-sufficiency problem in preliminary examinations is the inability of eyewitnesses to identify the defendant, with certainty, as the perpetrator of the offense charged. In Illustration No. 4, the reason for the uncertain identification is obvious. In Illustration No. 3, when the doubt as to identification was interjected by the witness himself, the causes are largely speculative and could be the product of the dishonesty or faulty memory of the witness, or even of a poorly conducted line-up.

In Detroit, the inability of eye-witnesses to make certain identification is one of the two major causes of dismissals at preliminary examinations. In Illustration No. 4, the doubt as to identification is probably not sufficient to prevent a bindover, although some judges of Recorder's Court are especially careful to determine whether the witness seeing the offender is able to make a certain identification. The time of day the offender was seen and the distance from which the witness saw him thus assume greater importance and are inquired into in more detail before these judges. In Illustration No. 3, a dismissal is almost a certainty.[69] No doubt the press of business rather than strict adherence to theoretical norms accounts for dismissals in some borderline cases.

2. *Reluctance of victim to testify.*

Illustration No. 5: In a preliminary examination on a charge of statutory rape, the complainant, seventeen years old, was embarrassed when the prosecutor questioned her.

69 Indeed, an assistant prosecutor in Detroit indicated that he would recommend a dismissal in such a situation.

The judge said he knew the complainant did not want to prosecute but that her father was forcing her to do so. The defendant was bound over.

Illustration No. 6: In a preliminary examination on a charge of statutory rape, the complainant proved to be an unwilling witness, apparently because she had made up with the defendant between the time of the initial charging decision and the preliminary. The defendant was dismissed.

The reluctance of the complainant-victim to testify presents recurring evidence-sufficiency and discretionary problems in statutory rape cases, as well as in other cases involving sex victims. Unlike the evidence-sufficiency problems created by uncertain identification, the doubt created by the reluctance of the complainant to testify normally relates to the question whether a crime was committed, not to the defendant's participation in it. The discretionary problem is created because prosecutors are hesitant to prosecute when the victim does not wish to do so.

In Detroit, the reluctance of the complainant-victim to testify is one of the two major causes of dismissals at preliminary examinations. Even when the defendant is bound over for trial, a prosecutor is likely to accept a plea to a considerably reduced charge or to dismiss the case, because of the combination of evidence-sufficiency consequences of a reluctant complainant[70] and of a belief that prosecution is undesirable in some situations when the victim does not feel sufficiently aggrieved to desire to prosecute.[71] As Illustrations Nos 5 and 6 indicate, the reluctance to testify normally arises from a fear of embarrassing questions or from an unwillingness to hurt the defendant, or from both.

3. *Circumstantial evidence.*

Illustration No. 7: In a preliminary examination on a charge of breaking and entering during the nighttime, it had definitely been established that somebody stole cigarettes and money from a vending machine in a service station. There were no eye-witnesses and no confession. The

70 Other aspects of the problems experienced in conducting preliminaries involving young statutory rape victims have been discussed in Chapter 4 *supra*. The problem discussed there was largely the partial disclosure which sometimes results because of the embarrassment of the victim or her difficulty in understanding the questions. These problems, as well as the victim's reluctance to testify, together account for any doubt which is created as to the sufficiency of the evidence.

71 It is likely that the discretionary problem created by the reluctance of the victim to testify is regularly handled by the prosecutor's office, not by the examining magistrate, although it is not unlikely that the latter will recommend dismissal of the case for nonevidence-sufficiency reasons. See notes 31 and 66 *supra* and accompanying text.

defendant was linked to the crime because his fingerprints were found on the machine. The defendant was dismissed.

In Illustration No. 7, the state was forced to rely on circumstantial evidence of the identity of the offender, requiring the magistrate to give more careful attention to whether the inferences were supported by the evidence than would be necessary had there been eye-witnesses or a confession.[72] The judge stated that a dismissal was in order because it would be easy for the defendant to take the stand and testify that he had previously purchased cigarettes from the machine, thus explaining the existence of his fingerprints on it.

Often the doubt concerning circumstantial evidence is whether a crime has been committed.[73] In many cases, particularly in

[72] In his concurring opinion in United States v. Masiello, 235 F.2d 279 (1956), *cert. denied*, 352 U.S. 882, Judge Frank noted this difference with regard to motions for directed verdicts in criminal cases: "When, in a jury case, a witness testifies to the occurrence of a fact, the jury, if it believes him, may properly infer the occurrence of that fact from that testimony. Such an inference, based directly on testimony, is a *'testimonial inference'* (or a direct or primary inference). It rests entirely on the jury's belief in the credibility — reliability — of the testimony of some witness: A witness has directly testified to a fact which the jury, believing him, takes as a fact. Accordingly, such an inference is often (misleadingly) called 'direct evidence.'

"From one or more testimonial inferences, however, further inferences of the occurrence of other facts may be drawn, i.e., inferences as to the existence or occurrence of facts concerning which no one has testified. Any such inference, for convenience, may be described as an 'indirect' or 'derivative inference.' Often it is labelled 'circumstantial evidence' to distinguish it from 'direct evidence.'

"A testimonial inference involves an evaluation of witnesses' credibility; but once a fact is inferred on the basis of a testimonial inference, then any fact derivatively inferred from that fact (i.e., any 'circumstantial evidence') will in and of itself involve no evaluation of credibility." Id. at 289 (italics in original).

In addition, there is some indication that the magistrate's decision might be subject to more intensive appellate scrutiny if it were based on circumstantial evidence. Again in United States v. Masiello *supra,* Judge Frank noted: "In a federal civil case tried by a judge without a jury, the upper court must (except in unusual circumstances) accept the findings of the trial judge, insofar as they consist of testimonial inferences based on testimony of orally-testifying witnesses whose demeanor the trial judge observed. But the upper court may reject any of the trial judge's rational derivative inferences if other alternative rational derivative inferences are open. . . .

"Whether the same is true when an upper court reviews the findings of a trial judge sitting in a criminal case without a jury, has not yet been considered, so far as I know. I see no good reason for a difference." Id. at 290 n.9.

[73] In a preliminary examination on a charge of larceny, the testimony indicated that between January 1 and June 26, approximately 13,000,000 spark plugs were produced in a plant, and an inventory disclosed that 21,541 of them were missing. Although defendant had confessed to the crime, he was dismissed. The doubt here about the commission of an offense, in spite of the confession, arose from the possibility that the discrepancy had arisen from some error in inventory procedures in counting the large number of plugs involved or from some other failure of bookkeepers to keep track of the plugs.

arson prosecutions, the corpus delicti, as a practical matter, must be proved by circumstantial evidence because of the rarity of eye-witnesses.[74] A circumstantial evidence problem which recurs with some frequency is the difficulty of proof of the mental element of the offense. Unless there is a confession, and even with a confession in Michigan,[75] proof of the mens rea — guilty mind — must be made by circumstantial evidence.[76] If there is no proof of a guilty mind, then, in the absence of a presumption supplying the requisite mental state, the prosecution has failed to prove that a crime was committed, even though the defendant's participation may be clear. Finally, a problem of proving factual causation by circumstantial evidence occasionally arises — that is, whether defendant's act caused, for example, the death of a purported homicide victim.[77]

It can be seen that these circumstantial evidence issues can

[74] In a preliminary examination on a charge of arson, the testimony indicated that the building had been unoccupied for some time prior to the fire, that the fire was discovered about 1:30 in the morning, that a mattress and some rags were found burning in a corner, that the door to the house was found open, and that an empty gas can and a partially empty kerosene can were found on the kitchen table. Defendant had confessed to the crime. He was bound over. There is a rule of evidence, applicable in this case as well as in the case described in note 73 *supra*, which prevents the prosecution from relying solely on a confession to establish the commission of an offense.

"The most widely prevailing form of the American rule is that in a prosecution for any crime where the state relies on a confession, it must also produce evidence independent of the confession tending to establish the corpus delicti, that is, the fact that the crime charged has been committed." McCormick, Evidence 230 (1954). The rule in Michigan, both at trial and at preliminary examination, is probably unique in its strictness because it does not require merely corroboration of the corpus delicti but requires that it be proved without any aid from the confession at all. See authorities cited note 35 *supra*. Thus, the rarity of eye-witnesses, coupled with the inability of the prosecution to rely on confessions alone, forces reliance on circumstantial evidence to a large extent. That kind of evidence, existing independently of a confession, was apparently felt to be strong enough in the above arson prosecution to support a bindover, although it was not in the case described in note 73 *supra*.

[75] See note 74 *supra* and accompanying text.

[76] See People v. Asta, 337 Mich. 590, 60 N.W.2d 472 (1953).

[77] In a preliminary examination on a charge of first degree murder, two eye-witnesses testified to seeing the defendant shoot the victim. The victim's physician testified that the immediate cause of death was hypostatic pneumonia, which was, in turn, caused by a psychosis. The judge inquired into the causal connection between the gun shot and death. The doctor said that in his opinion the gun shot caused the psychosis which, in turn, caused the pneumonia, resulting in death from pneumonia. Defendant was bound over. In this case the identity of the offender and the conclusion that some crime had been committed by him were not in doubt. Whether the crime was murder or a nonhomicidal assault was placed into doubt by the unusual circumstances of the death. The judge's bindover for murder was made only after careful consideration of the evidence on causation and with some doubt on the issue.

become technical matters which can be adequately handled only by defense counsel. The defendant himself may not even perceive the defects in circumstantial evidence giving rise to these issues. If he does perceive them, he is likely to be unable to articulate an effective defensive stand on them. Therefore, the efficacy of this proceeding as a screening device is in part at least dependent on the extent to which counsel is afforded for defendants at this stage. The trend is in the direction of guaranteeing counsel by constitutional mandate, although this has been predicated on rather unusual procedural characteristics of preliminaries in some jurisdictions and has not yet been held to be generally applicable to all preliminaries.[78] Closely related to this trend are suggestions for increasing the educational level and professional competence of magistrates for considering the technical legal issues that might arise and for up-grading the preliminary generally as an independently significant phase in administration.[79]

4. *Uncertain legal standards.*

> *Illustration No. 8:* Eight tavern owners were prosecuted for operating gambling devices in violation of a statute. It was alleged that they paid nickels for games won on their pinball machines. Defendants were dismissed at preliminary examination.
>
> *Illustration No. 9:* Defendant was prosecuted for violating a criminal syndicalism statute. It was alleged that he distributed literature on the teachings, doctrines, and purposes of the I.W.W. Defendant was bound over at preliminary examination.

A problem which could arise with frequency at preliminary examinations is that posed by a vague statutory definition of what conduct is criminal. Whether the statute is vague because of the limitations of language or for other reasons, it becomes necessary to determine what conduct should be included and excluded on

78 See Chapter 4, notes 28 and 54-55 *supra* and accompanying text.

79 See generally Hearings on S. 1343 Before the Subcomm. on Improvement in Judicial Machinery of the Comm. on the Judiciary, 89th Cong., 1st Sess., on the United States Commissioner System (1965). Senator Tydings indicated in those hearings that he considered the preliminary to be a somewhat superfluous proceeding in federal prosecutions, although others disagreed with him. He even stressed, among other possible defense advantages, the opportunities for discovering the state's evidence. One point repeatedly discussed was the prospect of increasing the level of education of United States commissioners whose duties include the holding of preliminary examinations. This was a central consideration in Tydings's introduction of the Federal Magistrates Act, S. 3475, 89 Cong., 2d Sess. (1967), which recommended changing their title from commissioner to magistrate.

a case-by-case basis, because to apply the statute to its fullest leads to obviously absurd results.

It should not be surprising, however, to find that little of this necessary statutory interpretation is done at the preliminary examination. The typical attitude is that, if the conduct is arguably within the terms of the statute, probable cause exists and a bindover for trial is in order.[80] Thus, the examining magistrate can avoid a number of legal problems if he feels that it is unnecessary to consider them in light of the possibility of a trial and an appeal.

In Illustration No. 9, the magistrate found probable cause to believe the defendant guilty of the offense charged. On appeal from a conviction, the appellate court noted simply that some of the pamphlets which defendant distributed were clearly within the scope of the statute,[81] implying that the magistrate's conduct in failing to go into the issue was proper. In Illustration No. 8, the magistrate dismissed the defendant on the grounds that the pinball machines, even as operated, were not gambling devices. Thus it is arguable that here the magistrate perceived the legal issue implicit in the vague statute and decided the case on that basis. It is likely, however, that the case was dismissed as a technical violation because of the small amounts involved and the apparent lack of relation to organized crime.

[80] In re Danton, 108 Kan. 451, 195 Pac. 981 (1921); see In re Stilts, 74 Kan. 805, 87 Pac. 1134 (1906).

[81] In re Danton, *supra* note 80.

CHAPTER 6

Waiver of the Preliminary Examination

In the typical criminal case in which a preliminary examination is authorized by law, no preliminary examination is conducted because it is waived. During a single year, 5231 criminal defendants who appeared before Recorder's Court in Detroit could have been given a preliminary examination under Michigan law. Seventy-two per cent of those defendants waived their examinations.[1] Approximately 2/3 of the defendants in Sedgwick County, Kansas, waived preliminary examinations in that same year.[2] And, again, survey teams reported that, during the same year, a large (although unspecified) percentage of Milwaukee defendants waived preliminary examinations.[3] Furthermore, official statistics indicate that during the period between January 1, 1958, and July 1, 1961, the preliminary examination waiver rate for Milwaukee County was almost 90 per cent.[4] Because concern here is with the preliminary examination as an institution assumed in law to serve the function of eliminating from the crim-

1 Annual Report for the Recorder's Court of the City of Detroit, Michigan, 1956, 11 (Mimeo. 1957).

2 It is likely that the percentage is even higher in other Kansas counties.

3 For example, mention was made that a certain judge was not responsible for the high percentages of waivers in his court. Also, during the spring of 1957, the district attorney in Milwaukee County issued a memorandum in which he proposed a plan to stop the "rash" of remands for preliminaries under the new statute permitting such a procedure when the preliminary examination is waived without advice of counsel.

4 This figure is an average of the waiver rates for each of the years involved as computed by the Wisconsin Judicial Council. See Wisconsin Judicial Council, Biennial Report J-153-158 (1959); Wisconsin Judicial Council, Judicial Statistics B-108-113 (1959); Wisconsin Judicial Council, Biennial Report I-108-13 (1961); Wisconsin Judicial Council, Judicial Statistics B-108-13 (1961).

Caution should be used in transferring these figures from Milwaukee County to the remainder of the state, or from any urban to rural area. During this same period, although the waiver rate for Milwaukee County was 90 per cent, the waiver rate for all the other counties was only 77 per cent. Ibid.

inal process those persons against whom there is insufficient evidence to justify continuation of the restrictions on their liberty inherent in a charge of crime, attention is focused on the impact of extensive waivers of the preliminary on the effectiveness of the institution in performing this function.

A. Current Waiver Practices

Statutes in each of the three states expressly permit defendants to waive their preliminary examinations.[5] The field studies show that three distinct types of waivers were used in one or more of the three jurisdictions under authority of those statutes, although this pluralistic waiver practice is in no way reflected in the statutes and only partially reflected in case law.

Defendants may have several opportunities to waive their preliminary examinations. In Michigan at the time of the field studies, as well as under an earlier Wisconsin practice, defendants were asked to plead at their initial appearances. The purpose of the plea was not to obtain a judicial admission of guilt, nor was it to preclude a later plea of not guilty: its sole purpose was to determine whether the defendant wished to have the preliminary examination guaranteed him under the law. If the response to the request for a plea was "guilty," the only consequence was that the preliminary examination step was not taken.

In the absence of any practice of seeking implied waivers of preliminaries by requiring pleas at the initial appearance, as well as in those situations in which the "plea," when it was required, was "not guilty," defendants in both Wisconsin and Michigan were given an opportunity to waive a preliminary examination expressly. They were simply asked whether they wanted one. Under some circumstances the same opportunity was accorded defendants in Kansas.

5 Kan. Stat. Ann. §62-805 (1964); Mich. Stat. Ann. §28.982 (Supp. 1958); Wis. Stat. Ann. §§955.18 (Supp. 1968) and 954.34 (1958).

The American Law Institute Code of Criminal Procedure provides that the accused may waive his right to a preliminary examination. ALI, Code of Criminal Procedure §40 (1930). For a listing of statutes and cases which authorize waiver of the preliminary see id. at 276-279.

In State ex rel. Dilworth v. Braun, 31 Wis. 600 (1872), Justice Lyon said: "It is very questionable, if the examination be waived, and the accused recognize to appear before the circuit court to answer the charge against him, without any adjudication of probable cause by the justice, whether that court can take jurisdiction of the proceeding. I am strongly inclined to the opinion that it cannot." Id. at 605. Although this case has never been overruled, Justice Lyon's dictum that the preliminary examination cannot effectively be waived was expressly rejected two years later in Rindskopf v. State, 34 Wis. 217 (1874).

In addition, neither of these practices prevented a defendant from waiving his preliminary examination anytime before it was actually held, although under some circumstances, notably when the defendant was unrepresented by counsel in Kansas, no waiver would be accepted.[6] It is also clear that developments occurring subsequent to the field studies may make waiver more difficult today, or at least make subsequent attacks on the validity of waiver practices more likely to succeed.

1. *Implied waiver — pleading to the warrant.* Shortly after his detention has begun, an arrestee must be brought before a magistrate in a proceeding that is termed the "initial appearance" or the "arraignment on the warrant."[7] This proceeding marks the first time judicial officers (magistrates) might participate in determining whether previously arrested defendants will be formally charged and thus required to enter the adjudication stage. In practice, however, magistrates do not discontinue prosecutions either for evidence-sufficiency or other reasons at this stage. Instead, if defendants attempt to make exculpatory remarks, magistrates tell them that questions of guilt or innocence are reserved for later proceedings. Magistrates do make bail determinations at the initial appearance,[8] but its chief importance here is that

6 Since an express waiver may occur at almost anytime prior to the preliminary examination, or even while it is being conducted, it might be thought inaccurate to speak of only three opportunities to waive the preliminary. It is true, however, that at only three stages in the pretrial process is a defendant required to decide whether to waive or not — twice at the initial appearance and once at the arraignment on the information. Waivers not given at one of these occasions must stem from the initiative of the defendant, an important distinction which will later receive elaboration. Perhaps a better word than opportunities would be "invitations."

7 Although these terms are used interchangeably in the formal law and practice, for purposes of discussion in this chapter, the proceeding will be called an "initial appearance" when the offense charged is serious enough to require a preliminary examination (see Introduction, notes 6-8 *supra* and accompanying text) and an "arraignment on the warrant" when the offense is minor enough to be within the criminal trial jurisdiction of the magistrate or justice of the peace conducting the proceeding. If the offense is within the trial jurisdiction of a magistrate or justice of the peace, but the official conducting the proceeding does not have that trial jurisdiction, the proceeding is not an arraignment on the warrant as that phrase is used here. If the offense is too serious to be within the trial jurisdiction of a justice of the peace but not serious enough to require preliminary examination (for example, "high misdemeanors" in Kansas), the proceeding is neither an arraignment on the warrant nor an initial appearance. None of the discussion in this chapter should be considered necessarily applicable to the proceeding when it is used in either of the latter two circumstances. For a discussion of the problems arising in determining the length of time and the circumstances under which a person can be detained by the police prior to being brought before a magistrate, see LaFave, Arrest (1965).

8 See LaFave, Arrest 206-207 (1965).

it serves as a vehicle for waiver of a preliminary examination. The result is that defendants might either be held in custody or required to supply bail as a condition of freedom without any judicial determination that they were probably guilty of the offense charged — either to the time of the preliminary if there is one, or more often to the time of adjudication, either by plea of guilty or after trial.

In the typical initial appearance, when his name is called, the arrestee steps before the bench and the charge contained in the complaint or warrant is read to him, or he is informed generally of the charge against him. He may be immediately required to plead to that charge, a procedure which is termed "pleading to the warrant."[9] The extent to which it was utilized varied significantly among the three states. Before entering into a detailed analysis of these variations, it is important to consider how the practice of pleading to the warrant at the initial appearance began.

Initial appearances and arraignments on the warrant are conducted by the same official in the same proceeding.[10] Yet the functions performed by the initial appearance and the arraignment on the warrant differ radically. If the offense is within the trial jurisdiction of the official conducting the proceeding, formal law in each of the three states requires the defendant to plead to the charge contained in the complaint or warrant.[11] If he pleads guilty, the magistrate sentences him immediately;[12] if the plea is not guilty, a date is set for trial.[13] The arraignment on the warrant, then, is the proceeding at which a trial plea is given in cases triable by a magistrate. In more serious cases, which are not tri-

[9] This term will be used here even though in some circumstances it may include a practice which is literally "pleading to the complaint." It is clear, however, that in most jurisdictions the warrant is regarded as the significant document at the initial appearance. For a discussion of this and related problems, see Chapter 1.

[10] For example, in Sedgwick County, persons charged with felonies make their initial appearance in the early morning session of the Court of Common Pleas, along with persons charged with low misdemeanors who are arraigned on the warrant.

[11] Mich. Stat. Ann. §28.1196 (1954) provides: "The charge made against the accused, as stated in the warrant of arrest, shall be distinctly read to him at the time of his arraignment and he shall be required to plead thereto, which plea the court shall enter in its minutes; if the accused refuse to plead, the court shall enter the fact with a plea of not guilty in behalf of such accused in its minutes." For comparable provisions see Kan. Stat. Ann. §63-301 (1964) and Wis. Stat. Ann. §960.09 (Supp. 1968).

[12] Kan. Stat. Ann. §63-309 (1964); Mich. Stat. Ann. §28.1198 (1954); Wis. Stat. Ann. §960.11 (1958).

[13] Kan. Stat. Ann. §63-302 (1964); Mich. Stat. Ann. §§28.1197 to 28.1199 (1954); Wis. Stat. Ann. §960.10 (1958).

able by the magistrate and for which preliminary hearings are required unless waived, the trial plea is not made until arraignment on the information before a court of general trial jurisdiction to which the defendant has been bound over. The law contemplates that a defendant should plead at the arraignment on the warrant in the former kind of case. When, however, the proceeding is simply an initial appearance, as in the latter kind of case, there is no formal law authorization of (and little formal law advertence to)[14] the practice of requiring a plea to the warrant. It is probable that the requirement of pleading to the warrant when the offense charged is triable by the magistrate led to an unauthorized carryover of that practice to the initial appearance in serious cases not within the trial jurisdiction of the magistrate. At the time of the survey, the practice was observed at initial appearances extensively in Michigan, to a lesser extent in Kansas, and scarcely at all in Wisconsin.

In Michigan, as soon as the accused was informed of the charge against him, he was asked "How do you plead?" If he offered to relate exculpating or mitigating circumstances, he was told that the initial appearance was not the time for the trial of his case.[15] If he asked for counsel, he was told that no attorneys were appointed at this stage because the statute then provided for court-appointed counsel only at the arraignment on the information.[16] He was instructed to plead one way or the other.

In Kansas, while pleading to the warrant at the initial appearance was utilized, the procedure differed somewhat from that in Michigan. If a defendant made his initial appearance before the Court of Common Pleas for Sedgwick County with an attorney, he was required to plead to the warrant, just as he

[14] For the only formal law advertence to the practice uncovered in any of the three states, see State v. Kornstett, 62 Kan. 221, 61 Pac. 805 (1900); Stecher v. State, 237 Wis. 587, 297 N.W. 391 (1941); Montgomery v. State, 128 Wis. 183, 107 N.W. 14 (1906). See also Latimer v. State, 55 Neb. 609, 76 N.W. 207, 70 Am. St. Rep. 403 (1898); Note, 36 U. Det. L.J. 202, 204 (1958).

[15] In one case observed, a defendant charged with breaking and entering in the nighttime entered a plea of not guilty, waived preliminary examination, and requested the judge to allow him to say something. The judge agreed. The defendant stated, "I didn't do it." The judge replied that he did not want to hear anything about the case at this time and set a date for the preliminary examination. The judge told the accused that he would have an opportunity to say something in court at that time.

[16] Mich. Stat. Ann. §28.1253 (1954). In 1957, this section was amended to permit the appointment of counsel prior to the preliminary examination. Mich. Stat. Ann. §28.1253 (Supp. 1968). For an extended discussion on the formal law and practice in all three states with regard to the appointment of counsel at the preliminary examination, see Chapter 4.

would have been in Michigan. If he appeared without counsel, however, he was first asked whether he had or planned to retain an attorney. If he already had an attorney or said he did not want one, he was required to plead. If he did not have an attorney and wanted one, the court set a date for a preliminary without requiring a plea to the warrant and without asking the defendant whether he wished a preliminary. If the defendant was indigent, the court concluded his initial appearance by informing him that an attorney would be appointed in time to represent him at the preliminary examination.[17]

If a defendant made his initial appearance with an attorney before City Court in Kansas City, he was required to plead. If he had no attorney with him, a date for his preliminary examination was automatically set, without inquiring into the reasons for his not having counsel with him. Except in rare cases, no attorneys were appointed to represent defendants at the preliminary examination.[18] There is some indication, however, that in parts of Kansas outside of Sedgwick County and Kansas City, the practice of pleading to the warrant at the initial appearance approximated that found in Michigan.

Although it is not known whether it more closely resembled the Michigan or the Kansas practice, it is clear that pleading to the warrant of some variety was at one time the practice in Wisconsin.[19] In 1949, however, the statutes were amended to provide that "In cases not triable before the magistrate, the defendant shall not be required to plead."[20] The practice of asking defendants to plead to the warrant charging a serious offense is no longer followed as a matter of routine in Wisconsin. There were, however, four instances observed in which a volun-

17 Kan. Stat. Ann. §62-1304 (1964) provides, similarly to the Michigan statute in note 16 *supra*, for appointment of counsel only when the information or indictment has been filed in the trial court. The judges of both the Court of Common Pleas and the District Court in Sedgwick County feel, however, that counsel should be appointed in time to represent the defendant at the preliminary examination. Pursuant to an agreement made with the District Court, the judges of the Court of Common Pleas for Sedgwick County regularly make appointment of counsel at the initial appearance.

18 The judge of division 2 of City Court in Kansas City indicated that occasionally he would assign counsel at the initial appearance to an indigent defendant who was rather young. He continued by saying that, if the defendant were indigent, between 16 and 20, and involved in a case which had attracted a substantial amount of publicity, he would probably appoint counsel in time for the preliminary examination.

19 Stecher v. State, 237 Wis. 587, 297 N.W. 391 (1941); Platz, The 1949 Revision of the Wisconsin Code of Criminal Procedure, 1950 Wis. L. Rev. 508.

20 Wis. Stat. Ann. §954.04 (1958).

tary plea — made without request by the court — was accepted as a waiver.[21] The practice as observed in these instances would seem to be entirely consistent with the wording of the amendment, which provided that the defendant is not to be required to plead, rather than the implication that a plea does not have the effect of a waiver.[22]

When the accused is required to plead to the warrant, he faces his first opportunity to waive the preliminary examination. If he pleads guilty, the amount of bail is determined and he is immediately bound over to the trial court without further proceedings, because a guilty plea is regarded as an implied waiver of the preliminary examination.[23] Waiver of the preliminary can be avoided by expressly pleading not guilty and also by the interesting practice observed in Michigan of defense counsels' having their clients "stand mute" when asked to plead to the warrant. The effect of standing mute is that a plea of not guilty is entered for the defendant.[24] None of the pleas at the initial appearance has standing as a trial plea, hence the accused is required to plead over at the arraignment on the information regardless of what his plea to the warrant may have been.

21 The police detective attached to the district court for Milwaukee County informed the accused of the charge contained in the warrant. The defendant then stated that what the detective said was true and the judge treated this statement as a waiver of the preliminary examination. In another observed instance, the accused, although not asked to plead, did so knowing that it would result in a waiver of the preliminary examination. His plea of guilty was accepted.

Two instances were observed in outlying Wisconsin in which pleading to the warrant was permitted in spite of the 1949 amendment. Both occurred in the Eau Claire County Court. In both cases the defendant made his initial appearance with an attorney and in both cases he pleaded not guilty to the warrant, although he was not asked to plead in either case. In both cases, the defendant then expressly waived the preliminary examination.

22 For a summary of the Wisconsin amendment see Platz, *supra* note 19. See also Odell v. Burke, 281 F.2d 782 (7th Cir. 1960); Wis. Stat. Ann. §954.04, Comment of Advisory Committee, 1949 (1958).

23 State v. Kornstett, 62 Kan. 221, 61 Pac. 805 (1900). Although there is no formal law on this proposition in Michigan, the field studies make it abundantly clear that this is invariably the practice. The practice, as observed in Michigan, is for the examining magistrate to announce as soon as a guilty plea is entered, "There will be a waiver of the examination and the case will be set for trial." The preliminary may be impliedly waived in ways other than by pleading to the warrant, but they are of only minor importance in the practice. Thus, the giving of bail or the simple failure of the defendant to appear in court on the date set for his preliminary examination may be construed as an implied waiver. See 2 Wis. Ops. Att'y Gen. 345 (1913).

24 For the effect of pleading to the warrant, and particularly the practice of standing mute, on defects in the warrant, see Chapter 3. One judge of Recorder's Court told a field interviewer that all good defense attorneys have their clients stand mute at the initial appearance.

Even a guilty plea may not, under certain circumstances, result in a waiver of preliminary examination. It is the practice of at least some Michigan judges not to accept a waiver of a preliminary if the charge is serious, the defendant does not have counsel and does not seem to comprehend the nature of the proceedings.[25] Except under these unusual circumstances, a guilty plea will be accepted even if the defendant is not aware he is thereby waiving the preliminary examination.

2. *Express waiver.* A defendant in Michigan who did not plead guilty to the warrant immediately faced his second opportunity at the initial appearance to waive the preliminary examination, this time expressly. The same held true for a defendant in Sedgwick County or Kansas City who made his initial appearance with counsel and did not plead guilty. For the Wisconsin defendant, and for some defendants in Sedgwick County and Kansas City,[26] this represented the first opportunity to waive, since pleading to the warrant was not required.

The procedure typically takes the form of a question from the magistrate or clerk such as, "Do you waive a preliminary hearing?" or "Do you wish a preliminary examination or would you rather go directly to trial?" If the defendant indicates a desire for a preliminary, a date is set and he is freed on bail or reincarcerated. If he indicates that he does not wish a preliminary examination, it is treated as waived and he is immediately bound over for trial. This latter alternative is what is here termed "express waiver" of the preliminary examination, in opposition to the waiver which is implied by a plea of guilty to the warrant.

It has previously been noted that statutes in each of the three states explicitly authorize the defendant to waive his right to a preliminary examination.[27] Although there is little material on this point, the available evidence indicates that express waivers — not implied waivers by pleading to the warrant or pleading to the information — were contemplated in drafting these statutes.[28]

25 In one initial appearance observed in Michigan, a woman, charged with first degree murder, when asked to plead, replied, "Yes, I is guilty." At this point, the judge interrupted the sobbing defendant and stated, "I refuse to accept this plea. Let her stand mute and get an attorney before deciding whether or not she wishes a preliminary examination."

26 See notes 17 and 18 *supra* and accompanying text. Of course, if a defendant pleads guilty to the warrant, he is immediately bound over for trial and is not given a second opportunity to waive the preliminary.

27 See note 5 *supra* and accompanying text.

28 See State v. Myers, 54 Kan. 206, 38 Pac. 296 (1894); People v. Quicksall, 322 Mich. 351, 33 N.W.2d 904 (1948); Stewart v. People, 42 Mich. 255, 3 N.W. 863 (1879). Additional evidence lies in the statutes. Thus, although statutes in each of

This proposition will not be found in the formal law. Indeed, from appellate opinions it is frequently impossible to distinguish between an express waiver and a plea to the warrant, for typically, when the issue of waiver is raised, it will be disposed of by a statement that the defendant "waived this examination, as shown by the return of the examining magistrate."[29] It is even possible that the magistrate's return normally will not distinguish between an express waiver and a waiver by plea to the warrant,[30] hence, it is likely that the appellate court itself (on the basis of the record) may not know which type of waiver was utilized. In contrast, if the court relies on a waiver made at the arraignment on the information, it will typically indicate that this was the case.

Occasionally a defendant may seem hesitant to indicate whether he wishes a preliminary or he may manifest his uncertainty as to what a preliminary examination is. The field studies reveal that the magistrate usually gives the defendant ample time to make up his mind. In addition, a brief explanation of the preliminary is frequently given. The explanation is usually limited to a statement that the purpose of the preliminary examination is to ascertain whether there is probable cause to hold the defendant for trial.[31]

If the defendant has completed his initial appearance without waiving the preliminary examination, he is scheduled to receive a preliminary in the near future. Nevertheless, he may waive it at any time between the initial appearance and the conclusion of the examination itself. He could, of course, effect such a

---

the three states recognize the power of waiver, and although statutory provisions in each of these states require a plea to the warrant in cases triable by a justice of the peace, there is no statute authorizing or recognizing, even inferentially, the practice of waiving the preliminary examination by pleading to the warrant. See notes 5, 10-14 *supra* and accompanying text. Further evidence is found in the 1949 Wisconsin amendment which abolished pleading to the warrant. For many years, two statutes explicitly recognized the power to waive the preliminary. See Wis. Stat. Ann. §§955.18 and 954.34 (1958). In 1949, Wis. Stat. Ann. §954.04 (1958) was amended to abolish pleading to the warrant in cases not triable by justices of the peace. The other two statutes referring to waiver were allowed to remain unchanged, presumably on the theory that they are consistent with abolishing pleading to the warrant.

29 People v. Losinger, 331 Mich. 490, 496, 50 N.W.2d 137, 140 (1951).

30 It was noted previously that under the Michigan practice the magistrate states, when a guilty plea is entered, that there will be a waiver of the preliminary examination. See note 23 *supra*. If the statement and not the plea is recorded, the record would not reveal the manner in which the waiver occurred.

31 One court clerk used this prepared explanation: "An examination is simply a hearing to see if there is enough evidence to hold you for trial."

waiver before the date set for the preliminary simply by appearing before the examining magistrate and indicating his desire to waive. In like manner, he could effect a waiver at any time during the course of his preliminary by manifesting the appropriate intent.[32] Although these possibilities exist, the field studies indicate that virtually all the waivers at this stage in the charging process do not occur until after the case is called for preliminary examination and before the prosecution begins to offer its evidence. What is being discussed here, then, is express waiver of the preliminary examination at the time the preliminary itself is scheduled to begin.

This particular opportunity for waiver differs materially from the implied waiver by pleading to the warrant and even from the express waiver at the initial appearance: all waivers occurring at this point are solely the result of the initiative of the defendant. No suggestion or even mention of waiver is made by the court. Thus, waivers occurring at this point would seem to be stripped of any feature of coercion or suggestion on the part of administrative officials, but would rather seem to be simply the result of desire to waive on the part of the defendant.[33] The relevancy of this distinction will be made clear later.[34]

The field studies in Michigan indicate that this opportunity for waiver is a significant one. The judge of Detroit Recorder's Court who has the examining duties handles approximately fifteen preliminaries per day. Although almost twenty are set for hearing each day, an average of five are not heard because of last minute decisions on the part of the defense counsel to waive. It will be recalled that, if a defendant in Kansas makes his initial appearance without counsel, he is not given an opportunity to waive the preliminary at that stage. Instead, a date is set for his preliminary examination without consulting him.[35] Thus, in these cases — a substantial percentage[36] — there is no opportunity to waive the preliminary examination until after the initial

32 People v. Sartori, 168 Mich. 308, 134 N.W. 200 (1912). See also People v. Fishel, 270 Mich. 82, 258 N.W. 217 (1935); 2 Wis. Ops. Att'y Gen. 345 (1913).

33 See note 6 *supra*. This is not to indicate, however, that an express waiver at the preliminary examination stage cannot be the result of bargaining between prosecutor and defense counsel, although bargaining at this stage is infrequent.

34 See note 38 *infra* and accompanying text.

35 See notes 17 and 18 *supra* and accompanying text.

36 Although no figures are available in Kansas, in Detroit Recorder's Court 43 per cent of all felony defendants were represented at one time or another by court appointed counsel. Annual Report for the Recorder's Court of the City of Detroit, Michigan, 1956. P. 11 (Mimeo. 1957). Of a series of 13 initial appearances observed in Detroit, the defendant was represented in only 4.

appearance. As might be anticipated, the vast majority of waivers occur immediately before the preliminary itself is to begin.[37]

3. *Persuading defendants to waive.*

Illustration No. 1: Two women were charged with embezzling $2500 from a department store. They entered the court without counsel for their initial appearance. As they stood before the bench they were asked whether they waived a preliminary examination. The judge repeated the question and then said, "Now, again, ladies, I ask you, what do you want to do? Do you want me to adjourn this matter so you can think it over, or do you want to waive the preliminary examination. It's up to you." The women shrugged their shoulders and, looking about in a somewhat puzzled fashion, said, "Gee, we don't know what to do." The judge replied, "Well, I'll give you a few minutes to discuss this among yourselves and then you let me know if you want to waive the preliminary hearing." As the judge left the bench, a police detective said to the defendants, "Look, there is nothing to this procedure. Take my word for it, just waive. When the judge gets back, tell him you waive." A court attendant said, "Look, we're not trying to influence you in this matter whatsoever, but the best thing for you to do is to waive the preliminary examination. When the judge comes back, tell him you waive the preliminary examination." When the judge returned, the women waived the preliminary.

Although occurrences such as this are by no means routine, they were observed from time to time in Michigan and Wisconsin. They were observed only at that part of the initial appearance when the defendant was asked if he wished a preliminary examination[38] and only when counsel was not present with

37 It would, of course, be expected that there would be more waivers at the preliminary examination stage in Sedgwick County than in Kansas City, because of the practice of appointing counsel at the initial appearance in the former jurisdiction. Surprisingly enough, however, very few of the waivers occurring at the preliminary examination are the result of bargaining betwen defense counsel and the prosecutor.

38 The discussion here must be limited to attempts to persuade a defendant *in open court* to waive the preliminary examination. Although there was some speculation as to possible persuasion in the detention pen where defendants are kept immediately before making their initial appearances, no instances were observed. Of all the pretrial court appearances which a defendant makes, persuasion was observed only in that portion of the initial appearance when the preliminary may be waived by express waiver. This is the only time the defendant is expressly asked

the defendant. Perhaps because this practice is of doubtful legality,[39] information was difficult to obtain, resulting in uncertainty as to its details. Apparently police officers attached to the court more often engage in persuading than do court clerks or bailiffs. The indication is that it is practiced more often in Wisconsin than in Michigan, although no estimate of the percentage of cases in which it is practiced is available for either state. There is no indication that the practice exists at all in Kansas.[40]

Only three instances were observed in Michigan in which officials attached to an examining magistrate's court attempted to persuade a defendant to waive the preliminary examination. All three occurred at the initial appearance and all three occurred when defense counsel was not present. In two of the instances the persuasion was attempted by a court bailiff and in the third instance the persuading official was a member of the Detroit Police Department. In the latter instance the accused pleaded not guilty to larceny from a store. The court then asked him if he wanted an examination. The police officer, in a low tone, advised the accused to waive the preliminary examination. The accused stated "yes" he did want a preliminary examination as soon as he could have one. An assistant prosecuting attorney in

---

his desires with regard to waiving a preliminary examination. In pleading to the warrant and in pleading to the information, the defendant is required to make a decision which could result in a waiver, but the question is in the form of requiring him to plead. The express waiver which is given at the preliminary examination is not solicited by the court. Hence, the express waiver at the initial appearance is the only occasion on which the defendant is directly required to waive or request a preliminary examination. It seems to be the only time when court-attached officials consider it appropriate to advise defendants about waiver decisions.

39 No cases have been uncovered in which this issue was raised. There is some indication, however, that a waiver occurring in such a situation would be regarded as being involuntary and, hence, void. See In re Secrest, 36 Kan. 725, 14 Pac. 144 (1887) in which the court held that a waiver of the preliminary examination was void when given out of a fear that mob violence would result if a preliminary were held. See also State v. Sweet, 101 Kan. 746, 168 Pac. 1112 (1917). But see State v. Lewis, 19 Kan. 260 (1877) in which the court held that the mere fact that the defendant waived the preliminary while handcuffed did not make the waiver involuntary.

40 It is likely that no instances were observed in Kansas because of the peculiar lack of opportunity for their occurrence. Observations in the other two states indicated that officials will attempt to persuade a defendant to waive the preliminary only if he is not represented by counsel at the initial appearance. The Kansas practice permits a waiver of the preliminary examination only if the defendant is represented by counsel at the initial appearance. Hence, if the defendant is not represented by counsel, no pressure to waive can be used because he could not waive the preliminary even if he wanted to do so; conversely, if he has counsel, he is permitted to waive the preliminary, but the presence of counsel will preclude any attempt to persuade him to do so.

Detroit told a field reporter that he had never seen police officers assigned to the examining magistrate's court attempt to influence a defendant to waive the preliminary examination.

The practice seems to be more extensive in Wisconsin. Observations indicate that typically there must be two conditions present before persuading the defendant to waive the preliminary will be attempted. The defendant must make his initial appearance without counsel. No attempt to persuade was observed when the defendant was represented. In Wisconsin many defendants do not have counsel at the initial appearance since the applicable statute does not require appointment of counsel as a matter of routine this early in the proceedings. The second condition is that the defendant must express some doubt whether he wishes to waive the preliminary. Although there were one or two exceptions, no pressure is exerted unless the defendant manifests uncertainty in making his waiver decision. As a general proposition if the defendant appears without counsel and manifest uncertainty as to waiving the preliminary, he is very likely to receive "advice" to waive it.[41]

This practice — both in Michigan and Wisconsin — seems to be the product of an attitude which certain officials hold toward the usefulness of the preliminary examination. Most preliminaries that are held result in bindovers to the trial court.[42] But holding a preliminary examination will normally entail a two to three weeks' delay in bringing the case to trial.[43] The police officers and court officials who engage in this practice consider the preliminary to be a serious waste of everybody's time. They

41 A Milwaukee County defense attorney, admittedly a biased observer, told a field reporter: "There ought to be a law against the police officers and the clerks talking the defendant into waiving a preliminary hearing. Not only does it have the defense attorney in a spot when this defendant, if he is indigent, later gets court-appointed counsel on the municipal court level, but it just tends to be a bad situation altogether. I know the police officers are guilty on this inducement to waiver; they figure they don't have to do as much work later on if preliminary examination is waived. The clerks do it also, but this isn't very often. I've only seen it a couple or three times. I don't really want to say that it is a practice."

42 See text accompanying notes 1 and 2 *supra*.

43 Thus, in Detroit the average time from waiver of the preliminary to filing of the information is ten days. The average time between request for a preliminary and time of the hearing is one week. It then takes from ten days to two weeks for the magistrate's stenographer to prepare the transcript. The case is then in the prosecutor's office (where it would be sent immediately if the preliminary were waived), and it takes the usual ten days to prepare the information for filing. Thus when a preliminary is requested, the case is from two and a half to three weeks longer in getting to trial or other disposition in the trial court. The clerk for Recorder's Court explained that this is the major delay in processing a defendant charged with a serious offense.

feel that the situation justifies their persuading the defendant to waive.[44] An additional factor present in Wisconsin is that the defendant can always obtain a remand for a preliminary if it is waived without advice of counsel — the very situation in which persuasion is normally attempted. Therefore, the persuading officials might feel that their behavior can have no lasting adverse effects upon the defendant since he can obtain a preliminary later anyway.[45]

B. Innovations in the Waiver Practices

Three devices have been developed in an effort to correct what have been perceived as defects in waiver practices. The first of these is the Wisconsin amendment abolishing pleading to the warrant as a waiver technique.[46] The second is the practice in two Kansas communities of refusing to accept a waiver of the preliminary examination unless the defendant is represented by counsel.[47] The third is the remand statutes found in Michigan and Wisconsin.[48]

It is emphasized in this section that these innovations have not significantly decreased the overall waiver rate. Various reasons will be suggested why informed defendants or defense counsel might find waiver to be advantageous from the standpoint of defense strategy. These reasons may account for the continuing high rate in spite of the innovations. The importance of the changes must then be measured by how well they assure that waiver will result only from an informed assessment of defense strategy.

1. *Abolishing pleading to the warrant.* In 1949, the following sentence was added to the section of the Wisconsin statutes which provides for the initial appearance: "In cases not triable before the magistrate, the defendant shall not be required to plead."[49] A writer, commenting upon this amendment, said

44 If a preliminary examination is waived, the police officer will have one less court appearance to make. See note 41 *supra*. One field reporter felt that the judge sometimes unconsciously encourages waiver of the preliminary. Some judges ask "Do you waive preliminary examination?" rather than "Do you want a preliminary examination?" In addition, if a defendant is uncertain whether he wishes to waive, he is sent back to the police detention pen to think the matter over. In the trial court, silence after a request to plead is one way of "standing mute," which, of course, results in a plea of not guilty.

45 See note 75 *infra* and accompanying text.

46 See notes 19-22 *supra* and accompanying text.

47 See notes 17-18 *supra* and accompanying text.

48 See text accompanying note 45 *supra*.

49 Wis. Stat. Ann. §954.04 (1958).

> It has been almost a universal custom, so far as this writer has observed, for the magistrate to ask the defendant in such cases "whether he pleads guilty or not guilty." Although the proceedings are clearly not an "arraignment" in cases where the magistrate has no trial jurisdiction, it is customary to refer to them as such. Of course, a true arraignment can be held only in a court having trial jurisdiction, and where the case is not triable by the magistrate, the accused can only be arraigned in a court of record upon an information or indictment. The statute enacts the correct rule. The Wisconsin Supreme Court has pointed out that a "plea of guilty" taken at this stage of the proceedings amounts in legal effect to no more than a waiver of preliminary examination.[50]

This amendment, enacted to correct a usurpation of trial court arraigning functions by magistrates in cases not triable before them, does not directly meet the waiver aspects of pleading to the warrant. Thus, it abolished the practice of magistrates *requiring* a plea, instead of abolishing the practice of inferring a waiver of preliminary examination from a plea of guilty. For this reason the pre-amendment practice is unchanged with regard to pleas given without a request from the magistrate.[51]

With this exception, the amendment has effectively abolished the implied waiver by pleading to the warrant in Wisconsin. Two different practices have arisen under the amendment. In one, after the defendant is informed of the charge, the magistrate simply omits the pleading step in the initial appearance and proceeds directly into the express waiver step. But in such courts defendants occasionally volunteer pleas before they are asked if they wish a preliminary, and when they do, waivers are inferred as they were under the pre-amendment practice.[52] Under the second practice, the court, instead of omitting the pleading step entirely, announces to the accused that since the offense is one which requires a preliminary examination, he is not permitted to plead at this time but will be allowed to plead at the arraignment on the information instead. Even with this added precaution, pleas are sometimes volunteered, and the usual waiver consequences are imputed to them.[53] Of course, if no plea of guilty is volunteered, the magistrate proceeds to the express waiver step.[54]

When pleading to the warrant is utilized as an implied waiver,

50 Platz, The 1949 Revision of the Wisconsin Code of Criminal Procedure, 1950 Wis. L. Rev. 508.

51 See notes 21-22 *supra* and accompanying text.

52 See note 21 *supra*.

53 Ibid.

54 See text accompanying note 38 *supra*.

the plea is accepted even though the defendant is not aware he is waiving the preliminary.[55] Although abolishing pleading to the warrant has not decreased the waiver rate substantially, it has changed this feature of the practice. The result is that normally only express waivers occur at the initial appearance — waivers given only by defendants who are informed that they are being asked to waive the preliminary examination.[56]

2. *Requiring the advice of counsel.* At the time of the survey, statutes in the three states did not require appointment of counsel to represent indigent defendants at preliminaries, although a statute in Michigan now requires this, and a recent enactment in Wisconsin, although not explicitly requiring it, has apparently had the effect of causing counsel to be appointed in time for preliminaries as a matter of routine, at least in Milwaukee County.[57] At any rate, at the time of the survey, no attorneys were appointed, with relatively minor exceptions, in time for preliminaries in Michigan and Wisconsin, and, except for Sedgwick County, the same was true in Kansas.

When a defendant made his initial appearance before the Court of Common Pleas in Sedgwick County unaccompanied by counsel, he was asked whether he had or intended to employ counsel. When the response was negative, the judge inquired into the defendant's indigency. A defendant who appeared without counsel was given no opportunity to waive the preliminary at the initial appearance, either expressly or by pleading to the warrant.[58] Counsel was then appointed for indigent defendants between the initial appearance and the date set for the preliminary examination. Thus, when his case was called for the preliminary, the defendant was usually represented by counsel.[59]

Two facets of this procedure are significant at this point. First, no defendant could waive the preliminary at the initial appear-

[55] See text accompanying note 41 *supra.*

[56] Although no specific data are available, persuasion would seem necessarily to increase the waiver rate. It is clear that the purpose of officials doing the persuading is to increase the number of waivers. See notes 41-45 *supra* and accompanying text.

[57] Kan. Stat. Ann. §62-1304 (1964); Mich. Stat. Ann. §28.1253 (1954); Wis. Stat. Ann. §957.26 (1958). In 1957, the Michigan statute was amended to permit the appointment of counsel prior to the preliminary examination. Mich. Stat. Ann. §28.1253 (Supp. 1968).

[58] The presence of counsel, appointed or retained, at the preliminary and its effect on evidence-sufficiency screening are discussed in Chapter 4.

[59] Counsel is appointed for an indigent defendant unless expressly refused. At the preliminary examination, assuming that all retained counsel are present, the only defendants without counsel are the nonindigent who have not hired one and the indigent who refused to have one appointed. Virtually all defendants are in fact represented at the preliminary examination.

ance unless he first had the advice of counsel. Second, when the defendant faced his final waiver opportunity at the beginning of the scheduled preliminary examination, he was normally represented by counsel. The significance of this procedure is that preliminary examinations were waived in Sedgwick County only by defendants represented by counsel.[60] The procedure used in Kansas City, Kansas, was comparable except in certain mystifying respects. Just as in Sedgwick County, a preliminary examination was automatically given to those defendants who make their initial appearances without counsel.[61] The Kansas City procedure differed, however, in that counsel was not appointed to represent the defendant at the preliminary examination. No appointments were made, with rare exceptions, until the defendant was arraigned on the information in the trial court.[62] Thus, the Kansas City procedure was similar to the Sedgwick County procedure in that no waivers were permitted at the initial appearance unless the defendant was represented by counsel, but it was also similar to the former procedure used in Michigan, Wisconsin, and most of Kansas in that no appointments were made until the arraignment on the information. The apparent conclusion from the Kansas City practice is that the preliminary is so important it cannot be waived without advice of counsel, but it is not important enough to justify appointment of counsel to represent the defendant at the examination itself.

What consequences do the Sedgwick County and Kansas City procedures have on the waiver practices? It has been noted that elsewhere defendants have frequently pleaded guilty to warrants without knowing they are waiving the preliminary examination.[63] This aspect of the waiver practices observed in Michigan was effectively abolished both in Sedgwick County and in Kansas City by requiring the advice of counsel as a condition precedent to permitting the defendant to plead to the warrant. Defendants occasionally expressly waived the preliminary examination at the initial appearance without fully knowing what they were waiving, even if an explanation was given.[64] This aspect of the waiver practices, observed both in Michigan and Wisconsin, was not found under the Kansas City and Sedgwick County procedures.

60 Even if a defendant appears for his preliminary examination without counsel, it is extremely doubtful that the court would permit him to waive it, since this is not permitted at the initial appearance.

61 See note 18 *supra* and accompanying text.

62 See note 18 *supra*.

63 See text accompanying note 25 *supra*.

64 See text accompanying note 31 *supra*.

Under the Sedgwick County procedure a defendant was represented by counsel when he faced his final opportunity to waive prior to the presentation of the state's case at the beginning of the preliminary itself. Virtually all of the preliminaries waived in Sedgwick County were waived at this point, with advice of counsel. In Kansas City, where counsel was not appointed for the preliminary, a defendant faced his final waiver opportunity without advice of counsel. There is, however, no evidence that a waiver proferred at that time would have been accepted, and it would have been inconsistent if it were. In addition, no solicitations of waivers were made at the beginning of the preliminary examination.[65] Thus, even if waivers occurred at that point without advice of counsel, they would have been of the same character as volunteered pleas made in Wisconsin without the advice of counsel.[66]

An additional consequence of both the Sedgwick County and the Kansas City procedure is that the practice of persuading the defendant, at the initial appearance, to waive the preliminary examination was not permitted. In both Michigan and Wisconsin it was found that persuasion was applied only to those defendants who were not represented by counsel.[67] In the two Kansas communities under discussion, if a defendant made his initial appearance with counsel he was permitted to waive the preliminary, but no persuasion could be applied because of the presence of an attorney. If, however, he appeared without counsel, persuasion could be applied, except that the defendant was not permitted to waive even if he wanted to. Thus, in either event, the possibility of court officials persuading the defendant to waive was precluded by the procedures used in Sedgwick County and Kansas City. In accord with this conclusion, no instances of persuasion were observed in either of these jurisdictions.

What consequences should procedures such as those in the two Kansas communities have upon the waiver rate? Because waiver statistics are not available for Kansas City, the discussion must be limited to Sedgwick County, although there is reason to believe that the consequences are different in the two jurisdictions.[68] Since many defendants are not represented at the initial

65 See text accompanying notes 33-34 *supra*.

66 See text accompanying note 21 *supra*.

67 See text accompanying note 38 *supra*.

68 No solicitations of waivers are utilized in either Sedgwick County or Kansas City at the preliminary examination. Fewer waivers probably occur in Kansas City

appearance,[69] a requirement of advice of counsel before waiver is permitted would seem to be a severe limitation on the opportunities for waiver at that stage. In practice very few waivers occurred at the initial appearance in Sedgwick County. Because the first opportunity to waive in a large percentage of cases occurred at the time the preliminary examination was scheduled to begin — after counsel has been appointed for the defendant — it might be expected there would have been a substantial reduction in the waiver rate and hence, an increase in the use of the preliminary.

That has not been the result. In fact, the waiver rate in Sedgwick County has been approximately 67 per cent for a number of years, while in Detroit, where pleading to the warrant and other practices that would appear to induce a high incidence of waivers were observed and where no policy like that of Sedgwick County regarding counsel was followed, the waiver rate was found to be only 72 per cent.[70] This figure is contrary to the assumption that when a defendant has counsel, he will not waive the preliminary, and when he does not have counsel, he will waive. This assumption takes account only of the role which lack of information plays in the waiver practices. Thus, defendants frequently plead guilty to warrants without knowing they are thereby waiving the preliminary. In addition, defendants occasionally expressly waive the preliminary not fully knowing what they are waiving, even if an explanation is given. If defense counsel were present, uninformed waivers would be much less likely. Finally, the presence of counsel precludes any attempt at persuasion by court officials, thereby preventing any waivers which might otherwise result from such practices. It is clear, then, that preliminary examinations have been waived in some situations in which they would have been demanded had defense counsel been present.

But this does not fully explain the relationship between coun-

---

at this stage because the defendant does not have counsel, and, in all probability, a waiver will not be accepted if volunteered. The Sedgwick County defendant, on the other hand, has counsel who is aware that a waiver given at that time will be accepted.

69 Field observations indicate that over two-thirds of the defendants do not have counsel at the initial appearance in Detroit. There is no reason to believe that the percentage is lower in Sedgwick County.

70 Since the Sedgwick County procedure was instituted such a long time ago (the exact date is uncertain), it is not possible to compare the waiver rate there before and after the procedure was begun. The comparison to the Michigan waiver rate admittedly is inconclusive; it assumes, of course, that all the other forces tending to raise or lower the waiver rate are equal.

sel and waivers, because it is based on the assumption that the preliminary examination is always an advantage to the defendant. There are certain situations in which a preliminary examination is a genuine detriment to the defendant.[71] To these must be added the large number of cases in which the preliminary, while not affirmatively harmful, does not produce sufficient benefits to outweigh the time and expense which a defendant must sacrifice in order to be given one, with the result that a preliminary examination would be a net disadvantage to him. Thus, it is clear that there are some situations in which defense counsel would waive the preliminary while a defendant acting without advice of counsel might demand one. Perhaps the existence of these situations accounts for constancy of a high waiver rate. Perhaps the waiver rate itself is a less significant factor in current administration than affording defendants or their counsel the opportunity to make an intelligent waiver decision by weighing the strategic defense advantages of a preliminary against its possible disadvantages. The Sedgwick County practice would appear to afford this opportunity.

3. *Remanding the defendant for a preliminary.* The most elaborate device is the remand statute found now in Michigan and Wisconsin. In 1953, the basic preliminary examination statute in Wisconsin was amended by adding the following subsection:

> (2)(a) Upon good cause shown the trial court may in its discretion remand the cause to the magistrate for a preliminary examination, upon motion made pursuant to §955.09. Good cause means:
>
> 1. Preliminary examination was waived and
> 2. Defendant had not had advice of counsel prior to such waiver; and
> 3. Defendant denies that probable cause exists to hold him for trial; and
> 4. Defendant intends to plead not guilty.[72]

71 Thus, the state's right to a preliminary examination is never asserted unless the defendant waives his right. See State v. Pigg, 80 Kan. 481 (1909) for a discussion of the circumstances in which the giving of a preliminary examination would be to the disadvantage of the defendant. The field studies in Michigan indicate that occasionally when a defendant waives the preliminary at the initial appearance, a police officer or an assistant prosecutor insists on an examination for the purpose of preserving the testimony of the state's witnesses.

72 Wis. Stat. Ann. §955.18(2) (1958). This provision presents a number of procedural problems, especially whether the motion has to be made prior to the plea to the information and whether "waived" includes waiver by plea to the information as well as waiver before the magistrate. These problems are explored in Chapter 7.

The statute seems designed to meet this recurring problem: a defendant makes his initial appearance without counsel and waives his preliminary examination, perhaps as a result of persuasion by court officials. At his arraignment on the information he claims indigency and counsel is appointed to represent him, or he does not retain counsel until that time. Counsel then faces the problem of quickly gathering all the facts of the case in order to bargain, plead, and perhaps try the case in the best interests of his client. If he had been appointed or retained prior to the preliminary examination, he could have used that proceeding as a device to discover the nature and strength of the state's case. Under this statute he can secure a remand for that purpose.

The statute seems to have been employed extensively by counsel, such as the one hypothesized above, who enter the case later in the proceedings. When a motion for a remand is made, the judge typically asks the assistant district attorney handling the case if he has any objections. Regularly, no objections are interposed, except in rare cases when the prosecution feels that the defendant was not entitled to a preliminary examination in the first place.[73] This practice resulted in such a volume of remands that the district attorney for Milwaukee County decided to object to the motion in certain cases. In March 1956 a memorandum was issued to the assistant district attorneys, directing them to oppose remand if the defendant has admitted guilt either to the police or the prosecutor.[74]

It is abundantly clear, then, that the remand statute has seen extensive use. What effect has it had on the waiver practices and the waiver rate? The statute has done nothing toward abolishing the practice of persuading the defendant to waive the preliminary examination. Indeed, there is some evidence that it has increased that practice.[75] It has, however, altered certain prejudicial effects of the practice. Thus, even though the unrepre-

[73] Thus, a motion was successfully opposed on the ground that since the defendant was a fugitive from justice, he had no right to a preliminary examination which could be waived.

[74] "Recently there has been a rash of motions in the Municipal Court to remand to the District Court under 355.18 [955.18] Stats., where the defendant has waived preliminary examination. We have not opposed these motions in the past, but [in the future] consider these matters more closely with a view to preventing abuses.

"In the future, enter an objection to the motion where the state has a strong case by way of admission either to the police or to us. A defendant cannot logically contend under Section 3 of the statute that probable cause does not exist to hold him for trial where he has admitted the offense. If it appears that the justice would not be done by arbitrarily opposing the motion, do not oppose it."

[75] See text accompanying note 45 *supra*.

sented defendant may waive the preliminary without realizing what defense advantages he may be losing, perhaps as a result of official persuasion, he is entitled to another chance for a preliminary when counsel is later appointed for him. If the net strategic advantages of a preliminary — for example, the opportunity to discover what evidence the state is prepared to offer into evidence — outweigh any disadvantages, that opportunity is not irrevocably lost by an uninformed waiver decision.

It was observed that, when remands were requested, they were given despite inconvenience to the court, the prosecutor, and the witnesses in the case. In a number of cases observed, it was clear that the granting of a remand would result in an added burden upon the court's docket and in added expense for the state.[76] The trial judges felt, however, that they had no discretion in granting remands; they attempted to expedite matters as much as possible by requesting that the preliminary be held on the same day the motion was made. In any event, the effect upon the trial court's docket was considerable.[77]

Between January 1, 1958, and July 1, 1961, the preliminary examination waiver rate in Milwaukee County was almost 90 per cent — the highest of any of the three states.[78] By 1958, the remand statute had been in operation for five years. Initially, then, it would be easy to conclude that it has had no effect on the waiver rate. The difficulty however, is that these waiver statistics were very likely obtained from magistrate's returns, which reflect only those waivers occurring before the magistrates. It is likely that the preliminary examination is waived in 90

[76] In one instance observed court-appointed counsel stated to a judge of the municipal court of Milwaukee: "This defendant did not have counsel at the time he waived preliminary hearing. Your Honor, please at this time, on behalf of my client, I request a preliminary hearing." Whereupon the judge stated, "The state has four witnesses subpoenaed at this time, counsel, and are ready for trial." The assistant prosecutor stated: "We don't object to this motion, Your Honor. All we do is request of counsel that if he is going to present such a motion as this, he notify the office of the district attorney, or the court, or the clerk in enough time so that we can allow the witnesses to be excused from appearing on this date. It makes it quite difficult for the witnesses who have to appear on this date." The motion for remand was granted.

[77] Presumably, the statute prevents the trial judge from conducting the preliminary examination himself, even though he is authorized generally to conduct preliminaries. See text accompanying note 72 *supra*. In those cases in which all the witnesses are present, the proceedings would certainly be expedited if the preliminary were conducted immediately by the trial judge, especially when he has already reserved all the time necessary in anticipation of trying the case.

Michigan recently adopted the remand procedure. See Mich Stat. Ann §28.985 (Supp. 1968).

[78] See notes 1-4 *supra* and accompanying text.

per cent of the cases, but a sizable number of those cases are remanded for preliminaries, a fact which probably is not shown on the justice's return since the defendant is already under the jurisdiction of the trial court as a result of a prior bindover. In terms of percentage of preliminaries ultimately given (including those given on remand) of all preliminaries which could have been given, the waiver rate for Milwaukee County is probably considerably lower than 90 per cent. This would seem necessarily to be the case from the extent of the use of the remand provisions.

C. Summary

An analyst of current criminal administration might well take a position along the following lines the preliminary examination is such an important and integral part of the pretrial process that the high waiver rate reflects serious defects in administrative practices relating to waiver. More intensive analysis appears to reveal, however, that a deceptive significance is likely to be attached to that rate as an indication of administrative adequacy. The example of Sedgwick County, Kansas, reveals that, in routine cases, the preliminary may not perform significant enough functions to merit concern over a high waiver rate in and of itself. From the standpoint of the adequacy and efficiency of criminal administration, an important potential function of the preliminary is that of evidence-sufficiency screening; that is, assuring that defendants are not carried further in the criminal process than can be justified by the degree of probable guilt or convictability which appears. But evidence-sufficiency screening by the police and prosecutor is so complete — at least in the three states under consideration — that no need for additional screening remains in the great majority of cases. Thus, evaluated exclusively in terms of evidence-screening capacity, a system might be functioning properly with a waiver rate of 67 per cent, or even higher, although this might not be true in other jurisdictions where pre-preliminary screening by police and prosecutors has been found to be less intensive.

Of course, any view of the adequacy of current administration must be rounded out by considering functions which the preliminary might fulfill from the standpoint of defense strategy. First of all the defendant has an interest in having his case screened early for evidence sufficiency. Given a high incidence of waiver, the possibility remains open that many defendants will be retained in custody, or have their release conditioned on an amount of bail, without any judicial determination in advance of adjudication that probable cause exists to justify carrying them further in the criminal process. Again, however, if this screening function is being performed intensively by police and prosecutors, the absence of judicial participation in it as a matter of routine may be of no great concern since more or less the same results are achieved anyway.

There remains the probably atypical case in which pre-preliminary screening has not identified evidentiary defects which could be presented for resolution at a preliminary; the possibility of dismissal if perceived by the defendant because of these defects might make waiver in these cases unlikely. A high waiver rate has little direct correlation to this problem. What is significant is whether practices assure that those defendants who could possibly receive this benefit will not make an uninformed decision to waive the preliminary. Concern over waiver has narrowed to a relatively small group of cases. Some of the innovations in practice discussed in this chapter are most directly relevant to these cases; by preventing all defendants from making uninformed waiver decisions which are irrevocable, the practices help assure that some of the defendants will not lose unusual defense advantages relating to evidence-sufficiency screening. From this perspective it is perhaps not unusual that practices designed to prevent uninformed waiver, notably the appointment of early counsel in Sedgwick County apparently have not significantly reduced high waiver rates.

The matter is complicated by the introduction of possible defense advantages other than those which relate to evidence-sufficiency screening. Even in a perfect system of pre-preliminary screening, a preliminary might be requested for purposes of discovering specifically what evidence the state is prepared to offer, even though there is no doubt that it is of a net sufficiency to pass the test of a preliminary. But some persons believe this consideration to be irrelevant to questions about the preliminary because the matter of discovery should be faced squarely in pretrial procedures devoted specifically to discovery by the defendant. At any rate the consideration may not be as pivotal as one might assume it to be, at least if the experience in Sedgwick County is a valid indicator. There a high waiver rate has persisted in spite of the almost uniform presence of counsel to assess the possibilities of incidental discovery from the holding of a preliminary. As indicated earlier, there may be strategic disadvantages from a defendant demanding a preliminary, and these may outweigh any discovery benefits that might accrue. Perhaps it is only when special circumstances make discovery unusually important that the balance will fall in favor of demanding a preliminary. What becomes the focus of concern again is whether the waiver decision is one which takes account of the advantages and disadvantages. The most significant question is not the desirability of the high waiver rate, but whether the waiver decisions are informed ones.

Two sets of practices received the focus of attention in this chapter. Some practices have tended to induce a high incidence of waiver and some of these, like official persuasion, have caused uninformed waiver. Other practices have been designed to prevent uninformed waiver. The requirement of pleading to the warrant, coupled with the practice existing in Michigan at the time of the survey of treating a plea of guilty as a waiver, caused waivers by defendants who did not realize that there was such a thing as a preliminary examination. The combination of lack of counsel, the probably inherent inadequacy of proffered explanations of the meaning and significance of a preliminary, and efforts to persuade defendants to waive was found to cause waivers by those who knew that they were entitled to a preliminary examination but, in varying degrees, lacked understanding of its significance. In the former situation — waiving in ignorance of any right at all — it is significant that the waiver is accomplished by an admission of guilt.

It may be that waivers are usually inferred from early guilty pleas only in cases in which an informed assessment of defense strategy would result in a waiver for the reason that a preliminary would unnecessarily delay the ultimate disposition following upon guilty pleas which the defendants are willing to make at the arraignment on the information. This is not to say, however, that no defendants ever will suffer from uninformed waivers inferred from guilty pleas made at the initial appearance. It is inconceivable that laymen know in all instances whether they are guilty, and even less believable that they know the precise nature of their offenses. A preliminary examination could save some of those defendants the expense, inconvenience, and disgrace of a trial and could assure that others would be tried for an appropriate offense, ordinarily a less serious one. In this limited but important sense, then, the requirement of pleading to the warrant and implying from a guilty plea a waiver of the preliminary has evidence-sufficiency significance.

When the preliminary is waived by one who knows that he is waiving a right of some sort, but without full realization of the possible importance of that right, a quite different relationship between the waiver and evidence sufficiency can be established. Of controlling importance in making the distinction is the fact that such a waiver is not accomplished by an admission of guilt: indeed, such a waiver occurs only after an express denial of guilt in jurisdictions where pleas at the initial appearance are required. It is, therefore, much more likely that the waiver would be made by a defendant against whom the evidence is inadequate to bind over. It is just such a person — one who has slipped through the police and prosecutor screening nets — to whom the evidence-sufficiency screening function of the preliminary is of real importance.

Both in Kansas and in Wisconsin reforms have been instituted which are designed to prevent waivers, or, at least, uninformed waivers, of preliminary examinations. To prevent waivers by those defendants who are ignorant that they are waiving anything, the obvious reform would be to eliminate pleading to the warrant or refusing to infer waiver from a plea of guilty if a plea remains necessary. The former alternative was in substance chosen in Wisconsin, and in Kansas a plea is not required of an unrepresented defendant. Obviously these reforms, with the exception of a limited number of volunteered but unrequired pleas in Wisconsin, effectively prevent waivers made in total ignorance of the right to a preliminary examination. To the extent alluded to above, they enhance the evidence-sufficiency screening function of the preliminary.

Solution of the problem of express waivers made by defendants who understand they are waiving something, but not the significance of it, is equally obvious: either refuse to accept waivers of any kind by unrepresented defendants, or appoint counsel prior to, or early enough at, the initial appearance to ensure that all waivers are intelligently made. None of the three states accepted the latter alternative, but in Kansas an unrepresented defendant may not waive a preliminary even if he wishes to. Obviously under such a system, no unintelligent waivers can occur, and the evidence-sufficiency screening function of the preliminary examination will be fully utilized in all cases in which it is to the defendant's advantage to so utilize it.

Wisconsin and, more recently, Michigan have adopted a much less direct approach to this aspect of the problem. Their remand statutes initially permit waivers by defendants who are not fully cognizant of the significance of the preliminary, but they seek to safeguard against the detrimental effects of such waivers by permitting a remand for a preliminary upon a showing, in effect, that the waiver was an uninformed one by emphasizing the absence of counsel as a requirement. Indeed, by confining the right to a remand to defendants who intend to plead not guilty and who maintain that probable cause to hold them for trial is lacking, this device tends to isolate and focus upon those defendants who wish the benefit of the evidence-sufficiency screening function of the preliminary examination, although in practice the suspicion is strong that the device is utilized primarily to aid in discovering the state's evidence. To be weighed against this advantage is the fact that, by postponing the decision, dockets are disrupted and witnesses are seriously inconvenienced. Because of this, as well as because the discovery function of the preliminary may be even more important than its screening function, other alternatives may be preferable.

It could be asserted that preliminaries ought to be waived only if they do not serve either of their primary functions in protecting defendants: evidence-sufficiency screening and discovery of the state's case. In many situations, they will not serve those functions to a sufficient extent to warrant the additional delay which imposes such heavy burdens on defendants, especially those who cannot make bail. When that is true, waiver is beneficial, not detrimental. But defendants can make the decision intelligently only with the help of counsel. For that reason, only appointment of counsel sufficiently early to enable him to advise the defendant about the advantages and disadvantages of waiving in the first instance would solve the problem fully. In addition the presence of counsel would insure against court attachés persuading defendants to waive.

CHAPTER 7

Reviewability of the Decision to Dismiss or Hold for Trial

Of particular importance in the administration of a relatively undefined standard such as "probable cause" is the extent to which the initial application of that standard is subject to review and reversal. On the other hand, for the parties involved, review of decisions made at the preliminary examination is not as important as it is at other stages, because the examining magistrate's decision is by no means the final one in the criminal administration process—for either the defendant or the prosecution. Because of the undeniably "preliminary" character of the magistrate's decisions, review has been carefully limited, at least in comparison with the availability of review for decisions made at the trial. This, in turn, creates a limitation on the number of formal law pronouncements of norms applicable to the preliminary examination, permitting the probable cause standard to remain in a relatively undefined form.

A. Review of the Decision to Dismiss

Of central importance to an analysis of the location of ultimate power to make the charging decision in serious cases is the extent to which a prosecutor must accept an examining magistrate's dismissal of a defendant for want of probable cause and, conversely, the methods by which he may seek review of, or otherwise challenge, that decision. It is clear that a dismissal at a preliminary examination prevents a prosecutor from then filing an information against the dismissed defendant.[1] To that extent, the magistrate's decision is final.

[1] Kan. Stat. Ann. §62-805 (1964); Mich. Stat. Ann. §28.982 (Supp. 1968); Wis. Stat.

It is also clear in Kansas[2] and in Wisconsin[3] that a prosecutor has no right to appeal from an order dismissing a defendant at a preliminary examination. Although no Michigan case speaks directly to the point, the state apparently has no right to appeal in that jurisdiction either.[4] Other methods of direct review of the decision of the examining magistrate, such as mandamus or injunction, are apparently unlitigated in the three states.[5] An indirect method of review — commonly referred to as holding a second preliminary examination — remains then as the only[6] method by which the prosecution may seek review of a dismissal at a preliminary examination.[7]

Ann. §955.18(1) (Supp. 1968). A conviction under an information filed against a defendant dismissed by an examining magistrate is void. State v. Goetz, 65 Kan. 125, 69 Pac. 187 (1902); People v. Evans, 72 Mich. 367, 40 N.W. 473 (1888).

2 In State v. McCombs, 164 Kan. 334, 188 P.2d 922 (1948), the court dismissed the state's appeal, noting: "Under the authorities heretofore cited, dealing generally with the legal status of magistrates while holding preliminary hearings and with questions pertaining to rights of appeal from their action in discharging persons accused of offenses at such hearings, and without more, we would have little difficulty in concluding the appellant has no right of appeal under the provisions of G.S. 1935, 62-1703, or any other statute, from Judge Robb's ruling discharging the appellee during the course of the preliminary examination he was conducting as a magistrate." Id. at 337-338, 188 P.2d at 925. The statute referred to is the Kansas provision governing the right of the state to appeal in criminal cases. In McCombs, defendant had been discharged before a justice of the peace. A second preliminary before a district court judge resulted in dismissal. The supreme court held that the fact the examining magistrate was a trial judge was immaterial to disposition of the appeals question.

3 State v. Friedl, 259 Wis. 110, 47 N.W.2d 306 (1951); 4 Ops. Wis. Att'y Gen. 489 (1915). The Wisconsin statute governing state's appeals in criminal cases is Wis. Stat. Ann. §958.12 (1958).

4 Mich. Stat. Ann. §28.1109 (1954) provides for appeal from a ruling of a court of record in only three instances, none of which would encompass a dismissal by an examining magistrate, even if he sat as a court of record like Recorder's Court in Detroit. See People v. Fairman, 59 Mich. 568 (1886), holding that this statute does not authorize an appeal from a discharge on habeas corpus by a court of record and dismissing the appeal because it was not permissible under the strict common law limitations.

5 See, however, Peterson v. Oceana, Circuit Judge, 243 Mich. 215, 219 N.W. 934 (1928), permitting, without discussion, a mandamus action to compel a trial judge to reverse his decision refusing to quash the information for failure to provide a preliminary examination.

6 This assumes, of course, that the conclusion on the condition of the Michigan law with regard to the state's right to appeal from the magistrate's decision expressed in note 4 *supra* is correct.

7 Other situations in which the state might be able to appeal — such as from a discharge of a defendant on habeas corpus for lack of probable cause at the preliminary or from an order granting a motion to quash or a plea in abatement for lack of probable cause at the preliminary — are arguably indirect methods of reviewing the examining magistrate's action by the state. They are considered later in connection with habeas corpus and the trial court challenges to the information.

Formal law in each of the three states is clear that jeopardy does not attach until sometime after the preliminary examination stage of the prosecution.[8] For this reason, the constitutional provisions in each of the three states which prohibit double jeopardy[9] do not prevent a prosecutor from re-initiating the prosecution of a defendant for an offense for which he has been discharged at a preliminary examination.[10] On the subsequent prosecution, the defendant must, of course, be given his right to request a preliminary examination.[11] If a bindover is secured in the second preliminary, or if the preliminary is waived, the case proceeds as if no discharge had occurred.

The question arises whether there are any limits on the number of times a prosecutor may re-initiate prosecution if the defendant is discharged at the preliminary examination on each attempt. A Kansas case indicates the limitations are slight:

> There is no constitutional or statutory inhibition against holding more than one preliminary examination for the same offense. . . . In this state, as many preliminary examinations may be held as the prosecution may in good faith desire, and the defendant has no just cause for complaint.[12]

In Wisconsin, the authority of the prosecutor to subject a discharged defendant to further prosecution was codified:

> If a preliminary examination has been had and the defendant has been discharged for want of evidence, and the district attorney afterwards discovers evidence sufficient, in his judgment, to convict the defendant, he may cause another complaint to be made, and thereupon a *second arrest and examination should be had.*[13]

The language raises the issue whether the statute, authorizing a second examination, impliedly prohibits more than two examinations. This doubt was dispelled by an amendment which de-

[8] The usual statement is that jeopardy does not attach until the jury is impaneled and sworn. See, e.g., State v. Stiff, 117 Kan. 243, 234 Pac. 700 (1924); People v. Bigge, 297 N.W. 70 (1941); McDonald v. State, 79 Wis. 651, 48 N.W. 863 (1891).

[9] Kan. Const. Bill of Rights §10; Mich. Const. Art. I §15 (Const. of 1963); Wis. Const. Declaration of Rights Art. I §8.

[10] State v. Jones, 16 Kan. 608 (1876); Gaffney v. Missaukee Circuit Judge, 85 Mich. 138 (1891); Campbell v. State, 111 Wis. 152, 86 N.W. 855 (1901). See Boyer, The Riddle of Double Jeopardy in Wisconsin: The Defendant's View, 1954 Wis. L. Rev. 395; Orfield, Criminal Procedure from Arrest to Appeal 93 (1947).

[11] See note 1 *supra*.

[12] State v. Curtis, 108 Kan. 537, 539, 196 Pac. 445, 445-446 (1921). There is apparently no Michigan formal law authority speaking to the point.

[13] Wis. Stat. Ann. §955.20 (Supp. 1968) (emphasis added).

leted the italicized portion of the statute and substituted "further proceedings shall be had."[14]

A closely related problem is whether the reasons for which a prosecutor might re-initiate prosecution against a discharged defendant are subject to limitations. The Wisconsin statute quoted above implied that the discovery of additional evidence sufficient to secure conviction is a prerequisite to a subsequent prosecution. Case law interpretation has in substance eliminated this implication; a prosecutor's judgment as to the sufficiency of the evidence is not subject to review and he is not required to show that he discovered new evidence,[15] although certainly the discovery of new evidence would constitute one reason for re-initiation of prosecution.

A Kansas case indicates that prosecution may be re-initiated simply to find a more willing magistrate:

> [D]ischarge by a magistrate is not a bar to another preliminary examination. The state has supplied itself with many magistrates . . . including the judges of the supreme court. Out of all these we rather imagine it would not be too difficult to find some magistrate who would lend a responsive ear in any case where the state seeks to bind over a person charged by a complaint with the commission of a crime if the facts or the law warrant its position.[16]

A third occasion on which a prosecutor might wish to re-initiate prosecution arises because of the almost universal policy of revealing just enough of the state's case at the preliminary to secure a bindover.[17] Implementation of this policy results in an unexpected dismissal of the defendant on rare occasions. In such an event, use of all the evidence at the prosecutor's disposal virtually assures a bindover at the second preliminary examination.[18]

While the position of the formal law appears to be that there are no substantial[19] limitations on the power of the prosecutor

14 Wis. Stat. Ann. §955.20 (Supp. 1968). It has been suggested that repeated arrest and examination of a defendant might give rise to a claim of denial of the constitutional right to a speedy trial. See Boyer, The Riddle of Double Jeopardy in Wisconsin: The Defendant's View, 1954 Wis. L. Rev. 395, 401 n. 23.

15 Drops v. State ex rel. Kaiser, 219 Wis. 279, 262 N.W. 700 (1935). See Boyer, The Riddle of Double Jeopardy in Wisconsin: The Defendant's View, 1954 Wis. L. Rev. 395, 400.

16 State v. McCombs, 164 Kan. 334, 337, 188 P.2d 922, 924 (1948).

17 See Chapter 4.

18 A Kansas judge related such a case. He analogized the situation to the discovery of new evidence.

19 The opinion has been expressed that the prosecutor must simply avoid acting in bad faith. 10 Ops. Wis. Att'y Gen. 551 (1921). See note 12 *supra* and accompanying text.

to subject a defendant to repeated prosecutions for the same offense so long as each terminates before jeopardy attaches, in current administration this rarely occurs. In Detroit, it is the policy of the prosecutor's office to examine the evidence in any case dismissed at the preliminary examination in order to determine whether a *different* charge would be more appropriate on the evidence.[20] In one Kansas jurisdiction, reprosecution for the same offense of a defendant discharged at the preliminary examination has occurred only once in twelve years.

In practice, then, a discharge by an examining magistrate finally terminates prosecution for the offense examined. It is extremely doubtful if a discharged defendant is ever subjected to a subsequent prosecution for a different offense of comparable seriousness — one which would require another preliminary examination. Probably, if anything happens, a discharged defendant is tried for (or pleads guilty to) an offense of much less seriousness. If a defendant pleads guilty to or is tried for an offense less serious than that for which he was discharged at the preliminary examination, this second prosecution is clearly not a review of the magistrate's action. Even when there is a subsequent prosecution for a different offense which is serious enough to require a second preliminary, the latter preliminary is not a review of the first. Only when the second preliminary is for the same offense can it be described, in any sense, as a review of the decision of the examining magistrate.[21] Then it is comparable to a trial de novo, but it occurs only rarely in current administration.

B. Review of the Decision to Hold for Trial

The focus of attention shifts to the defendant's right to seek review of the sufficiency of the evidence to bind him over for trial. The discussion is limited by the assumptions that a pre-

[20] There is no indication whether this departmental review is fruitful in any significant number of cases. The desire to avoid such a procedure occasionally leads to charging multiple offenses in the warrant, thus anticipating difficulty when the facts seem to lend themselves to it and enabling the magistrate to bind over on one charge and dismiss the other, depending upon how the evidence develops at the preliminary.

[21] Even on such facts, the reasons for the second preliminary are material in determining to what extent it is a review of the first preliminary. Thus the discovery of new evidence or the use of all the evidence at the state's disposal for the first time would seem to mitigate the review aspects of the second preliminary. See text accompanying notes 15-18 *supra*.

liminary examination was given and the defendant was bound over for trial for the offense charged in the complaint-warrant. If the defendant was discharged at the preliminary examination, the review problems are the prosecutor's; they were discussed in the preceding section. If, at the preliminary examination, the defendant was held for trial by the examining magistrate himself, review of that decision may be sought in an appeal from the justice court conviction.[22]

Review of the extent the information can differ from the magistrate's bindover order and the evidence at the preliminary examination, review of the right to counsel and other rights at the preliminary examination stage, and review of the magistrate's authority to conduct the preliminary present no problems distinct from review of the sufficiency of the evidence to bind over for trial. Review of waivers of preliminary examinations given at the initial appearance also present no distinct problems other than the fact that in Michigan and Wisconsin special remand provisions are available.[23]

It is important to distinguish several stages at which review may be sought: after the bindover but before the filing of the information; after the filing of the information but before conviction; and after conviction. The problems differ for each stage.

1. *Review prior to the filing of the information.* After the evidence is in and the usual motions and arguments made, the examining magistrate must make his determinations. If he decides that there is probable cause to believe the defendant guilty of the offense charged, he will fill in a "justice's return" stating that finding. In Detroit, an average of from ten days to two weeks are consumed before the transcript of the preliminary is completed by the examining magistrate's stenographer. The justice's return, the transcript, and the other documents in the case file are then sent to the prosecutor's office. It takes about ten days for the personnel in the prosecutor's office to prepare the information. The information is filed in the trial court and a date is set for the arraignment on the information. The question of concern here is what methods are available to the defendant before he is arraigned on the information for review of the sufficiency of the evidence to hold him for trial?

While formal law does not speak directly to the point, it is reasonably certain in each of the three states that a defendant

22 See, e.g., the provisions for appeal from justice court convictions in Wisconsin. Wis. Stat. Ann. §958.01 (Supp. 1968).

23 For a discussion of the operation of these remand provisions, see Chapter 6.

has no right to appeal directly from an examining magistrate's bindover decision.[24] It is clear in Wisconsin that a writ of prohibition may not be used to prevent the trial court from assuming jurisdiction of a case on the ground that the examining magistrate's bindover was based on insufficient evidence.[25] In Kansas it seems certain that a writ of mandamus will not lie to test the sufficiency of the evidence to support the bindover decision.[26]

Habeas corpus seems the most appropriate remedy to test the sufficiency of the evidence before the information is filed, although it is certainly not confined to pre-information review.[27] In Kansas, a writ of habeas corpus, issuing out of a court of general criminal trial jurisdiction[28] or directly out of the supreme court,[29] may be used to test the sufficiency of the evidence to support the bindover decision. In Wisconsin, a writ of habeas corpus issuing out of a court of general criminal trial jurisdiction may be used for the same purpose.[30] No Michigan case has been found which granted or denied relief on habeas corpus for lack of evidence sufficiency.[31]

[24] The right of the defendant to appeal is governed by statute. See Kan. Stat. Ann. §62-1701 (1964); Mich. Stat. Ann. §28.1100 (1954); Wis. Stat. Ann. §958.11 (1958). In the following cases, it was held or stated that an appeal would not lie until after a judgment of conviction. State v. Brown, 144 Kan. 573, 61 P.2d 901 (1936); People v. West, 143 Mich. 586, 107 N.W. 283 (1906); Bennet v. State, 24 Wis. 57 (1869). See also 16 Ops. Wis. Att'y Gen. 710 (1927).

[25] In re Weaver, 162 Wis. 499, 156 N.W. 459 (1916). The decision was placed on two grounds: failure to conduct a proper preliminary examination is not a jurisdictional error, and an adequate remedy exists in a plea in abatement of the prosecution in the trial court.

[26] Sayfer v. Bloomer, 132 Kan. 877, 297 Pac. 681 (1931). The court held that a plea in abatement in the trial court was an adequate remedy.

[27] See State ex rel. Wojtycski v. Hanley, 248 Wis. 108, 20 N.W.2d 719 (1945) in which habeas corpus was brought after the information had been filed and during trial to contest the sufficiency of the evidence at the preliminary.

[28] See Gates v. Zimmer, 152 Kan. 616, 106 P.2d 650 (1940); King v. McKnight, 120 Kan. 692, 245 Pac. 105 (1926); State v. Pfeifer, 109 Kan. 232, 198 Pac. 927 (1921); State v. Ray, 81 Kan. 159, 105 Pac. 46 (1909).

[29] See McIntyre v. Sands, 128 Kan. 521, 278 Pac. 761 (1929); In re Danton, 108 Kan. 451, 195 Pac. 981 (1921); In re Stilts, 74 Kan. 805, 87 Pac. 1134 (1906).

[30] See Hancock v. Hallmann, 229 Wis. 127, 281 N.W. 703 (1938); State ex rel. Durner v. Huegin, 110 Wis. 189, 85 N.W. 1046 (1901). No case has been found in which the Wisconsin supreme court was asked to issue a writ of habeas corpus in an original proceeding.

[31] Perhaps the absence of cases is explained by Mich. Stat. Ann. §27A. 4310 (1962) which provides: [a]n action for habeas corpus to inquire into the cause of detention may not be brought by or on behalf of the following persons: . . . (2) Persons committed for treason or felony, or for suspicion thereof, or as accessories before the fact to a felony, where the cause is plainly and specially expressed in the warrant of commitment. . . ." In LaFave, Arrest (1965), the regular use of habeas corpus in Detroit to test the legality of detention prior to the initial appearance was detailed. This apparent inconsistency might be explicable because

The scope of habeas corpus in Kansas, both in the trial court and as an original proceeding in the supreme court, is what might be termed a full review of the facts upon which the magistrate made his determinations. An early Kansas case indicates that the scope of review is the fullest possible, in effect, a second preliminary examination:

> The hearing in the district court in this case was only an inquiry as to the existence of probable cause to hold the prisoner for trial—a mere preliminary examination—and the result only determined that upon the evidence then produced probable cause was not shown.[32]

In Wisconsin a markedly different attitude prevails. There the scope is limited to determining whether there was any competent evidence upon which the magistrate could act.[33] Habeas corpus may not be used to review whether the evidence before the magistrate supports the inference of probable cause which he made. A landmark Wisconsin case, establishing habeas corpus as a review device for preliminary examinations, found it necessary to limit its scope in order to be consistent with the rule that habeas corpus may not be used to test the sufficiency of the evidence at a trial:

> Sufficient has been said to demonstrate that counsel for plaintiff in error have confused the scope of a habeas corpus suit calling in question the validity of a final judgment or order and the scope thereof as to reaching the proceedings of a committing magistrate. It is not understood, it seems, that failure to comply with the statute requiring such magistrate, in his inquiry, to act upon evidence, is not an error committed in acting within his jurisdiction,

---

there is usually no "warrant of commitment" (if by that phrase is meant arrest warrant) at that stage in the pretrial process. If this is the case, then the statutory disability would not apply until the post-arrest warrant was issued.

32 State v. Ray, 81 Kan. 159, 161, 105 Pac. 46, 47 (1909). See the cases cited in notes 28 and 29 *supra*, which contain a noticeable lack of language limiting the scope of review and in which the court usually fully recites the evidence at the preliminary and makes what appears to be a de novo determination of probable cause or its lack.

33 In Hancock v. Hallmann, 229 Wis. 127, 281 N.W. 703 (1938) the defendant was bound over for trial on a charge of rape. He sought habeas corpus in the trial court on the grounds that the complaining witness was incompetent to testify. His contention was rejected and, on appeal to the supreme court, the judgment was reversed and the defendant discharged. The court said: "[i]t is well established that one who is charged with crime may be held for trial only when the evidence establishing substantial grounds for such action is competent. . . . It follows that when the action of the magistrate in holding a defendant for trial rests solely upon the testimony of an incompetent witness, he acts without jurisdiction, and the defendant is entitled to be released upon habeas corpus." Id. at 131, 281 N.W. at 785.

as is the act of entering a judgment by a court, upon the trial of an issue, without competent evidence to warrant it,—but is error in going beyond his jurisdiction.[34]

Thus, in Kansas, while neither the prosecution nor the defendant has a right to appeal directly from a decision of an examining magistrate,[35] the defendant may use habeas corpus to obtain a full review of the evidence at the preliminary. The proceeding may be brought directly in the supreme court or, if it is brought in a trial court, the defendant may appeal to the supreme court from an adverse decision.[36] In Wisconsin, where a similar inability to appeal directly from a decision of an examining magistrate apparently exists,[37] the defendant may bring habeas corpus and obtain a limited review in the trial court,[38]

34 State ex rel. Durner v. Huegin, 110 Wis. 189, 242, 85 N.W. 1046, 1059 (1901). The court said: "[t]here is no need to go further to demonstrate that the common-law office of the writ of habeas corpus, as it came to us and has been preserved by our state constitution, is as indicated by the decision referred to. While it is true that such writ never takes the place of a writ of error, and is confined to jurisdictional defects, when it is resorted to merely for the purpose of liberating a person detained in custody to await his trial on a charge of being guilty of a criminal offense, the questions of whether there was any evidence for the magistrate to act upon and whether the complaint charges any offense known to the law are jurisdictional matters. The reviewing court, in the exercise of its function, must necessarily pass upon and reverse or affirm the decision of the committing magistrate, if such matters are properly presented for its consideration, according to its determination thereof, and in doing so it does not go beyond jurisdictional defects. It can examine the evidence only sufficiently to discover whether there was any substantial ground for the exercise of judgment by the committing magistrate. It cannot go beyond that and weigh the evidence. It can say whether the complaint will admit of a construction charging a criminal offense, or whether the evidence rendered the charge against the prisoner within reasonable probabilities. That is all. When it has discovered that there was competent evidence for the judicial mind of the examining magistrate to act upon in determining the existence of the essential facts, it has reached the limit of its jurisdiction on that point. If the examining magistrate acts without evidence, he exceeds his jurisdiction; but any act, upon evidence worthy of consideration in any aspect, is as well within his jurisdiction when he decides wrong as when he decides right." Id. at 236-237, 85 N.W. at 1057-1058.

35 See note 24 *supra*.

36 See note 28 *supra*. The prosecution has no right to appeal from a decision of a trial judge discharging a defendant on habeas corpus. State v. Ray, 81 Kan. 159, 105 Pac. 46 (1909), holding the state has no right to appeal because the habeas corpus proceeding was simply a second preliminary examination and the state has no right to appeal from a discharge at a preliminary examination. See note 2 *supra* and accompanying text. But see King v. McKnight, 120 Kan. 692, 245 Pac. 105 (1926), holding that the state has the right to appeal from an order discharging the defendant because of an alleged lack of authority in the magistrate to transfer the examination to another magistrate and limiting the Ray rule to discharges based on a lack of probable cause.

37 See note 24 *supra*.

38 See note 30 *supra* and accompanying text.

and either the defendant or the prosecution may appeal to the supreme court from an adverse decision.[39]

2. *Review after the filing of the information but before conviction.* After the information has been drafted by the prosecutor's office, it is filed with the trial court and a date is set for the arraignment on the information, where the defendant is formally notified of the charge against him, is required to plead to the information, and is assigned counsel if he is indigent.[40] At the arraignment on the information a date is set for the trial of the case if trial is necessary.[41] After the information is filed, review takes the form of a challenge to the information as violating the basic preliminary examination statute.[42]

In each of the three states, a defendant may obtain a review of the sufficiency of the evidence to support the examining magistrate's bindover decision by making a request in the appropriate form[43] prior to the trial of his case.[44] But, if a request for review is made in incorrect form[45] or if it is not timely interposed,[46] the judge may properly refuse to hear the alleged grounds for complaint.

39 See Hancock v. Hallmann, 229 Wis. 127, 281 N.W. 703 (1938) granting, without discussion, the defendant the right to appeal from an adverse decision in a trial court habeas corpus proceeding. See State ex rel. Durner v. Huegin, 110 Wis. 189, 85 N.W. 1046 (1901), granting the state the right to appeal from a discharge in a trial court habeas corpus proceeding.

40 Other functions are served by the arraignment on the information, such as arranging to hold a hearing to determine the competency of the defendant to stand trial.

41 Literally, in many cases, a date is set on which the trial date is to be set. When the defendant pleads guilty, a date is normally set for some sort of post-plea hearing and for sentencing.

42 The basic statute in Michigan provides: "No information shall be filed against any person for any offense until such person shall have had a preliminary examination therefor. . . ." Mich. Stat. Ann. §28.982 (Supp. 1968). Comparable provisions exist in the other two states. See Kan. Stat. Ann. §62-805 (1964); Wis. Stat. Ann. §955.18(1) (Supp. 1968).

43 In Kansas, the appropriate form is the plea in abatement. State v. Saindon, 117 Kan. 122, 230 Pac. 301 (1924); State v. Woods, 49 Kan. 237, 30 Pac. 520 (1892); State v. Finley, 6 Kan. 366 (1870). In Michigan the appropriate form is a motion to quash, People v. Davis, 171 Mich. 241, 37 N.W. 61 (1912); Washburn v. People, 10 Mich. 372 (1862). In Wisconsin, the appropriate form was formerly a plea in abatement, but it is now a motion to dismiss. Wis. Stat. Ann. §955.18(1) (Supp. 1968). Stetson v. State, 204 Wis. 250, 235 N.W. 539 (1931); State v. Faull, 178 Wis. 66, 189 N.W. 274 (1922).

44 See Mich. Stat. Ann. §28.1016 (1954); Wis. Stat. Ann. §955.09 (1958). No Kansas statute or case on this point has been found.

45 State v. Saindon, 117 Kan. 122, 230 Pac. 301 (1924); Washburn v. People, 10 Mich. 372 (1862); State v. Faull, 178 Wis. 66, 189 N.W. 274 (1922).

46 People v. Davis, 171 Mich. 241, 137 N.W. 61 (1912); State v. Faull, 178 Wis. 66 189 N.W. 274 (1922).

A further problem arises from the doctrine of waiver. A plea of guilty[47] or not guilty[48] to the information given before the request for review is made precludes review of the sufficiency of evidence to bind over, because it is a waiver of the defendant's right to a preliminary examination. If the defendant chooses to "stand mute" when requested to plead to the information, a statutory plea of not guilty is entered for him,[49] but no waiver of the preliminary examination is imputed, so he may later challenge the sufficiency of the evidence by a request for review appropriately made.[50]

Waiver of preliminary examination by plea to the information is markedly different from the waiver discussed previously.[51] In the former instance, a waiver at the initial appearance results in an immediate bindover for trial without a preliminary examination. In this instance, a preliminary examination has been held prior to the filing of the information, and the plea to the information simply precludes the defendant from challenging the sufficiency of the evidence at the preliminary.

The scope of review in the trial court is limited, in effect, to determining whether the examining magistrate abused his discretion in binding the defendant over for trial on the basis of the evidence before him.[52] If the trial judge concludes that the evidence at the preliminary was insufficient to support the bindover decision, the defendant is discharged.[53] In such an event, the

47 Plasters v. Hoffman, 180 Kan. 559, 305 P.2d 858 (1957); Foster v. Hudspeth, 170 Kan. 338, 224 P.2d 987 (1950); Cooper v. Hudspeth, 166 Kan. 239, 199 P.2d 803 (1948); People v. Losinger, 331 Mich. 490, 50 N.W.2d 137 (1951); People v. Tate, 315 Mich. 76, 23 N.W.2d 211 (1946); People v. Harris, 266 Mich. 317, 253 N.W. 312 (1934); People v. Sanford, 233 Mich. 112, 206 N.W. 370 (1925); Maynard, Post Conviction Problems and Procedures in Michigan, 36 U. of Det. L.J. 202 (1958); Annot., Defendant's Plea to Indictment or Information as Waiver of Lack of Preliminary Examination, 116 A.L.R. 550 (1938).

48 People v. Paugh, 324 Mich. 108, 36 N.W.2d 230 (1949); People v. Williams, 93 Mich. 623, 53 N.W. 779 (1892); People v. Jones, 24 Mich. 215 (1872); Mark v. State, 228 Wis. 377, 280 N.W. 299 (1938), *appeal dismissed,* 303 U.S. 520 (1939). No Kansas case has been found. See Maynard, note 47 *supra;* Annot., note 47 *supra.*

49 Kan. Stat. Ann. §62-1305 (1964); Mich. Stat. Ann. §28.977 (1954); Wis. Stat. Ann. §955.08 (1958).

50 People v. Dochstader, 274 Mich. 238, 264 N.W. 356 (1936). Stetson v. State, 204 Wis. 250, 235 N.W. 539 (1931), dictum contra. No Kansas case has been found.

A plea of guilty or not guilty may be withdrawn in order to interpose the proper request for review in the discretion of the trial judge. People v. Harris, 103 Mich. 473, 61 N.W. 871 (1895); Richards v. State, 82 Wis. 172, 51 N.W. 652 (1892).

51 See Chapter 6.

52 See State v. McGinley, 153 Wis. 5, 140 N.W. 332 (1913); State v. Bailey, 32 Kan. 83, 3 Pac. 769 (1884).

53 Since trial court review occurs before the jury is impaneled and, hence, before jeopardy attaches, there would seem to be nothing to prevent the state from re-

prosecution may appeal directly to the state supreme court.[54] In current administration, it seems likely that defendants are only rarely discharged in the trial court for insufficient evidence at the preliminary.[55] If the trial judge concludes the evidence was sufficient, the defendant may not appeal from that decision until after conviction.[56]

3. *Review after conviction.* Generally, a defendant may obtain a review of the sufficiency of the evidence at the preliminary examination in an appeal from a conviction. Because the appellate review is regarded as a review of the trial judge's review of the sufficiency of the evidence at the preliminary, all of the prerequisites to review in the trial court must be met in order to secure appellate review.[57] The scope of review on appeal is limited to determining whether the magistrate abused his discretion in binding the defendant over for trial.[58]

The doctrine of nonprejudicial error causes considerable difficulty in appellate review of this type. Even if the appellate court is convinced that the evidence was insufficient at the preliminary, should it reverse the conviction if the evidence at the trial was sufficient to support the guilty verdict? How has the defendant been harmed? On the one hand the evidence was sufficient to persuade a jury of his guilt; on the other hand he should have been dismissed at the preliminary and in such an event he probably would not have been subjected to trial. In Michigan the conviction would be reversed in such a situation.[59] It is not altogether clear, however, that this would be the result in other jurisdictions. In Kansas, convictions have been reversed when

---

initiating prosecution against a defendant discharged after such a review. Wis. Stat. Ann. §955.09(6) (Supp. 1968) provides: "If the court grants a motion to dismiss based on a defect in the indictment, information or complaint, or in the institution of the proceedings, it may order that the defendant be held in custody or that his bail be continued for a specified time pending issuance of a new summons or warrant or filing of a new indictment, information, or complaint." See Richards v. State, 82 Wis. 172, 51 N.W. 652 (1892).

54 Kan. Stat. Ann. §62-1703 (1964); People v. Madley, 339 Mich. 486, 64 N.W.2d 708 (1954); People v. Weiden, 239 Mich. 169, 214 N.W. 120 (1927); State v. McGinley, 153 Wis. 5, 140 N.W. 332 (1913).

55 In Detroit Recorder's Court, only two informations were successfully challenged in 1956. Annual Report for the Recorder's Court of the City of Detroit, Michigan, 1956, 8 (Mimeo. 1957).

56 See note 24 *supra*.

57 See notes 43-50 *supra* and accompanying text.

58 See, e.g., People v. Karcher, 322 Mich. 158, 33 N.W.2d 744 (1948).

59 People v. White, 276 Mich. 29, 267 N.W. 777 (1936); People v. Lee, 231 Mich. 607 (1925). In Michigan the point cannot be raised by habeas corpus after conviction. People v. Harris, 266 Mich. 317, 253 N.W. 312 (1934).

the magistrate found a lack of probable cause,[60] but no case has been found which reversed a conviction when the magistrate found probable cause on insufficient evidence. The law in Wisconsin is even less clear.[61]

60 State v. Howland, 153 Kan. 352, 110 P.2d 801 (1941); State v. Goetz, 65 Kan. 125, 69 Pac. 187 (1902).

61 A number of Wisconsin appellate opinions have given what appears to be serious consideration to claims of evidence insufficiency at the preliminary examination even though the defendant was subsequently convicted. See, e.g., State v. Goodchild, 272 Wis. 181, 74 N.W.2d 624, *cert. denied*, 351 U.S. 958 (1956). On the other hand, no case has been found which reversed a conviction on the basis of evidence insufficiency at the preliminary; nor has any case been found which applied the doctrine of nonprejudicial error to prevent reversal. In State v. Faull, 178 Wis. 66, 189 N.W. 274 (1922), however, the court said that a bindover on irrelevant evidence was erroneous, but it refused to reverse the conviction because the point was not raised in the trial court until after the verdict. See People v. McCalla, 63 Cal. App. 783, 220 P. 436 (1923), where the court refused to reverse the conviction because the complete absence of a preliminary examination was not prejudicial.

PART IV

Discretion and the Charging Decision

If every policeman, every prosecutor, every court, and every postsentence agency performed his or its responsibility in strict accordance with rules of law, precisely and narrowly laid down, the criminal law would be ordered but intolerable.

BREITEL, Controls in Criminal Law Enforcement, 27 *University of Chicago Law Review* 427 (1960).

. . . A society that holds, as we do, to belief in law, cannot regard with unconcern the fact that prosecuting agencies can exercise so large an influence on dispositions that involve the penal sanction, without reference to any norms but those that they may create for themselves. Whatever one would hold as to the need for discretion of this order in a proper system or the wisdom of attempting regulation of its exercise it is quite clear that its existence cannot be accepted as a substitute for a sufficient law. Indeed, one of the major consequences of the state of penal law today is that administration has so largely come to dominate the field without effective guidance from the law. This is to say that to a large extent we have, in this important sense, abandoned law—and this within an area where our fundamental teaching calls for its vigorous supremacy.

WECHSLER, The Challenge of a Model Penal Code, 65 *Harvard Law Review* 1097, 1102 (1952).

Full enforcement of the criminal law in the sense that every violator of every statute should be apprehended, charged, convicted, and sentenced to the maximum extent permitted by law has probably never been seriously considered a tenable ideal.

Even if it were so considered, limitations on the amount of resources — broadly conceived to include not only the finite nature of the amount of wealth available but also the supply of and fallibility of the human beings who must administer the system — would prevent its realization. Judge Breitel, quoted above, points out that, even in the absence of those limitations, such a system would prove intolerable in any event.

A necessary corollary to that conclusion is that some known offenders will not suffer the full penalty for their violations of law. Although the law has steadfastly denied to the police the right not to arrest the probably guilty, and has similarly denied to the judiciary the right to acquit the proven guilty, judicial statements are not lacking concerning the absolute power of the jury to acquit even the most clearly guilty, and these are important ameliorating influences in our system of criminal justice; certainly the notion of "executive clemency" has ancient and respectable roots. Beyond this, there is widespread recognition of the desirability of selectivity at the sentencing level — usually under the rubric of "individualization of punishment," or "making the punishment fit the crime," with the word "crime" including the characteristics of the particular criminal.

The point of focus then is the extent to which the law has recognized the same right to select among the probably guilty those to be charged fully, less than fully, or not charged at all. Because the charging decision is traditionally the prosecutor's, the law has often described this power in terms of "prosecutor discretion." The law is by no means clear, however, about the precise meaning of the term "discretion" in this context. Most of the judicial statements clearly encompass within the meaning of discretion the exercise of judgment whether the evidence is sufficient to believe the suspect to be guilty and convictable. Here, as elsewhere in this series, the term "discretion" means the judgment to officially charge, or to use some informal alternative to charging, a suspect who is probably enough guilty to justify the action.

Discretion so defined is exercised every day at every step of the criminal justice process. In law, there are limits to discretion, but they are never set out in legislative enactments and rarely carefully considered in judicial opinions. It is perhaps because of this failure to be explicit about the limits of charging discretion, in the face of almost uncontrolled exercise of it in practice, that Professor Wechsler expresses concern over the implicit erosion of the "rule of law" ideal. An important question, then, is the extent to which it is feasible to provide criteria for the exercise of charging discretion. The criteria currently used in day-to-day administration may have important bearing on this issue.

Even the strongest advocates for the establishing of criteria to control discretion would admit that some considerable amount of judgment must remain, if only because of the variety of situations that arise and the limitations inherent in the use of language. Some, however, have urged that charging discretion should not reside exclusively in the prosecutor and the police and that the trial judiciary should participate more fully in the process. The reasons why the trial judiciary does not do so in current administration should also help to evaluate those suggestions.

CHAPTER 8

Charging Discretion

Many persons who are in fact guilty of a crime and who could be convicted are either not charged at all, are charged with a less serious offense or a smaller number of offenses than the evidence would support, or are subjected to informal control processes which do not require formal accusation.[1] Although some decisions not to charge or not to charge fully for reasons unconnected with probability of guilt are made by the police, the primary concern here is with those made by the prosecutor. With rare exceptions, legislatures and appellate judges officially approve of this allocation of power to prosecutors, but the precise issue is infrequently confronted in appellate litigation and is only occasionally dealt with specifically in statutes.[2]

One important explanation for the paucity of direct decisions is that occasions are not common in which it is administratively necessary — or even desirable — to differentiate judgments based on discretion from those about the sufficiency of the evidence. In many instances, warrant or complaint requests are denied by

1 The chapters that follow contain detailed treatment of the various alternatives and their utilization in the three states under observation. For further descriptions of practice in the offices of prosecutors, see, e.g., Baker, The Prosecutor — Initiation of Prosecution, 23 J. Crim. L. 770 (1933); Brenner, How the Prosecuting Attorney's Office Processes Complaints, 27 Det. Law. 3 (1959); Kaplan, The Prosecutorial Discretion — A Comment, 60 Nw. U.L. Rev. 174 (1965); Klein, District Attorney's Discretion Not to Prosecute, 32 L.A.B. Bull. 323 (1957); Seymour, Why Prosecutors Act Like Prosecutors, 11 Record of N.Y.C.B.A. 302 (1956); Worgan and Paulsen, The Position of a Prosecutor in a Criminal Case — A Conversation with a Prosecuting Attorney, 7 Prac. Law. 44 (Nov. 1961).

2 United States v. Cox, 342 F.2d 167, 171 (5th Cir.), *cert. denied* 381 U.S. 926 (1965): "The discretionary power . . . in determining whether a prosecution shall be commenced or maintained may well depend upon matters of policy wholly apart from any question of probable cause." See, e.g., Pugach v. Klein, 193 F. Supp. 630, 635 (S.D.N.Y. 1961); Howell v. Brown, 85 F. Supp. 537, 540 (D. Neb. 1949); Williams v. Cave, 138 Kan. 586, 590, 27 P.2d 272, 274 (1933); Hassan v. Magistrates' Court, 20 Misc. 2d 509, 514, 191 N.Y.S.2d 238, 243 (Sup. Ct. 1959).

prosecutors both because the evidence is doubtful and because the desirability of prosecution is not clear in any event. When this occurs, marking "insufficient evidence" on the request for a warrant requires less refined articulation of reasons than an express statement that the suspect is probably guilty and convictable but prosecution is not in the community interest, so the former and not the latter is the course chosen.[3] Even when there is no question about the sufficiency of the evidence to demonstrate guilt, the same "insufficient evidence" notation is likely to be found — indeed it has become a shorthand way of saying that one or both of two conclusions has been reached: (1) the evidence is insufficient to prove guilt (or to assure conviction) or (2) prosecution is otherwise undesirable. It is certainly so understood by prosecutors, and almost certainly by trial judges as well. Indeed, inertia may play a role here: "We always do it that way."

Perhaps as a carryover from the warrant practice, perhaps because lack of evidence is viewed as a more defensible explanation if the decision is called into question, the same practice is found if the prosecutor decides to dismiss without filing an information, or even to quash an information, and must accompany his dismissal with a statement of reasons. This pattern obtains whether judicial approval of the dismissal is required. In Michigan, for example, the typical statement of reasons is couched in terms of lack of evidence that the defendant had a "criminal intent." In some circumstances that description would be technically correct, but in others the consideration that makes the "intent" other than "criminal" is that it would not be in the community interest to prosecute. Perhaps the outstanding illustration of a similar approach by the appellate judiciary is found in the Kansas case of *Fox v. Eaglin*.[4] A probate judge had "remarried" without divorcing his wife and had lived for many years with his second "wife" within 300 miles of the institution in which his wife resided. In the ensuing will contest, the Supreme Court of Kansas approved, at least by implication, a prosecutor's decision not to charge in this language:

> Mayhap the fact that he had openly espoused another wife and lived openly in ostensible wedlock with her for twenty years within 300 miles of the lunatic asylum which his first wife had

[3] See Klein, District Attorney's Discretion Not to Prosecute, 32 L.A.B. Bull. 323, 327-333 (1957).

[4] 132 Kan. 395, 295 Pac. 662 (1931). The judge was the beneficiary of his "wife's" will, and the issue in the will contest was whether he was legally married to the deceased.

> entered . . . tended to convince the state's prosecuting officers that the important fact of *intent* to commit the crime was wanting and that a prosecution would fail.[5]

What is significant is that, even if a judge might have a mistaken notion that he was not guilty of a crime under these circumstances, his mistake would not constitute a defense in any event, so the suggestion of lack of "criminal intent" can only be given a nontechnical meaning — in short, that this is the kind of case in which the law is violated but the violator ought not to be prosecuted. Furthermore, the idea that a jury would be likely to acquit a defendant they believe to be guilty is so intertwined with the first idea that one cannot determine the appropriateness of nonconvictability as a criterion separately from the question of appropriateness of other factors which do not bear on guilt.

Indeed, it is even more likely that careful separation of evidence-sufficiency and discretion problems would be viewed as undesirable by front-line enforcement agencies when the case has progressed to the point that a formal charge has been made. The decision to discontinue prosecution of a suspect already charged is a much more visible one — one which is more likely to come to the attention of the public through newspaper publicity or otherwise. That public reaction is a matter of concern to police and prosecutors is clear,[6] and no doubt the same may be said of many trial judges as well. Any general newspaper campaign asserting directly or even implying "softness" in law enforcement is likely, therefore, to have some effect on the decisions made by those officials.[7] It is clear, for example, that prosecutors are less willing to "bargain" in cases which have received considerable public attention.[8] That the evidence is insufficient is likely to be a more palatable explanation to the public than would an explanation that reflected a conclusion that a probably guilty man should not be prosecuted despite adequate evidence of guilt.

A second factor, and one of probably even greater causative

[5] Id. at 400, 295 Pac. at 665.

[6] See, e.g., Kaplan, The Prosecutorial Discretion — A Comment, 60 Nw. U.L. Rev. 174, 190 (1965).

[7] See Note, 48 J. Crim. L.C. & P.S. 526, 531 (1958).

[8] Ludwig, The Role of the Prosecutor in a Fair Trial, 41 Minn. L. Rev. 602, 610 (1957). Conspicuous press coverage might make a lenient disposition impractical for reasons other than the prosecutor's desire to avoid harsh criticism. The deterrent effect of the laws may be reduced if would be offenders are notified of tendencies toward leniency. Polstein, How to "Settle" a Criminal Case, 8 Prac. Law. 35, 40 (Jan. 1962).

significance, is that decisions not to seek maximum enforcement are less likely to be opposed by people with a sufficient legal standing to raise the issue. Most issues in or about the administration of criminal justice are raised either by the defendant or the state, since they are the formal parties to the proceeding. When the interest of the two coincide, the likelihood of judicial determinations of the propriety of the action diminishes greatly. This conclusion is reinforced by two sets of observations: (1) when the victim or other complaining witness is insistent on prosecution, his wishes are given very serious consideration by prosecutors and often prove controlling;[9] and (2) when the prosecutor is enforcing under circumstances which do not normally call for that full enforcement, there is an increasing likelihood that he will be faced with an argument that the defendant has been denied equal protection of the laws as a result of selective enforcement practices. Although the argument rarely meets with success, it is raised often enough, particularly in recent years, to account for a relatively greater body of specific decisions concerning limits on the amount of enforcement than can be found on the question of underenforcement.[10]

In point of fact, the relatively few cases in which statements are made about the limits of prosecutor power not to enforce fully do arise simply because someone other than the prosecutor — and usually someone other than the trial judge — objects to a pattern of underenforcement practices.[11] Attempts to oust prosecutors from office, to disbar them, or to prosecute them

9 The insistent complainant is discussed in Chapter 19.

10 See generally Comment, 61 Colum. L. Rev. 1103 (1961).

11 As indicated in Chapter 20, higher state officials and even private citizens initiate actions calling prosecutors to account for enforcement policies and charging decisions that allegedly reflect an undesirable attitude toward their position of trust. Often the issue necessarily arises of the extent of the prosecutor's discretion to conduct himself in office as he did, and its resolution often revolves around evaluation by the appellate court of particular charging decisions made by him in certain concrete situations. See Chapter 20, note 12 and accompanying text. General statements are sometimes made in other kinds of cases about discretion to not fully enforce, typically in cases involving a dispute between the prosecutor and some other official about who is authorized to exercise certain types of decision-making functions. E.g., State ex rel. Griffin v. Smith, 363 Mo. 1235, 258 S.W.2d 590 (1953), dispute between prosecutor and trial judge about which has authority to unilaterally discontinue prosecutions. The issue here does not necessarily focus on the permissibility of specific decisions made in concrete situations recounted in the opinions, for it is typically resolved by reference to common law or statutory sources allocating general types of decision-making functions pertaining to law enforcement. General statements regarding the scope of prosecutor discretion should be extracted from context in these cases with caution because of the absence of concern over some concrete situation.

criminally do occasionally result in appellate decisions in which may be found some guidance for the exercise of prosecutorial discretion.[12] Similarly, efforts to have particular cases prosecuted against the wishes of the prosecutor — mandamus actions, the appointment of substitute prosecutors, the intervention of the state attorney general, the insistence on the right to continue privately instituted prosecutions — provide sources of legal attitudes toward factors that in current administration cause prosecutors to make negative charging decisions.[13] Most of the factors which form the subject matter of Chapters 9-19 have been discussed, often with approval, in appellate decisions. But these actions are relatively uncommon, and resulting appellate decisions show the same tendency to mix evidence-sufficiency judgment with discretion, thus leaving the law less clear than commentators have seemed generally to assume. Furthermore, the body of law which has developed is nearly exclusively concerned with the corrupt or the inefficient, and not with the problems of the honest, competent man who is seeking guidance.

Although the remedies for controlling prosecutor-charging discretion are rarely used, nevertheless they are available. It would be a mistake, however, to draw the inference that the law is chary of recognizing prosecutor discretion. A more accurate analysis is that it is the prosecutor who is expected to make the thousands of decisions, often difficult ones, in this area, and that so long as his decisions fall within a normally expected pattern, they will not be overturned. Power to overturn his decisions exists, but in current administration and in law, the power to intervene and override the honest judgment of the prosecutor is conceived by "the law" and its "administrators" as a residual power, to be used sparingly. The point is probably best illustrated by the following provision of the Kansas statutes:

> The district judge may *in extreme cases,* upon affidavits with him filed of the commission of crime, require the prosecuting attorney to prosecute any criminal by information for such crime, and may compel, by attachment, fine or imprisonment, the compliance with this section.[14]

In short, both in law and in fact the discretion of the prosecuting attorney is very great, and, although the power to control it is

[12] Chapter 20 discusses these methods of "indirect control" in a separate subsection.

[13] See Chapter 20 for a discussion of these methods of "direct control."

[14] Kan. Stat. Ann. §62-807 (1964) (emphasis added).

clear, there is no expectation that, in the normal pattern of events, someone else's judgment will be substituted.

Regardless of what position might be taken in law, there is general recognition everywhere that resources are simply not adequate to fully enforce every penal law.[15] Recognition of the necessity for charging discretion, therefore, is most widespread in terms of limited resources. Enforcement practices designed to utilize resources most efficiently are adopted by prosecutors everywhere. A Detroit prosecutor reported, for example, that cases of nonsupport, conversion, fraud, and embezzlement are growing at such a rate that his office cannot prosecute all offenders;[16] instead, private compromise settlements between the complainants and the offender are encouraged actively.[17]

Once again, there is less explicit recognition of this problem in appellate judicial opinions than might be anticipated, but, when the issue must be met, the courts have been clear that prosecutors must weigh competing demands on their time and resources and make judgments about the importance of prosecuting some offenses more vigorously than others.[18] Instead, many cases in which a prosecutor has been called to account for less than maximum enforcement turn ultimately on whether he can demon-

15 E.g., Abernathy, Police Discretion and Equal Protection, 14 S.C.L.Q. 472, 475 (1962); Baker, The Prosecutor — Initiation of Prosecution, 23 J. Crim. L. 770, 786, 791 (1933); Brezner, How the Prosecuting Attorney's Office Processes Complaints, 27 Det. Law. 3 (1959); Goldstein, Police Discretion Not to Invoke the Criminal Process: Low-Visibility Decisions in the Administration of Justice, 69 Yale L.J. 543, 561 (1960); Jackson, The Federal Prosecutor, 24 J. Am. Jud. Soc. 18 (1940); see Note, 112 U. Pa. L. Rev. 881 (1964).

16 Brezner, How the Prosecuting Attorney's Office Processes Complaints, 27 Det. Law. 3, 4 (Jan. 1959).

17 Ibid. The encouragement of private restitution as an alternative to prosecution is discussed in Chapter 18. A related consideration is that prosecution of a fugitive offender might not be worth the expense it would require to extradite. See Attorney General v. Tufts, 239 Mass. 458, 518, 132 N.E. 322, 339 (1921); Worgan and Paulsen, The Position of a Prosecutor in a Criminal Case — A Conversation with a Prosecuting Attorney, 7 Prac. Law. 44 (Nov. 1961); Wright, Duties of a Prosecutor, 33 Conn. B.J. 293 (1959); see also the discussion of extradition in Chapter 10.

18 "Still other factors are the relative importance of the offense compared with the competing demands of other cases on the time and resources of investigation, prosecution and trial. All of these and numerous other intangible and imponderable factors must be carefully weighed . . . in deciding whether or not to prosecute." Pugach v. Klein, 193 F. Supp. 630, 635 (S.D.N.Y. 1961). See Attorney General v. Tufts, 239 Mass. 458, 508, 519, 132 N.E. 322, 334, 339, docket congestion as a factor in determining what standards of diligence a prosecutor should meet in bringing cases to trial; People v. Brady, 257 App. Div. 1000, 13 N.Y.S.2d 789 (1939), prosecutor decides whether it is worth time and expense to bring a bigamy case to trial; Johnson v. Boldman, 24 Misc. 2d 592, 203 N.Y.S.2d 760 (Sup. Ct. 1960); People v. Black, 156 Misc. 516, 282 N.Y. Supp. 197 (Otsego County Ct. 1935) prosecutor with undermanned staff justified in leaving minor offense prosecutions to other officials.

strate that he had focused his resources with sufficient vigor that it could be said that he was following a good faith policy of enforcement.[19] Usually the cases go only so far as to permit a prosecutor to enforce certain laws selectively, but in one case[20] the court permitted a prosecutor, in a particularly difficult situation in which general lawlessness was rampant, to go further and pick out certain laws which he would not enforce generally. He was authorized, said the court, to take into account which laws could be most effectively enforced and could even consider in this connection the prevailing sentiment in the community with regard to those choices, a factor whose legitimacy some courts have denied.[21]

Although particular resource considerations which loom important in current administration, as well as the extent to which the law has recognized the propriety of considering those factors, can be identified, it is enough here to point out that courts,

19 Compare State ex rel. McKittrick v. Graves, 346 Mo. 990, 144 S.W.2d 91 (1940), with State ex rel. McKittrick v. Wallach, 353 Mo. 312, 182 S.W.2d 313 (1944); see Ferguson, Formulation of Enforcement Policy: An Anatomy of the Prosecutor's Discretion Prior to Accusation, 11 Rutg. L. Rev. 507, 515 (1957).

20 State ex rel. Bourg v. Marrero, 132 La. 109, 140-141, 61 So. 136, 146-147 (1913).

21 See Wilbur v. Howard, 70 F. Supp. 930, 934 (E.D. Ky. 1947), *rev'd as moot,* 166 F.2d 884 (6th Cir. 1948); People ex rel. Hoyne v. Newcomer, 284 Ill. 315, 324-325, 120 N.E. 244, 247 (1918); Michael v. Matson 81 Kan. 360, 365, 105 Pac. 537, 539 (1909); State ex rel. Johnston v. Foster, 32 Kan. 14, 27, 3 Pac. 534, 538, *aff'd,* 112 U.S. 201 (1884); In re Voss, 11 N.D. 540, 547-548, 90 N.W. 15, 19 (1902). The Kansas courts have probably isolated the main concern of these cases. They do not allow community sentiment to be the only or even the principal consideration leading to nonenforcement, for fear that prosecutors might allow state laws to be suspended generally in one part of the state if people there dislike them. State ex rel. Coleman v. Trinkle, 70 Kan. 396, 400-401, 78 Pac. 854 855 (1904); State ex rel. Johnston v. Foster, *supra;* see Brown v. State, 177 Md. 321, 332, 9 A.2d 209, 214 (1939); Cates, Can We Ignore Laws? — Discretion Not to Prosecute, 14 Ala. L. Rev. 1, 7 (1962). Courts and commentators appear more willing to approve consideration of community sentiment if it is one of several factors that influence the decision not to prosecute. State ex rel. Bourg v. Marrero, *supra* note 20 gave its approval of the factor when combined with considerations of resource allocation. See Pugach v. Klein, 193 F. Supp. 630, 635 (S.D.N.Y. 1961); Howell v. Brown, 85 F. Supp. 537, 540 (D. Neb. 1949); Abernathy, Police Discretion and Equal Protection, 14 S.C.L.Q. 472, 478-482 (1962); Hoey, The Prosecuting Attorney and Organized Crime, 8 Crime & Delinquency 379, 381-382 (1962); Kaplan, The Prosecutorial Discretion — A Comment, 60 Nw. U.L. Rev. 174, 183 (1965). One point made in some of these sources is that prosecution for violation of an unpopular law might be futile because the chances of getting an unbiased jury are slim. This appears to be why prosecutors in Sedgwick County, Kansas did not attempt to rigorously prosecute violations of the Prohibitory Law, in spite of the concern manifested in the appellate cases over not letting local populations suspend a state legislative policy. Prosecutions were undertaken only when violations became especially extensive or notorious or were combined with other vices. But see State ex rel. McKittrick v. Graves, 346 Mo. 990, 1001, 144 S.W.2d 91, 97 (1940).

commentators, and prosecutors themselves have emphasized the seriousness of the offense as of prime importance,[22] but they have also stressed the nonconvictability of the suspect because of factors unrelated to probability of guilt.[23] Nonconvictability is of prime importance for two reasons: (1) subjecting the guilty but unconvictable suspect to trial, which is itself a form of punishment, may be regarded as fundamentally unfair;[24] (2) the prosecutor may be concerned over the possibility that too many acquittals may undermine public confidence in the working of the criminal justice system generally and the functioning of his office in particular.[25]

There is also wide recognition that factors other than limited resources may provide adequate bases for failure to enforce the law fully against the guilty.[26] The wide variety of situations which may arise, including important differences in the characteristics of particular offenders, as well as inherent limitations in the use of language, force legislatures to proscribe conduct in broader terms than might be considered ideal.[27] Indeed, there is evidence that full enforcement apart from resource limitations

22 It is commonly assumed that the prosecutor should give precedence to cases involving serious crimes in allocating his time and resources. See Attorney General v. Tufts, 239 Mass. 458, 508, 132 N.E. 322, 334 (1921); Baker, The Prosecutor — Initiation of Prosecution, 23 J. Crim. L. 770, 794-795 (1933); Kaplan, The Prosecutorial Discretion — A Comment, 60 Nw. U.L. Rev. 174, 181 (1965); Polstein, How to "Settle" a Criminal Case, 8 Prac. Law. 35, 40 (Jan. 1962). Authorities favoring prosecutor discretion not to prosecute, for example, when extradition is too costly or private restitution is a possible alternative, typically insert the reservation that this discretion should be restricted to cases involving minor offenses. In re Ridgely, 48 Del. 464, 471, 106 A.2d 527, 531 (1954); Wright, Duties of a Prosecutor, 33 Conn. B.J. 293 (1959); see State ex rel. Coleman v. Trinkle, 70 Kan. 396, 407, 78 Pac. 854, 857 (1904).

23 See Kaplan, The Prosecutorial Discretion — A Comment, 60 Nw. U.L. Rev. 174, 180-184 (1965).

24 Worgan and Paulsen, The Position of a Prosecutor in a Criminal Case — A Conversation with a Prosecuting Attorney, 7 Prac. Law. 44, 53 (Nov. 1961); see 1 Davis, Administrative Law Treatise §4.07, 256-257 (1958).

25 See Arnold, Law Enforcement — An Attempt at Social Dissection, 42 Yale L.J. 1, 10 (1932); Cates, Can We Ignore Laws? — Discretion Not to Prosecute, 14 Ala. L Rev. 1, 6 (1962); Waite, The Legal Approach to Crime and Correction, 23 Law & Contemp. Prob. 594, 598 (1958).

26 Abstention from federal prosecution because of deference to state policies is discussed in the following authorities: Pugach v. Klein, 193 F. Supp. 630, 635 (S.D.N.Y. 1961); Schwartz, Federal Criminal Jurisdiction and Prosecutors' Discretion, 13 Law & Contemp. Prob. 64, 70-81 (1948). Additional nonevidence-sufficiency factors are discussed in detail in the chapters that follow.

27 See Church of the Holy Trinity v. United States, 143 U.S. 457 (1892); Pound, Criminal Justice in America 40-41 (1930); Breitel, Controls in Criminal Law Enforcement, 27 U. Chi. L. Rev. 427, 431-434 (1960); Goldstein, Police Discretion Not to Invoke the Criminal Process: Low-Visibility Decisions in the Administration of Justice, 69 Yale L.J. 543, 586 (1960).

is not consistent with legislative expectations in some situations.[28] On these assumptions, it follows that detailed distinctions must, in some measure, be drawn by front-line administrative officers, whether prosecutors, police, or trial judges;[29] that charging discretion is necessary to transform broad legislative proscriptions into pragmatically satisfactory social policy.[30]

28 See LaFave, Arrest 87-96 (1965). For example, it is arguable that legislatures are aware of patterns of infrequent prosecution for violations of sexual deviancy laws and that they have given tacit approval to these patterns by not imposing stiffer enforcement standards in recent revisions of these laws. See Note, 1965 Wash. U.L.Q. 220, for a discussion of revisions, including that of Wisconsin; see generally Cates, Can We Ignore Laws? — Discretion Not to Prosecute, 14 Ala. L. Rev. 1 (1962). It has also been suggested that legislatures proscribe certain deviant behavior as a means of expressing community ideals without any contemplation that the laws will be vigorously enforced. Remington and Rosenblum, The Criminal Law and the Legislative Process, 1960 U. Ill. L.F. 481, 493; see Abernathy, Police Discretion and Equal Protection, 14 S.C.L.Q. 472 (1962); Arnold, Law Enforcement — An Attempt at Social Dissection, 42 Yale L.J. 1, 14 (1932). Another suggestion is that legislatures intend some criminal statutes to be utilized obliquely for purposes other than securing convictions of the offenses defined in the statutes. Note, The Fugitive Felon Act: Its Function and Purpose, 1964 Wash. U.L.Q. 355.

29 Some authorities appear to contemplate that administrators will carry out unexpressed but implicit legislative intent in situations that could not be provided for explicitly when the generally relevant legislation was drafted. See State ex rel. Parker v. McKnaught, 152 Kan. 689, 692. 107 P.2d 693, 695 (1940); Ewell v. State, 207 Md. 288, 114 A.2d 66 (1954); Abernathy, Police Discretion and Equal Protection, 14 S.C.L.Q. 472, 477 (1962); Comment, 61 Colum. L. Rev. 1103, 1115-1120 (1961). This means, however, that decisions vitally affecting the lives and livelihood of individuals are guided in large measure by the biases inherent in the exercise of personal judgment by enforcement personnel. This appears to conflict with the rule of law ideal. See Baker, The Prosecutor — Initiation of Prosecution, 23 J. Crim. L. 770, 771 (1933). Scholars have pointed out that the rule of law is a considerably more subtle concept than is implied by framing the issue in these terms. 1 Davis, Administrative Law Treatise 53-64 (1958); Breitel, Controls in Criminal Law Enforcement, 27 U. Chi. L. Rev. 427-428, 435 (1960). See Arnold, Law Enforcement — An Attempt at Social Dissection, 42 Yale L.J. 1, 6, 17-19 (1932); Miller, The Compromise of Criminal Cases, 1 So. Calif. L. Rev. 1 (1927) (pointing out difference between law in action and law in books).

30 "*Just because a crime has been committed, it does not follow that there must necessarily be a prosecution* for it lies with the District Attorney to determine whether acts which may fall within the literal letter of the law should as a matter of public policy not be prosecuted." Hassan v. Magistrates' Court, 20 Misc. 2d 509, 514, 191 N.Y.S.2d 238, 243 (Sup. Ct. 1959). Other cases agree with the statement in Pugach v. Klein, 193 F. Supp. 630, 634 (S.D.N.Y. 1961), that the prosecutor's problems of determining what prosecutions will be in the community interest "are not solved by the strict application of an inflexible formula. Rather, their solution calls for the exercise of judgment." Howell v. Brown, 85 F. Supp. 537, 540 (D. Neb. 1949); State ex rel. McKittrick v. Wallach, 353 Mo. 312, 323, 182 S.W.2d 313, 319 (1944); State v. Loose, 120 Wis. 115, 97 N.W. 526 (1903); State v. Seiler, 106 Wis. 346, 82 N.W. 167 (1900). One prosecutor reports that he would not prosecute a young man for statutory rape if the girl was just under the age of consent and the two had been planning to marry: "Although the letter of the law makes the act of intercourse a crime in such a case . . . the purpose of the criminal law is really not subverted by a failure to prosecute. The law intends to punish those older men who seek to take advantage of young girls, . . ." Worgan and Paulsen, The Posi-

Commentators have pointed out that, given unlimited resources, full enforcement of all technical violations would subject practically every member of society to some form of penal sanction.[31] It is clear that no one has seriously suggested that full enforcement in that sense would be desirable, much less tolerable. For example, if prosecution would cause great harm to the suspect or his family,[32] or even to the victim of the crime,[33] that

---

tion of a Prosecutor in a Criminal Case — A Conversation with a Prosecuting Attorney, 7 Prac. Law. 44, 51 (Nov. 1961). It has been reported that a United States Attorney's office for awhile prosecuted every person guilty of airplane bomb hoaxes but soon discovered that this policy had to be modified, especially when one of the jokesters turned out to be a priest. Kaplan, The Prosecutorial Discretion — A Comment, 60 Nw. U.L. Rev. 174, 191 (1965); see Cates, Can We Ignore Laws? — Discretion Not to Prosecute, 14 Ala. L. Rev. 1 (1962).

31 Jackson, The Federal Prosecutor, 24 J. Am. Jud. Soc. 18-19 (1940); see generally Kinsey, Pomeroy and Martin, Sexual Behavior in the Human Male (1948).

32 The significance of this consideration in the three states under consideration is discussed in Chapter 13. Authorities generally approve of prosecutors considering (1) the age of the accused, State ex rel. Coleman v. Trinkle, 70 Kan. 396, 78 Pac. 854 (1904), youthful defendant with rehabilitation potential; Attorney General v. Tufts, 239 Mass. 458, 520, 132 N.E. 322, 340 (1921), advanced age and feeble health; (2) the lack of a previous record, Hoey, The Prosecuting Attorney and Organized Crime, 8 Crime & Delinquency 379, 381-382 (1962), first offense or a technical violation may be disposed of by a warning; and (3) the fact that leniency may avoid the unduly harsh result of parole revocation, Attorney General v. Pelletier, 240 Mass. 264, 343, 134 N.E. 407, 435 (1922). All three were found, among other considerations, to be reasons for discontinuance of prosecutions in one large city. Note, 103 U. Pa. L. Rev. 1057, 1066-1067 (1955). Other considerations given approval by the authorities are that leniency may allow offenders to avoid deportation or to qualify for the armed forces, Wright, Duties of a Prosecutor, 33 Conn. B.J. 293 (1959), and that conviction of emotionally disturbed persons is not necessarily socially desirable, State v. LeVien, 44 N.J. 323, 209 A.2d 97 (1965); Copeland v. Donovan, 124 Misc. 553, 554, 208 N.Y. Supp. 765, 767 (Erie County Ct. 1925); Commonwealth v. Ragone, 317 Pa. 113, 176 Atl. 454 (1935); Brezner, How the Prosecuting Attorney's Office Processes Complaints, 27 Det. Law. 3 (1959); Kaplan, note 30 *supra* at 188-190 states that one United States Attorney's office encountered difficulty in not having enough alternative charges provided in the statutes for certain types of conduct, and that the only available charge often carried a penalty out of proportion to the seriousness of the criminal act. This motivated the office to decline prosecution in many instances of clear criminal conduct. See State v. Loose, 120 Wis. 115, 97 N.W. 526 (1903).

33 See Brezner, note 32 *supra,* and Wright, Duties of a Prosecutor, 33 Conn. B.J. 293, 295 (1959), sparing female victim of sexual deviancy cases the discomfort of testifying at trial. A related occurrence is the failure to prosecute because the victim does not desire prosecution. See Attorney General v. Pelletier, 240 Mass. 264, 348, 134 N.E. 407, 437 (1922), no proof that prosecutor acted in bad faith in not pressing adultery case for trial when wife of defendant had withdrawn her complaint; Goldstein, Police Discretion Not to Invoke the Criminal Process: Low-Visibility Decisions in the Administration of Justice, 69 Yale L.J. 543, 573 (1960), discussion of practice of Oakland, California, police, when victim of felonious assault refuses to sign complaint; Klein, District Attorney's Discretion Not to Prosecute, 32 L.A.B. Bull. 323, 326-329 (1957); Note, 103 U. Pa. L. Rev. 1057, 1069 (1955). The posture of the victim as it bears on the charging decision is discussed more extensively in Chapter 9.

harm might be thought to outweigh the benefits of prosecution, and discretion to decline prosecution would be regarded as socially desirable. Beyond this, however, are instances which typically call for some form of action in current administration but in which charging would be socially unwise. It is at this point that a consideration of what social objective a particular proscription was intended to facilitate becomes important.[34] For example, the nonsupport and desertion laws are designed not only to permit application of their sanctions to violators, they are also intended to compel heads of families to support their families. If some means short of charging accomplishes that objective — an advisory discussion with a prosecutor resulting in the violator's resumption of his support obligations, for instance — it might be thought preferable not to use the stronger sanction.[35] The same may be said of bad checks or certain other wrongful appropriation of property situations; if the objective of protecting individual property interests can be accomplished by return or restitution of the property, perhaps that should end the matter.[36] Again, if in assault situations of a not too serious nature,[37] the assumption is made that the purpose of the criminal statute is to protect against nonconsensual interference with the

[34] The position of the prosecutor in formulating public policy is discussed in notes 28-30 *supra;* see also Worgan and Paulsen, discussed note 30 *supra.*

[35] This is discussed more extensively in Chapter 18. See Ewell v. State, 207 Md. 288, 114 A.2d 66 (1955); Brezner, How the Prosecuting Attorney's Office Processes Complaints, 27 Det. Law. 3 (1959).

[36] Discussed more extensively in Chapter 18. Authorities generally approve of prosecutors making this consideration. In re Ridgely, 48 Del. 464, 106 A.2d 527 (1954); Attorney General v. Tufts, 239 Mass. 458, 519, 132 N.E. 322, 339 (1921); Gould v. Parker, 114 Vt. 186, 42 A.2d 416 (1945); see Jaffe, The Individual Right to Initiate Administrative Process, 25 Iowa L. Rev. 485, 508 (1940). Some legislatures have made special provision for the handling of cases in which restitution is a possible alternative to prosecution. E.g., Idaho Code Ann. §19-3401 (1948); Me. Rev. Stat. Ann. tit. 15, §891 (Supp. 1967); N.D. Cent. Code §29-01-16 (1960); S.D. Code §34.2101 (1939); Wash. Rev. Code §10.22.010 (1961). Authorities also approve of prosecutors' decisions that certain matters would be handled more appropriately in civil than in criminal litigation, Attorney General v. Pelletier, 240 Mass. 264, 344-345, 134 N.E. 407, 435-436 (1922), and that suspension of criminal prosecutions to await the results of pending civil litigation is desirable, Attorney General v. Tufts, 239 Mass. at 518-519, 132 N.E. at 339; see 14 Ops. Wis. Att'y Gen. 317 (1925). But cf. State ex rel. Coleman v. Trinkle, 70 Kan. 396, 78 Pac. 854 (1904), contemplated prosecution by a city does not relieve county prosecutor of responsibility for prosecuting violation of prohibition law. The avoidance of use of the prosecutor's office as a "coercive collection agency" by person involved in essentially private financial disputes appears to be another legitimate consideration in refusals to prosecute. Brezner, How the Prosecuting Attorney's Office Processes Complaints, 27 Det. Law. 3 (1959); see Wright, Duties of a Prosecutor, 33 Conn. B.J. 293 (1959); Note, 103 U. Pa. L. Rev. 1057, 1069 (1955).

[37] See note 22 *supra.*

person, it may be thought that uncoerced forgiveness by the victim — a not unlikely event if a charging decision is delayed until the parties have had a chance to reflect — ought to stop the criminal law machinery short of charging.[38]

Both traditionally and in current administration, charging discretion resides ultimately in the public prosecutor.[39] Many explanations have been advanced, ranging from a rather uncritical assumption that this was the situation at common law,[40] through the mere conclusion that discretion "may arise out of the very nature of the office"[41] to the contention that fundamental separation of powers doctrine requires that particular allocation of power.[42] It now is obvious that none of these is a satisfactory

[38] One of the considerations that led the Wisconsin legislature to expressly exempt the county prosecutor from the duty of prosecuting assault and battery cases, Wis. Stat. Ann. §59.47 (1957), was that his office has more important matters to attend to than involvement in neighborhood and family squabbles. Note, 1953 Wis. L. Rev. 170, 171. The implications of this statute with respect to private prosecution and the practice that has emerged under it are discussed in Chapter 20. It has been recognized that prosecution would merely aggravate friction and controversy in some situations, Pugach v. Klein, 193 F. Supp. 630, 635 (S.D.N.Y. 1961), and that it might moreover be unjustified because the parties to certain quarrels, notably those occurring in families or neighborhoods, are equally at fault. Wright, Duties of a Prosecutor, 33 Conn. B.J. 293 (1959); see Brezner, How the Prosecuting Attorney's Office Processes Complaints, 27 Det. Law. 3 (Jan. 1959); Note, 103 U. Pa. L. Rev. 1057, 1069 (1955). A further consideration is that complainants might desire to utilize the criminal process as a mode of private vengeance, which is apparently contrary to the American theory of public prosecution. See, e.g., Wilson v. State, 24 Kan. 189 (1880); Meister v. People, 31 Mich. 99 (1875); Biemel v. State, 71 Wis. 444 (1888); 14 Ops. Wis. Att'y Gen. 317 (1925); Cates, Can We Ignore Laws? — Discretion Not to Prosecute, 14 Ala. L. Rev. 1, 2 (1962). But see Note, Private Prosecution: A Remedy for District Attorneys' Unwarranted Inaction, 65 Yale L.J. 209, 227-228 (1955).

[39] As discussed in Chapter 20, other persons — judges, higher state officials, and private citizens — can through various formal means influence charging practices and enforcement policies of the prosecutor, but these means have only been effective in extraordinary circumstances. Influence has been exerted perhaps most effectively as a matter of routine by citizens, police, and other officials through informal channels. Nevertheless, "The policy . . . would appear to be to insure orderly procedure by, in the main, funnelling all law enforcement through the prosecuting attorney . . . ." People v. Holbrock, 373 Mich. 94, 97, 128 N.W.2d 484, 486 (1964).

[40] It is commonly assumed that prosecutors are clothed with common law powers. E.g., United States v. Brokaw, 60 F. Supp. 100 (S.D. Ill. 1945); Curran, A Federal Prosecutor Looks at the New Federal Criminal Rules, 13 J.B.A.D.C. 3 (1946). The contention often runs that the prosecutor's duties are to be identified with those of the Attorney General of England, which is called a misinterpretation of history in State v. Winne, 12 N.J. 152, 164, 96 A.2d 63, 69 (1953).

[41] See State v. Winne, 12 N.J. 152, 164, 96 A.2d 63, 69 (1953), quoting State v. Weleck, 10 N.J. 355, 366, 91 A.2d 751, 756 (1952).

[42] See, e.g., United States v. Cox, 342 F.2d 167, 179 (5th Cir.), *cert. denied*, 381 U.S. 926 (1965); People ex rel. Woll v. Graber, 394 Ill. 362, 371, 68 N.E.2d 750, 755 (1946); State ex rel. Pitchford v. District Court, 323 P.2d 999 (Okla. Crim. 1958). It has been authoritatively pointed out that the increased complexity of relationships

explanation, and there remains little doubt that legislatures have power to restrict prosecutorial discretion.[43]

At this point it is imperative to distinguish the initial charging decision sometimes reflected in a complaint alone, sometimes in a complaint and warrant, from the final charging decision reflected in an indictment or information in serious cases. Indeed, it is usual to include the power to discontinue proceedings already begun as part of the discretion whether to prosecute. Legislative efforts to control discretion in the latter situation by forcing the prosecutor to share his power with the trial judiciary have been common.[44] In some jurisdictions, a prosecutor may not decline to file an information after a preliminary determination of probable cause reflected in a magistrate's bindover order without judicial approval.[45] Although such approval is nearly automatic, there can be no doubt that the passage of legislation of this type reflects some concern over the extent of prosecutorial charging discretion. There has, however, been no substantial agitation to restrict the prosecutor's discretion at the initial charging stage by giving that discretion to some other official.[46] Certainly, the entire tendency has been to restrict the use of private prosecution.[47] In short, there seems to be no substantial body of opinion to support a shift of this core decision in the general run of situations, although one apparent exception should be noted. When crimes are committed which involve no victim, and especially when there is divided community sentiment about the desirability of enforcement in any event, some legislatures have enacted statutes which seem literally to remove discretion from the prosecutor not to enforce.[48] Prohibition statutes form the

---

between the branches of government has surpassed the usefulness of the traditional formulation of the doctrine as a prescriptive as well as a descriptive device. Youngstown Sheet & Tube Co. v. Sawyer, 343 U.S. 579, 593-596 (1952) (concurring opinion of Frankfurter, J.); 1 Davis, Administrative Law Treatise 64-74 (1958).

43 See State v. Coubal, 248 Wis. 247, 21 N.W. 2d 381 (1946); see generally Baker and DeLong, The Prosecuting Attorney, 24 J. Crim. L. 1025 (1934).

44 Discussed notes 50-51 *infra* and accompanying text.

45 The statutory provisions of the three states under consideration in this series are discussed in Chapter 20, notes 65-69 *infra* and accompanying text.

46 Commentaries do indicate concern over the lack of methods to correct instances in which prosecutors have exceeded the range of expectability. E.g., Note, Prosecutor Indiscretion: A Result of Political Influence, 34 Ind. L.J. 477 (1959); Note, Private Prosecution: A Remedy for District Attorneys' Unwarranted Inaction, 65 Yale L.J. 209 (1955). They do not appear to go further than suggesting administrative procedures to handle abuse of discretion, and they do not appear to favor a transfer of the discretionary charging function as a matter of routine to some other point in the system of law enforcement.

47 Private prosecution is discussed in Chapter 20.

48 See generally Baker and DeLong, The Prosecuting Attorney, 24 J. Crim. L.

best example, but there are others, mostly subsumable under the general rubric of vice crimes.[49] What is significant at this point in the discussion is not that discretion has been transferred to some other front-line administrative agency,[50] but that it has been denied completely[51] if those statutes are given literal effect. But it is extremely doubtful that such statutes were intended

---

1025 (1934); Note, 30 Ind. L.J. 74, 80-81 (1954); Note, 103 U Pa. L. Rev. 1057, 1058 (1955). The typical pattern is the existence in each state of a general statute pertaining to the prosecutor's responsibility to prosecute crimes in general, and some special statutes pertaining to his responsibility to prosecute particular crimes. No case was located in which a general statute was definitely construed as precluding selective enforcement against persons who are probably guilty, although language suggestive of this is found in Watts v. Gerking, 111 Ore. 641, 222 Pac. 318 (1924). It is clear, however, that the special statutes do purport to establish enforcement standards. Baker and DeLong, *supra* at 1034, note that few of these pertain to mala in se offenses. Perhaps a more comprehensive observation is that they usually pertain to offenses that have no individual victims. See Newman, White-Collar Crime, 23 Law & Contemp. Prob. 735, 745 (1958). Certainly legislatures would be concerned that, in the absence of complaining victims to bring violations to attention and insist upon prosecution, laws proscribing conduct like gambling might be laxly enforced. See State ex rel. McKittrick v. Graves, 346 Mo. 990, 144 S.W.2d 91 (1940). Another possible concern is that respectable public sentiment may not uniformly favor enforcement of laws, for example, those prohibiting liquor, and there is need for special provisions to assure that one segment of a community does not suspend the legislative policy in a portion of the state. See State ex rel. Johnston v. Foster, 32 Kan. 14, 3 Pac. 534 (1884); State ex rel. Timothy v. Howse, 134 Tenn. 67, 183 S.W. 510 (1916).

49 See State ex rel. Coleman v. Trinkle, 70 Kan. 396, 78 Pac. 854 (1904); In re Voss, 11 N.D. 540, 90 N.W. 15 (1902). In both cases prosecutors were called to account for lax enforcement of prohibition laws. The effect of special provisions for enforcement of gambling laws was at issue in State v. Langley, 214 Ore. 445, 323 P.2d 301 (1958).

50 There have been, however, some statutory requirements for the prosecutor to prosecute certain kinds of offenses when directed to do so by an administrative agency. These are surveyed in Baker and DeLong, The Prosecuting Attorney, 24 J. Crim. L. 1025, 1056-1057 (1934); Note, 30 Ind. L.J. 74, 82 (1954).

51 Special provisions are typically located within the legislative acts pertaining to certain crimes, and they provide for criminal sanctions or ouster from office when prosecutors fail to meet whatever enforcement standards are imposed. The authoritative interpretations of the special statutes are found in cases discussing whether prosecutors have made themselves liable to these sanctions because of noncompliance with the enforcement standards. Perhaps the leading representative cases of this kind are State ex rel. Coleman v. Trinkle, 70 Kan. 396, 78 Pac. 854 (1904), and State v. Langley, 214 Ore. 445, 323 P.2d 301 (1958). In parts of both opinions it is noted that the special statutory language does literally preclude selective enforcement. A different interpretation of the language emerges, however, in the parts of the opinions in which the courts voice their holdings. The enforcement standards that emerge from these constructions do not require the conscientious prosecutor to prosecute probable violators in every instance called to his attention. The provisions were regarded as designed to prevent laxness in enforcement for which no good faith reasons like inadequacy of resources, State ex rel. McKittrick v. Wallach, 353 Mo. 312, 182 S.W.2d 313 (1944), or personal judgment about the community interest [Coleman *supra*] can be offered by the prosecutor as excuses for inaction.

to be read so literally as to compel prosecution no matter what circumstances were present.[52]

Even the limited efforts to restrict prosecutorial power to discontinue prosecution once begun have been criticized by commentators and have rarely been utilized.[53] One reason for this criticism is that, pragmatically, it is easier to work out complex matters in the give and take of the relatively less formal setting of a prosecutor's office than in a judge's chambers.[54] Another is that the importance of insuring impartiality in the court, which may ultimately be called upon to decide guilt or innocence on the basis of evidence before it, may be greater than the benefits to be gained from earlier judicial involvement in the case.[55] Finally, and most often asserted, is the argument that the prosecutor as an elective official with a relatively short term of office is more likely to be responsive to the wishes of the polity than the judge who is conceived as a more remote figure.[56]

[52] One exception to this observation may exist, however, in some statutory provisions that charges of recidivism be brought against every accused who the prosecutor has reason to believe has had prior convictions. California interpretations appear to preclude selective charging of recidivism, People v. Dunbar, 153 Cal. App. 2d 478, 314 P.2d 517 (Dist. Ct. App. 1957), and the peculiar development of the Oregon law leaves little doubt that selectiveness is condemned. Bailleaux v. Gladden, 230 Ore. 606, 370 P.2d 722 (1962); State v. Hicks, 213 Ore. 619, 325 P.2d 794 (1958); State v. Cory, 204 Ore. 235, 282 P.2d 1054 (1955); Macomber v. State, 181 Ore. 208, 180 P.2d 793 (1947). Contra, People v. Casias, 73 Colo. 420, 216 Pac. 513 (1923); State v. Tatum, 61 Wash. 2d 576, 379 P.2d 372 (1963). Another possible exception is the Wisconsin law defining certain lobbying offenses. See State ex rel. Arthur v. Superior Court, 257 Wis. 430, 43 N.W.2d 484 (1950). A special enforcement policy in regard to this law, the enforcement of which is primarily the responsibility of the attorney general, does little violence to the proposition that the prosecutor has discretion to prosecute selectively the types of offenses that are routinely called to his attention.

[53] Discussed in Chapter 20.

[54] See, e.g., Pugach v. Klein, 193 F. Supp. 630, 635 (S.D.N.Y. 1961); Howell v. Brown, 85 F. Supp. 537, 540 (D. Neb. 1949); People ex rel. Woll v. Graber, 394 Ill. 362, 371, 68 N.E.2d 750, 755 (1946); State ex rel Spencer v. Criminal Court, 214 Ind. 551, 556, 15 N.E.2d 1020, 1022 (1938); Hassan v. Magistrates' Court, 20 Misc. 2d 509, 515, 191 N.Y.S.2d 238, 245 (Sup. Ct. 1959). These cases suggest that the courts lack either the time or the competency to participate in the pre-charge screening process. See Hodgsen, Administration of Criminal Justice as Viewed by the State's Attorney's Office, 25 Conn. B.J. 244, 247-248 (1951); Note, 103 U. Pa. L. Rev. 1057, 1072 (1955).

[55] See Howell v. Brown, 85 F. Supp. 537, 539-540 (D. Neb. 1949); State ex rel. Griffin v. Smith, 363 Mo. 1235, 1241, 258 S.W.2d 590, 594 (1953); Smith v. Gallagher, 408 Pa. 551, 585, 185 A.2d 135, 152 (1962); Note, 48 J. Crim. L.C. & P.S. 531, 540 (1958).

[56] See People v. Florio, 301 N.Y. 46, 92 N.E.2d 881 (1950); Hassan v. Magistrates' Court, 20 Misc. 2d 509, 512-515, 191 N.Y.S.2d 238, 243-244 (Sup. Ct. 1959); Note, 48 J. Crim. L.C. & P.S. 531, 538 (1958). The prosecutor's responsibility to the electorate is discussed in Chapter 20.

These contentions may be of greater weight when the problem becomes one of charge selection or of informal disposition than when the problem is one of outright release. Although it has been suggested that, in order to meet its responsibility in achieving the rehabilitation ideal of the criminal process, a trial court must be able to control charge selection to prevent limitation on its sentencing discretion,[57] the law in general has not taken this position, and judicial opinions instead reflect the view that one of the essential functions of the prosecutorial office is the selection of the charge which the prosecutor deems most appropriate.[58] Bargaining for guilty pleas, as well as promises of leniency for supplying evidence are usually complex matters which require the balancing of desires to achieve more objectives than resources would permit, and there is some opinion that the prosecutor may make that judgment more skillfully than a trial judge, simply because he knows more about the myriad of problems which confront law enforcement.[59] But the position in law is by no

[57] See United States v. Morin, 26 Fed. Cas. 1316 (No. 15,810) (D. Ind. 1866); People v. Sidener, 58 Cal. 2d 645, 665-666, 375 P.2d 641, 654-655 (1962) (dissenting opinion).

[58] State v. Faught, 97 Ariz. 165, 398 P.2d 550 (1965); Mervig v. Municipal Court, 226 Cal. App. 2d 569, 572-573, 38 Cal. Rptr. 232, 234 (1964); State v. Bastedo, 253 Iowa 103, 111 N.W.2d 255 (1961); State ex rel. Dowd v. Nangle, 365 Mo. 134, 276 S.W.2d 135 (1955); People v. Malavassi, 248 App. Div. 784, 289 N.Y. Supp. 163, *aff'd*, 273 N.Y. 460, 6 N.E.2d 403 (1936); People v. Lefkowitz, 232 App. Div. 18, 248 N.Y. Supp. 615, *aff'd*, 257 N.Y. 560, 178 N.E. 794 (1931); Allen v. Raines, 360 P.2d 949 (Okla. Crim. 1961); Wilson v. State, 89 Okla. Crim. 421, 209 P.2d 512, 514 (1949); Jones v. State, 84 Okla. Crim. 81, 179 P.2d 484 (1947). It must be acknowledged, however, that some aspects of charge selection do spill over into an area dominated by the judiciary. "Motions to dismiss or require election on the grounds that multiple counts are duplicitous, motions for correction of illegal sentences, and pleas of double jeopardy, all present in context issues appropriate for judicial determination — and incidentally, create an opportunity for courts to define the area of choice open to the Prosecutor." Ferguson, Formulation of Enforcement Policy: An Anatomy of the Prosecutor's Discretion Prior to Accusation, 11 Rutg. L. Rev. 507, 524 (1957); see Ladner v. United States, 358 U.S. 169, 79 Sup. Ct. 209, 3 L. Ed. 2d 199 (1958). See generally Comment, 76 Harv. L. Rev. 1668 (1963).

[59] See Whiskey Cases, 99 U.S. (9 Otto) 594, 603-604, 25 L. Ed. 399, 402-403 (1878); Pugach v. Klein, 193 F. Supp. 630, 635 (S.D.N.Y. 1961); State ex rel. Bourg v. Marrero, 132 La. 109, 139-140, 61 So. 136, 147 (1913); State ex rel. McKittrick v. Wallach, 353 Mo. 312, 322, 182 S.W.2d 313, 318-319 (1944); People v. Florio, 301 N.Y. 46, 53, 92 N.E.2d 881, 885 (1950); Jackson, The Federal Prosecutor, 24 J. Am. Jud. Soc. 18, 19 (1940); Snyder, The District Attorney's Hardest Task, 30 J. Crim. L.C. & P.S. 167, 169-171 (1939). Flexibility in law enforcement may result from the prosecutor's failure to prosecute persons who have cooperated in the arrest and conviction of other, more strategically positioned offenders. This was approved in Attorney General v. Tufts, 239 Mass. 458, 517, 132 N.E. 322, 338 (1921); see State v. Jourdain, 225 La. 1030, 74 So. 2d 203 (1954). The Florida position is that the prosecutor has discretion to enter into contracts to exchange leniency for cooperation; the public interest in breaking up conspiracies is thereby served. McKeown v. State, 54 So. 2d

means as clear as it is in practice, and there is more than a little authority denying power to prosecutors to accomplish some of these objectives without judicial approval.[60] Indeed, even in current administration, some charging practices directly reflect the attitudes of the trial judiciary.[61]

One proposal is of sufficient importance to merit separate consideration. Without any suggestion about the propriety of charging discretion resting in the prosecutor, the draftsmen of the American Law Institute's Model Penal Code have recommended that trial judges be given discretion to acquit in what are called de minimis violations.[62] Although the Code contains no implication that this proposal should be regarded as a substitute for charging discretion residing in the prosecutor, it is arguable that the factors which presently cause prosecutors not to charge, or not to charge fully, could be utilized instead by the trial judge in dismissing charges.[63] A possible criticism of such a proposal is that it would be extraordinarily wasteful of already limited resources with little compensating advantage in protecting the

---

54 (Fla. 1951); see State v. Finch, 128 Kan. 665, 280 Pac. 910 (1929); Lowe v. State, 111 Md. 1, 73 Atl. 637 (1909); 1941-1942 Rept. of Mich. Att'y Gen. 416.

60 There are statutory schemes providing for immunity from prosecution in exchange for testimony to be formally dispensed and made binding as a matter of record. In California the applicable statute is Cal. Pen. Code §1099 (1961). The court has made it clear that the grant of immunity can only be made by a judge; the prosecutor's role is merely that of applying for the grant. People v. Indian Peter, 48 Cal. 250 (1874); see Erskine, Arraignment, Pleadings, and Motions, in California Criminal Law Practice 350-352 (1964). Wis. Stat. Ann. §325.34 (1958) allows a judge to solicit or even compel incriminating testimony in exchange for immunity. It has been authoritatively asserted that the judge has the final discretion to refuse or to grant immunity, State ex rel. Kowaleski v. District Court, 254 Wis. 363, 371-372, 36 N.W.2d 419, 424 (1949), but it also has been acknowledged that it is within the province of the prosecutor to make the first move toward securing the agreement of the accused and the judge to the arrangement, Wight v. Rindskopf, 43 Wis. 344 (1877); 11 Ops. Wis. Att'y Gen. 57 (1922). Accord, People v. Walther, 27 Cal. App. 2d 583, 590, 81 P.2d 452, 455 (1938). A reservation is voiced in State ex rel. Jackson v. Coffey, 18 Wis. 2d 529, 118 N.W.2d 939 (1963) (state has interest in selection of offender to be immunized, and immunity cannot be given if sufficient evidence against accomplices is otherwise available). In Michigan, although the judge has the final authority to grant immunity, it is clear that he cannot do so on his own motion, but only on the motion of the prosecutor. Thus, contemplation of a form of shared discretion is made explicit. Petition of Hickerson, 301 Mich. 278, 3 N.W.2d 274 (1942); Petition of Dohany, 301 Mich. 273, 3 N.W.2d 272 (1942).

61 See the discussion of informal controls in Chapter 20.

62 Model Penal Code §2.12 (Proposed Official Draft, 1962).

63 As discussed in Chapter 20, note 162 and accompanying text, some states have already enacted statutes allowing judges to dismiss on their own motion, and these have been interpreted as granting authority to the judges to consider the discretionary factors.

public against poor prosecutors by making the decisions more visible.

A different suggestion also aimed at controlling the exercise of charging discretion is that legislatures provide, with some measure of particularity, the criteria to be exercised in using discretion.[64] While examples cannot be found in current legislation, it would be possible to construct general principles which might or might not conform with the factors isolated in current empirical studies as those which are employed with some measure of uniformity in current administration to select the appropriate charging action. In recent years there has been increasing concern over selective law enforcement resulting in part from uncontrolled (prosecutor) discretion, and the contention that selection of a particular suspect denies him equal protection of the laws is increasingly urged on the ground that others similarly situated have not been prosecuted, or have been treated less harshly at the charging stage.[65] Despite the fact that the argument has been rejected out of hand in the bulk of the cases on the ground that what happens to other criminals is of no concern to the suspect,[66] some limitations have been recognized.

First, an occasional case has been found in which an explicit effort by a legislature to give a prosecutor a choice of which statute to proceed under,[67] or whether to charge a felony or a misdemeanor for the same conduct,[68] or whether to invoke the habitual criminal statute,[69] has been struck down as an unconstitutional delegation of legislative power. But such cases are rare, in a distinct minority, and seem to overlook the fact that many statutes exist which may be violated by a single act, thus giving the prosecutor in fact just this kind of choice whether it is spelled out in the statute or is merely implicit in the fact of over-

64 See generally Breitel, Controls in Criminal Law Enforcement, 27 U. Chi. L. Rev. 427 (1960); Goldstein, Police Discretion Not to Invoke the Criminal Process: Low Visibility Decisions in the Administration of Justice, 69 Yale L.J. 543 (1960).

65 See generally Comment, 61 Colum. L. Rev. 1103 (1961).

66 For a collection of the cases, see id. at 1106 n.12.

67 See State v. Wentler, 76 Wis. 89, 44 N.W. 841 (1890). This holding has, however, been severely limited by subsequent cases. Ex parte Bentine, 181 Wis. 579, 196 N.W. 213 (1923); State v. Loose, 120 Wis. 115, 97 N.W 526 (1903); State v. Seiler, 106 Wis. 346, 82 N.W. 167 (1900). See also Brown v. United States, 299 F.2d 438 (D.C. Cir.) *cert. denied,* 370 U.S. 946 (1962); Deutsch v. Aderhold, 80 F.2d 677 (5th Cir. 1935).

68 Olsen v. Delmore, 48 Wash. 2d 545, 295 P.2d 324 (1956). See also State v. Pirkey, 203 Ore. 697, 281 P.2d 698 (1955).

69 State v. Cory, 204 Ore. 235, 282 P.2d 1054 (1955). But see State v. Hicks, 325 P.2d 794 (Ore. 1958).

lapping provisions.[70] Second, and more significant, is the emergence of a line of cases which deny selective enforcement when the selection is based on unacceptable criteria. Race, religion, and political affiliation are perhaps the most obviously unacceptable criteria for selective enforcement, but the Supreme Court has formulated the rule in slightly broader fashion to prohibit any arbitrary classification.[71]

It is clear that any formulation of criteria to guide the exercise of discretion would have to meet these constitutional minima, but that is the simplest part of the problem. More fundamental is the same kind of consideration which underlies the entire long-ranging debate about the necessity for and proper control of the administrative process in general. Whether a reasonable compromise can be reached between the necessity for discretion and flexibility which usually justifies a relatively uncontrolled administrative process and the desirability of affording the citizenry the kind of protection against arbitrary action usually associated in the minds of lawyers and laymen alike with the judiciary is by no means clear. It is probable that the severity of the sanctions involved has deterred courts from making any substantial concessions to the police in this field and explains as well the lack of forthright recognition of the administration of criminal justice as simply another species of administrative law.

70 One commentator has noted the many charging possibilities open to the prosecutor against a person accused of committing robbery in New York. Polstein, How to "Settle" a Criminal Case, 8 Prac. Law. 35 (Jan. 1962); see Barber v. Gladden, 309 P.2d 192 (Ore. 1957).

71 See Oyler v. Boles, 368 U.S. 448, 82 Sup. Ct. 501, 7 L. Ed. 3d 446 (1962).

C H A P T E R 9

The Decision Not to Proceed Further Because of the Attitude of the Victim

An important factor considered by prosecutors in making day-to-day decisions whether to charge is the expressed desire of the victim of the crime. Sometimes the problem encountered is whether to prosecute when the victim — initially, at least — is insistent but the prosecutor does not desire to charge, either for reasons of evidence sufficiency or because he believes that prosecution would not be in the community interest. Frequently, however, the problem he faces is whether to charge when the victim does not wish him to do so. This may be a determining factor even though the formal law rarely requires the consent of the victim as a condition to prosecution. Although prosecutors may subpoena the victim as well as other witnesses and compel them to testify (provided, of course, that they may not be compelled to incriminate themselves), reluctant witnesses, such as the willing female participant in a statutory rape, or "guilty" victims, such as a prostitute who has been beaten or robbed, do not make good witnesses from the viewpoint of the prosecutor. If only because the likelihood of conviction is lessened, prosecutors are thus inclined to accede to the wishes of the victim in all but the most serious cases.

Those statutes which penalize physical attacks are clearly designed to encourage the settlement of disputes by means other than force. Uncoerced forgiveness reflects the lack of importance attached to the incident by the victim and, perhaps, by the aggressor; the absence of such forgiveness indicates both that the incident is regarded as more serious by the victim and that the disposition contemplated by the statute was not achieved. If, within certain cultural subgroups, objectively more serious assaults are routinely regarded as not serious, it is not surprising that police and prosecutors tend to accept the group judgment about intra-group affairs and to abide by the victim's wishes with respect to prosecution. But those wishes are acceded to even when it is evident that the underlying objectives of the criminal statutes have not been satisfied. In many cases, it is clear that the disputants simply prefer to settle the dispute in their own way and do not desire official intervention.

Obviously, when the wishes of the victim are considered by prosecutors in making the charging decision, a complex interrelation of many factors is involved. The material in this chapter is designed to identify those recurring situations in which prosecutors simply concur with a victim in his desire not to prosecute.

A. Negro Assaults

In a large majority of cases involving assaults between Negroes, the offender is released without charge. Indeed, most of these cases are disposed of by the police without prosecutor participation, either by not making an arrest, or by releasing the suspect after arrest without requesting a warrant from the prosecutor's office. Officials commonly believe that Negro victims of assaults, even of very serious assaults, will not willingly prosecute their assailants; that belief is well supported by the field observations made in Detroit.[1] When the victim is a Negro and is unwilling to sign a complaint, the reluctance of the victim is usually accepted by police and prosecutors.[2] The following case is typical:

> *Illustration No. 1:* A scout car was dispatched to the home of a Negro man and wife on complaint of a disturbance. The wife indicated that the husband had cut her with a knife on

1 An incident was reported in Pontiac in which a Negro woman stabbed her common law husband with a large scissors, inflicting about a six-inch penetration in his shoulder. When the police arrived, he was bleeding profusely, but he told them that he did not desire to prosecute her, stating: "We're just a little upset, that's all." The police officer observed that the victim's attitude was typical of these cases. In perhaps the most extreme case of this sort reported, the victim expressed the desire to postpone his decision whether to prosecute until he ascertained whether he would recover from the wounds inflicted upon him.

2 A police official in a small Michigan city said that for some time he had instructed his police officers to endeavor to get the assault victim to sign a complaint in all cases in which a weapon had been used. He stated to the field researcher: "Of course you can't force people to sign complaints, so this order was somewhat unrealistic." A Detroit police supervisor indicated that assaults of this nature occurred so frequently in his precinct that, if all of them resulted in prosecution, officers would have to spend a considerable amount of time in court. So his decision not to encourage the victim to prosecute felonious assault cases if the victim is initially unwilling reflected a desire to conserve system resources, as discussed in Chapter 10.

her stomach and lower part of the chest. She had run from him and called the police. The husband was arrested for felonious assault. The complainant stated that she wanted to prosecute. When the detectives interviewed her later, she indicated that she did not want her husband charged but wanted him placed on "peace bond."[3] The officers informed her that the peace bond procedure could not be used unless she was willing to prosecute. She then indicated that she wanted him released without charging. The arrestee was released without being charged.

Similar offenses occur frequently both between Negro husbands and wives and between neighbors. Although the harm inflicted by the assailant is often extremely serious,[4] almost invariably the victim refuses to participate in prosecution of the offender. When such unwillingness is indicated, that attitude is usually allowed to control the disposition of the case. Indeed, as Illustration No. 1 indicates, the police are even loathe to invoke the informal alternative of placing the assailant on a peace bond. The factors which influence the official acceptance of nonprosecution of these offenders seem to derive both from the fact of the victim's reluctance to testify as well as from the fact that the victim is a Negro. The latter part of that statement, however, is difficult to establish. Although it is clear from the observed practice in Negro assaults that the vicim's attitude will be allowed to control the charging decision if the victim is still alive and indicates an unwillingness that the offender be charged, it is not known how far such official acceptance of victim attitude would go in cases involving whites. Some officials have indicated, however, that official acceptance of the victims' attitude in the latter cases would be more limited and would depend upon the seriousness of the assault. Apparently the reason for the lack of observation of such cases is that whites are more willing to testify in serious assault cases.[5]

[3] For a description of this procedure, see Chapter 18.

[4] In one case, the wounds inflicted were believed to be so serious that the police initially referred investigation of the case to the homicide bureau. It was later returned to the precinct detectives when it was learned that the victim was expected to live. When, despite some urging by the police, the victim refused to sign a complaint, the assailant was released without charge.

[5] One assistant prosecutor in Detroit expressed the belief that the moral code among the Negro subgroup was so low that if all such offenses were prosecuted the courts would be overloaded. The case that prompted this statement concerned cohabitation with a twenty-year-old girl. The assistant indicated that the charging decision would have been different if white persons had been involved.

Because of this uncertainty, these cases cannot unqualifiedly be classed as those in which prosecutors concur in the unwillingness of the victim to prosecute. Despite the fact that such conduct may not be viewed as serious in the Negro community, charges would be brought if the victim were willing to prosecute. Thus, it appears that official acceptance of the reluctance of Negro victims to prosecute derives from official perception of the cultural subgroup norms governing conduct among Negroes combined with the difficulty of prosecuting when the victim is not willing. In those cases in which the attitude of the victim derives not from a lack of belief in the seriousness of the offense but from a generalized dislike of official intervention into what is considered a private dispute, the prosecutor or police concur in the attitude, but not for the reason that underlying objectives of the law would be realized without such intervention. Instead, more reliance is placed on the attitude of the victim without concern about the factors which led the victim to adopt that attitude.[6]

B. "Guilty" Victims

> *Illustration No. 2:* Complainant told the assistant prosecutor that the female suspect had solicited him to have intercourse with her. He accepted and followed her to her apartment where he gave her five dollars. The complainant then changed his mind and asked for the return of his money. The suspect refused and ordered the complainant out of her apartment. No warrant was issued.

In many cases involving "guilty" victims, the prosecutor is successful in convincing the complainant that prosecution would be undesirable. In Illustration No. 2, for example, victims of this sort can often be dissuaded from pressing charges by the reminder that trial testimony would necessarily involve an admission that they had engaged in dealings with prostitutes. Only when the victim is adamant will a warrant be issued; only then will the victim's attitude cause a charge to be filed when normally the suspect is released.

Even though the attitude of the insistent victim may overcome

6 Police officers are quite critical of the Negro victim's attitude. They generally believe that the police are called only so that the victim can obtain free transportation to the hospital. One officer reflected that, if the policemen should begin to sign complaints in such cases over the protests of the victim, fewer cases would be reported to the police; the combination of victim reluctance and the deterrent effect of conviction would reduce complaints.

the reticence of the prosecutor, it remains unlikely that either the judge or the jury will be convinced that conviction is warranted due to the "guilt" of the victim. Thus the primary factor which leads the prosecutor to discourage prosecution in these solicitation cases is the improbability of conviction.[7] The final charging decisions in cases involving guilty complainants are not uniform, yet it is clear that in most there is an initial clash between the attitude of the victim and the prosecutor's perception of the undesirability or difficulties of obtaining a conviction.

C. Statutory Rape

In terms of the probable frequency of occurrence of the crime of statutory rape, relatively few offenders are ever charged. This is true because prosecutors usually allow their charging decision to be controlled by the attitude of the victim — either the girl or her parents — when they are opposed to charging. In those cases, the decision is based upon a consideration of the same factors, such as embarrassment and inconvenience, that led the victim to adopt a negative attitude. Occasionally, however, the prosecutor is faced with a decision whether to charge when the parents of the girl insist that the offender be charged. If the parental "victims" are insistent enough, the prosecutor may concur and will charge the suspect with statutory rape, but more often the prosecutor is successful in dissuading the victims from prosecuting. A multiplicity of factors enter into the decision to attempt to persuade them not to prosecute, two of which are of general application. First, the law is generally considered an "unpopular" one and prosecutors are not unmindful of their political responsibility. Indeed, prosecutors themselves concur in the perceived general attitude that the law should not be enforced. Secondly, the "collateral harm" which would be caused to the offender by conviction for the "sex offense" would, prosecutors believe, far outweigh the degree of culpability inherent in the commission of the offense.

Apart from those generalized objections to charging violators of this law, the merits of individual cases very often militate against charging. Often, the couple may be willing to resolve the problem created by pregnancy by getting married. Prosecutors clearly prefer this alternative to the prosecution insisted upon

[7] A secondary consideration is the "collateral harm" that would be imposed on the complainant if the case went to trial.

by the parents. It is pointed out that in this way the offender can undertake the support burdens which otherwise would fall upon the parents. In other cases, the prior unchaste character of the female may be indicated. Because prosecutors rely on a conviction standard in making their determination whether to charge, and because they are aware that juries are less willing to convict an offender when the complainant is guilty or immoral herself, the character of the girl is an important factor in individual cases. Indeed, in a sense, the girl may always be considered "immoral" because of her willing participation in the act.

It is impossible, of course, to say which of these factors is the most important in influencing the prosecutor's decision not to prosecute. In the usual case, the attitude of the victim coalesces with other factors leading to a decision not to charge. Even if the victim desires prosecution, other factors may outweigh her attitude, and charging may not occur. Occasionally, however, if prosecution is insisted upon by the girl or her parents the attitude of the victim may control.

CHAPTER 10

The Decision Not to Proceed Further Because of Cost to the System

A desire to conserve the limited resources of the criminal justice system may cause the prosecuting attorney to decide not to charge an offender who would otherwise be prosecuted. This factor is independent of evidence-sufficiency questions and produces a pattern of non-enforcement even if the prosecutor's charging standard — probability of conviction — has been met. Such a release is predictable if the case is one in which the suspect is presently in another jurisdiction or about which there is strong public sentiment.

When extradition proceedings are not instituted, the prosecuting attorney has usually concluded, in effect, that the cost in system resources (the expense of returning the suspect for purposes of prosecution) is too great to justify the issuance of a warrant. In other cases, although full enforcement is the normal pattern, no charge may be filed if the statute allegedly violated is an unpopular one, the suspect is a person of some reputation in the community, or the implications of the offense would reflect adversely on the police or the prosecutor. There, the cost in system resources is seen as a loss of public approval of and respect for administrative officials, which may materially increase the expenses of law enforcement.

A. Extradition

One of the clearest examples of the influence exerted on the decision to prosecute by the limitations of enforcement resources is presented when the costs of taking a suspect into custody are materially increased because he is not presently within the territorial jurisdiction of the state in which the crime was committed. Since, in such a situation, the decision to charge and the decision to take the suspect into custody must be made simultaneously,[1] often no charge is filed because taking the suspect into custody would be too expensive in the judgment of the officials responsible for making this decision. When the suspect must be returned from a foreign jurisdiction for prosecution, the charging decision is the result of balancing the burden imposed on available resources by taking him into custody against the desire to prosecute him.

The availability of sufficient funds to pay the costs of returning the suspect[2] and his willingness to waive formal extradition rights[3] are among the many factors involved in this balancing process. But the factor most directly affecting the prosecutor's decision is the distance which the officials from the demanding state must travel to return the suspect for prosecution, since it is in direct proportion with the cost of extradition. Thus, a suspect is less likely to be returned from California to Kansas than from Michigan to Kansas. Even if the suspect is within the borders of the state which desires to prosecute, his distance from the county in which venue lies is an important consideration.[4]

1 It would be a great waste of resources to take a suspect into custody in a foreign jurisdiction and return him to the state where the crime was committed for prosecution only to have the prosecutor refuse to charge him. Thus the decisions to take such a suspect into custody and to charge him are made at the same time by the same official — usually the prosecuting attorney. If formal extradition is pursued, a charge is a prerequisite. U.S. Const. art. IV, §2; 18 U.S.C. §3182 (1964); Uniform Criminal Extradition Act §3. It is clear in current administration that a suspect is not returned from another state until a decision has been made to carry through with prosecution.

2 In Michigan, the prosecutor's decision to extradite sometimes has been effectively "vetoed" by the county auditor's determination that too much of the county's funds has already been expended for extradition. In Wisconsin, police are frequently willing to extradite at any expense, but prosecutors sometimes refuse to extradite on the grounds of lack of funds.

3 If, as in most cases, the suspect is willing to waive extradition, the only expense involved in taking him into custody is the cost of sending a police officer to the foreign jurisdiction to return him to the prosecuting state. But if the suspect refuses to waive extradition, the responsible officials must send an attorney as well as a police officer to represent them at the governor's hearing (if there is one) and habeas corpus hearing (which the suspect may demand of right) in the foreign jurisdiction. This entails traveling expenses for two officials as well as additional expenses incurred as a result of the time spent in the foreign jurisdiction while the hearings are conducted. Since the officials of the prosecuting jurisdiction invariably learn whether the suspect is willing to waive extradition before they attempt to take him into custody, it is understandable why the return is more likely to be effected if he will waive extradition than if he insists upon all the formalities of that procedure.

4 A prosecutor in rural Wisconsin said that even a suspect apprehended within the state would rarely be brought back to stand trial on a bad check charge if the costs of such a return approached half the amount of the check.

In cities which are situated on state borders next to "sister cities" in an adjacent state, the return of suspects from one such city to the other is an everyday occurrence and is effected almost without regard to the seriousness of the offense. Since formal extradition is never used, the cost incident thereto is avoided. This combination of factors permits the wholesale return of suspects between such cities with little more cost than is incurred in obtaining custody of one who is discovered in the same city in which the crime was committed. It is clear in such a situation that the suspect's presence outside the state does not materially influence the charging decision.

The interest that must be balanced against the cost of obtaining custody is the desire to prosecute the suspect. The seriousness of the offense may be a determining factor; many prosecutors indicate they would never seek extradition of a suspect who has committed what amounts to only a misdemeanor.[5] Others indicate that they are more cautious in extraditing when the suspect has committed a white-collar crime. For some minor property crimes, such as bad check offenses, the complainant may be required to sign an agreement of indemnification, promising to reimburse the county for its expense if custody of the suspect cannot be obtained in the other state, if prosecution is not pursued due to lack of cooperation by the complainant, or if the suspect is found not guilty at trial.

In their efforts to avoid the expenses necessarily incident to obtaining the return of a suspect for prosecution, the responsible officials are careful to ascertain whether alternative remedies are available to the aggrieved party. This attitude is particularly prevalent in bad check and nonsupport cases. In the check cases, officials urge the complainant to seek restitution in lieu of the return of the suspect for prosecution. If the complainant is unable or unwilling to obtain restitution, an agreement of indemnification may be used in an attempt to discourage his efforts in securing extradition. In the nonsupport cases, the Uniform Reciprocal Enforcement of Support Act (URESA), adopted in all three states[6] — indeed, in all states[7] — permits the suspect to submit himself to the jurisdiction of the courts of the foreign state for support orders. If he complies with such orders, he is

[5] This criterion is a factor in the usual decision whether to extradite, although not in the "sister cities" situation.

[6] Kan. Stat. Ann. §§23-419 to 23-446 (1964); Mich. Stat. Ann. §§25.225(1) to 25.225(2) (Supp. 1968); Wis. Stat. Ann. §52.10 (Supp. 1968).

[7] 9C U.L.A. 10-12 (Supp. 1967).

deemed immune from extradition. In each of the three states, it is the policy to refuse to charge a suspect and take him into custody until the procedures of this Uniform Act have been exhausted. Nevertheless, in spite of these efforts to discourage prosecution, bad check and nonsupport cases constitute a substantial proportion of the instances in which a suspect is returned from a foreign jurisdiction for prosecution.

The length of time elapsed since the commission of the offense, the probable rehabilitation of the suspect in the foreign state, whether he is serving a sentence in the foreign state for an offense committed there, as well as the suspect's presence outside the territorial responsibilities of the officials making the decision, are all factors affecting the desire, or lack of it, on the part of the prosecuting officials to charge the suspect and seek his extradition.[8] The entire decision process is illustrated by a bad check case.

> *Illustration No. 1:* The suspect had been living with a girl, not his wife, and had written a number of "no account" checks. The girl had been passing the checks at various places in the county. The two left Kansas and were finally apprehended in Los Angeles. The man was convicted of a similar offense and served time in California. His sentence was almost finished and the California officials wanted to know whether to hold him for extradition. When it was discovered the girl had become pregnant in California, no charges were brought against her. The checks passed before the couple fled Kansas had amounted to only $60. The Kansas prosecutor indicated that it would cost the county $500 to take the man into custody. To him it was a simple matter of economics to decide not to charge the suspect. He indicated that, if the checks amounted to more than $100, he would not hesitate as much in extraditing.

Although prosecution of the casual bad check passer is discouraged in favor of restitution,[9] when the evidence points to the operations of a professional passer, prosecution is not discouraged; it is clear in Illustration No. 1 that the suspect would have been charged had he been within the state. The prosecuting attorney made a negative charging decision because he believed

[8] For a discussion of the obverse situation and the factors involved in the decision whether to release an arrested suspect to the custody of officials of the demanding state, see Chapter 14.

[9] See Chapter 18.

the burdens imposed by extradition on the system's limited resources clearly outweighed the benefits from prosecution.

B. To Avoid Loss of Public Support and Respect

Public opinion about the desirability of enforcing or not enforcing a given criminal statute influences decision-making at all stages of the administrative process. There is a feeling among many enforcement officials that criminal justice administration must, within certain limits, be responsive to public opinion in order to be effective. In a number of situations, when the feelings of the community have been particularly strong in favor of full enforcement of certain laws, officials have deferred to this opinion, at least until the criticism subsided.[10] In other situations, the attitude of the community has resulted in nonenforcement of certain laws against particular persons when they would otherwise have been subjected to partial or full enforcement. At still other times, the charging decision is affected by a desire to avoid what officials anticipate will be adverse or undesirable community reaction.

> *Illustration No. 2:* Two young men were arrested with beer illegally in their possession. One of the suspects was a local boxer of some fame, greatly admired by various members of the police department. The suspects identified the person who sold them the beer. They were not charged.
>
> *Illustration No. 3:* The defendant was charged with selling liquor without a license, a misdemeanor. At his trial, two sheriff's deputies who made "buys" from the defendant testified. The jury, rather quickly, returned a verdict of not guilty.

The charging decision is sometimes affected by the popularity which the suspect enjoys or the popular dislike for the law which he has violated. In Illustration No. 2 there are elements of both. Other important factors in the decision not to charge were the youth of the suspects and their willingness to inform on the seller. The police anticipated an adverse public reaction because of one of the suspect's reputation as a boxer and, in addition, because prosecution would create difficulties for a local boys' club, with which the suspect was connected.

10 See Chapter 19.

There are certain unpopular laws which are not enforced unless the facts present an extreme case or there is strong community pressure. The classic example of an unpopular law is, of course, national prohibition. Other less sweeping examples exist in current administration. Adultery and fornication cases are almost never prosecuted, except occasionally as disorderly conduct offenses; the statutory rape law is also difficult to enforce, particularly when the parties involved are close to the same age and there is no evidence of force. For this reason, every effort is made in the latter cases to reconcile the parties in interest, including the girl's parents. Counselling marriage or an acknowledgment of paternity if she has become pregnant is the usual method of inducing the girl, with her parents' approval, to drop the charges.[11]

After the jury returned the not guilty verdict in Illustration No. 3, the prosecutor trying the case stated that he was little surprised at this outcome. He said that the "big hurdle in this type of prosecution is a general willingness on the part of the public to let the bootleggers operate so long as there is no other vice connected with the sale of whiskey without a license." For this reason, the prosecutor's office had made very little effort until this time to enforce the statute against the illegal sale of liquor. Since a negative reaction was observed in this test case of public opinion, the prosecutor indicated that the general pattern of nonenforcement would, as a result, probably continue.

> *Illustration No. 4:* A group of college boys presented themselves to the police department with a story about a fellow student who was leading many college students astray, teaching them highly irregular and immoral sexual practices. A young police woman was planted in the suspect's circle of friends. She attended a large, wild party given by the suspect at his hotel, where she gathered enough evidence to permit the police department to ask for a warrant. The prosecuting attorney said he did not wish to approve a warrant until the chief of police was consulted, because the evidence uncovered by the police woman revealed that a young police officer had become involved with the suspect. The prosecuting attorney stated he would dismiss the case if the chief of police did not wish to have it prosecuted.

In Illustration No. 4, the officials had intended to prosecute the leader and instigator of the parties, but not the other partici-

11 See Chapter 9.

pants; neither an unpopular law nor a popular defendant was involved. Nevertheless, since prosecution would publicize the police officer's participation in the parties and, consequently, reflect adversely upon the entire police department, the officials felt the objectives of the system would be better served by dropping the case. Of course, if the decision not to prosecute were given publicity along with the reason, the public reaction would be even more adverse and would affect the prosecutor's office as well as the police department. By releasing the subject, the police provided themselves with an opportunity to discipline the police officer in question with relatively little publicity. Thus the officials were willing to permit the offender to go free in order to protect the enforcement system against the loss of public respect.

CHAPTER 11

The Decision Not to Proceed Further Because of Undue Harm to the Suspect

Obviously guilty persons may not be charged when, in the judgment of police or prosecutor, the consequences of prosecution and conviction seem unduly harmful in relation to the criminal conduct involved or the social and economic circumstances of the suspect. Two recurring situations of this type are the decision not to institute a second prosecution and the release without charge of drunks and minor traffic offenders.

Although prosecutors in Michigan and Wisconsin clearly have authority to institute second prosecutions on the basis of offenses known to them prior to the first prosecution, they rarely do so in current practice. This is apparently based on a feeling that, despite clear legal precedent, successive prosecutions due to official dissatisfaction with the disposition of prior cases are unfair to the defendant. Officials state that their duty is to prosecute offenders, not to persecute them.

Police are frequently faced with the problem of whether to seek prosecution of certain persons arrested for drunkenness or minor traffic offenses. When the arrested person has stable family and employment ties, and a recurrence of the offense seems unlikely, police must decide whether the benefits of prosecution, if any, outweigh its harmful effects on the suspect's reputation. This decision, normally made at the precinct "desk," frequently results in immediate release of the suspect without charge.

A. The Decision Not to Institute a Second Prosecution

Illustration No. 1: The defendant and two others allegedly entered a tavern and robbed five persons — A, B, C,

D, and E. Defendant was prosecuted for robbing A, B, and C. At the trial all five victims testified they had been robbed but only E could make a certain identification of the defendant as one of the robbers. The defendant offered an alibi defense, and he was acquitted. He was then prosecuted for robbing E. At this trial, the prosecution called only E, who testified that he had been robbed and that the defendant was one of the offenders. The defendant called the four other victims, who repeated their previous testimony, and himself repeated the alibi he had offered at the first trial. This time he was convicted.

Illustration No. 2: The defendant's wife and three children were found dead in a burning building. The defendant was prosecuted for the murder of his wife. He was convicted and the jury sentenced him to twenty years imprisonment. He was then tried for the murder of one of his children. He was convicted and sentenced to forty-five years imprisonment. He was tried again, this time for the murder of another of his children. Upon conviction, the jury imposed the death penalty.

Two United States Supreme Court cases, *Hoag v. New Jersey,*[1] upon which Illustration No. 1 is based, and *Ciucci v. Illinois,*[2] summarized in Illustration No. 2, have held that a prosecutor does not violate the Fourteenth Amendment by subjecting a defendant to successive prosecutions for separate offenses arising out of the same conduct. Opportunities for second prosecutions arise daily. In addition to the instances in which the defendant's conduct injures several persons, second prosecutions are possible when the same act violates the laws of two sovereigns, such as both federal and state law, and thus gives rise to separate offenses, as well as when in the clean-up process a number of offenses are admitted for which the defendant has not been prosecuted. The instances in which second prosecutions occur tend to be quite dramatic if the *Hoag* and *Ciucci* cases may be used as an indication.

In Kansas, a statute prohibits a second prosecution when evidence of the subsequently prosecuted offense was admitted at the previous trial.[3] Several provisions in the Model Penal Code prohibit successive prosecutions under certain circumstances.[4]

1 356 U.S. 464, 78 Sup. Ct. 829, 2 L. Ed. 2d 913 (1958)
2 356 U.S. 571, 78 Sup. Ct. 839, 2 L. Ed. 2d 983 (1958)
3 Kan. Stat. Ann. §62-1449 (1964).
4 Model Penal Code §§1.07-1.11 (P.O.D. 1962).

In many situations, however, successive prosecutions are not presently barred by statute. Although statements are frequently made, both to defendants and to others, that the prosecutor stands ready to prosecute those offenses not charged in the first trial, this threat has almost never been executed in the three states. No official in the Milwaukee police department or prosecutor's office could remember an instance in which such a prosecution was actually instituted. In Michigan, very few second prosecutions could be recalled. Enforcement officials in Kansas have interpreted their statute to prohibit second prosecutions entirely — an interpretation not supported by the statutory language.[5]

The second prosecutions that have been instituted were the result of a feeling of outrage by prosecutors at the disposition of the first case. In each such case, the defendant was dismissed on a technicality of pleading, was acquitted by a jury for what appeared to the prosecutor to be unjustifiable reasons, or was convicted of a much less serious included offense. The sentences imposed in by far the greatest percentage of cases — all those disposed of by guilty pleas and almost all of those going to trial — are not considered so inadequate by prosecutors as to warrant instituting a second prosecution.[6]

B. Drunks and Minor Traffic Offenders

Illustration No. 3: A woman in an extremely intoxicated condition was brought before the lieutenant in charge of the precinct desk. He asked if she had a family and she informed him she did. She also told the lieutenant she was ashamed of herself for being in such a condition. He quickly decided not to charge this woman, but he booked her as a Golden Rule Drunk to be released after she had sobered.

Illustration No. 4: Two uniformed officers brought in a man whom they had stopped for reckless driving. The sus-

[5] The Kansas statute prohibits a subsequent prosecution only for those offenses known to the prosecutor before the first trial and of which evidence is admitted in the first trial. A Kansas prosecutor stated that the underlying policy against harassment by successive prosecutions expressed in this statute would prohibit him, after a prosecution for robbery, from prosecuting the defendant for a bad check passed six months before the robbery of which he knew at the time of the robbery trial, even though evidence of the bad check offense was not admitted or even admissible at the robbery trial.

[6] Those cases in which second prosecutions were actually instituted are examined in more detail in Chapter 19.

pect was intoxicated and admitted he had recently been drinking. The lieutenant in charge of the precinct desk informed the suspect that, if he agreed to leave his car at the station and promised to take a taxi home, no charge would be lodged. The suspect agreed to this and he was released. The officers brought his car into the station garage.

Each day the police handle large numbers of cases involving public drunkenness and minor traffic violations.[7] To prosecute all such cases would place a considerable burden on the criminal justice system; thus, other considerations are used by the prosecutor to effect selective enforcement at the charging stage. The desire to avoid undue collateral harm is one

The maximum offense in Illustration No. 3 would be public intoxication; in No. 4 reckless driving. In each case, prosecution and conviction would be likely to result only in a small fine or probation. The relatively minor character of the offenses, the expense of prosecution, and the harm to the suspects' reputations by prosecution and conviction were all factors in the decision not to charge commission of the offenses that the evidence supported. The expenses of prosecution[8] and the harm to the suspects' reputations would not be substantially mitigated if less serious offenses had been chosen, especially since the maximum offenses were relatively minor.

In Illustration No. 3 the woman was booked as a "golden rule drunk"[9] and placed in a cell overnight because she was unable to conduct herself in a manner consistent with her own safety. The man in Illustration No. 4, less intoxicated, was sent home to "sleep it off." Neither suspect was an habitual drunkard, at least so far as the police knew. It seems probable, then, that the police thought prosecution would do little more to prevent a recurrence than was accomplished by the methods used.

Illustration No. 5: Two men, each age 35, were brought before the lieutenant in charge of the precinct desk. The arresting officer, a detective, informed the lieutenant that the two men stopped him as he was driving across an intersection, told him they were detectives, and fled when he reached for his revolver. The men denied they impersonated

[7] See LaFave, Arrest, 439-449 (1965).

[8] It seems unlikely that a charge reduction would effect much of a saving of enforcement resources by inducing a guilty plea, since guilty pleas to minor offenses such as the maximum offenses in these cases are regularly entered anyway.

[9] For a detailed discussion of the golden rule drunk program in Detroit, see LaFave, Arrest 439-449 (1965).

an officer and said they were simply informing traffic violators of their offenses. They admitted they had been drinking at several bars and were "feeling good." They were released and no charges were brought.

In this case, the maximum offense would have been impersonating a peace officer. It is uncertain what punishment upon conviction would be likely, but it is clear from the lieutenant's treatment of the problem that he thought substantial punishment not unlikely. Thus, it is possible that no charge was lodged because the punishment harm was regarded as too severe for the conduct. Before he made his decision, however, the lieutenant was careful to ascertain that both suspects were family men and had been steadily employed for over 12 years. If he had been concerned about undue punishment harm, a charge of disorderly conduct would seem appropriate. On the other hand, if unnecessary collateral harm or the limitations on enforcement resources were considered, charging a less serious offense would be of little aid. A stern lecture was administered to the suspects on the subject of their lack of authority to stop traffic violators. When they were released, the lieutenant concluded that they had probably learned their lesson and would be unlikely to repeat their performance.

CHAPTER 12

The Decision Not to Charge Fully Because of Cost to the System

It is clear that the common practice of making concessions to a suspect in exchange for a plea of guilty will reduce the cost to the system by obviating a formal trial on the question of guilt. Although the form and direct effect of this practice varies in the three states studied, the functional result is the same — a trial is avoided because the suspect's chances for a reduced sentence or probation are increased.

Although the legislatures have prescribed different ranges of sentences within which the trial judge may exercise his discretion, the prosecutor's awareness of judicial sentencing patterns is everywhere a factor in the choice of a charge. Thus, the decision is often made to specify a less serious offense, or fewer than the maximum number of offenses that could be supported by the facts, when it is believed that the probable effect on the sentence would be minimal. Charge is not made of past instances of criminal activity — previously undiscovered offenses that are distinct from those for which the suspect was arrested but were admitted during in-custody interrogation — for a number of reasons related to the conservation of system resources. Similarly, when the prosecuting attorney believes that proof of prior convictions will not affect the sentence, he will not invoke the habitual criminal statute.

A. The Negotiated Plea

Careful allocation of limited enforcement resources is most dramatically reflected in current administration in the practice of making concessions to induce pleas of guilty. Commonly referred to as "bargaining for guilty pleas," the encouragement of such pleas in the interest of efficiency in administering the system is common in the United States.[1]

A "bargain" exists only when it involves actual or apparent advantages to both parties. Prosecutors bargain to save the time and expense attendant on trials; defendants bargain for (1) reduced charges,[2] (2) less severe sentences,[3] (3) conviction of fewer offenses, or (4) avoidance of the stigma attaching to conviction of certain classes of crimes, particularly sexual offenses. Although these considerations can be theoretically separated, in practice they are dependent and interrelated.

When the trial judge is not given adequate sentencing discretion, a bargain requires charge reduction as well as sentence promise. Sometimes avoidance of the stigma attaching to sex-motivated crimes can be accomplished only through charge reduction.[4] Under other conditions, the principal benefits, or at least the benefits consciously sought, can be obtained without any charge reduction. For example, in Wisconsin, where great sentencing discretion is vested in the trial judge,[5] no bargaining over the charge is necessary, so both the charge contained in the warrant and that named in the information and pleaded to reflect the prosecutor's decision about charge propriety as divorced from considerations of negotiated pleas.[6]

When a legislature restricts the sentencing discretion of the trial judge, as has been done in both Kansas[7] and Michigan,[8] a

1 See Newman, Pleading Guilty for Considerations: A Study of Bargain Justice, 46 Crim. L.C. & P.S. 780, 787-788 (1956).

2 Usually the reduction is from a felony charge to a misdemeanor charge.

3 This is normally the defendant's primary motive for entering into a bargain; he wishes to avoid a high statutory mandatory minimum or maximum sentence, although often he may seek to avoid conviction of a nonprobationable offense, e.g., murder, rape, or armed robbery.

4 Typically, this takes the form of a less serious, though related offense, one which does not reflect sex motivation quite so explicitly.

5 The sentencing judge is given complete discretion, within statutory limits, over the maximum sentence. The minimum sentence is fixed by the legislature at a uniform period of two years or less. This is discussed at greater length in Dawson, Sentencing (1969).

6 This is not to say, of course, that in Wisconsin the prosecutor always selects and charges the most serious offense that can be supported by the evidence. Many times, a less serious offense will be selected on discretionary grounds unrelated to a desire to induce a guilty plea. For example, see Chapter 13.

7 In Kansas, the trial judge must impose both the statutory minimum and the statutory maximum. See Dawson, Sentencing (1969).

8 The Michigan situation is more complex, having some of the characteristics of both the Kansas and Wisconsin systems. For some offenses, the trial judge has discretion with regard to both the maximum and minimum. In others, the legislature has fixed a mandatory minimum. For most offenses, however, the judge must impose

sentence promise sufficient to secure a plea of guilty often requires an accompanying reduction in formal charge. It is for this reason that in both states, bargaining, even when its primary objective is sentence minimization, is reflected in reduced charges. In each of the three states studied, the initial charge specified in the warrant in no way reflects a desire to secure a plea of guilty; this is an "on the nose" charge. The consequence of bargaining in Kansas and Michigan, however, is that the initial charge is not the charge to which the plea of guilty is entered at the arraignment on the information.

The practices, although their result is the same, vary in the two states. The chief difference is the point at which the bargain is formally evidenced by a charge reduction. Probably because counsel is appointed earlier in Kansas,[9] bargaining there usually occurs between the time of the initial appearance and the formal arraignment, and thus is reflected in the information. In contrast, bargaining in Michigan usually occurs after the information is filed but prior to the arraignment. Thus the information originally contains an "on-the-nose" charge as does the warrant in each state and the information in Wisconsin. But, as a result of bargaining, a count is added to the information before the arraignment, a count containing the lesser charge sometimes necessary to permit the judge to carry out the sentence promise.[10] Thus the charge to which the plea of guilty is entered is not, in Kansas and Michigan, the charge specified in the warrant or, in Michigan, the charge originally contained in the information.

Superficially, it might be contended that, since the final form of the charge to which the guilty plea is entered reflects a bargain in both Kansas and Michigan, but not in Wisconsin, the Wisconsin procedures are not relevant to charge selection. Again, perhaps still superficially, it might be said that the criterion of relevancy should be the extent to which bargaining is handled by the prosecutor, free from interference by the trial

the statutory mandatory maximum, but has discretion in fixing the minimum. See Dawson, Sentencing (1969).

[9] In Kansas, counsel is appointed at the initial appearance, although in Michigan no appointments are made until the arraignment on the information. See Chapter 6 for a discussion of one of the reasons for the early Kansas appointment practice. Another reason is the trial judge's lack of sentencing discretion.

[10] The usual effect of reducing the charge in Michigan is simply to reduce the severity of the statutory maximum sentence; this in no way affects the sentencing judge's power to set the minimum. In some situations, however, the charge is reduced to avoid conviction of a nonprobationable offense or the imposition of a high statutory mandatory minimum. In these cases, the sentence promise could not be carried out without such a charge reduction.

judge. Under this criterion, Michigan would be classified with Wisconsin, because the charge to which the guilty plea is entered can be formulated only with the approval of the trial judge;[11] this process is closely related to the adjudication of guilt. Conversely in Kansas, where the prosecutor reduces charges at a stage sufficiently early to obviate judicial participation,[12] it would be arguable that the primary relevance is to charging.

These suggested distinctions overlook the functional similarity of these practices in current administration. Although it is true that only in Wisconsin does the charging process fail formally to reflect at any stage the desire to induce guilty pleas, it would be a gross distortion of the significance of current practices to distinguish these procedures on the basis of differences at most technical. Therefore, the "bargained for" or "negotiated" plea practices are given detailed but unitary treatment in the volume on conviction.[13]

B. The Decision to Charge a Less Serious Offense Because Charging the Greater Offense Would Not Materially Increase the Sentence

When a police officer brings the report of his investigation to the attention of an assistant prosecuting attorney, it already carries a tentative charge agreed upon by the officer and his superior. Normally, this tentative charge is "on the nose"; in a limited class of cases, however, it is evident that the investigating police officer tends to "undercharge" or "downgrade" the offense — to select a tentative charge less serious than the "on-the-nose" charge — in order to avoid certain administrative or judicial procedures.

> *Illustration No. 1:* A woman made an improper turn in the street. The police followed her and when she noticed them she accelerated her car. She could not negotiate a left turn and as her car jumped the curb she threw out several handsful of yellow pieces of paper, which were mutuel bet slips. After stopping her, one police officer issued a ticket

11 See Mich. Stat. Ann. §28.969 (1954). Since the bargain in Wisconsin is over sentence without an accompanying charge reduction, the approval of the sentencing judge clearly is needed.

12 See Williams v. Cave, 138 Kan. 586, 27 P.2d 272 (1933); State ex rel. Mitchell v. Court of Coffeyville, 123 Kan. 774, 256 Pac. 804 (1927).

13 See Newman, Conviction 78-104 (1966).

for the traffic violation while the other picked up the bet slips. The on-the-nose charge for carrying the bet slips would have been possession of gambling paraphernalia. The police recommendation for a warrant charging engaging in an illegal occupation was accepted by the prosecutor's office.

Under Michigan law, possession of gambling paraphernalia is a high misdemeanor and engaging in an illegal occupation is a low misdemeanor. In Detroit, bet slip carriers are usually charged with the low misdemeanor despite the prevailing view that the high misdemeanor more closely fits the conduct. High misdemeanors and felonies are subject to the same pretrial procedural steps under Michigan law. Both require an initial appearance, a preliminary examination or its waiver, and a trial or guilty plea, each on separate dates.[14] Final disposition of low misdemeanors occurs at the arraignment on the warrant, held at the same time as the initial appearance in high misdemeanor cases. A high misdemeanor case, then, may require as many as three court appearances by the arresting officer, although a low misdemeanor requires only one. The police justify selecting the less serious charge in the bet slip cases on the grounds of sentence leniency. They believe that the sentence imposed will be within the statutory range applicable to the charge of engaging in an illegal occupation, whether that offense or the greater offense of possession of gambling paraphernalia is charged.

The prosecutor's office usually accepts the police downgrading, although sometimes reluctantly. One assistant prosecutor stated:

> This is one of my peculiar grievances here. Possession is a high misdemeanor but engaging in an illegal occupation is a low misdemeanor. The police feel that the offense should be charged as engaging in an illegal occupation because it involves less paper work, when the facts really amount to the crime of possession. Possession is a high misdemeanor, and you have to have a preliminary examination and the police have to appear on several occasions before the case comes to a conclusion. This is one of those instances in which the police themselves are responsible for downgrading the offense.

Another assistant prosecutor replied to that statement:

> It isn't that the police are particularly lazy or that they do not want to do any work; the fact of the matter is that the judges will give the same sentence in a high misdemeanor as in a low misdemeanor in such cases. The police attitude can be summed

[14] See Mich. State. Ann. §§28.1192, 28.922 (1954).

> up as "why bother?" They know if a case, the facts of which are no more than that the arrested person had yellow bet slips in his possession, is taken to court, the suspect will be given a penalty which amounts to nothing more than 90 days, whether he had been charged with a high misdemeanor or a low misdemeanor. So there is the question of why the officer should go through all the foolishness of charging the man with a high misdemeanor when he will be given a low misdemeanor penalty.

The charging attitude held by members of the Detroit Police Department toward minor property offenses committed by bums is based on the same combination of a perceived pattern of sentencing leniency and a desire to conserve enforcement resources.

> *Illustration No. 2:* A "wino" stole some shoes from a bowling alley for the purpose of pawning them to pay for wine. After reading the write-up, the assistant prosecutor asked, "Do you want to take him on larceny from a building or simple larceny?" The detective indicated that the charge had been put on the police register as simple larceny and to take him for larceny from a building would require re-registering the man and going through a lot more records and red tape. Although the assistant prosecutor protested, "Well, I know, but look at the record of petty thefts on this man according to his rap sheet. How can you ever get rid of these people if you don't prosecute them?" He later approved a warrant for simple larceny.

The police attitude is that, since the suspect will be given the same sentence whether he is charged with simple larceny or with larceny from a building, they book him on a charge of simple larceny and are reluctant to change the booking. Police undercharging in this class of cases is accepted less frequently than it is in the bet slip cases, especially if the bum has a long record. One assistant prosecutor summed up his views:

> If a man is arrested for a sufficiently serious crime, he must be processed through a rather elaborate administrative routine. So the policemen simply try to get him on the lightest charge to avoid paper work. Of course they don't always do this—the deciding factor in these cases is that they feel that the bums are just not worth it. The police feel that the courts will release them and they'll be back on the street again. However, we contend that, if we charge them with a fairly serious offense, they will become known to the court and that perhaps something more substantial will be done.

C. The Decision to Charge Fewer Than the Maximum Number of Offenses Because Charging the Maximum Number Would Not Materially Increase the Sentence

If the in-custody interrogation of the suspect has produced a confession, he may be urged to incriminate his cohorts if the police have reason to believe that other persons who were not named in the confession participated in the offense. If it seems likely that the suspect has committed similar offenses he will also be urged to admit them. This final stage of in-custody interrogation is termed the "clean-up."

> *Illustration No. 3:* Four young men were apprehended in the act of breaking into and entering a business establishment. During in-custody interrogation, one of the suspects admitted that he and the other three were guilty of the offense for which they had been arrested. The detective who was conducting the interrogation then said to the suspect: "Now is the time to clean yourself up. So long as you've been apprehended for this one thing, we can give you a clean record by going through the police reports and picking out all other cases in which you've been involved." The suspect proved cooperative and immediately admitted breaking into a large number of places. As a result, one of the detectives spent several hours at various precincts going through all the breaking and entering reports for the year preceding the arrest, and the suspect indicated in which cases he or any of his friends had been involved. While one detective was typing a warrant recommendation, the other was completing the "clean-up sheet," which contained descriptions of 45 offenses admitted by the suspect.

Once the clean-up is completed, the case against the newly discovered multiple offender is taken to the prosecutor's office for the charging decision. Not all the offenses admitted by the suspect are charged against him.

> *Illustration No. 4:* A suspect was apprehended in the act of breaking into and entering a business establishment in the nighttime. During in-custody interrogation, he admitted to 37 separate breaking and entering offenses. An assistant prosecutor approved a warrant charging the suspect with

the single offense of breaking into and entering the business place where he had been arrested.

In Kansas and Michigan it is uniform practice to charge only one offense, no matter how many the suspect may have admitted. In Wisconsin, two offenses are selected from the suspect's admitted criminal activity to be charged against him.[15]

In addition to urging the suspect to "clean himself up," the detective conducting the interrogation may inform him that the offenses which he admits are "free" — that he will not be prosecuted for them. But the suspect may also be informed that, if he fails to admit any offense he has committed and his participation is later discovered, he will be prosecuted for it separately. Instead of giving the prosecutor's office detailed information about the "free offenses," the investigating officers will usually select what they consider to be their best case and request prosecutor approval of a warrant charging it.[16]

The result of the clean-up process is a clean-up sheet, which is simply a tabular description of the offenses admitted by the suspect. It is distributed to the precincts that have reports of the offenses described in it, enabling each precinct to clear the admitted offenses from its records. The clean-up, then, serves a bookkeeping function by enabling the police to keep up to date on the crimes that remain unsolved.

A wide variety of reasons are offered by officials engaged in current administration for not charging all the offenses discovered during the clean-up. Although some of the reasons offered are obviously of less importance than others, several of them are important enough to merit discussion.

1. *To accommodate the charging decision to the uniform practice of concurrent sentencing.* Concurrent sentencing for multiple offenses is used almost without exception in the three states. In Michigan, with only minor exceptions, consecutive sentences are prohibited;[17] in Kansas and Wisconsin, consecutive sentences

15 Charging the multiple offender in the federal system is quite different. For example, Federal Narcotics Bureau officials functioning in Michigan charge three separate offenses for every narcotics sale — importation, purchase, and sale. The same practice is used by the Alcohol and Tobacco Tax Unit of the Treasury Department when reviewing a case of a still operator — they charge possession of an unregistered still, possession of nontax-paid mash, and possession of nontax-paid spirits.

16 The prosecutor selects the offense which carries the most severe penalty unless there is reason to believe that, in the event of a trial, conviction on this charge would be difficult or unlikely. In Wisconsin, using these same criteria, two offenses are selected.

17 In re Allison, 322 Mich. 491, 33 N.W.2d 917 (1948).

may be imposed but this is done only rarely. Therefore, under these concurrent sentencing practices, whether required by law or not, a defendant who is convicted of more than one offense will not be sentenced to a longer period of incarceration than that permissible for the most serious offense of which he was convicted.[18] Nevertheless, prosecutors are reasonably certain that, when trial judges have sentencing discretion, they will impose a more severe sentence upon a multiple offender than on a single offender, even though they are unlikely, if permitted, to impose consecutive sentences extending beyond the statutory limits set for the most serious offense.

If there were no other way of informing the trial judge of the defendant's multiple criminal activity than by charging him with a large number of offenses, multiple charges might be more common. But this is considered to involve significant drawbacks, such as an increase in the paper work necessary at the warrant-issuing stage. Multiple adjudication, in cases disposed of at trial, would entail considerable expenditure of resources to prove all the offenses charged.[19]

The dilemma created by the desire to inform the trial judge of the defendant's multiple criminal activity without the resource expenditures necessary for multiple charging has been solved by informing the judge of the extent of the defendant's criminal activity in the presentence report,[20] thereby avoiding the paper work and resource expenditures incident to prosecution for multiple offenses. This report, submitted to the judge before sentence is imposed, contains a summary of the clean-up sheet, which was given to the investigating probation officer. Police and prose-

[18] Since the most serious offense is selected, charging the other offenses could not possibly increase the punishment beyond the statutory limits for that offense without the imposition of consecutive sentences; charging the other offenses will only increase the judge-imposed sentence to the statutory limits for the most serious offense. See note 16 *supra,* and accompanying text. For example, in Michigan, where the judge, for most offenses, must impose the statutory maximum sentence but has discretion to fix the minimum sentence, two charges might be brought, one carrying a fifteen-year maximum and the other a ten-year maximum. Suppose, further, that the judge imposes a two-year minimum on the first offense and a three-year minimum on the second. If the sentences could be imposed consecutively, the defendant would be sentenced to a minimum term of five years and a maximum term of twenty-five years. Under concurrent sentencing practices, the sentence would be three to fifteen years.

[19] One reason offered was avoiding the necessity for frequent police appearances in court in order to prove each of the offenses charged.

[20] In Wisconsin, any uncharged previous criminal activity may be brought to the judge's attention by stipulation of counsel. The judge will almost invariably discover the extent and nature of such uncharged crimes in one way or another in serious cases; in *minor* cases, such as joy-riding, this is not the practice.

cutors believe that most judges impose a more severe sentence when they see a long list of "free offenses" in the defendant's presentence report.[21]

2. *To provide added leverage for guilty plea bargaining.* Another explanation for the practice of charging fewer than the maximum number of offenses relates to the official desire to conserve system resources by encouraging guilty pleas.[22] Thus, it would be possible for the prosecutor to "hold back" several offenses and threaten to charge them later if the suspect fails to accept the guilty plea offer. This was not, however, observed as a part of the plea bargaining process, the natural place for such a threat to be made. A more promising course would seem to be a practice of charging all the offenses initially, then agreeing to drop the other charges if the suspect pleads guilty to the most serious.

3. *To insure the possibility of subsequent prosecutions if the first is terminated unsatisfactorily.* A third explanation is that the uncharged offenses are "held back" to permit their prosecution in the event the first case is not terminated to the complete satisfaction of the officials. If the defendant is acquitted on the first charge, or given a light sentence, he could, at least theoretically, be prosecuted again and again until the desired sentence is imposed or the officials exhaust their supply of free offenses. Although it is clear that threats of subsequent prosecution are sometimes utilized to induce suspects to admit their criminal activities fully,[23] it is equally clear that successive prosecutions

[21] One Detroit judge recognized that the "free offenses" are brought to his attention in order to influence his sentence decision. The presentence report, he explained, is very explicit in describing the crimes of which the defendant is apparently guilty, or has confessed, but is not charged with committing. Although indicating that it was difficult to verbalize the criteria by which he decides to increase the minimum sentence, he stated that a good general rule would be that the severity of the minimum varies directly with the number and aggravation of the uncharged criminal activity brought to his attention.

Bad check cases present a clear example of the close relationship between charging and sentencing the multiple offender. Frequently, a bad check passer has admitted a considerable number of such offenses before he is charged with any one of them. The sentencing judge is invariably informed of the extent, in terms of total dollar amount, of the uncharged bad checks. Probation may then be conditioned upon the defendant's making restitution for his known bad check activity, both charged and uncharged. Furthermore, the prisoner's uncharged crimes are contained in the report that accompanies him to the penitentiary. This report is kept in the files of the parole board, which uses this information in making its decision to grant or deny parole.

[22] See text at notes 1-13.

[23] See text accompanying note 16 *supra*.

are indeed rare in current administration.[24] It thus seems unlikely that officials withhold the free offenses in order to permit subsequent prosecutions that will rarely be instituted.[25]

4. *To avoid evidence-sufficiency problems on the "free offenses" caused by the perfunctory nature of the clean-up.* Clean-up sheets sometimes list as many as 150 felonies, some of which were committed more than a year previous to the current arrest. There is no question that all the offenses listed were committed by somebody — the police have a report on each of them in the precinct files. The promises and threats made during the clean-up to secure cooperation from the suspect,[26] however, create doubt that all the offenses admitted by a particularly cooperative suspect were really committed by him. No attempt is made to check the authenticity of the admissions, to return the property stolen to its owners, nor to discover the suspect's method of disposing of it. Further, there is considerable competition among police detectives in securing the largest number of admissions. Sometimes, there is a suspicion that unsolved crimes have been included in a particular clean-up sheet in order to enhance the investigating officer's reputation for securing admissions, when in fact the suspect did not admit them.[27]

It is arguable, then, that only one offense is charged because the police doubt they can prove the others. This theory is supported by the pattern of charging the offense for which the suspect was apprehended in the first place. The clean-up, as it is currently conducted, does not produce the proof that assistant prosecutors insist upon before approving a warrant; this is the result, rather than the cause, of the practice of not charging all the offenses admitted by the suspect. Since the clean-up does not form the basis for charging, the rigid standards of evidence sufficiency imposed for warrant approval need not be used.[28]

5. *To comply with the formal law rules of joinder and double*

24 See Chapter 11.

25 It is clear that Kansas practice is not explicable in terms of enabling subsequent prosecutions, because Kan. Stat. Ann. §62-1449 (1964) has been interpreted by prosecutors to prohibit virtually all subsequent prosecutions. See Chapter 11.

26 See text accompanying note 15 *supra*.

27 For example, in one case a clean-up sheet listed 127 admissions of separate offenses of breaking and entering. To the comment that the suspect must have maintained an excellent bookkeeping system in order to recall all 127 offenses, the police sergeant responded with a snicker and then implied that the investigating officers had "loaded" the clean-up sheet.

28 If sentence severity is related to the number of uncharged offenses appearing in the presentence report, then the propriety of dispensing with all methods of checking into the accuracy of the clean-up sheet is drawn into question.

jeopardy. A final explanation seeks to base the practice on formal law compulsion. It is clear that practical interpretations of the rules of joinder may limit, in a particular case, the choice of offenses which will be joined in a single prosecution.[29] The Wisconsin joinder rules[30] have not, however, prevented the practice of regularly charging the two best offenses in a single prosecution. Since multiple charges are lodged when officials desire full enforcement,[31] the rules of joinder can hardly explain the practice of charging only one offense when full enforcement is not particularly desired.

A police officer was asked if he has ever requested more than one charge against a suspect. He responded, "My God, no! You can only charge a man with one crime. To charge a man with more than one crime — that would be what they call double jeopardy. Our objective is simply to prosecute the man — not to persecute him."

Multiple charging does not, of course, normally violate the provisions against double jeopardy. It seems extremely unlikely that double jeopardy could serve as a reason for a high-level policy decision to charge fewer than the maximum number of offenses. The police detective's statement does, however, point out the difficulty that enforcement officials encounter in their attempts to explain the practice.

D. The Decision Not to Invoke the Habitual Criminal Statute

The suspect who has been convicted one or more times prior to committing the offense for which prosecution is currently sought may be subject to increased punishment as an habitual offender.[32] Use of an habitual criminal statute is of charging significance for two reasons: (1) the allegation of a prior con-

[29] One Kansas prosecutor said that he would never permit offenses of markedly different seriousness to be joined in a single prosecution — that first degree murder, for example, would never be joined with a bad check offense.

[30] Wis. Stat. Ann. §955.14(1) (Supp. 1968) provides that "different crimes and different degrees of the same crime may be joined in one information, indictment or complaint." For a discussion of the law and practice on joinder of offenses, with emphasis on Wisconsin, see Remington and Joseph, Charging, Convicting, and Sentencing the Multiple Criminal Offender, 1961 Wis. L. Rev. 528.

[31] See Chapter 19.

[32] Most states, including Kansas, Michigan and Wisconsin, have habitual criminal statutes. See Kan. Stat. Ann. §21-107a (1964); Mich. Stat. Ann. §§28.1082 to 28.1085 (Supp. 1968); Wis. Stat. Ann. §§939.62 and 959.12 (Supp. 1968); Habitual Criminal Statutes, Ill. Legis. Council Pub. No. 122 (1955).

viction required to invoke the statute may be regarded as a charge by the formal law;[33] (2) the invocation of the statute, because it increases the possible severity of the sentence, accomplishes that which would otherwise be possible only if a more serious offense or more than one offense were charged. The decision to invoke the habitual criminal statute may then properly be treated as a charging decision in practice, even though it might not be so regarded in formal law.

1. *Use of habitual criminal statutes in Michigan.* In Michigan all felonies and some misdemeanors are subject to habitual criminal provisions. Those relating to felonies are contained in a single statute, although the misdemeanor provisions are scattered throughout the sections defining misdemeanor conduct. If a defendant has been convicted of a felony prior to his present felony, proceedings may be initiated to prosecute him as an habitual offender. The defendant must be "charged" with the prior conviction either in the information charging the present offense or in a supplemental information filed after adjudication of guilt of this offense. Formerly, it was mandatory for the prosecutor to allege the prior conviction(s) whenever a defendant came within the provisions of the habitual criminal statute and, if this was done, the judge was required to impose the minimum sentence specified in the habitual criminal statute.[34] Judges throughout the state were dissatisfied with this procedure because it deprived them of their normal sentencing discretion. The present provisions, which amended the former law, declare that, if the statute is invoked at the prosecutor's discretion, the judge may sentence the defendant to any term of years not exceeding the maximum prescribed by the statute or place the defendant on probation if he is charged as a second offender.[35]

After adoption of this discretionary statute, assistant prosecutors in Detroit filed supplemental informations when they thought the circumstances warranted the imposition of the increased punishment. When Recorder's Court judges refused to impose a more severe sentence than would have been possible

33 The allegation of a prior conviction has been regarded as a charge for purposes of a statute requiring a preliminary examination of persons charged with an offense. See Note, 11 Okla. L. Rev. 76 (1958).

34 Mich. C.L. 1948, §§769.10 to 769.12.

35 Mich. Stat. Ann. §§28.1082 to 28.1085 (Supp. 1968). A second felony offender may be sentenced to a term, the maximum of which is no longer than one and one-half times the statutory maximum for the present offense. A third felony offender may receive a maximum term not longer than twice the statutory maximum for the present offense. Fourth offenders may be dealt with even more severely. Ibid.

without the invocation of the statute, the prosecutors concluded that this invocation involved an unnecessary expenditure of resources and produced no corresponding increase in the punishment. Nevertheless, prosecutors and judges agreed that some offenders should be subjected to a more severe sentence than that permissible upon conviction of the present offense alone.

For several years, the prosecutor's office in Detroit has not invoked the statute unless a judge of Recorder's Court, after studying the presentence report, decides that it should be used, contacts the prosecutor's office, and suggests that supplemental information be filed.[36] Judicial requests for invocation in Detroit have been limited to situations of an extremely aggravated nature[37] which exhibit the same characteristics that lead to full enforcement at the charging stage generally.[38] In other Michigan courts, unrequested invocation of the statute has been met with similar resistance by trial judges.[39]

Many Michigan statutes defining misdemeanor conduct have repeater provisions — sections which provide for increased punishment when the defendant has previously been convicted of the same offense.[40] Although a few are regularly used,[41] other

36 In rare instances, the prosecutor's office may invoke the habitual criminal statute without judicial request, for example, when public pressure for full enforcement in a particular case is unusually strong. Invoking the statute shifts the brunt of public pressure from the prosecutor's office to the trial judge. See Chapter 19.

37 One judge of Recorder's Court said the habitual criminal statute has not been used in his court for the last seven or eight years unless he had requested it. He further stated that the judges of Recorder's Court will request invocation only when the defendant, as evidenced by his record and current conduct, is really a "bad egg" and should be incarcerated for a longer period of time than would be permissible under the crime for which he currently stands convicted. An assistant prosecutor said that when a Recorder's Court judge requests invocation of the statute the defendant has usually demonstrated his "habitualness" with a record of four or five felony convictions.

38 See Chapter 19.

39 The Michigan habitual criminal statute has not been used in Wayne County, Michigan, in over thirteen years because the judges of the Wayne County Circuit Court prefer not to have it used. In one outstate Michigan city, the habitual criminal statute is apparently never used, even in full enforcement situations.

40 Such a section was a part of the disorderly conduct statute, which defined numerous common misdemeanors. Mich. Stat. Ann. §§28.364 to 28.365 (1962). The first violation of this statute was a misdemeanor and the punishment was limited to ninety days. If a defendant was convicted a second time under this statute, and charged as a second offender under its repeater provisions, he was incarcerated, if at all, for a period of not less than thirty days nor more than three months. For a third or subsequent conviction, the period of incarceration, if any, was not less than six months nor more than two years. The statute, however, has recently been amended. Mich. Stat. Ann. §§28.364 to 28.365 (Supp. 1968).

41 See Chapter 19.

misdemeanor repeater provisions are used only very sporadically, and most are not used at all.[42]

2. *Use of habitual criminal statutes in Kansas.* The effective decision to invoke the habitual criminal provisions in Kansas is made by the prosecutor.[43] The judge's discretion is limited: invoking the statute against a defendant currently convicted of a felony, who has one previous felony conviction, automatically doubles the statutory penalty for the current conviction; invoking the statute against a defendant who has two previous felony convictions requires that the trial judge set a definite sentence between fifteen years and life for the third or subsequent felony conviction.[44]

> *Illustration No. 5:* The deputy county attorney was attempting to persuade the defense attorney to plead his client guilty to the offense charged, in return for a promise not to invoke the habitual criminal statute. Defense counsel stated that he had not talked with his client about the matter. The deputy county attorney responded that, once the defendant saw the evidence the state would produce at the preliminary examination, he was sure he would go for such a deal. He then described the expected testimony of one of the police officers, and counsel looked quite discouraged when he heard it. Later, the deputy county attorney explained he was confident the deal would be consummated, because the defendant was an "old timer" who "knew the ropes."

The most extensive use made of the Kansas habitual criminal statute is in bargaining with defendant and his counsel over a

[42] One assistant prosecutor, when asked if persons arrested for persistent mutuel betting violations are prosecuted under the repeater provisions for that offense, said: "Many of the people we have in here on these mutuel bet operations have had twenty or thirty charges and convictions. The judges tell us not to clutter up the courts with charging a lot of habitual offenders since the process is the same as for a felony. They prefer that if we do any work at all we try to 'clear up crimes of violence.' There is no charging anyone as an habitual offender in this class of crimes because, if they got a sentence at all, it would be handed out in such a way that it would either be suspended or it would amount to just a very few days in jail."

A police officer described the charging activities of the Detroit bum squad: "If the bum doesn't have too lengthy a record, and if we don't know him too well, we will golden rule drunk him. If he has a long recent record, we will charge him with drunkenness or vagrancy. There is no sense in going for an habitual because that could not easily be got, and anyway, the judge only gives a sentence which would be equal to the plain charge."

[43] This is in marked contrast to the Detroit practice, where the decision is made, in effect, by the trial judge.

[44] Kan. Stat. Ann. §21-107a (1964).

plea of guilty. Often, such bargaining results in the defendant's pleading guilty to the present offense in return for the prosecutor's promise not to use the habitual criminal statute against him. If the defendant refuses to plead guilty, the prosecutor is likely to invoke the statute after conviction. Prosecutors may refuse to offer some defendants, particularly those with two prior felony convictions, the opportunity to plead guilty and avoid invocation of the statute.[45] In spite of fairly frequent invocation of the statute, the most significant characteristic of its use is its noninvocation in exchange for a guilty plea.

3. *Use of habitual criminal statutes in Wisconsin.* The Wisconsin "repeater" statute provides for an increased permissible sentence upon conviction for a second or subsequent offense, whether a felony or misdemeanor.[46] The effect of invocation is to broaden the scope of judicial sentencing discretion by permitting, although not requiring, the imposition of a longer maximum sentence than that permissible for conviction of the present offense alone. The statute is rarely used in current administration, although police or prosecutor might, on appropriate occasion, threaten its use in order to secure cooperation of various kinds from a suspect. It is not entirely clear why the statute is not used, but a likely explanation is that officials feel that the maximum sentence permissible for most offenses affords sufficient sentencing flexibility to deal with the habitual offender in a severe manner, when that course seems appropriate. One prosecutor mentioned that, even though he does not use the statute, he is careful to see to it that the sentencing judge is informed of the defendant's criminal record. The implication is clear that a longer judicial maximum sentence, although still within that permissible for the current offense alone, can be reasonably expected simply by making the defendant's record known to the trial judge. Thus, in a manner similar to the decision to charge fewer than the maximum number of offenses, officials feel they have solved the sentencing problems posed by the habitual offender without the resource expenditures needed to invoke the statute.

[45] See Chapter 19.
[46] Wis. Stat. Ann. §939.62 (1958).

CHAPTER 13

The Decision Not to Charge Fully Because of Undue Harm to the Suspect

In many cases a prosecutor may decide to charge an offense less serious than that which could be justified by the facts despite the sufficiency of the evidence to convict the suspect of the maximum offense. One reason for such a decision may be the desire to avoid unnecessary infliction of collateral or punishment harm. It could be argued that the decision to charge a less serious offense for such a reason constitutes a deliberate frustration of legislative intent — a circumvention of the statutory penalty. This is true only if it is assumed that the legislature intended prosecution for the maximum offense on every violation, an assumption clearly unwarranted in some circumstances. In any event, avoidance of legislative efforts to prevent leniency at the sentencing stage is accomplished by manipulating the charge.

A charge may be reduced to avoid infliction of punishment harm that administrative officials regard as too severe in relation to the suspect's conduct. Usually, a less serious offense is charged because conviction of the maximum offense carries a statutory mandatory minimum sentence or a statutory ineligibility for probation; the new charge will allow the judge greater discretion in imposing a minimum sentence — which term determines the prisoner's eligibility for parole — or in granting probation.

Because charge reduction in theory is likely to result in a reduction in the punishment harm, it is arguable that the desire to reduce punishment harm is the moving factor in these decisions, and the avoidance of collateral harm is at best secondary. Nevertheless, a close examination of the system reveals that a reduction of the formal charge will not necessarily produce a reduction in the punishment imposed, because the trial judge has been appraised of the circumstances surrounding the offense and is able to determine for himself what the maximum offense would have been. Thus, in many cases the decision to reduce the charge is wholly or partly the result of a desire to avoid unnecessary collateral harm.

A. The Decision to Charge a Less Serious Offense to Avoid Undue Collateral Harm

1. *Young offenders.*

Illustration No. 1: The sheriff's office had received reports of several loud parties in a certain house. The names of all the participants had been secured and they, with their parents, were assembled in the sheriff's office. It was soon learned that beer had been purchased by two eighteen-year-old boys who had distributed it to the other participants, all of whom were sixteen or seventeen years old. The minimum age for legal purchase of beer was eighteen. Although they could have been charged with contributing to the delinquency of a minor, the assistant prosecutor approved a warrant against them for disorderly conduct.

In Illustration No. 1, the maximum offense that could be charged was contributing to the delinquency of a minor. One of the suspects had previously been convicted of that offense — apparently under similar circumstances — and had received a fine. The assistant prosecutor gave two reasons for not charging contributing: (1) The difference in ages between the two suspects who violated the law and those who participated in the parties but did not violate the law was so slight that it seemed to him unfair to punish them and release the others, and (2) it was his policy in such cases not to charge contributing to the delinquency of a minor because it is a rather serious charge with overtones of sexual misconduct, and when it appears on the records there is no accompanying explanation of the nature of the offending conduct.[1] No reason was given for not dismissing the case, except the prosecutor's statement that "it was the law."

2. *The respectable offender.*

Illustration No. 2: The state police received information that gambling equipment and an indecent floor show would

[1] Similarly, a young offender who violates the concealed weapons statute is prosecuted for disorderly conduct if his behavior was not too serious. The suggestion has been made that the disorderly conduct statute ought to be amended specifically to include minor concealed weapons offenses, in order to remove any possibility that a young offender would have a record for conviction of a concealed weapons charge.

> be found in the clubhouse of a fraternal organization. The clubhouse was raided and, although the charge of engaging in an illegal occupation could have been brought, the officers of the organization were charged with disorderly conduct.

When this case was brought before him, an assistant prosecutor indicated that the maximum offenses would be the felonies of illegal occupation and permitting gaming equipment on the premises. Prosecution probably would have resulted in probation or a relatively light fine. When he refused a felony warrant, the assistant prosecutor stated that, "because of the caliber of the men involved, the complaint should be for a misdemeanor." All the suspects pleaded guilty to disorderly conduct and were fined $10 and $4.30 costs.

3. *Sex offenders.*

> *Illustration No. 3:* The suspect was clearly guilty of sodomy. He had twice before been charged with sodomy but each time the charge was reduced to disorderly conduct. The assistant prosecutor refused to issue a warrant for sodomy and instead issued one for disorderly conduct.

In Wisconsin, offenses which technically constitute adultery are normally prosecuted on a charge of disorderly conduct. In Detroit, a statutory rape against a promiscuous and obviously willing victim who in physical appearance seems to be older than the statutory age is quite likely to be prosecuted as a common assault. With these and similar cases, it is difficult to determine whether the less serious offense is charged to avoid undue collateral harm, punishment harm, or both. Prosecution for offenses against morality may result in severe injury to the defendant's reputation, while a conviction creates a more harmful criminal record than is true of offenses of other types. Also, some judges may regard these offenses as particularly serious and impose quite severe sentences.

It seems clear in Illustration No. 3 that the less serious offense was charged to avoid the unnecessary collateral harm evolving from a record of a sodomy conviction. The suspect had committed the offense twice before, so it seems unlikely that the assistant prosecutor would consider the punishment harm as too severe for the conduct. Nevertheless, the stigma attached to a conviction for sodomy is considerable. The police officer who investigated the case indicated that the suspect's attorney had approached him and attempted to persuade him to request a warrant for disorderly conduct, stressing the detrimental effects of a record of a sodomy conviction; this plea was apparently successful.[2]

B. The Decision to Charge a Less Serious Offense to Avoid Undue Punishment Harm

1. *To avoid a statutory mandatory minimum sentence.*

Illustration No. 4: A woman with no previous criminal record was arrested for forging a $10 check. The assistant prosecutor decided to charge her with issuing a bogus check rather than with forgery.

Illustration No. 5: A 22-year-old narcotics addict had sold a few capsules of heroin to another addict. The assistant decided to charge the suspect, who had never been convicted of possession or sale, with possession of narcotics rather than with their sale, since the latter charge is nonprobationable and carries a twenty-year minimum sentence.

In Illustration No. 4, the maximum offense would have been forgery, which carries a mandatory minimum sentence of one year[3] in Wisconsin unless probation is granted. The assistant prosecutor stated that the judge, who feels that this sentence is much too severe, had instructed him that the charge should be reduced to bogus check issuance whenever the suspect is a first offender and the amount of the check is small. Under the reduced charge the judge can sentence the suspect up to one year in the local jail.

In Illustration No. 5 the maximum offense would have been sale of narcotics, carrying a statutory mandatory minimum sentence of twenty years. The judges of Detroit Recorder's Court, the assistant prosecutors, and some members of the police department feel that imposing the mandatory minimum is unwarranted in certain sale cases. The policy is to reduce the charge from sale to possession, or addiction, on the basis of the presence of some or all of these factors: (1) the suspect (an addict) was apprehended while selling a small quantity of narcotics

[2] A concern for the collateral harm involved in this case — the stigma attached to the particular violation — underlies decisions categorized in the other illustrations in this chapter. In each situation, the maximum — in one case, contributing to the delinquency of a minor and in the other, illegal occupation — carries overtones of sexual misconduct particularly harmful under these particular circumstances.

[3] See Wis. Stat. §343.56 (1951). This mandatory minimum is no longer in effect. Wis. Stat. Ann. §943.38 (1958).

to another addict (an accommodation sale); (2) the suspect has no prior record or arrest or convictions for narcotics violations; (3) the suspect has only recently become addicted to narcotics; and (4) the suspect is willing to cooperate with the police in identifying his source of supply.[4]

2. *To increase the probability of probation.*

Illustration No. 6: The suspect had suffered a financial setback and was having difficulty feeding his family. He was apprehended in a grocery store under such circumstances that the maximum charge would be breaking and entering in the nighttime, a nonprobationable offense. The assistant prosecutor refused to charge that offense and instead charged breaking and entering in the daytime, a probationable offense.

Illustration No. 7: The suspect had stolen $250 from his employer under such circumstances that the maximum charge would be larceny of that amount. He turned himself in to his employer, who contacted the police. A warrant was issued charging him with larceny of $93. The assistant prosecutor reminded the suspect that he still had to make restitution for $250.

In Illustration No. 6 the maximum offense, breaking and entering in the nighttime, was under Michigan law an offense for which the defendant could not be placed on probation.[5] When the defendant was apprehended in the grocery store, it was apparent to the police that he was not after money but was attempting to steal food supplies and, indeed, he was seen eating some of the items he had just taken from the shelves. The charge was reduced to breaking and entering in the daytime, even though the occurrence was late at night, so the defendant would be eligible for probation.

In Illustration No. 7, the maximum offense was grand larceny, a probationable offense. Since an amount over $100 had been taken, the case would go to a particular judge who would refuse probation because the suspect was a second offender. A warrant

[4] See Chapter 17. Another factor is the knowledge that a jury trial is necessary if a conviction for sale of narcotics is to be sought, and that even then, conviction is difficult.

A similar situation prevails in Wisconsin, where the offense of possession of obscene literature carries a mandatory minimum sentence of one year. If the suspect is willing to inform the police of his source of supply, the charge is normally reduced to disorderly conduct.

[5] Mich. Stat. Ann. §28.1131 (1954). This is no longer true. See Mich. Stat. Ann. §28.1131 (Supp. 1968).

was issued for larceny of $93 which, as a lesser offense, would place the case in the court of another judge who, it was believed, would be quite likely to place the defendant on probation.

3. *To increase the probability of a more lenient sentence generally*. Under Michigan law, a person who steals something worth less than $50 from a building, such as a shoplifter would commonly do, can be charged with larceny from a building or with petty larceny. The former is a felony, the latter, a misdemeanor. Although there is no mandatory minimum sentence for either offense, and although probation is available for either offense, the police and prosecutor use sentencing considerations in their decision to charge under one statute or the other. If the suspect has no prior record, he will be charged with petty larceny. If he has a record, or is the type of suspect who has given the police or prosecutor trouble, or if they suspect him of committing several crimes which they cannot prove he committed, he is charged with larceny from a building.

CHAPTER 14

The Decision Not to Charge Because Alternative Procedures Provide Adequate Incarceration Potential

An important exercise of charging discretion occurs when a prosecutor decides to accomplish the incarceration of the defendant by means other than the normal sequence of prosecution, adjudication, and sentencing. In current practice, this decision is made in four major situations: the civil commitment of insane criminal defendants, the civil or criminal commitment of so-called sex psychopaths, the revocation of the probation or parole of a person suspected of committing a new offense, and the release of a suspect to another jurisdiction for prosecution or revocation of conditional liberty.

Although these four alternatives to prosecution differ among themselves in significant ways, they have one important feature in common. At the time the decision is made whether to prosecute the suspect in the normal fashion or to use one of the four alternatives to prosecution, it is a virtual certainty that the suspect will be incarcerated no matter which way the decision goes and that the incarceration will be relatively lengthy. Indeed, an important consideration in the decision is whether the available alternative is adequate in terms of the length of incarceration permissible by its use. If the length of incarceration permissible through use of the alternative seems to the prosecutor to be inadequate, he may prosecute the suspect in the normal fashion. If it seems adequate, the prosecutor is likely to use the alternative for several reasons. In some situations, the use of the alternative effects a savings in expenditure of enforcement resources. This seems to be a major consideration in the decision to seek revocation of probation or parole in lieu of prosecution and in the decision to release the suspect to another jurisdiction for prosecution or revocation of conditional liberty.

In other situations, the resource savings factor does not seem as important. In the decision to seek civil commitment of an insane criminal defendant, and in the decision to seek commitment of sex psychopaths, there is the feeling that the alternative to prosecution is better in terms of achieving treatment objectives. Rehabilitation is more likely when the alternative is used. In the sex psychopath situation, there is the added factor that the incarceration length provided for under the criminal law may be regarded as inadequate for purposes of protecting society from recidivism.

A. Insanity Commitments

A belief on the part of legislators that arrested persons with a suspected mental disease or disorder should be handled separately and differently from normal offenders has led to the enactment of statutes[1] that delineate alternatives to the normal charging procedure. These statutes provide that such an offender should be channeled out of the usual charging-adjudication process into a noncriminal system for treatment and rehabilitation.

In all three states, the question of the defendant's insanity at the time of the criminal offense may be raised at his trial for the substantive offense,[2] at which time the court will apply the legal standards by which it is directed to evaluate possibly insane behavior. The statutes direct that examinations shall be made of any defendant who is allegedly insane, a hearing held on the results of these tests and observations, and, possibly, a jury empanelled if requested by the defendant.[3] These procedures do not allow for exercise of the prosecutor's discretion, since the defendant has

1 Kan. Stat. Ann. §§59-2001 to 59-2008, 59-2271 to 59-2276a, 62-1531 to 62-1532 (1964); Mich. Stat. Ann. §§28.966(11) to 28.966 (12) (Supp. 1968); Wis. Stat. Ann. §§51.001 to 51.50, 957.13 (Supp. 1968).

2 Kan. Stat. Ann. §§62-1531 to 62-1532 (1964); Wis. Stat. Ann. §957.13 (Supp. 1968); Mich. Stat. Ann. §28.966(11) (Supp. 1968).

3 Kansas law clearly indicates that a jury determination of insanity at the time of the commission of the offense is a matter of right. See Kan. Stat. Ann. §§62-1531 to 62-1532 (1964). See also State v. Cox, 191 Kan. 326, 328, 380 P.2d 316, 317 (1963), *vacated,* 376 U.S. 191 (1964); State v. Latham, 190 Kan. 411, 428, 375 P.2d 788, 801 (1962); State v. Hickock and Smith, 188 Kan. 473, 481, 363 P.2d 541, 547 (1961). In Wisconsin, though the defendant has waived his right to a jury trial on the basic question of his guilt or innocence of the substantive offense, he may request the selection of a special jury to hear the insanity issues. Wis. Stat. Ann. §§51.03, 957.13, (1958).

been formally charged and is being tried in the usual fashion, and the prosecuting attorney, in opposing the insanity plea,[4] is merely fulfilling his role as an adversary, the proponent of the state's case. However, if the defendant is allegedly suffering from some mental disease at the time of arrest, charging, or arraignment, the prosecutor's decision whether to institute commitment proceedings is likely to be the most important event in the case, since it determines the course of subsequent treatment of the suspect.

Illustration No. 1: One of the assistant prosecutors received a police request for a warrant against a woman who had seriously beaten her infant child. She had admitted the act and attributed her loss of control to the fact that the three-month-old child would not drink his milk. At the time of arrest, the woman was hysterical and thought the child dead; however, by the time the warrant was requested, it had been determined that the child would recover. The assistant contacted the family physician to obtain the suspect's medical history and requested the psychopathic clinic to make a preliminary examination of the woman to determine if there was a sufficient basis for filing an insanity petition.

Illustration No. 2: A defense attorney whose client had just been arrested by the police contacted an assistant prosecuting attorney with regard to the issuance of an insanity petition. The lawyer had sufficient doubts about his client's sanity to seek commitment but was not absolutely sure that the subsequent examination would reveal a mental disease, so he desired this request for action on the part of the assistant to avoid embarrassment if the suspect were declared sane.

Illustration No. 3: The defendant was arraigned on an information charged with armed robbery and carrying a concealed weapon. When informed of the charges against him and requested to plead, he seemed rather oblivious to the whole situation. He stared at the foot of the judge's bench, grunted inaudible expressions to questions propounded to him by the judge, and had a general demeanor and appear-

4 One might conclude that there is little if any judicial discretion at this stage either, because the language of the statutes is mandatory rather than permissive. For example, if the defendant is not committed by the judge during the trial after a special hearing has been held on the question of sanity, then the Kansas directive (Kan. Stat. Ann. §62-1532 [1964]) is for automatic commitment upon a verdict of not guilty by reason of insanity.

ance of not being aware of the world around him. Since the defendant was obviously of unsound mind, the only order entered was one referring the defendant to the psychiatric clinic for an examination. The judge then notified the prosecutor's office of this action and requested that the assistant who handled such cases prepare and submit an insanity petition.

When the issue of the defendant's *present* sanity is faced by the prosecuting attorney at the time the usual warrant decision would be made, this charging decision, whether negative or positive, will be accompanied by some other positive action designed to insure that the defendant's mental condition will be expertly ascertained. The information necessary for making this decision — generally derived from first-hand observations of the defendant's behavior — is gathered into the prosecutor's office[5] through reports from (1) investigating or arresting police officers,[6] which are made available to the assistant prosecutor when the warrant decision would typically be made, and (2) defense counsel, mentioning unusual conduct of the suspect.

If the prosecutor determines, after a warrant has been issued, that an alternative to prosecution should be used, his decision will be manifested by a suspension of the criminal proceedings or an entry of a *nolle prosequi* along with formal institution of alternative proceedings. Although the information on which this decision will rest is normally provided by the investigating policeman or prosecutors, the issue may also be raised, at this stage, by a complaint regarding the defendant's courtroom behavior from a judge who had conducted the initial appearance, preliminary examination, or arraignment.

Though the sources of the factual basis of the prosecutor's decision to seek commitment of the suspect before trial are similar in the three states, the procedures for such commitment vary. In

[5] The Detroit situation is typical: all cases of suspected insanity are referred to one assistant prosecuting attorney, who is solely responsible for the initiation of commitment proceedings, though he may not select the specific charge to be included in the warrant. See notes 21 through 23 *infra*.

[6] The assistant prosecutor in Detroit with the responsibility for reviewing such cases and filing insanity petitions stated that the police, though they may wish to see the defendant incarcerated rather than committed, have been cooperative in revealing all the facts of the arrest situation and the defendant's accompanying behavior. This assistant "harps" at them, trying to impress on them that part of a detective's job is to see that mental incompetents and persons suffering from mental disorders are treated and processed through the courts in a manner in keeping with the theme of the statutes which tend to define such persons as sick rather than criminal.

Kansas and Wisconsin, the prosecuting attorney, having failed to charge or having dismissed the charges, will utilize the procedures for civil commitment of any person suspected of dangerous insanity.[7] Thus, he will assume the role of the "reputable citizen" required by statute[8] in filing the petition vesting the probate court with jurisdiction in the case. It is clear that the prosecutor will not refuse to charge or dismiss charges already filed unless he is reasonably certain that the defendant does indeed have some mental problem of the degree to require commitment; a preliminary mental examination of the suspect in his jail cell is not uncommon.

In Michigan, the prosecuting attorney is not free to refuse to issue a warrant or enter a *nolle prosequi*. Under the statute,[9] he *must* charge the suspect before petitioning the district court[10] for a hearing to determine the defendant's sanity.[11] Criminal proceedings are then suspended until a verdict is reached concerning the defendant's competency to stand trial.[12] The ultimate

7 Kan. Stat. Ann. §§150-2202, 150-2203, 150-2005 (1964); Wis. Stat. Ann. §§51.01(1), 51.02, 51.03, 51.05 (Supp. 1968).

8 Kan. Stat. Ann. §59-2271 (1964). Wis. Stat. Ann. §51.01 (1958) requires "at least 3 adult residents of the state, one of whom must be a person with whom the patient resides, or at whose home he may be or . . . (a close relative or) the sheriff or a police officer or public welfare or health officer."

9 Mich. Stat. Ann. §28.966(11) (Supp. 1968).

10 Such a petition contains: (1) a request that two doctors and one psychiatrist be named as a sanity commission; (2) the facts and circumstances of the case; and (3) a court order appointing the three physicians, which is ready for the judge's signature.

11 The precise issue at this hearing is stated explicitly in the insanity petition filed with the court: "This petition is filed in order to determine whether or not at this time the defendant is capable of understanding the nature and object of the proceedings against him, and of comprehending his own condition in reference to such proceedings of assisting in his defense in a rational and reasonable manner . . . ." In one case which had received considerable notoriety, the court had appointed three psychiatrists, rather than just one and two general practitioners as was the normal procedure, because the judge did not wish to have any public criticism over the verdict. The final order was phrased thus "The findings of the court were that the defendant was psychotic, unable to comprehend or understand her position in the case with relation to the charges filed against her and she was of sufficient mental deterioration that she could not assist her counsel in conducting her defense. The defendant is insane within the meaning of (the statutes) . . . and was committed . . . until such time as she is cured of her mental illness so as to no longer be a danger to society."

If the Michigan suspect is adjudged sane, the prosecuting attorney will apparently reconsider his warrant decision and possibly redetermine the charge, since in large measure a warrant was only issued to invoke Mich. Stat. Ann. §28.967 (1954), repealed by Mich. Pub. Acts 1966, No. 266, which read, "When a person accused of any felony shall *appear* to be insane . . . ." (Emphasis added.)

12 While held in courts of different jurisdiction in the three states, insanity proceedings follow a common pattern; notification of the defendant, appointment of

responsibility is upon the prosecuting attorney if the alternative to prosecution, whatever it may be, is to be invoked before trial. The standard used is the defendant's capacity to stand trial, to assist his counsel in his own defense.

In contrast, if the issue of the defendant's present sanity is raised at his trial, the role of the prosecutor is of less importance. Because the statutes[13] require an examination to be ordered by and the subsequent hearing held before the trial judge, the civil commitment proceedings are not used in Kansas and Wisconsin; in Michigan, the prosecutor files the same petition with the district judge, invoking the mental health act provisions. The actions of the prosecutor, raising a new issue to be determined by the court, will not affect the court's jurisdiction over the defendant.

B. Sex-Deviate Commitments

In most states, there are statutory provisions for handling criminal defendants differently when they have been diagnosed as suffering from a mental disorder that leads them to commit sex-motivated offenses. These sex-deviate or sex-psychopath provisions vary significantly from state to state, but they have two major features in common: the period of potential incarceration is increased by use of the provisions and there is more emphasis on treatment of persons committed under these provisions than of criminal defendants sentenced under the criminal code. Kansas, Michigan, and Wisconsin all have sex-deviate statutes.[14] In Kansas and Michigan, the statutes provide for a completely indeterminate civil commitment to the state mental hospital system; in Wisconsin the statute provides for a criminal commit-

a commission to examine him, and subsequent hearing on the commission's findings, which hearing may or may not take on the attributes of a full-blown trial with the introduction of expert and lay witnesses, presence of counsel, and the adjudication of sanity by a jury. One Detroit psychiatrist on the staff of the state psychopathic clinic indicated that the more informed and educated a judge, the more psychiatrists he would appoint to the sanity commission. Mich. Stat. Ann. §28.966(11) (Supp. 1968); Kan. Stat. Ann. §62-1531 (1964); Wis. Stat. Ann. §§51.01, 51.02 (Supp. 1968).

13 Kan. Stat. Ann. §§62-1531 to 62-1532 (1964); Wis. Stat. Ann. §957.13 (Supp. 1968); Mich. Stat. Ann. §28.967 (1954).

14 Kan. Stat. Ann. §§62-1534 to 62-1537 (1964); Wis. Stat. Ann. §959.15 (1958); Mich. Stat. Ann. §§28.967(1) to 28.967(9) (1954). See 38 Mich. L. Rev. 1316 n.2 (1940) where it is stated: "These statutes are not criminal in their nature. They are designed in scope and purpose to protect the public from sex offenders. Though such statutes are included under different titles in the statute books, they all aim at the correction or segregation of sexually delinquent persons." See Annot., 24 A.L.R.2d 350, 353 (1952).

ment for the maximum term permitted for the offense of which the defendant was convicted with the addition of an unlimited number of court-ordered five-year extensions. The statutes in the three states vary significantly in their effect on the charging decision. In Kansas and Wisconsin, the sex-deviate statute can be invoked only when the defendant has been convicted of certain specified offenses. Charging is involved in these states only to the extent the charge may be manipulated to bring the defendant within or without the statutory category of offenses that permits invocation of the provisions. In Michigan, the statute may be invoked prior to adjudication; if a sex-deviate commitment follows invocation the charge will be dismissed without conviction. Clearly in Michigan, at least, the sex-deviate procedure must be regarded as an alternative to prosecution.

> *Illustration No. 4:* The defendant was tried in common pleas court on a charge of "committing an open and notorious act of public indecency, grossly scandalous," a misdemeanor. After he had pleaded guilty and a probation officer had submitted a presentence report which indicated that the defendant might be a good probation risk, the prosecutor reminded the judge that there had been a reduction from the original charge of sodomy and moved that the defendant be committed to a state mental hospital for a ninety-day examination; this was ordered by the judge. At the completion of the examination, the judge followed the recommendation of the psychiatrist, put the defendant on probation, and imposed those conditions suggested by the doctor.

In Kansas, the statute authorizes examination and determination of the defendant's mental condition only upon conviction "for any offense against public morals and decency, as relating to crimes pertaining to sex. . . ."[15] The suspect is charged with and tried for the sex offense; upon conviction, the prosecuting attorney,[16] when convinced of the existence of some significant psychiatric problem, will request deferment of the imposition of sentence until an examination has been conducted and a hearing held on the report.

> *Illustration No. 5:* A twenty-year-old man was charged with the forcible rape of a fifteen-year-old girl. Although he

15 Kan. Stat. Ann. §62-1534 (1964).

16 Kan. Stat. Ann. §62-1534 (1964). Though other persons are free to request such a deferment of the imposition of sentence, the motion normally comes from the prosecutor.

normally would have been charged with statutory rape, under these facts, the forcible rape charge was selected so that, upon conviction, the sex-deviate law would have to be used.

Illustration No. 6: The defendant and another had committed larceny of the person of two individuals. When they were apprehended and the defendant's car searched, the police found a gunny sack containing numerous lewd pictures. Defendant was charged with and convicted of the possession of obscene literature. Since this is not one of the offenses for which examination is mandatory, the prosecutor had to request such examination. The judge agreed because the defendant had a history of sexual maladjustment.

The Wisconsin statute[17] provides that upon conviction for named crimes (forcible rape, sexual intercourse without consent, indecent behavior with a child)[18] an examination shall be held; for other sex-motivated crimes this procedure is optional. Thus, if the prosecuting attorney feels that the suspect is so sexually deviant as to require commitment, he may seek to specify in the warrant a charge that will require the judge to order the mental examination; this is the situation presented in Illustration No. 5. Another way in which the charging decision may be influenced by the provisions of the sex-deviancy statute appears in Illustration No. 6, where the prosecutor had the choice of charging larceny from the person, possession of obscene literature, or both. Because of the defendant's history of sex abnormality, he chose to charge possession of obscene literature, since that would permit invocation of the sex-deviancy provisions.

The defendant convicted of an offense that makes invocation of the sex-deviate statute mandatory or discretionary will be committed to the State Department of Public Welfare for psychiatric examination if invocation of the statute is sought. If the psychiatric report determines that the defendant is deviated and in need of treatment, the trial judge has the option of committing him to the State Department of Public Welfare for the maximum term permitted for the offense of which he was con-

17 Wis. Stat. Ann. §959.15 (1958).

18 The 1951 Act provided that persons convicted of statutory rape (carnal knowledge and abuse) shall be committed for a presentence examination to the state mental health department. Law of July 6, 1951, c. 542, §2, [1951] Wis. Laws 401. However, a recognition that a large number of such cases did not involve deviancy led the 1953 Legislature to amend the act and delete statutory rape from the enumerated crimes for which examination is mandatory. Law of April 24, 1953, c. 85, [1953] Wis. Laws 58. Now the trial judge has discretion, upon a statutory rape conviction, to order the investigation.

victed, subject to unlimited five-year extensions, or of placing him on probation on the condition that "he receive outpatient or inpatient treatment. . . ."[19] If the psychiatric examination results in a finding that the defendant is not deviant and not in need of treatment, the judge may make any disposition of the case permitted for the offense of which the defendant was convicted.

> *Illustration No. 7:* The defendant was charged with assault and battery after having molested the complainant in a movie. He pleaded guilty at his initial appearance, was placed on bond, and waived preliminary examination but failed to appear for his arraignment. After extradition from a neighboring state, an assistant prosecutor filed a petition for a Goodrich hearing. He indicated that the defendant's long criminal record of similar conduct with middle-aged women was considered sufficient to establish the necessary criminal sexual intent.

The procedure provided for by the Michigan statute[20] is quite different from that found in Kansas and Wisconsin, since the arrestee suspected of sex deviation is to be examined before trial and, upon determination of a mental disorder, completely removed from further routine criminal proceedings.

The assistant prosecuting attorney who handled the initiation of proceedings under the Goodrich Act will both request a regular warrant[21] and file a petition[22] to the trial court judge requesting the appointment of a "Goodrich commission."[23] Within fifteen days after he is notified that the court has set a date for his

19 Wis. Stat. Ann. §959.15(6) (Supp. 1968).

20 Mich. Stat. Ann. §§28.967(1) to 28.967(9) (1954). This statute is known as the "Goodrich Act," and other procedures are referred to as a "Goodrich commission" or a "Goodrich hearing." The law was held to be constitutional, as "a valid and proper exercise of State police power as a measure of public safety," in People v. Chapman, 301 Mich. 584, 608, 4 N.W.2d 18, 28 (1942).

21 Although commitment proceedings can be initiated at any time in the regular criminal process prior to the imposition of sentence, every effort is made to decide the propriety of invoking the act at the initiation of prosecution. An early determination is thought desirable because it not only conserves system resources but also permits earlier commencement of treatment of the suspect.

22 The petition reads in part: "The defendant is a person who is suffering from a mental disorder and is not feeble-minded, which mental disorder has existed for a period of not less than four months and is coupled with criminal propensities to the commission of sex offenses." After a presentation of the facts of the present offense and the past criminal history of the suspect, the petition will close: "Wherefore, your petitioner prays that this honorable court will appoint the commission herein requested." The Michigan Supreme Court, in People v. Artinian, 320 Mich. 441, 445, 31 N.W.2d 688, 689 (1948), ruled that the petition must state such facts fully or else be considered fatally defective

23 The commission consists of three psychiatrists who are to be qualified by at least five years of exclusive practice in psychiatric diagnosis.

hearing, the defendant may request a jury verdict at the hearing on the precise issue of his sexual deviation.[24] If the trier of fact determines by a preponderance of the evidence that the suspect does come within the provisions of the act, he is committed to a mental institution for an indefinite period of time.[25] After he has been ordered committed, he may not be subsequently tried for the substantive offense specified in the warrant. Great care is exercised in making the decision to invoke the act, because the provision for indefinite commitment may amount to a life sentence despite the amendment to the act[26] that provides for release upon a showing that the person is sufficiently recovered so that he is no longer a menace to others. One result of this caution is a very high commitment rate in Goodrich cases compared to the numbers of petitions filed.

The information necessary to make the decision to invoke the sex psychopath law is gathered from reports submitted to the assistant prosecuting attorney by the investigating or arresting policeman, another assistant prosecutor who had previously reviewed the case, the defense counsel, or the trial judge. The overall behavior of the suspect is evaluated. Thus, if the prosecutor believes that the defendant is deviant to the point of insanity, he will, in Kansas and Wisconsin, either decline to issue a warrant or move to dismiss charges already filed and then invoke civil commitment proceedings. The Michigan prosecutor, on reaching the same conclusion, will charge in the usual fashion and then petition for an insanity commitment.

If the suspect is believed to be sane, other criteria are used in judging his conduct. Factors such as a past record of sex-related offenses,[27] the relative ages of the offender and his victim, the

24 In Simon v. Craft, 182 U.S. 427, 437, 21 Sup. Ct. 836, 840, 45 L. Ed. 1165, 1171 (1901), the Supreme Court indicated that a failure to accord the defendant a jury trial would not be a denial of due process of law.

25 It has been held that since a Goodrich hearing is not a criminal proceeding, the commitment order cannot be equated with a sentence. People v. Piasecki, 333 Mich. 122, 147, 52 N.W.2d 626, 631 (1952).

26 Mich. Stat. Ann. §28.967(7) (1954).

27 The sex psychopath laws are usually invoked only when the suspect has a prior conviction for a sex-motivated offense. If possible, the details of the prior offenses are obtained, for the offense charged does not necessarily reveal the presence of sexual motivation. For example, many types of sexual activity may be charged as mere "disorderly conduct." Occasionally, instances arise in which the act will be invoked despite the lack of prior convictions for sex-motivated crimes. Thus, when it is evident that the defendant has engaged in a pattern of sexual misconduct of a deviant nature but has not been prosecuted because of reluctance of the persons concerned to press charges, the defendant may be prosecuted under the act if the victims are then willing to testify in the proceedings.

aggravated nature of the offense, and the presence of any mitigating circumstances are all weighed by the prosecutor before turning to the sex-deviate law. Two additional criteria are prescribed by the Michigan statute: the prosecuting attorney must also determine that the defendant is not feeble-minded[28] and that he has suffered from this mental disorder (deviation) for at least four months.[29]

C. Revocation of Probation or Parole

The procedures for handling insane persons and sexual psychopaths, as discussed previously in this chapter, are authorized and regulated by statutory provisions, but no such formal law exists to guide the prosecuting attorney in his processing of cases involving renewed criminal conduct of probationers and parolees. Therefore, any alternative to charging and prosecuting persons in this category is strictly informal, though quite regularized; the alternative developed and used by many prosecutors is to request a revocation of the probation or parole of the suspect.

The statutes of Kansas, Wisconsin, and Michigan vary with respect to whether probation or parole is violated by a new criminal offense, and, if so, how the alleged violator should be handled. The Kansas statutes in effect when the survey was conducted[30] indicated in express terms that the commission of

[28] When the reports of the police or others having personal contact with the defendant indicate only borderline feeble-mindedness, the assistant allows the case to follow the normal prosecution channels because another evaluative report will be made as part of the normal presentence investigation. Then, if the judge feels it necessary, the Goodrich Act could be invoked after conviction but before sentencing.

[29] The statute requires both that the mental condition be shown to have existed four months prior to the action and that it is "coupled with criminal propensities to the commission of sex offenses." Even though there is no requirement of prior conviction for sex offenses, the assistant prosecutor expressed the opinion that proof of prior convictions of sex offenses is usually the only way in which the burden of proof on those issues could be met. The duration of the mental disorder can be established by the use of the previous sex offense conviction.

[30] The Kansas parole and probation service, when the pilot project survey was conducted, operated under Kan. Gen. Stat. Ann. §62-2201 to 62-2214 (1949) (parole/probation/granted by a court); §§62-2215 to 62-2222 (parole granted by the governor); and §§62-1522 to 62-1531 (parole granted by the prison board) (1964). As the survey reports indicate, the vagueness of the statutory language was reflected in the ambiguous use of the term "parole" by judges and probation officers, so that it might mean suspension of sentence in one situation and a conditional release from prison in another. Some of the difficulties of a poorly organized and administered system were resolved by the repeal of these provisions (L. 1957, c. 331, §37, July 1) and the passage of a comprehensive new statute, Kan. Stat. Ann. §§62-2226 to 62-2255 (1964). §62-2227 provides definitions sufficient to eliminate the prior

a new offense would be sufficient to constitute a violation of probation or parole. The statutes presently in force[31] do not state this explicitly, but the policy of the Kansas Probation and Parole Department in treating a new crime as a violation has continued. This same policy prevails in Wisconsin,[32] where the statutes[33] do not include a new offense among those violations that justify a revocation. The statutes in Michigan[34] are clearer, since one requirement of probation or parole is that the prisoner not violate any state criminal law.

Regardless of the exact language of the governing statute, once the attention of the prosecuting attorney is brought to the commission of a new criminal offense by a probationer or parolee,[35] he may, at his option, (1) request the revocation of the conditional liberty by the parole board or the sentencing judge, or (2) prosecute the suspect in the normal fashion. The formal alternative is extensively used in Wisconsin and Kansas; one assistant prosecutor in the latter state mentioned that parole revocation is often used as a penalty for a new crime, or a substitute therefore, if the new crime is not of greater magnitude than the previous one.

---

ambiguity, and provisions for retaking prisoners upon a violation of probation and parole are to be found in §62-2244 and §62-2250, respectively.

31 Kan. Stat. Ann. §62-1528 (1964) (parole). Kan. Stat. Ann. §62-2244 (1964) (probation).

32 The district supervisor of the parole office for Milwaukee County indicated that, as a matter of policy, a conviction of a new felony constitutes automatic revocation of parole, although there might be exceptions to this rule where courts, in handling such cases, might want to place a man on probation and the department would go along with the court and not revoke parole.

33 Wis. Stat. Ann. §§57.01 (probation), 57.06 (parole) (1957). A typical parole agreement as drawn up by the state parole and probation department will read in part:

"PROBATION AND PAROLE AGREEMENT

"In consideration of Probation or Parole being granted to me, I agree to the following:

"1. I will make a sincere attempt to avoid all acts which are forbidden by law and contrary to public welfare or my own best interests. . . ."

34 Mich. Stat. Ann. §28.1133 (Supp. 1968) (probation); Mich. Stat. Ann. §28.2308 (1954) (parole).

35 In Michigan, the Identification Bureau of the Detroit Police Department maintains a record of all persons paroled from the various penal institutions in the state. When a paroled prisoner is taken into custody, the officer in charge is required to notify the Michigan State Parole Department immediately. In booking a parolee for a violation of parole, the arresting officer is required to follow that procedure which would be used in the booking of a prisoner for the offense for which the individual was sentenced and is presently on parole. In all cases in which a defendant is placed on probation, the officer who brought the case into court is required to establish contact with the probation department, and this procedure is noted on the request for a warrant that is submitted to the prosecutor's office.

Illustration No. 8: The previous year the defendant had been sentenced to the state prison for a period not to exceed ten years on a charge of burglary in the second degree, then placed on probation. This man thereupon committed, and admitted, six burglaries and larcenies. Upon proof of these, his probation had been revoked, but was reinstated the same day. Since that time, he had participated in six other burglaries and larcenies from which he gained mainly cigarettes and beer. The county attorney explained that just one of these offenses would have been sufficient to revoke the probation, but this man had committed a total of twelve felonies; a revocation was formally requested and granted.

If the request for revocation of parole or initiation of probation revocation proceedings in court by a supervising officer is made to the probation and parole department, the practical result is that control over the suspected violator is also relinquished,[36] although he may remain in custody until some final disposition of his case is made. If the request is made to the trial judge[37] for revocation of probation, neither custody nor jurisdiction is surrendered since, if the revocation request is denied, the process of prosecution will resume.

It is possible to identify the criteria and influences weighed by the prosecuting attorney in making his decision to request revocation of parole or probation or to proceed with prosecution. Possibly the most important of these is a desire to conserve system resources. As one assistant prosecutor mentioned, the institution of revocation proceedings not only saves the state or county the expense of a new trial but also serves the same purpose as a new trial on the second offense, since the offender is, in any event, at

[36] In one reported case, a parolee was arrested after selling heroin to a police undercover agent, whereupon a warrant was issued and the parolee detained overnight in jail. His parole officer was notified and a "hold" placed for the division of paroles; the next day bail was set at his initial appearance. The police discussed the possibility of releasing the suspect in order for him to cooperate in making a case against his reported New York connection. The parole officer stated that it was impossible for him personally to order a release of a man wanted for violation. Apparently the parole division supervisor's express approval was needed to permit physical disposition of this accused violator.

[37] A Kansas judge stated that one of the major problems he encounters in deciding whether probation should be revoked is the constant requests by police officers, the county attorney's office, and the FBI to have probation revoked on a person suspected of a crime. He said that he absolutely and positively refused to revoke probation merely because a law enforcement officer or a prosecutor suspected the probationer of having committed an offense. He continued that when there is tangible proof, the type which would bring about a guilty verdict in a jury trial, then it was a horse of a different color and he would probably revoke.

least incarcerated for the period for which he was originally sentenced. The prosecuting attorney's attitudes and practices are likely to vary as he deals with different classes of offenders — for example, one Wisconsin police officer complained that the local prosecutor's office was too lenient with juveniles, preferring to permit them to commit many violations before taking any action to invoke the criminal justice process. He cited one case of a seventeen-year-old youth with a juvenile record, presently on parole from the state reformatory, who was arrested for burglary. Following the general procedure, the police had simply turned him over to the supervising parole office in at least four instances, with nothing having been done until the subject was arrested on the most recent charge of burglary.

> *Illustration No. 9:* A man presently on probation for nonsupport of his family was charged with the statutory rape of his thirteen-year-old stepdaughter, who had become pregnant. Even though there was a family history of illegitimacy, this was considered a flagrant sexual offense. The arresting sheriff stated that he was going to request that a charge be brought against this man, rather than simply having his probation revoked. He explained that, if the probation were revoked, the man could serve a short period (for nonsupport) and get out from under both raps. A new charge would impose a definite prison sentence for this new offense.

A third consideration is police attitude; in some cases the decision to charge or utilize revocation, while made by the prosecutor, is directly influenced by police requests. This practice of declining to charge the suspect is also found in Michigan, but the prosecutors there are more apt to proceed with the prosecution of the probationers and, less frequently, parolees suspected of criminal activity, even though a suspended sentence will often be recommended so as to permit the probation and parole department, after conviction, to dispose of the case according to its own standards and policies.

> *Illustration No. 10:* The defendant had been convicted of breaking and entering a motor vehicle. On the strength of a presentence report, which revealed that at times in the past he had used narcotics but was presently abstaining, he was placed on probation and ordered to pay court costs and make restitution to the owner of the automobile. As time progressed, it became apparent that the probationer had reverted to the use of heroin and had no intention of

paying the costs assessed against him as a condition of his probation. Upon pleading guilty to a new charge of petty larceny, he was again placed on probation and the case referred to the probation division. The request by this division for revocation of the probation was honored by the judge who had originally granted probation to the defendant.

The effect of this practice is to place responsibility for the disposition of such a case in the hands of the sentencing judge, rather than the prosecuting attorney. Though this decision to request a revocation of the conditional liberty or to continue the criminal justice process against the accused is thus made at a different stage in the process, by a different participant, the results in Michigan are likely to be similar to those in Kansas and Wisconsin, where the prosecutor makes the effective determination, since a sufficiently serious new criminal offense will almost inevitably result in a revocation.

D. Release to Another Jurisdiction

Those alternatives to the normal charging-prosecution procedure which are used by a prosecuting attorney in handling cases in which the accused has committed a crime in another jurisdiction are, like those used in cases involving probationers and parolees, unauthorized in formal law. This decision to charge or to release the suspect to another authority will differ according to the nature of and relations between the two jurisdictions. Three situations are of importance in current administration: release to another jurisdiction within the same state, release to another state, and release to the federal government.

If the suspect is wanted for a criminal offense in one or more other subjurisdictions of the same state,[38] the authority which first apprehends him will normally prosecute if all else is equal. If the charge is much more serious or the evidence more convincing elsewhere, the prosecutor's office is likely to suggest delivering the defendant to the jurisdiction with the best case. When there is a possibility of relinquishing custody and jurisdiction to a municipality, rather than pressing charges on the state level, other factors may be considered — the age of the suspect,

[38] Although the FBI acts as a clearing house for many such offenses, when the different authorities are from subjurisdictions of the same state, it is most probable that information is gathered by circular, letter, or phone.

his prior criminal record, and the relationship between the suspect and complainant-victim.[39] In any case, the delivery of the suspect and any relevant evidence can usually be effectuated, and no problems of the availability and admissibility of testimony from officers of different localities should arise. In the event of a lack of cooperation between these subjurisdictions, however, serious problems concerning reciprocal use of facilities and manpower can and do arise.[40]

If the suspect is named in a criminal warrant issued in another state, the prosecuting attorney may be forced to decide if the defendant should be extradited to that state. Of the criteria used by the prosecutor in making this determination, perhaps the most important is the relative severity of the offense charged in the demanding jurisdiction. One Michigan prosecutor reported that he personally presents the charges pending in both his and the demanding jurisdiction before the presiding judge for evaluation, and if the judge acquiesces, a *nolle prosequi* is entered, allowing the other officials to extradite the defendant.[41]

> *Illustration No. 11:* The suspect had been arrested in Kansas City, Missouri, on a charge of flourishing a dangerous weapon (revolver). During questioning, it was learned that (1) the "dangerous weapon" was a plastic toy gun, and (2) the suspect had left Kansas without the permission of his supervising probation officer. The Missouri authorities dropped their charges but held the suspect for Kansas City, Kansas, officials on the probation violation.

39 For a full discussion of the factors considered in deciding whether to proceed under statute or ordinance, see Chapter 15.

40 Some Wisconsin local officials indicated that, because relations with the state authorities are poor, when they need any investigative assistance, as with crime analysis, they refer to the FBI instead of the state office. Likewise, Oakland County, Michigan, police officers complained about a lack of cooperation from the police of adjoining Wayne County (Detroit). In the past when the Oakland police had sought a person suspected of the commission of an offense within Oakland County, the Detroit police were apt to hold and secrete the suspect so that the Oakland officers could not interrogate him. The Oakland officers now seek the assistance of the state troopers in such a situation.

41 If the apprehending authorities are willing to relinquish complete jurisdiction over the defendant they will also normally drop all pending charges. For example, after a warrant was issued in Platte County, Missouri, for burglary, the defendant was apprehended in Kansas City, Kansas, and he agreed to sign an extradition waiver. The arresting detective told him that, if he had committed crimes in Kansas, and particularly in Kansas City, he should confess these crimes so that his name could be cleared on the books. The officer indicated that, if Missouri was going to prosecute, Kansas officials would not press any charges against him for crimes committed in Kansas. The boy admitted two auto accessory thefts, and the detective took down the information and thanked him.

Another criterion is the status of the suspect — a different procedure may be used if he is on a conditional liberty from another jurisdiction. For example, the use of a request for revocation as the alternative to charging is normal practice in Kansas and Wisconsin if the suspect is a probationer or parolee.

When the suspect may be prosecuted under both state and federal law, the considerations weighted by the local prosecuting attorney are of somewhat secondary importance, since in large measure the effective decision is made by the United States Attorney as he selects cases for federal prosecution. The federal prosecutor normally presses charges only if (1) the case has substantial national implication, i.e., is not primarily of local concern or a minor nature;[42] and (2) he is completely satisfied that there is sufficient evidence to obtain a conviction. If these criteria are strictly applied, resentment may be engendered among the state officials; such was the reaction of two Wayne County, Michigan, assistant prosecutors who complained that the United States Attorney "throws junk our way" simply because the crime in question appears to be too petty to handle or the possibility of a conviction is not strong enough to fit his high standards.[43]

Nevertheless, certain situations are routinely referred to the federal prosecutor, either to notify him of a violation of a federal statute or to otherwise facilitate investigation or prosecution in an area of joint jurisdiction.

> *Illustration No. 12:* After release from the state prison in Lansing, Michigan, the defendant committed a burglary in Wichita. Kansas placed a "hold" on him after he was recommitted to Lansing on another charge. Though the federal government subsequently filed a similar hold, the Wichita charge would have priority for trial after the defendant's final release from prison. At that time, however, the Kansas charge could not be heard for five months, but the federal authorities could prosecute immediately. The assistant prosecutor stated that he did not recall the nature

42 E.g., interstate shipments of (traffic in) narcotics.

43 As an example, they mentioned a case dealing with some agency that was using the local railroads to defraud the public, in which the amount in controversy was slightly under $200. At the time of the investigation, when the problem of joint jurisdiction arose, the United States Attorney took the position that the crime was of a relatively minor nature and so should be handled by the local prosecutor. The assistants were disturbed over this attitude because the case proved to be a difficult one to prosecute and they felt that the federal prosecutor did not want to "dirty his hands" with such a case unless it was of enough significance to impress the general public.

of the federal charge, but he knew that it carried a minimum sentence of five years, so that this man would be out of circulation for a good long while. In light of this, the second degree burglary charge in Wichita seemed unimportant and was dismissed.

Illustration No. 13: The suspect, charged in Detroit with forging and uttering checks, was wanted on a similar charge by the federal government. The local prosecutor pressed charges, and upon conviction the judge called the United States Attorney to discover the federal attitude and recommended penalty. The judge stated that he thought that if he gave enough of a sentence the other state jurisdictions seeking this suspect would deem this sufficient punishment. However, since he also wanted the federal government to impose a sentence, he did not wish to make the sentence so hard that the federal government would lose interest entirely. He imposed a sentence of from one to five years, and three months later the federal court imposed two years, to be served at completion of state sentence.

When the local prosecuting attorney seeks the employment of the federal criminal justice process in addition to the state proceedings, he may be seeking to guarantee that a sufficiently heavy sentence for the offense will be imposed or that the defendant will have a federal criminal record, viewed as a more serious blight on one's reputation than a local or state conviction. Or he may wish to resolve a search and seizure problem which has threatened the possibility of conviction in state courts. Again, use will be made of federal facilities if the suspect is believed to have fled the state. The FBI will then issue a warrant under the Fugitive Felon Act,[44] and, if apprehension is effected, the subject will be returned to the local authorities and, usually, the federal charge dismissed. If the subject is found not guilty locally, federal prosecution may then be undertaken.

Cases involving persons under federal supervision or jurisdiction are also referred to the United States Attorney. For example, if the local police discover a federal probationer or parolee in the commission of a new offense, the federal probation service would prefer that the case be given to the federal officials for revocation of the conditional freedom rather than be prosecuted in the state courts for a violation of state statute.

The prosecuting attorney will notify a federal agency that is

[44] 74 Stat. 87 (1960), 18 U.S.C. §1073 (1964).

charged with the investigation and prosecution of certain types of violation of the Federal Criminal Code if he is apprised of conduct that contains some elements of this particular offense. As an example, all reports coming to the attention of local police officers that involve the illegal manufacture of liquor are given to the alcohol and tobacco tax division of the Internal Revenue Service, which, although it engages in its own investigation, does depend in large measure on local police information Likewise, if a complaint is made of any allegedly counterfeit money, the agents of the Treasury Department are contacted.[45] Since the local police department will typically turn over to the postal authorities all cases of thefts of mail from a residence, the area in which any substantial amount of investigative overlap occurs is that of frauds and lotteries. Use of the mail as the principal means of communicating a scheme to other persons will result in a handling of the case by postal inspectors; if the mails were used only incidentally or occasionally, the local agency will manage the case. In the latter instance, the Post Office Department will lend investigative help and support as it sees fit. The postal authorities are also notified of conduct relating to the mailing of obscene literature.

The local-federal jurisdictional overlap is greater in cases of narcotics violations because federal narcotics law prohibits possession and sale of drugs whether or not interstate transportation is involved. If much interstate activity is discovered, the local agency informs the Federal Bureau of Narcotics which can investigate on both ends. If, on the other hand, the FBN stumbles on a large local operation, the police are notified so they can take primary responsibility. The FBN also notifies the local department in cases of sales to juveniles.

There is another type of case which is normally referred to the federal prosecutor's office — those involving transportation of a stolen auto across state lines, even though this could be handled on the local level. Three reasons were cited for this policy: (1) under the federal Dyer Act there is no venue problem and the defendant can be prosecuted in any one of the states in which he was in illegal possession of the automobile; (2) many local police departments and prosecutors' offices are understaffed and it is the feeling of the federal authorities that the local authori-

45 The (Detroit) police had found what they thought to be a counterfeit $100 bill and called the local office of the Treasury Department. Upon determination by the Treasury agent that the bill was indeed genuine, the suspect was released from police custody.

ties are happy to see others handle such problems; (3) there is no need for the costly procedure of extradition. The United States District Attorney for Detroit indicated that he never experienced any criticism from local law enforcement agencies about the federal practice of prosecuting all such cases.

CHAPTER 15

The Decision Not to Charge Because Use of Formal Alternatives Prevents Undue Harm to the Suspect

A desire to avoid imposition of undue harm to the suspect is sometimes a primary motive for the use of alternatives to prosecution. Use of the juvenile justice system and proceedings under local ordinance rather than state statute are two such alternatives. Although the decision to use one of these alternatives may be based on several motives, it is likely to be viewed also as a grant of leniency both in terms of the likely punishment that will result from use of the alternative and in terms of the consequences of the record created by its use. The decision to use such an alternative represents a belief that full, or even partial, implementation of the criminal process will impose undue harm on the suspect, but other considerations dictate that something more than a complete dismissal should occur.

A. Use of the Juvenile Justice Process

The basic decision to subject some juveniles to a process other than the formal criminal law process has been made by legislatures in every state. In some states the classification is a simple one: assuming that some formal measures are taken, all persons below a certain age are channeled into the juvenile justice system and all above that age go into the criminal justice system.[1] Kansas

[1] Kan. Gen. Stat. Ann. §38-401 to 38-432 (1949); Mich. Stat. Ann. §27.3178 (598.1 to 598.28) (1962); Wis. Stat. Ann. §§48.01 to 48.47 (1957). The Kansas legislature adopted a new juvenile code in 1957; therefore the field observations made in Kansas are not helpful in determining how the new code is administered. Kan. Laws, 1957, c. 256, §39. See Kan. Stat. Ann. §§38-801 to 38-838 (1964). The

is a state with that system: all boys under sixteen and girls under eighteen are treated as juveniles, and all that age or over are processed as adults.[2] Obviously under such a system, neither prosecutor nor trial judge may exercise discretion about shifting an individual from one system to another,[3] although the prosecutor is still free, of course, to take no action at all or to use informal alternatives.[4]

Wisconsin code has also been changed. See Wis. Stat. Ann. §§48.01 to 48.47 (Supp. 1968).

2 Kan. Stat. Ann. §38-402 (1949); now see Kan. Stat. Ann. §§38-802 38-806 (1964).

3 A procedure apparently unique to the Kansas juvenile courts is presently authorized by Kan. Stat. Ann. §38-808 (1964), which gives the judge discretion to refer to the district court, the court of general criminal jurisdiction, any juvenile whose behavior would constitute a statutory felony if engaged in by an adult. Until the case is referred by the juvenile court, the district court has no jurisdiction and any sentence by that court is void. But once the case is referred, the district court has jurisdiction only until the return of the verdict; it has no authority to pronounce sentence on that verdict. The juvenile court determines what disposition will be made of the convicted juvenile offender.

4 In cases of truancy or minor disorderly conduct, the youth is usually lectured rather sternly at the police station and/or at home in the presence of the parents, then released to the custody of the latter. The juvenile is often referred to a special juvenile division of the police department for counseling. For example, Kansas City, Kansas, police have a special youth bureau and welfare office which handles juvenile suspects. The members of this department feel that a juvenile, if not a chronic repeater, deserves a chance to work out the problems that cause him to misbehave without being sent to juvenile court. In some cases contact will be made with the school authorities in an effort to help the child, or an attempt made at supervision, although usually not for periods longer than one month.

Milwaukee police refer the offender and his parents to the sheriff's office if the efforts of the police investigation division have proved ineffective in handling the suspect. If the problem should continue after the participants in the offense and their parents have been ordered into the sheriff's office, the matter is then turned over to juvenile authorities. However, the practice of conducting a hearing in the sheriff's office is usually a very effective technique. For one thing, the parents are called away from their regular daily duties, causing them considerable inconvenience, since such an appearance involves an average of over three and one-half hours; while a good part of this time is spent in waiting, the personnel in the office feel that even this is an essential part of the entire procedure. At the hearing, a stern warning is given that investigation and court proceedings will ensue upon a resumption of the delinquent behavior, because it is felt that, with this warning hanging over their heads, the juveniles will behave themselves and their parents will exercise more care to see that they do so. Such a hearing is most apt to be held in cases in which a charge would prevent a young male offender from entering military service.

Detroit police also hold a similar hearing with the offender and his parents, terming this procedure the "Court of No Record." In other instances, the charging decision is simply delayed by placing the youth's name on the "thirty-day list," so that the matter is reviewable at the end of this period to determine whether the offender has complied with any instructions or conditions and, if he has, no prosecution occurs, nor is the offender subjected to juvenile court procedures.

It should be noted that in each of the three states the motivation behind such dispositions of cases is to save trouble for both the offender and the administrative agencies. As another example of this approach, if a juvenile suspect is known to be

In many states a more complex system has been devised so that several age groupings became significant. In Wisconsin, there are three groups: everyone under age sixteen must be processed in juvenile court if he or she is processed at all; everyone age eighteen or over must be processed in the criminal courts, if at all; but for those who are sixteen or seventeen, there is an option. At the time of the survey, those in the latter age group fell within the jurisdiction of the circuit court but could be transferred to juvenile court at the discretion of the prosecutor.[5]

Michigan's classification is yet more complex. In addition to the youngest group — under fifteen, who must be processed as juveniles — and the oldest group — nineteen or older, who must be processed in the criminal justice system, there are two other groups. Children fifteen and sixteen years of age initially fall within the jurisdiction of the juvenile court, but this jurisdiction may be waived by the juvenile judge on request of the prosecutor. Children seventeen and eighteen years of age, as in the middle group in Wisconsin, may be charged as adults or treated as juveniles at the discretion of the prosecutor.[6]

It is readily apparent that, in the middle groups in Michigan and Wisconsin, the law contemplates that discretion shall be exercised in determining whether the child should be channeled out of the criminal law process and treated as a juvenile. It is also apparent that the decision, however and by whomever made, is a decision to charge with a crime or a decision not to charge with a crime; clearly it is a decision reached at the charging level, in some instances shared by the prosecutor and the trial judge, in others made by the prosecutor alone.

---

presently on probation or parole, the police are apparently reluctant to charge him again with a new offense but will just turn him over to his supervising officer. This of course, may result in a conditional releasee committing a series of delinquent acts before the juvenile court is notified.

5 Wis. Stat. Ann. §§48.01, 54.02 (1935). This statute vested in the prosecutor the discretion to determine how and where the juvenile offender of the ages of sixteen or seventeen was to be tried. Wis. Stat. Ann. §§48.03, 48.13, 48.44 (Supp. 1968) now vests this discretion in the juvenile court judge.

6 Mich. Stat. Ann. §27.3178 (598.2 to 598.6) (Supp. 1968). In Detroit, one assistant prosecuting attorney handles all such cases; referrals to him for a determination as to whether the prosecutor's office should petition the juvenile court for a "waiver of jurisdiction" come primarily from two sources: (1) police officers who think the juvenile should be prosecuted as an adult, (2) another assistant prosecutor who reaches the conclusion when reviewing a case that the juvenile court proceedings are not the appropriate remedy for the juvenile's illegal conduct. This assistant will never request a waiver unless he feels either that all the juvenile facilities have been used to no avail or that the behavior is of such a serious nature as to warrant disposition in Recorder's Court.

Illustration No. 1: Two men had been apprehended while burglarizing the apartment of a seriously ill elderly couple. The police discovered a sixteen-year-old boy lying down on the floor of the back seat of what was intended to be used as the get-away car. The boy was on probation from the juvenile court at the time. The assistant prosecutor reviewing the case decided to seek a waiver of juvenile court jurisdiction so that the boy could be tried in the criminal court.

Illustration No. 2: A sixteen-year-old youth had surrendered to the police after killing his stepfather under circumstances suggesting possible self-defense. He was charged with manslaughter rather than murder, and a request was made to the juvenile judge to waive jurisdiction of the boy to the criminal court. The judge did so.

In Michigan, some juveniles who are prima facie within the jurisdiction of the juvenile court may eventually be tried as adult criminals. Before they can be brought into the criminal justice system, two officials, the prosecutor and the juvenile judge, must concur.[7] In addition, certain Michigan juveniles who are seventeen or eighteen years of age,[8] sixteen and seventeen in Wisconsin,[9] are subject to the concurrent jurisdiction of both the juvenile and criminal courts and may be treated as juveniles if the prosecutor decides that they should be so treated. No judicial official need concur with the prosecutor in this instance.[10] Because in both groupings the initiative is in the prosecutor, it is accurate to say that he "selects" the procedure.[11] Criteria used in current administration by the prosecuting attorney and the juvenile court judge are isolable.

1. *The rehabilitation potential of the suspect.* A consideration important to the prosecutor who must decide whether to attempt to channel the suspect into the criminal or the juvenile justice

7 Mich. Stat. Ann. §27.3178 (598.4) (1962).

8 Mich. Stat. Ann. §27.3178 (598.2)(d) (Supp. 1968).

9 Wis. Stat. Ann. §48.01(5)(am) (1953). The present Wisconsin provision places this discretion with the juvenile court. Wis. Stat. Ann. §48.18 (Supp. 1968).

10 Mich. Stat. Ann. §27.3178 (598.2)(d) (Supp. 1968).

11 If the case is waived to or retained in the juvenile court, normal procedures for the disposition of youthful offenders will be followed; if waived to or retained in the district court, the prosecutor will then make the usual decision to charge and continue the prosecutorial process. However, there is an evident tendency toward undercharging or downgrading of the offense, apparently based on a desire to avoid giving the youthful offender a criminal record with an unnecessary social stigma (an original charge of attempted rape might be reduced to disorderly conduct) or one carrying an unduly harsh sentence (attempted murder reduced to felonious assault).

process is whether the juvenile process is likely to accomplish its ideal of rehabilitation of the individual. If anything, this consideration resumes even greater importance in the mind of the juvenile judge who must decide whether to surrender jurisdiction over a juvenile when requested to do so by the prosecutor. Thus, in Illustration No. 1, the juvenile's status as a probationer when he committed the new offense was enough to persuade the assistant prosecutor that his rehabilitation potential under juvenile processes was low. In most instances, as in this illustration, it is the past record of the juvenile on which the assistant relies in reaching a judgment about his rehabilitation potential.

Exclusive reliance on the past record to determine likelihood of rehabilitation is not necessary when the juvenile judge decides whether to accede to the prosecutor's request to waive jurisdiction. The juvenile judge in Detroit always requires that a report on the juvenile be in his hands by the time a hearing is held on the waiver request. The report — prepared by a court worker — will contain the social history as well as the past record of the juvenile and is likely to be oriented toward the specific question of the effect of various dispositions upon the juvenile. Detroit judges place heavy reliance on these reports in making a judgment about rehabilitation potential.

2. *Seriousness of the offense.* The severity of the crime with which the defendant is charged is likely to affect the waiver decision of the judge or the prosecutor. It is often felt that offenses deemed serious, even heinous by the general public, should be disposed of in the court of general criminal jurisdiction. The juvenile judge and prosecuting attorney are more likely to be receptive to and reflective of the community response to those crimes that have been widely publicized if they are elected officials. Disregard of public clamor over a shocking crime may well shake the security of their positions.[12]

3. *Physical appearance.* The consideration here is the actual size of the suspect. If the defendant is of such physical stature that he would not be out of place with normal adult men in a state reformatory or penitentiary, but would be considered out sized in a training school or detention center for juveniles, then a waiver of juvenile court jurisdiction is likely to be requested and granted. The converse is true if the youth is of slight build.

4. *Desire to invoke sex deviate provisions.* If it is suspected

[12] In 1956, in Detroit, only 22 of 85 requests for waivers of jurisdiction were granted.

that an arrested juvenile is suffering from a mental disorder coupled with a propensity to commit criminal offenses of a sexual nature, but he is not considered to be insane, the prosecutor may wish to use the sex deviate provisions so that the youth may be officially and competently examined and, if necessary, committed for treatment for an indefinite term. In such a case, if the youth falls within one of the age groupings over which there is discretion, the prosecutor will either request a waiver of jurisdiction or retain it in the circuit court. Probably the force prompting this decision is the knowledge that juvenile court jurisdiction does not extend beyond the minority of the juvenile;[13] so a juvenile court could not commit a young boy or girl for indefinite treatment.

5. *To avoid a criminal record.*

> *Illustration No. 3:* Several youths frequented a drive-in restaurant. They had purchased several large firecrackers, two of which they threw into a small room in the restaurant where the owner and his employees were working. The explosion necessitated medical treatment for two of the employees; it punctured the eardrum of one of them. Only two of the youths, both seventeen, were apprehended. It was decided to send them to the juvenile authorities.

In Illustration No. 3, since the suspects were between the ages of seventeen and nineteen, they could either be prosecuted as adults or processed through juvenile court.[14] The assistant prosecutor indicated that prosecuting them as adults would give them a criminal record, which would hamper them in obtaining employment or entering military service. On the other hand, he decided that, since the Fourth of July was approaching when these "firecracker cases" were common, something more serious should be done to the boys than simply permitting them to make restitution to the victims. It was decided to send the suspects to juvenile court, where proceedings do not create a criminal record,[15] but the juvenile judge can impose all the conditions when sentencing that other judges can, and, in addition, can place responsibility for the suspect's future behavior on the parents. The assistant prosecutor told the suspects: "As far as you boys are concerned, this will keep you from getting a record so that

13 Mich. Stat. Ann. §27.3178 (598.5) (1962).
14 Mich. Stat. Ann. §27.3178 (598.2)(d) (Supp. 1968).
15 Mich. Stat. Ann. §27.3178 (598.1) (1962).

when you grow up and have more sense and try to get a job you won't be dogged by this foolish prank. On the other hand, the juvenile judge is no softy."

These factors do not operate in isolation. If because of the preponderance of other factors the judge is inclined to grant the waiver, he may nevertheless deny it when the charge is one for which probation cannot be granted after conviction in the criminal courts. In Illustration No. 2, the judge indicated that, if the boy had been charged with murder — a nonprobationable offense in Michigan — he would have denied the waiver.

B. Use of the Ordinance-Statute Option

When criminal conduct occurs within the corporate limits of a municipality, it frequently violates both a state statute and a municipal ordinance. Since in practice no attempt is made to prosecute under both the statute and the ordinance, administrative officials must decide under which to proceed. For example, in Detroit, both a state statute and a municipal ordinance on disorderly conduct are in effect; fine or confinement may be imposed under either law. In deciding at the time of the arrest or later at the precinct station under which law to proceed, the police consider a number of factors: (1) prosecution under the ordinance will bring revenue to the city, which, officials feel, needs the funds more than the state does;[16] (2) proceeding under an ordinance requires only the issuance of a ticket, while fingerprinting and booking are required if the state statute is to be used; (3) disorderly conduct cases are likely to be dismissed under the statute when the conduct does not seem serious; and (4) it is felt that a record of a conviction for an ordinance violation is less serious than for a misdemeanor violation. Thus, police seek to charge under the ordinance in order to "give the defendant a break."[17]

The decision to charge under an ordinance is similar to a decision to send a young offender to juvenile court when he could

[16] The corporation counsel for the City of Detroit specifically denied that revenue was a motive in Detroit for proceeding under ordinance rather than state statute. He admitted, however, that it is a strong motive in other cities.

[17] The same factors are considered in deciding whether to prosecute a person for carrying a switch-blade knife with a blade longer than three inches. The Michigan statute prohibits blades over three inches long, while the ordinance prohibits blades under three inches as well as those over.

have been prosecuted as an adult, since in each case the suspect is not released but is instead handled in a fashion that will result in less collateral harm than would have accompanied full enforcement.

CHAPTER 16

The Decision Not to Charge Because Civil Sanctions Are Regarded as More Effective

With some classes of criminal offenders, the prosecuting attorney may, as an alternative to using the normal prosecution-adjudication pattern, institute civil actions designed to prevent or punish the commission of substantive criminal offenses. The use of three such actions, ostensibly created for some other purpose but adapted by the prosecutor to fill his own needs, forms the subject of this chapter. By statute the prosecutor is named as proper party plaintiff to initiate these civil proceedings in the name of the state to control vice. He may invoke equity jurisdiction to obtain an injunction to abate a public nuisance, such as a gambling house or a brothel; he may obtain an order of confiscation for a vehicle used in illegal activity; and he may seek revocation of the liquor license of a known liquor law violator.

In some instances, a civil action may be considered a supplement to normal prosecution because, by statute or as a matter of policy, the possession of evidence of at least one prior conviction is a prerequisite to filing the suit against the offender. This is true in the equitable abatement action, since a nuisance is defined, for these purposes, as a building or vehicle about which numerous complaints have been filed and convictions obtained.

In other situations, a suit filed for the purpose of invoking civil sanctions as an aid in law enforcement might better be viewed as a substitute for the routine criminal justice process. Thus, for example, if the prosecuting attorney receives a complaint and sufficient evidence concerning a liquor law violation, he may resort to the abatement-padlocking procedure or seek revocation of the owner's liquor license rather than prosecute for this offense. Since there is a widespread belief that the sentences and fines imposed upon conviction of such offenses have no deterrent effect, these alternatives are viewed as a more effective means of controlling organized crime. The substitutionary role of vehicle confiscation is somewhat different, because there is no court order given that purports to prevent the defendant from acting illegally; he is, in effect, merely prevented from using *that vehicle* for such purposes.

A. Padlock Laws

The legislatures in all three states have provided the prosecutor with civil procedures to abate nuisances,[1] available as alternatives to prosecution. Although the details of the statutes and the use made of them may differ, there is general agreement that they are necessary weapons to combat vice crimes, particularly prostitution and gambling.[2]

The "padlock laws," as they are commonly called, are used as alternatives to charging in a special sense. Charges are not refused in individual cases just because the prosecutor has available the alternative of proceeding in a civil action. Indeed, whether required by statute or not, the abatement provisions are not generally used unless there has been a prior conviction involving use of the premises to be padlocked.[3] But that procedure is resorted to as an alternative to *future* prosecutions. Law enforcement officers have pointed out that prostitution, gambling, and liquor violations are not controllable if the only control device used is arrest of the violators followed by prosecution, even if

1 Kan. Stat. Ann. §§21-918 to 21-922 (gambling establishments), §§21-937 to 21-942 (houses of prostitution), §§41-723 to 41-806 (liquor violations) (1964); Mich. Stat. Ann. §§27A.3801 to 27A.3840 (1961); Wis. Stat. Ann. §§176.72 (1957), 176.90 (Supp. 1968), 280.01 to 280.07, 280.09, 280.11 to 280.20 (1958), 280.08, 280.10 (Supp. 1968).

2 The most frequent use of the abatement procedure is against owners of premises in which there is prostitution or gambling, but there are instances of its use to combat illegal liquor sales or production and the sale or use of narcotics.

3 Mich. Stat. Ann. §27A.3815 (1961), for example, does not require proof of a conviction. The plaintiff must prove that the bill was filed within thirty days "after any act, any violation, or the existence of a condition herein defined as a nuisance. . . ." Since the circuit court is prone to dismiss the bill of complaint unless it can be shown that a conviction resulted from the most recent act for which the injunction is sought, the Detroit prosecutor will not usually file an abatement petition unless there have been three prior arrests for similar violations within the past year. While Wisconsin prosecutors also apparently require proof of such a record of violations, at least one Kansas County attorney indicated that he would institute civil abatement procedures whenever a conviction is obtained for a violation of the state liquor laws.

convictions are relatively easy to obtain. The sentences are so light that the violators are not deterred from returning to the same type of illegal conduct. Thus, it is often felt that the only efficient way to enforce the vice laws is to close down the premises in which the conduct occurs.[4] Enforcement officials feel that, unless the nuisance laws are used, an inordinate amount of resources would have to be expended in combating this type of conduct through many more arrests. To prevent the necessity for those arrests and prosecutions in the future, the alternative of padlocking the premises is utilized.[5] It is generally believed to be very effective.[6]

The regularized practices of the Detroit police department typify the procedure for the initiation of an abatement suit.[7] Daily reports are received at police headquarters from officers assigned to vice investigations in the various precincts. These reports are filed according to the premises involved, so that there is available in the vice bureau a record of policy activity relating to any building in the city. When such a record indicates a series of violations in a relatively short period of time, a warning is sent to the owner, stating that, unless the illegal activity complained of ceases, padlock proceedings will be initiated.[8] A continuation of offenses at the premises after such a warning will result in a review of the record by the inspector of the central vice bureau and referral by him to the prosecuting attorney's

[4] In addition to the perceived lack of deterrent power in the vice laws, police and prosecutors are not satisfied that judges are sufficiently motivated fully to enforce the law relating to prostitution, liquor, and gambling. Also, criticism of public acceptance of such conduct is not uncommon. A district attorney in a small Wisconsin town complained that the city council was composed of many businessmen who had financial interests in renting the premises in which the illegal conduct might take place and therefore were much too liberal in granting licenses to persons desirous of renting those premises.

[5] Since the padlock order is issued by a circuit court judge, this procedure is actually a form of prosecution and cannot be classed as a harassment technique.

[6] A prosecutor in one Wisconsin town said that the effectiveness of the law was demonstrated by the fact that there had never been a forfeiture of a bond required in such cases. See note 29 *infra*.

[7] It should be noted that this procedure is typical only of urban communities; in the rural areas, the prosecutor is most apt to gain his information concerning existence of nuisances from reports submitted by the state liquor control board's investigating field agents.

[8] Further indication of the effectiveness of this procedure is found by comparing the number of such letters and phone calls warning owners, with the number of actions actually instituted. In 1954 in Detroit, 62 actions were begun, but there had been 351 letters and 292 phone calls made to property owners advising them to take the necessary steps to abate the nuisance at the premises owned by them. Presumably, a large percentage of such nuisances are abated without the necessity of prosecutor participation.

office. The inspector decides whether to refer the case to the prosecutor on the basis of the number of offenses which have occurred on the premises, how many convictions have been obtained, and the period of time over which these offenses have occurred. The prosecutor normally concurs in the request of the vice bureau for an injunction[9] and then prepares all the necessary papers for initiation of the civil suit.[10]

The petition filed by the assistant prosecutor as plaintiff, representing the state in the court of equitable jurisdiction, must cite specific violations, arrests, and convictions; it must be based on more than information and belief.[11] That this suit is directed against the owners of the premises rather than the actual offenders also indicates that the abatement procedure is used as an alternative to the normal prosecution-adjudication pattern.[12] In Michigan, the defendant may, and usually does, then enter a consent decree; if he does not, or in Wisconsin and Kansas where such a plea is not used, the case is heard by one of the circuit court judges, who, upon a determination that the premises in question should be declared a public nuisance,[13] will issue a permanent injunction to supersede the temporary restraining

9 Independent of the review and referral by the police vice squad, a prosecutor might be moved to initiate abatement proceedings if a petition signed by residents of the area requesting such abatement is presented to him.

10 In Michigan, this must be done within thirty days after the most recent arrest for an offense which occurred on the premises in question. Mich. Stat. Ann. §27A.3815 (1961).

11 "The petition asks that the court issue a restraining order against appellant from keeping and maintaining a common nuisance, and on final hearing to adjudge the premises and building in question to be a common nuisance and that the nuisance be abated by order of the court, and the premises closed and padlocked for a period of not less than three months nor more than two years, or until the laws of Kansas are complied with and for other relief not material to the issues involved herein." State ex rel. Anderson v. Wilson, 170 Kan. 194, 224 P.2d 669 (1950). See Kan. Stat. Ann. §21-919 (1964).

12 Though the abatement proceedings are civil in nature, one might draw a parallel with a malum prohibitum offense, since the owners need not have personal knowledge of the existence of the violation on the premises. See Kan. Stat. Ann. §21-938 (1964); Mich. Stat. Ann. §27A.3815 (1961). Wis. Stat. Ann. §280.11 (1958); but see Kan. Stat. Ann. §§21-939, 41-805(1) (1964). This conclusion was also adopted by the Kansas Supreme Court in State ex rel. Graham v. Russell, 171 Kan. 709, 237 P.2d 363 (1951).

13 One Wichita judge mentioned that it was extremely hard to defend such an abatement suit, because the county attorney never filed a petition unless he had a "tight case." Indeed, the failure of defendants to appear for the hearing is not uncommon; in such a case, the injunction or padlock order issues by default judgment. Defendants might also decline to contest the suit in order to keep the injunction period to the statutory minimum.

order which was perfunctorily granted when the petition was filed.[14]

The order will usually close down the premises for a specified period[15] but enjoin the defendants from similar illegal activity in them forever.[16] If the prosecutor receives evidence of renewed criminal activity, he may resort to contempt proceedings[17] or seek forfeiture of the bond in those cases in which it was required.[18] Though the Detroit prosecutor relies on the effect of the court order to restrain vice offenses,[19] practice in other Michi-

14 Issuance of an injunction for at least the minimum period specified by the statute is clearly mandatory in Kansas, State ex rel. Graham v Russell, 171 Kan. 709, 237 P.2d 353 (1952), but apparently this question has not arisen in Wisconsin or Michigan.

15 Kansas — 90 days to two years; Kan. Stat. Ann. §41-806 (1964). Michigan — one year; Mich. Stat. Ann. §27A.3825 (1961). Wisconsin — one year; Wis. Stat. Ann. §280.3 (1958).

16 While padlocking the building, the police also dispose of property within premises used in the illegal activity. In Kansas, one prosecutor stated that the practice in padlocking buildings used to violate the liquor laws was to break all opened bottles and sell unopened ones. Disposal of gambling or other equipment may be prescribed by statute; Kan. Stat. Ann. §21-918 (1964) Mich. Stat. Ann. §§27A.3825 to 27A.3835 (1961); Wis. Stat. Ann. §§280.06, 280.13, 280.14 (1958). The owner may also be required to pay a reasonable attorney's fee to the prosecutor who instituted the abatement petition. Kan. Stat. Ann. §§21-918 to 21-941, 41-806 (1964); Mich. Stat. Ann. §27A.2421 (1961). Practices for obtaining and using this fee vary widely throughout the states.

17 Prosecutors in these states pointed out that it was much easier to proceed under the contempt laws than to attempt to prosecute for the violation itself, since a court of equity could act quickly and effectively. Further, the contempt proceedings would be against the owner of the premises himself, while the prosecutor may not be able to charge him with the violations in criminal proceedings. Kan. Stat. Ann. §21-918 (1964); Mich. Stat. Ann. §27A.3820 (1961); Wis. Stat. Ann. §280-12 (1958).

18 Records in the Detroit prosecutor's office indicate that in 1953 there were 30 cases, 24 consent decrees, and 6 dismissals; in 1954, there were 33 cases, 25 consent decrees, 8 dismissals; in 1955, 30 cases, 22 consent decrees, 8 dismissals; and in 1956, 52 cases, 42 consent decrees, and 10 dismissals. When the consent decree process is used, the defendant is required to pay $45 court costs. In the relatively small number of cases which were contested, the defendant was invariably required to post bond. In 1956, of the 52 cases, 35 consent decrees provided only for injunction, and 7 decrees were obtained providing for a bond of $1000 with the same provision for padlocking in case of violation. Ten cases were dismissed by the court because the nuisance had been abated, and no case resulted in an order to padlock the premises without a showing of a later violation. Kan. Stat. Ann. §41-806 (1964); Mich. Stat. Ann. §27A.3840 (1961). But see Kan. Stat. Ann. §§21-918 to 21-941 (1964).

19 The last actual padlocking of a building in Detroit took place over fifteen years ago. This is apparently due to the fact that a large majority of the cases involve hotels, and the Supreme Court of Michigan has held that only the rooms in which the illegal activities occurred can be padlocked. Since the illegal conduct could then be moved to any one of a number of other rooms, there is little incentive for padlocking. State ex rel. Brucker v. Robinson, 250 Mich. 99, 229 N.W. 403 (1930).

gan counties and in Wisconsin and Kansas is to actually padlock the building for the term of the injunction.[20]

B. Confiscation of Automobiles

Although the confiscation of automobiles in the states studied is based upon the same statutes that authorize the injunction proceedings to abate nuisances in buildings,[21] there are many differences between the procedures used in the two areas.

Illustration No. 1: A man had been stopped by a uniformed officer for a traffic violation and searched subsequent to the issuance of the ticket. Policy slips were found on him. The man was brought to the station and referred to the vice squad, where he was told that unless he cooperated they would take his car away. The lieutenant said "the man fell for this and agreed to cooperate with the police. He said he was supposed to transfer the policy slips to someone down on the corner, so we let him drive down there and look for the guy. He was really very nervous, especially when after a few hours no one showed up. We gave up and let the guy go, since we figured he had punishment enough sweating out the car confiscation."

Illustration No. 2: Two policemen had observed a known mutuel numbers man driving south, who, after seeing the officers, sped away. The officers stopped him, found a quantity of mutuel bet slips under the dashboard and arrested

20 In addition to the prescribed abatement procedures, the Detroit police have developed, with the tacit consent of the prosecutor, another alternative to prosecution for vice offenses. In one observed instance, a case against a club for gambling violations had been thrown out of court for lack of evidence. The vice bureau inspector then remarked that he was through fooling around with this group and informed the club officers that they must close down; if they failed to do so the vice bureau would arrange to move them out of their quarters and place all of their property in the confiscated property room of the police department. This action was apparently expected because the club members had already prepared a sign which read that the club premises were closed pending further notice. It was likely that the club members would attempt to secure an injunction against the police department in order to re-open their establishment. All the officers acknowledged that this was an extra-legal procedure really a harassment technique, but indicated that the inspector had been fairly successful with its use in the past.

21 Mich. Stat. Ann. §§27A.3801, 27A.3805, 27A.3825 (1961). These statutes apply equally to buildings, vehicles, boats, and aircraft. While confiscation of automobiles may be possible in the other states studied, instances of this practice were not observed, so the text refers only to Detroit, Michigan procedures. See Kan. Stat. Ann. §41-805 (1964) and Wis. Stat. Ann. §176.72 (1957) which declare automobiles used for the illegal sale of liquor to be nuisances, and Wis. Stat. Ann. §161.13 (1957) which designates vehicles nuisances when used in the narcotic trade.

him for violation of the state gambling laws. They confiscated ten current date mutuel bet slips, fifty envelopes, $5.50 in admitted gambling money, and a 1947 Ford coupe. The accused, who had a record of four previous car seizures, entered a consent decree.

Illustration No. 3: Defendant was arrested for driving on left side of the highway. When the car was searched, 417 current dated mutuel bet slips were found in the front seat. The record of the owner of the car, who was not the driver, indicated that five different cars owned by him had been confiscated by the police within the last five years. The defendant himself had been convicted twice for violation of the gambling laws. Because the prosecutor believed the evidence would be deemed admissible in court, he did not accept a consent decree from the defendant.

Confiscation may be used as an alternative to charging obviously guilty persons, or it may be used in addition to charging.[22] In the large majority of cases confiscation is used because a conviction could not be obtained since the evidence which convinces the prosecutor and the police that the suspect is guilty of a violation was illegally obtained and would not be admissible at trial.[23] Even when the prosecutor believes that a conviction could be obtained, the confiscation procedure is used as an alternative to the normal prosecution-adjudication pattern because it is thought that the punishment likely to follow successful prosecution would be insufficient to effectively deter the illegal conduct.[24] The offenders against whom this procedure is primarily used are those involved in the relatively lucrative occupation of gambling, although occasionally it is used when the offense involves the equally lucrative and illegal operations dealing with liquor, narcotics, or prostitution.[25]

It is usually clear to the officers making the initial arrest in these cases, as well as to the prosecutors, that the arrest is illegal

22 Cars are confiscated when they are involved in a pending criminal case. It is immaterial for this purpose whether the person arrested was booked on an investigation charge under the harassment program or on an arrest for a particular offense.

23 It has been estimated that the evidence seized in these cases would be admissible in a criminal action in only one out of every ten cases.

24 Several prosecutors stated they believed the gambling laws to be inadequate for just this reason.

25 One prosecutor stated that there are only four situations in which he presses for sale of the car as a nuisance: (1) narcotics violations, (2) prostitution, (3) violation of the liquor laws, and (4) gambling offenses which generally are charged as misdemeanor gambling or conspiracy to gamble.

and that prosecution will not follow the arrest. There is, indeed, often little effort to secure evidence that could be used for prosecution because of problems identified in past encounters with the search and seizure laws. In addition, the police share the prosecutor's attitude that, even if a conviction were possible, the likely sentence would have little deterrent effect. In this sense, the confiscation procedure is an adjunct of the police harassment program against this type of violator,[26] but differs from other harassment arrests because there is prosecutorial participation in the subsequent stages of the program. The fact that there is some doubt about the legality of the procedure[27] serves to underscore the prosecutor's use of the procedure as an opportunity to "punish" certain types of illegal behavior when use of the exclusionary rule clearly would bar the use of normal criminal sanctions.[28]

The confiscation procedure typically begins with an illegal search of an automobile in which the police believe that gambling paraphernalia will be found. When an officer finds evidence, such as policy slips, which convinces him that the automobile was being used in an illegal occupation, the occupants of the car are taken to headquarters and the car is driven to a police automobile pound. The police complete a confiscation report and forward it to the padlock division of the vice bureau, along with the previous records of the driver and the owner of the vehicle. The supervising officer then, in the name of the arresting officer, completes an affidavit which (1) states that, while acting in the capacity of a member of the police department, he observed the vehicle being used for such purposes as unlawfully

26 Confiscation of gambling money, and equipment (including telephones) is part of the more general harassment program used by the police. Such activity does not involve prosecutorial participation.

27 Although the constitutionality of the statutes has been upheld in People ex rel. Dowling v. Sill, 310 Mich. 570, 17 N.W.2d 756 (1945), the Supreme Court of Michigan has held that evidence seized in violation of the search and seizure clause of the constitution is inadmissible in civil trials as well as in criminal actions, Lobel v. Swincicki, 354 Mich. 427, 93 N.W.2d 281 (1958). See also Comment, 17 Ark. L. Rev. 207 (1963).

28 Commenting on this practice, an assistant prosecuting attorney who handles the confiscation proceedings acknowledged that he was distressed when, upon assuming these duties, he learned he must "follow procedures that in the ordinary practice of the law would be unethical, revolting, and shameful." Nevertheless, in becoming accustomed to the job, he learned the necessity for such procedures and now believes that the search and seizure laws were too stringent, resulting in exclusion of evidence in many cases and little or no punishment for such lucrative illegal conduct. It should be noted at this point that the exclusionary rule was in force in Michigan and Wisconsin, but not Kansas, at the time the survey was conducted. See Mapp v. Ohio, 367 U.S. 643 (1961).

transporting and possessing narcotics, liquor, or gambling paraphernalia, and (2) describes any evidence found in the vehicle.

All of these forms are then turned over by the vice bureau inspector to the assistant prosecutor responsible for the enforcement of the nuisance abatement statute. This official routinely prepares and forwards to the circuit court a bill of complaint and a restraining order, which together act to enjoin the defendant from filing any other action to recover possession of his car. Summonses will be sent to the owner of the vehicle and the holder of a lien, if one exists; the latter is made a party defendant to the action so that, upon notification of the action, he may intervene to protect his interests.

Most cases reach this procedural stage; occasionally, however, the assistant prosecutor does not concur in the request of the vice bureau and will order the car returned to the suspect. In one instance this occurred because the police had found only four current mutuel bet slips in the glove compartment, the defendant had no criminal record, and the defense attorney, whose opinion was highly respected, assured the assistant prosecutor that the suspect was not a gambler or a numbers operator. In the more usual case, when the complaint is filed in circuit court, one of two procedures will be followed.

The defendants enter into a consent decree in at least seventy-five per cent of such cases; the use of this decree is considered to be the most effective part of the entire program of automobile confiscation. This provides that the car is to be returned to the defendant but orders him to refrain permanently from using the vehicle in an illegal activity. Also included is an acknowledgment that the seizure and detention of the automobile was lawful, which is intended to free the arresting officers from any civil liability for damages. Such a decree manifests both the close cooperation between judge and prosecutor and the standardized nature of the procedures in these cases. Court costs are then assessed against the defendant and are clearly intended to be punitive. Actual court costs are about $20, but the standardized fee imposed by the prosecutor depends upon the age of the automobile; the costs are higher when the car is newer. Thus, return (in 1957) of a 1957 model car cost the defendant $119, of a 1953 car, $69.[29]

[29] There is some doubt about the legality of assessing such extra costs. In State ex rel. Dowling v. Martin, 314 Mich. 317, 22 N.W.2d 381 (1946), it was held that while the car involved in a gambling operation was properly confiscated and sold the assessment of $500 as costs out of money seized at the same time was improper

The other possible dispositions of the case occur when it is brought to trial. The defendant seldom insists on a trial despite the fact, as one prosecutor estimated, that 75 to 85 per cent of the cases would be dismissed due to the presence of illegally obtained evidence. The defendant is more likely to enter into a consent decree because (1) it would take several additional months to obtain the car by going to court, and (2) the attorney's fees would amount to more than the court costs assessed in the consent decree.[30]

The prosecutor will occasionally insist that the matter be brought to trial.[31] When this is done, and the state is successful in obtaining a conviction for the illegal activity, the court will order a public sale of the automobile.[32] If the prosecutor demands a trial, but the defendant fails to appear, a default decree is entered. In many cases, since an old car is involved, the prosecutor does not proceed with a public sale, but, after a six-month interval, requests the court to declare the car abandoned and then turns it over to the police for sale. Knowledge of this procedure results in the widespread use of old cars by many mutuel operators. If the car is confiscated, the gamblers are in a position to let a default judgment be entered against them without sustaining a heavy financial loss.

C. Revocation of Liquor Licenses

Although prosecutors do not seek revocation of a liquor license for every infraction of the state or local liquor control laws, license revocation presents an effective alternative to the normal

---

because there was no violation of a previous injunction. However, since the defendant in a typical confiscation case enters into the consent decree voluntarily instead of insisting on trial of the case, the assessments are probably better insulated from attack on such grounds.

30 While most gamblers threatened with confiscation have the services of an attorney retained by the gambling syndicate, the yearly retainer fee does not cover appearances in court. If the attorney is required to appear several times in court, his fee probably would exceed the amount of the court costs assessed if a consent decree is filed.

31 The prosecutor usually refuses to arrange for or accept a consent decree in (1) all narcotics cases, (2) gambling conspiracy cases, and (3) misdemeanor gambling cases when the defendant has an extremely bad record or is a known notorious violator of the gambling laws. Of course, even in these cases, the prosecutor will not press for trial unless he has a good case based on legally obtained evidence.

32 Funds obtained by the public sale are used to cover court costs, storage fees, and to pay off pending liens on the car. The balance goes to the county general fund. Certain policies of the prosecutor may determine whether the car will be returned to the suspect or sold — narcotics and gambling violators are more likely to completely lose the car through public sale.

pattern of charging the defendant with a violation of those laws. When there is an indication that the regular criminal processes and sanctions are not sufficient to deter the defendants from illegal conduct on certain premises, the prosecuting attorney may resort to the procedures provided by statute[33] to close the establishment permanently or for a limited time.[34] Prosecutors have adopted a policy of requiring proof of several prior convictions for liquor law violations before civil revocation proceedings will be commenced.[35]

If the prosecutor decides to forego charging the licensed defendant with the substantive offense, he will submit a petition[36] to, or otherwise notify, the authority that granted the defendant's liquor license — the local body in Wisconsin[37] — or a representative thereof — the director of the liquor control board in Kansas,[38] a commissioner in Michigan.[39]

A hearing is held by this body[40] or person[41] concerning the alleged violations which would justify revocation.[42] If the license

33 Kan. Stat. Ann. §§41-314, 41-320, 41-805, 41-806 (1964); Mich. Stat. Ann. §§18.975, 18.988, 18.991, 18.992 (Supp. 1969); Wis. Stat. Ann. §§176.11 to 176.121 (Supp. 1968).

34 Mich. Stat. Ann. §18.991 (1957) reads in part: "The suspension or revocation of a license and/or assessment of a penalty by the commission shall not prohibit the institution of criminal prosecutions for the violations of . . . this act. The institution of criminal prosecutions for such violations, or the acquittal or conviction of any person thereunder, shall not prevent the suspension or revocation of licenses and/or assessment of a penalty by the commission. . . ." However, there is no evidence that both procedures would be used against the same defendant for the same offense.

35 In Wisconsin, the state liquor agents have a policy of not requesting a prosecutor to institute a revocation action unless there have been at least two prior convictions; one prosecutor stated that the policy of his office was to require three convictions.

36 In State ex rel. Sullivan v. City of Tomah, 80 Wis. 198, 49 N.W. 753 (1891), the court, in reviewing a license revocation by the local common council, ruled that the petition must set forth the nature and date of the alleged offense(s).

37 There are apparently two procedures by which a license can be revoked in Wisconsin. The first is set forth in Wis. Stat. Ann. §176.11 (1957), the second in §176.121 (Supp. 1968). In the former, the local governing body, which has power to grant liquor licenses to residents, is also given power to revoke upon petition from any resident. In the latter, the director of the state liquor control commission brings a court action to determine if revocation is proper. It is unclear if the local prosecutor handles the state's case in such an action.

38 Kan. Stat. Ann. §41-320 (1964).

39 Mich. Stat. Ann. §18.991 (1957).

40 Mich. Stat. Ann. §18.991 (1957); Wis. Stat. Ann. §176.11 (1957).

41 Kan. Stat. Ann. §41-320 (1964).

42 This is not a criminal proceeding. In Shinavier v. State, 315 Mich. 188, 23 N.W.2d 634 (1946), the witnesses heard were the minor who had bought and consumed liquor on the defendant's premises and the state liquor agent who witnessed this. No mention was made of any participation by the prosecuting attorney.

is revoked or suspended, all accompanying privileges are forfeited,[43] liquor found on the premises is seized,[44] and the defendant is denied the privilege of holding another liquor license for a specified period.[45] A limited review of a decision to revoke is accomplished by certiorari to the district court in Wisconsin and Michigan[46] and by direct appeal in Kansas.[47]

43 Mich. Stat. Ann. §18.992 (1957).

44 Ibid.

45 Wis. Stat. Ann. §176.121 (Supp. 1968) (twelve months).

46 Wis. Stat. Ann. §§176.11 to 176.12 (1957); Mich. Stat. Ann. §18.991 (1957).

47 Kan. Gen. Stat. Ann. §41-323 (1964). Here the statute provides that if either the director or the licensed party is aggrieved by the decision before the full commission, he can appeal to the district court where the suit is docketed as a civil suit. The prosecuting attorney has the duty of presenting the state's case.

CHAPTER 17

The Decision Not to Charge Because the Suspect Is Willing to Cooperate in Achieving Other Enforcement Goals

Police perceive syndicated vice as the backbone of successful commercial crime. They tend to measure their success in controlling commercial crime in terms of their ability to control vice operations and are willing to make substantial charging concessions in order to accomplish that objective. Consequently, alternative procedures are used in cases involving lower echelon numbers runners and bootleggers and, particularly, narcotics violators who are willing in return to become informers.

Informants are extensively used in each of the three states, although, in general, their services are more highly cultivated in the larger cities. An attitude prevails among enforcement officials that effective control of vice — gambling, prostitution, and particularly narcotics — would be impossible without the aid of informants. As subsequent discussion will make clear, there are many types of informants but, generally, they are persons who regularly engage in criminal activity and who assist officials in the apprehension and prosecution of persons similarly engaged.

In Detroit, where informants do not receive money payments for their services, the primary inducement to cooperate is permission to continue their criminal activities, subject to police supervision designed only to keep them within the bounds of relatively minor offenses. But immunity from arrest alone is not sufficient in several situations; many offenders are made informants only after they have been arrested and have been given a charging concession as an inducement to assume informant status. And occasionally, when an informant is arrested by an officer who has no knowledge of his status, the charging decision must be accommodated to the needs of the informant system. One known to be an informant may be arrested if he commits an offense outside the scope of his arrest immunity; even then, his status is considered in making the charging decision.

Federal Bureau of Narcotics officials working in Michigan also make extensive use of informants. The policy of these officials is to make every person arrested on a narcotics charge an informant until the interstate shipper in the supply line is reached, although a suspect who has been a persistent, heavy local distributor will not be given informant status even though he is not an interstate shipper. The interstate shipper is usually prosecuted without the benefit of a charge concession, but over fifty per cent of the other persons arrested on narcotics charges are not prosecuted or are prosecuted on reduced charges in exchange for informant services.

In Milwaukee, the Intelligence Unit, a specialized division in the Milwaukee Police Department, is given responsibility for developing information from all sources on organized crime in order to assist the detective division in clearance of major crimes. The secrecy of the Unit's operations is carefully maintained but its members apparently have authority to make charging concessions in return for informant services. Detectives in the narcotics squad and in other sections of the vice squad have cultivated their own information sources, but the centralization of informant use in the Intelligence Unit operations prevents the development of a widespread, visible informant system of the Detroit type. In addition to inducement by charge concession, information is sometimes purchased.[1]

The informant system in Wichita is less highly developed. Informants are used by officials enforcing the narcotics and obscenity laws. Juvenile informants are used in an effort to control juvenile gangs. Charging concessions are made to induce informant services. Some information is purchased, usually at the rate of twenty-five dollars for each item.

In each of the three states, then, the need for an operating informant system influences the charging decision. Four kinds of situations in which the charging decision must accommodate the need for informants are analyzed below. Primarily, these are situations in which the charging decision is used as an inducement to make an informant out of an offender for the first time,

1 The 1955-1956 budget of the Milwaukee Police Department contained a $1500 secret service fund which, in part, was to be used to buy information.

or to induce him to take on new informant duties in addition to the ones he is already performing. A fifth category treats the charging decision as it is affected by the need to protect the anonymity of informants in the general expectation of their performing future services, but without immediately making a specific assignment.

A. The Casual Stoolpigeon

Prostitutes, petty gamblers, and habitual drunks, because of their continuous participation in criminal or borderline criminal activity, are good sources of information to the police. They are generally knowledgeable about the current criminal activity of others and, because they engage in illegal activity themselves, can be easily induced to pass on useful information.

> *Illustration No. 1:* A man entered police headquarters and told a detective he had information for him. The informant had been arrested a number of times for minor gambling offenses. In return for immunity from further arrest, and for charging concessions if he is arrested, he regularly informs the police department of current crap games and the activities of prostitutes.

This class of informant rarely influences the charging decision materially. His status as informant is the result of a personal relationship with a particular police officer, who rewards his information source with immunity from arrest for minor violations and, sometimes, money payments from a special police department fund. If the informant commits a serious offense, or if he is arrested for a minor offense by an officer who does not know of his status, his position as an informant then affects charging, but this occurs infrequently.

B. The Supervised Transfer

If a suspect is arrested on a charge of possession or sale of contraband, such as narcotics or gambling paraphernalia, he is likely to be offered a charge concession in return for making a supervised transfer.

> *Illustration No. 2:* A parolee sold four caps of heroin to a police officer acting undercover. He indicated he would aid in the apprehension of his source of supply, who was in New York City. The suspect was charged with sale of narcotics. The police notified the Federal Bureau of Nar-

> cotics of the suspect's connection in New York. The next day bail was set at the initial appearance and the suspect flew to New York to make a purchase of heroin under the supervision of federal officials. The police would not tell the suspect whether the sale charge would be dismissed or reduced to possession after he successfully completed the transfer.

In the supervised transfer the informant usually agrees to purchase contraband from another person under the supervision of the police or to arrange its sale to an undercover officer. The informant is never charged with the offense, if any, committed under police supervision. After the transfer is complete, the charge previously lodged against the informant is dismissed or reduced to one of less seriousness, to which it is expected the informant will plead guilty. Less frequently, promises of sentence leniency or probation are made as added inducements. The other transferee is then charged with the criminal activity that he engaged in under police surveillance. This charge may be dropped or reduced if he, in turn, is willing to aid the police in the prosecution of someone whom the officials wish to convict even more. Often, it is unnecessary for the informant making the supervised transfer to testify against his transferee. This is always the case when the transferee himself is made an informant or when he merely arranges a transfer with an undercover officer, but even under other circumstances the police officers who observed the transfer usually are able to supply the necessary testimony, although it may be necessary to place the informant's name on the information as a *res gestae* witness. In any event, the transferee is not arrested until sometime after the transfer in order to protect the informant as much as possible.[2]

C. The Witness Against Other Suspects

A suspect arrested on a vice charge, particularly sale or possession of narcotics, might be offered a charge concession in exchange for information about his source of supply and for testifying for the prosecution in the case against the source. This

[2] The supervised transfer, in one form or another, is used extensively by FBN officials functioning in Michigan. A typical arrangement is a charge concession in exchange for a promise to make a supervised buy from the suspect's principal supplier and from two other pushers known on a casual basis. When the deal is made, it is evidenced by the suspect signing a "special employee agreement."

agreement may include, in addition, a supervised transfer with the supply source.

> *Illustration No. 3:* A woman had been apprehended with a large quantity of heroin in her possession when her home was raided by officers of the narcotics bureau. She was a local distributor and agreed to identify her two carriers. The three, in turn, agreed to testify against three persons who were situated higher in the narcotics hierarchy in exchange for a charge of possession rather than sale. A warrant was issued against the three informants charging narcotics sale. Three other persons, higher in the narcotics structure, were arrested, charged with conspiracy to sell, and waived preliminary examination, but one was held at the request of the state because numerous threats had been made against the informants. The defendants were bound over for trial. The judge who conducted the preliminary indicated that if the three informants cooperated in testifying at the trial they would not even be charged with possession.

If an informant possesses information about persons whom officials are particularly anxious to prosecute, it is likely that his services as a witness will be necessary, because it is unlikely that the persons prosecuted will plead guilty. The usual agreement is a reduction in the charge in exchange for the necessary testimony and information. Typically, the informant will be initially charged with the most serious offense available in order to secure his complete cooperation in the prosecution of the other persons. Usually, a preliminary examination is held to put the informant's testimony on the record, because experience has taught the prosecutor that when the defendant is an important person in the underworld the informant may be induced not to testify at the trial, either by threats or bribe, and the preliminary examination record can be used at the trial in such an event.

Sometimes the informant's case is delayed until the disposition of the case in which he is testifying. He may then either plead guilty to a less serious offense than that contained in the warrant or he may be completely released. In other cases, the informant pleads guilty to a less serious offense, but the sentencing on that offense is delayed until he testifies against the other persons. After that case is complete, the informant is convicted of a less serious offense and given a very light sentence; whether he is convicted at all may depend upon how hard he bargains when he initially assumes informant status.

Informant testimony is used to some extent in each of the three states. Apparently, the feeling is that it is best to avoid the use of informant testimony if at all possible, because, for one reason, it destroys a large part of the witness's future use as an informant. The use of informant testimony seems to be largely limited to the narcotics field in each of the three states. In Detroit, it is almost exclusively limited to that use and is not used at all in gambling and liquor law cases.

D. The Witness Against Co-defendants

When two or more persons, apprehended while engaging in criminal activity, seem to the officials equally culpable, morally as well as legally, the prevailing attitude is to treat them as nearly alike as possible. Sometimes, however, it becomes necessary to grant a charge concession to one co-defendant in exchange for his testimony against the other. This is done only when conviction of both defendants seems unlikely. Although officials are willing, when necessary, to permit a co-defendant to plead guilty to a less serious offense in exchange for testimony, they will rarely agree not to charge the state's witness at all. Pandering cases present a major exception to this policy. Officials feel they do not have a case against a male solicitor unless the prostitute is willing to testify against him. The prostitute is taken before a judge and a detainer is placed against her as a witness. Bond is set, but, even if someone offers to post bail, she will usually prefer to remain in jail for her own protection. Even then, the risk is substantial that the prostitute will be deterred by threats or bribes from testifying at the trial because pandering cases usually involve criminal syndicates. To minimize that risk, a preliminary examination of the solicitor is held, even though he prefers to waive it, to preserve the prostitute's testimony for use at the trial. After the prostitute testifies against the pimp at his trial, she is released. No charge is ever lodged against her.

E. The Continuing Nature of the Informant Relationship

The most significant characteristic of the police-informant relationship is its continuing nature. Thus, if a police officer promises immunity from arrest for minor offenses, or can guarantee a charge concession in a pending case, when this specific informant assignment is completed in a relatively short time, other assignments are likely to follow. Some informants, because they persist in engaging in criminal activities, tend to take on the status of permanent informants.[3]

> *Illustration No. 4:* A woman had been arrested for narcotics addiction by officials in outstate Michigan. They learned she had been helpful in prosecuting two heroin pushers in Detroit. The lieutenant in charge of the vice squad promised her she would not be prosecuted for addiction if she informed on her local supplier.
>
> *Illustration No. 5:* The suspect had been informing for the Federal Bureau of Narcotics for some time. He had made supervised buys from several big dealers for them, in return for which he was never prosecuted. The suspect continued to push on his own and was apprehended when he sold four caps of heroin to an undercover state officer. A charge of narcotics sale was lodged against him but the case was delayed until the suspect had made supervised buys from five dealers for the state officials. The police wanted the narcotics sale charge dismissed, but the inspector refused to do more than recommend a reduction to possession until he was told by the federal authorities that the suspect's continued value as an informant would be destroyed if he were forced to plead to the possession charge.

If the informant has demonstrated his usefulness, he may be given a charge concession simply to keep him available for future use. The feeling among officials is that, once he is prosecuted for a less serious offense, his usefulness as an informant diminishes. Many times, the informant is given new assignments in exchange for the charge concession, but if he has proved particularly valuable he may be held generally in reserve for future use. In such a case a warrant may be issued, but nothing further done, in order to assure his cooperation whenever necessary. Officials continually warn informants that their status does not give them a "license to peddle," and that they will be arrested and prosecuted if they persist in making unauthorized narcotics sales.

[3] A federal prosecutor was observed in one case to argue for sentencing leniency when the defendant had been convicted of narcotics sale, an offense for which the prosecutor normally seeks a severe sentence, because the defendant had been particularly useful to his office in that he informed on 89 narcotic peddlers.

CHAPTER 18

The Decision Not to Charge Because Informal Administrative Procedures More Satisfactorily Achieve Objectives Underlying Criminal Statutes

In the handling of some classes of persons suspected of crime, the normal practice is to make a negative charging decision and to utilize some regularized procedure that is not provided by formal law for the prosecuting attorney's use. This chapter treats of seven such procedures, all of which are intended to relieve the criminal justice system of the intolerable burden that would be presented if every offender in those categories were processed through the system, as well as to provide an informal means of settling interpersonal disputes.

The objective of the informal alternative procedure, in most instances, is to insure that the offense complained of will not recur. This is true in cases of nonsupport, family and neighborhood assaults, distribution or exhibition of obscene materials or performances, disorderly conduct, or minor juvenile offenses. In each of these categories, the aim of the practice is to impress the suspect with the seriousness of his conduct and to warn him that probable prosecution will ensue with repeated offenses. The avowed objective of those who handle the informal disposition of statutory rape cases or minor property offenses is not so much preventive as it is conciliatory — to urge a settlement to the satisfaction of all parties through marriage or restitution.

A. Nonsupport Cases

Nonsupport statutes are frequently violated. Violations fall generally into three classes: (1) those in which the husband remains within the jurisdiction; (2) those in which he has taken up residence in another state; and (3) those in which the violator is not a husband, but merely the father of an illegitimate child. Discussion first centers on the problems and procedures common to all three situations, followed by an analysis of special problems caused by the fact that the defendant is not a resident of the state, and concludes with the handling of illegitimacy cases

In current practice, prosecutors prefer to use an alternative to prosecution for nonsupport. The primary reason for this reluctance to use the formal charging process is that the complainant is rarely interested in prosecution; usually she views the threat of it solely as a means of inducing her husband to support her and their children. Prosecutors tend to agree with the complainant's attitude toward prosecution for the same reasons. Causing a husband to be confined in jail eliminates the usual source from which support payments must come, and a fine necessarily decreases that fund as well. But even when the prosecutor is convinced that prosecution is desirable because the alternative procedures have not worked, it is still not feasible to prosecute unless the wife is willing fully to participate and she usually is not.

An important factor in the decision not to prosecute is the existence of alternative procedures — both formal and informal — designed to secure the underlying objectives of the criminal statutes: support of the family. These alternatives are plentiful and generally are more successful in achieving that objective than is prosecution. Although criminal prosecution may sometimes be predicated on desertion, apart from the resultant failure to meet financial obligations toward the spouse or children, often the two offenses are equated in the statutes.[1] This is generally done in practice; thus when a decision is made to rely on an alternative to prosecution, the prosecution which the officials have in mind would usually be for nonsupport rather than desertion, even if the husband had also deserted. The alternative procedures discussed here are, therefore, alternatives to criminal prosecution for nonsupport.

In Detroit, all complainants in nonsupport matters, when the defendant still resides locally, are referred to the adjustment division of the Recorder's Court Probation Department by all

[1] The Uniform Desertion and Nonsupport Act, 10 U.L.A. §1, states the elements of the offense in the alternative: either "desert or wilfully neglect or refuse to provide for the support. . . ." See Wis. Stat. Ann. §52.05 (Supp. 1968). Mich. Stat Ann. §28.358 (1962).

enforcement agencies, including the prosecuting attorney's office. In addition, many cases are referred by social agencies in the community. The staff of the adjustment division interviews both the wife, who is the complainant, and the husband. Arrangements are then made with the husband, under threat of prosecution for nonsupport, to make regular weekly payments to his wife through the adjustment bureau.

When the husband is unwilling to enter into arrangements that are satisfactory to the adjustment bureau, he may be prosecuted if the wife is willing to cooperate.[2] Probably the complainants in Michigan are more cooperative in prosecuting than in some states because the husband will be charged only with a misdemeanor and usually confined for not more than ninety days if convicted for a first offense.[3] If the adjustment bureau recommends to the prosecutor that a warrant be issued, the request is routinely granted because of the prosecutor's awareness that all efforts to arrange for continuing support have failed.

In Wisconsin, the decision whether to proceed against the husband by a civil action or by criminal action[4] is left largely to the complainant. When the husband and wife are in a middle or high income group, it is likely that a civil action will be used. In the more common situation, the family is in a low income group and has been on relief since the husband left. The statutes provide that state relief is not payable unless a warrant has been issued against the husband for a violation of the criminal provision relating to nonsupport.[5] Although it is not entirely clear, it appears that defendants are commonly charged in these cases when the wife is willing to prosecute and, if found guilty, are placed on probation on condition that they meet the support obligations.

Kansas prosecutors attempt to arrange informal settlement of support claims, whether the husband is a resident of the state

2 The division will not initiate proceedings for the issuance of a warrant if the man is unemployed or otherwise unable to pay. The department estimates that less than one per cent of the cases handled by the adjustment division result in the issuance of nonsupport warrants.

3 There are two statutory provisions relating to nonsupport. The one most commonly used is a part of the disorderly conduct statute, the violation of which is a misdemeanor. Mich. Stat. Ann. §28.364 (Supp. 1968). The second provision of the statutes relating to nonsupport is a section on "desertion and non-support," the violation of which is a felony. Mich. Stat. Ann. §28.358 (1962). If the defendant fails to respond or continues his refusal to provide support after punishment for the misdemeanor, then arrangements are made to have him charged with a felony.

4 Note, 1952 Wis. L. Rev. 544.

5 Wis. Stat. Ann. §49.19(4)(d)(5) (Supp. 1968).

or not.[6] As in the other states, if no provision can be worked out without prosecution, the wife is consulted to determine whether she is willing to prosecute, and her decision normally will control. Only if the prosecutor is convinced that the wife will carry through prosecution will the husband be arrested and charged.

If the wife is willing to prosecute after other methods of persuading the defendant to meet his support obligations have failed, the prosecution will be for either child or wife desertion, both of which are felonies.[7] The court has the power to enter a support order prior to trial and can punish for contempt in case of disobedience.[8] The court is also empowered to release the defendant on probation conditioned on his meeting the support arrangements.[9]

When the husband is found out of the jurisdiction, different formal procedures are available. In Michigan, as a substitute for criminal prosecution for nonsupport and the extradition of defendants who reside outside of the state, proceedings can be initiated under the Uniform Reciprocal Enforcement of Support Act (URESA).[10] The act, adopted in all states, is designed to create an effective civil remedy to enforce the support of abandoned wives and children when the husband has left the state.

The unit of the Detroit prosecuting attorney's office handling nonsupport matters has a staff of four assistant prosecutors who spend a substantial part of their time administering the act.[11] Complainants are interviewed by members of the staff, and all necessary information relating to the case is recorded. If the information provided by the complainant indicates that the defendant has neglected a duty to support, a petition is prepared

6 In Kansas, the practice is to treat all cases in which the persons are divorced as strictly a civil matter, and prosecutors refuse to charge on the basis of the availability of the civil actions. Such a distinction does not appear to be recognized by the formal law in Kansas. See Kan. Stat. Ann. §21-442 (1964). It has been held that a husband could be prosecuted for nonsupport of a child who had been awarded to the custody of the divorced wife. State v. Miller, 111 Kan. 231, 206 Pac. 744 (1922).

7 Kan. Stat. Ann. §21-442 (1964).

8 Kan. Stat. Ann. §21-444 (1964).

9 Kan. Stat. Ann. §21-445 (1964). This may be done either before trial with the consent of the defendant or after a plea of guilty at trial.

10 Mich. Stat. Ann. §§25.225(1) to 25.225(24) (Supp. 1965).

11 The uniform act was amended in 1953 in Michigan to provide: "In all instances in which a public support burden has been incurred or is threatened, it shall be the duty of the prosecuting attorney to represent the petitioner in initiating and conducting proceedings under this act: Provided, that the petitioner may be represented in any proceedings by private counsel, at his own expense." Mich. Stat. Ann. §25.225(10a) (1957).

for filing in the chancery division of the circuit court. The court routinely signs the necessary orders which are then sent to the responding state which makes an effort to find the defendant. When found, he is processed and taken to the appropriate court for disposition. The governor of the state has expressed opposition to initiation of extradition proceedings until the evidence before him indicates that all possible remedies under URESA have been exhausted.

As in Michigan, when a husband is out of the state of Wisconsin and accused of nonsupport, the policy of the district attorney's office is to utilize the civil proceedings under URESA[12] rather than extradition and prosecution. Under URESA, if the husband is determined to have a support duty and is ordered to meet it, upon failure of the husband to pay, it is possible to proceed against him by a contempt proceeding in the state in which he resides. It is also possible to charge him with a violation of the criminal statute in the state in which the wife is located and extradite him to stand trial for the crime of nonsupport. It is the policy of the district attorney's office in Milwaukee to avoid extradition and a criminal charge if that is possible. The assistant district attorney in charge of nonsupport matters will write as many as five or six letters requesting the husband to comply before taking any further proceedings. Even then she will request the state where the husband is resident to threaten a contempt proceeding hoping to persuade him to make support payments, and she may even go to the extent of actually starting a contempt proceeding with the hope that the husband will pay. If all this fails, then extradition may be instituted as a last resort.

In Kansas, URESA[13] civil actions do not appear to be used to the extent they are in Wisconsin and Michigan. It is much more likely to be the case that, if the Kansas wife convinces the prosecutor she will carry through prosecution if extradition is accomplished, the prosecutor will have the errant husband returned to the state. Still, as the result of past experience showing the likelihood that the wife will later change her mind, extradition is by no means automatic. As an example, in one case the husband had deserted and gone to Kentucky. He was extradited, returned to Sedgwick County, and placed on his own recognizance. When time for trial came, the man had jumped his bond and was later

12 Wis. Stat. Ann. §52.10 (1957).

13 Kan. Stat. Ann. §§23-419 to 23-446 (1964), adopted in 1953.

located in the state of Washington. He was again extradited and placed on a high bond, which he could not make. The wife continued to visit him in the county jail. When the time again came for trial and the wife was subpoenaed by the state, she absolutely refused to testify against her husband. The judge dismissed the case and the husband was released. The wife later returned to the prosecutor's office complaining that the husband had again left her. The deputy county attorney told her this time nothing could be done since she had her chance to avail herself of the criminal law in the first case and had refused to do so. The deputy refused to issue a warrant for the arrest of the husband.

All three states have statutes designed to secure the imposition of support obligations for illegitimate children.[14] Even though it may be theoretically possible to prosecute the father of an illegitimate child either under nonsupport statutes[15] or even fornication laws, in all the cases observed the procedure used was the bastardy or paternity action. Just as in cases involving nonsupport of the wife or legitimate children, it is obvious that prosecution will not achieve the goal of support. Further, the bastardy actions conveniently allow both of the major issues to be adjudicated in the same proceedings. Not only may the court establish the parenthood of the child, but the court is empowered to impose the exact amount of support that the father is required to pay.

In addition to those factors that influence the complainant to prefer the use of the bastardy proceedings over criminal prosecution, prosecutors are undoubtedly influenced by the statutory requirement that they represent the complainant in those actions. Because they must assist in the trial of the bastardy action, which normally results in the imposition of support obligations on the father, there simply is no need for criminal prosecution — the goal has been satisfied. If, after support orders are entered, a father neglects to make payment, the orders are enforceable through the use of civil contempt proceedings so that, again, re-

14 Mich. Stat. Ann. §§25.491 to 25.510 (1957). Both Kansas and Wisconsin have adopted the Uniform Desertion and Nonsupport Act which includes the support of illegitimate children. Kan. Stat. Ann. §§21-442 to 21-448 (1964); Wis. Stat. Ann. §52.05 (Supp. 1968). See also Wis. Stat. Ann. §§52.25-52.45 (Supp. 1968); Kan Stat. Ann. §§62-2301 to 62-2321 (1964). The support obligation may be imposed in the same action which establishes the parental relationship.

15 See, e.g., Wahl v. Walsh, 180 Kan. 313, 316, 304 P.2d 525, 527 (1956). The Kansas Supreme Court held that there was a common law duty to support illegitimate children. The case did not arise, however, as a result of a criminal prosecution.

sort to criminal prosecution is obviated. In the three states, bastardy actions are usually considered "quasi-criminal."[16] It is nevertheless clear that the prosecutor's participation in the procedure is much like that in criminal matters, except that the initial screening and investigation may be undertaken by welfare agencies rather than the police.

In Detroit, when the initial screening has been accomplished, the girl is sent to the office of the assistant prosecutor charged with administering the act. Two social workers are assigned to that office and one of them will interview her. Because of the large number of cases which must be processed,[17] the complainant is first informed of her right to have the matter handled by a private attorney who, she is advised, could bring the action much sooner. About one-third of the cases are disposed of in this manner. If she still wishes the prosecutor to handle the case, a letter is mailed to the putative father advising him to come to the prosecutor's office for an interview. During the interview, the assistant prosecutor advises him of his right to a blood test. He is also apprised of the evidence against him and the likelihood of his being named the father. The purpose of the interview is to get the father to admit parenthood. Whether or not he does, the mother signs a complaint and once a week all the mothers are taken to the circuit court where the complaints are sworn to and a summons is issued to the father informing him of the date of the hearing. If the alleged father is found guilty at the hearing, the court enters an order to this effect and designates the amount of support to be provided. Comparable procedures are provided in Kansas and Wisconsin.

B. Family and Neighborhood Assaults: The Misdemeanor Complaint Bureau

The number of complaints received in Detroit as the result of familial or neighborhood disputes is vast, yet very few of these complaints ever result in prosecution. Typically, the victim of an assault is initially insistent upon prosecution of the offender. For several reasons, prosecutors attempt to dissuade prosecution in these cases and are usually successful in that attempt.

Prosecutors are aware that, in many such cases, the complainant will desire not to prosecute after sufficient time has passed

16 See, e.g., Hodgson v. Nickell, 69 Wis. 308, 34 N.W. 118 (1887).

17 Approximately 600 such cases a year are brought to the attention of the prosecutor assigned to handle these cases.

for tempers to cool and second thoughts to be given to the seriousness of this course of action. Therefore, the simple expediency of delaying the charging decision for a few days often suffices. To charge immediately in these cases would usually be futile because, when the complainant later changes his or her mind, prosecution would be difficult if not impossible.

Another factor enters into the prosecutor's decision not to charge in many cases. Often the complainant is as "guilty" as the suspect in contributing to the dispute, even to the extent that his conduct amounts to a crime. In such cases, conviction would be improbable because of judge and jury reactions to complainants who are as guilty as defendants.

If prosecution were to be commenced in every case in which a drunken husband struck his wife, or a neighbor made threatening gestures at another, the charging decision would place an additional strain on an inevitably continuing relationship. Prosecutors prefer that the solution of the difficulties be an amicable one. Finally, if charging occurred in all of these cases, officials believe that an inordinate amount of resources would be expended in attempting to control infractions of a relatively minor nature which are generally viewed as the inevitable result of living in close communities. For these reasons, alternatives have been developed to resolve these disputes, and the very existence of these alternatives influences the decision not to charge and to convince the complainant that use of the alternatives is the better course of action.

Within the Detroit prosecutor's office, variously known as "the prosecuting attorney's detail" or "the prosecutor's bureau," are two divisions that process most of the cases involving this type of dispute.[18] The "assault and battery" detail receives the cases from the precinct offices. The two detectives assigned to that detail forward the cases to an assistant prosecutor who listens to the complaints and decides the disposition of each.[19] The assistant, after hearing the case, may decide: (1) that a warrant should be issued; (2) that the case should be dismissed; or (3) that the case should be referred back to another division in the "prosecutor's

[18] The third division which comprises the "prosecutor's bureau" is the felony detail.

[19] Unlike the usual procedure in the felony and high misdemeanor cases, a detective does not present the written request for a warrant to the prosecuting attorney's office. Instead, the request is generally brought to the office by the complainant who requested the warrant. If the defendant is in custody, the written request for a warrant is presented by the uniformed police officers assigned to transport the defendant to the prosecutor's office.

bureau" known as the "misdemeanor" or "domestic relations" detail.

The statistics available for 1953 show the typical type and disposition of the cases: 6170 complaints were received and processed by the assault and battery detail. Those complaints consisted of 5303 for assault and battery, 442 for simple assault, 69 for disturbing the peace, 165 for malicious destruction of property, 155 for indecent and obscene language, and 36 for miscellaneous offenses. Of the total of 6170 complaints received, the assistant prosecutors made the following dispositions: 913 warrants were recommended, 285 cases were dismissed, and 5329 were referred back to the domestic relations detail for mediation or imposition of "peace bonds." It is apparent that the operation of the domestic relations detail constitutes an important part of the administrative system in Detroit.

When the prosecutor decides that the mediation alternative to charging is appropriate, a hearing is set for the case, generally within a week from the initial contact by the complainant,[20] and notice is given to the interested parties to appear at that time. Only about half of the cases referred to the two detectives actually result in a hearing. If both parties fail to appear, it is concluded that conciliation has taken place and the case is dropped from the files of the prosecuting attorney's office. It is, in fact, primarily for this reason that a period of a week is set between the time the complaint is filed and the time the hearing is to be held. If one party fails to appear at a hearing in response to the notice, he is sent a second notice. If a "defendant" does not respond to a second notice and the complainant still wants to prosecute, a warrant is issued for his arrest.

The two detectives assigned to hear the cases occupy a room in the prosecuting attorney's office which consists of a desk in front facing chairs occupied by interested persons.[21] Occasionally one of the parties is represented by counsel. The hearing begins with the detective reading the report of the case submitted by the precinct detective initially involved with the case. After attempting to develop the facts from interviewing the interested persons, including the attorney, the "judge" decides on one of

20 When an individual is being detained in custody on a charge of assault, arrangements are made to hold the hearing as soon as possible so that it may be held prior to his release.

21 The character of the room is enhanced by a picture of a little boy which hangs on the wall. The boy is kneeling by his bed and offering a prayer: "Dear Lord, please make Mom and Pop stop fighting, cause it's hard to take sides when you love 'em both, and besides, I'm ashamed to face the kids."

four alternative dispositions available to him: (1) he may determine from the hearing that a warrant is justified; (2) he may convince the complainant that prosecution is not justified — or the complainant may so decide of his own volition — in which event the case is disposed of by having the complainant sign a statement to the effect that he or she does not wish to prosecute; (3) he may "adjourn the case without date"; or (4) he may place the defendant under a "peace bond."

Occasionally, the detective decides to refer a case back to the assistant prosecutor with a recommendation that the defendant be prosecuted. This occurs when facts that were not known at the time the case was initially reviewed and assigned for mediation come to the attention of the detective. For example, evidence that the victim had suffered severe physical injury at the hands of the defendant which was not apparent at first would cause reconsideration of prosecution. The case may also be referred back to the assistant prosecutor if it appears that there is no possibility of reconciliation.

In some cases the detective may determine that the infraction was minor and that both parties were equally guilty.[22] In those cases the detective may dismiss the matter himself. When the decision not to prosecute is mutually agreed to by the parties, the practice is to have the complainant sign a statement to the effect that he or she does not wish to prosecute.[23]

The third alternative available to the detective is to "adjourn the case without date." This alternative differs from outright dismissal only because it implies that, if further difficulties arise, official action will be taken. There is, however, no formal procedure by which a case which is "adjourned without date" is considered again unless it is at the initiative of the complainant and then only if a complaint of a new offense is made.

The fourth method of disposition of these cases is by far the most frequent. In 1953, of 5791 cases referred to the domestic relations detail, 5329 were terminated by placing the "defendant" on a "peace bond." The imposition of a peace bond under these circumstances has no foundation in Michigan law,[24] and the offi-

22 This normally is the result when a husband has assaulted his wife but the injury is not serious and it appears that there was "good cause" for him to do so.

23 Cases often arise in which the wife realizes after filing a complaint that prosecution is too drastic a means to accomplish the limited purpose she has in mind. For example, the detective will often point out that the husband may no longer be able to support the family for a period of time if he is successfully prosecuted.

24 Michigan law provides for security to keep the peace, but this may not be required by those detectives. Mich. Stat. Ann. §28.1154 (1954) provides: "The

cials are well aware of that fact. The only notation made that a "peace bond" is posted is a short pencil notation on the offense report prepared by the officers in the precinct. No bond, as such, is actually posted. The peace bond is merely a record kept of the particular case; it is intended that, if the person is involved in a similar offense within the period of the bond, the fact that he was involved in the prior offense will be considered in determining the disposition of the second offense.

Despite the lack of legal basis for the peace bond, the detectives responsible for its administration have developed criteria both to determine the sufficiency of the evidence to justify its imposition and to decide the duration of the bond.[25] Further, the prosecutor aids in increasing the efficacy of the peace bond by charging in cases in which normally no charge would be made on the grounds that the violator committed the minor offense while under peace bond. Even attorneys employed by "defendants" in these proceedings, although aware of its legal status, do not discourage its use. Indeed, they usually take a passive role in the proceedings and, when they do participate, they call the detectives "judge" or "your honor."

When the active endorsement of the system by police, prosecutors, and private defense attorneys is combined with the complainant's and defendant's unawareness of the lack of any official standing of the peace bond, it is not surprising that the procedure is effective both to satisfy the complainant that there has been "official" action taken with respect to the complaints,[26] and

---

justices of the supreme court, the several circuit judges, judges of courts of record having jurisdiction of criminal causes, circuit court commissioners, all mayors and recorders of cities, and all justices of the peace, shall have power to cause all the laws made for the preservation of the public peace to be kept and in the execution of this power may require persons to give security to keep the peace in the manner provided in this chapter."

25 The maximum period for which the bond is imposed is two years, and may be any period less than that.

26 One of the detectives underscored this function of the procedure:

"As you know, in many of these cases, one or both of the parties just want the police to do something about the other person. Considering the size of our city and the volume of these problems, you can imagine that if the police backed out of a case just because no one wanted to prosecute, in time there would be a lot of disgruntled people who would ask, 'What are the police and prosecuting attorneys doing for their salaries? We call the police and they tell us that they won't take action because the prosecuting attorney won't recommend a warrant.' This way, the people feel that the prosecuting attorney has done something in the case and there will not be so many embittered voters at the polls at election time."

This function appears to be especially important in resolving neighborhood disputes. It is felt that the complaining parties can derive some satisfaction from the fact that they have brought the matter to the attention of an official. Peace

to deter the defendant from future infractions.[27] The detectives in the domestic relations detail estimate that 85 per cent of the cases in which the defendant is placed on a peace bond achieve the desired result.[28] Indeed, frequently complainants go to the prosecutor's office requesting the imposition of the peace bond.

C. Minor Property Offenses: Restitution Instead of Prosecution

Victims of minor property crimes, such as recipients of bad checks, normally are interested only in restitution for the loss suffered by them, and they seek the aid of the prosecutor solely to achieve that end. Although they are usually willing to threaten prosecution, seldom are they willing to actually assist in prosecution, even if restitution is not made. Indeed, that situation is seldom presented because offenders readily make restitution if given the opportunity as an alternative to charging. Prosecutors, for the most part, are willing to allow the criminal processes to be used to gain that objective, although they often express some dissatisfaction with their status as "collection agencies."

Despite some dissimilarities in the details and scope of the informal procedures used in the three states, in all of them attempts are routinely made to encourage restitution for the issuance of a bad check as an alternative to charging.[29] In Detroit, a special police detail receives and processes all complaints for bad checks, and several attempts at restitution are made before the prosecutor is called upon to make a decision to charge. This

---

bonds will be resorted to in these cases when it appears that mediation is ineffective to resolve the differences.

[27] In one case the detective received a phone call from a man who wanted to find out if his son could be taken off "probation" so he could join the army. He had been placed on peace bond. The detective explained to the father that the boy did not have a criminal record.

In another case, a woman went to the prosecutor to determine if as she believed, her "bond" had "expired." The records were not immediately available so the prosecutor asked her if it was essential that she have the information immediately. She said that it was, that if the bond had expired, she wanted to get even with the other disputant.

[28] However, in practice, there is no routine procedure in use by which the fact that an individual is under peace bond comes to the attention of the detectives. The most common way in which this is discovered is through the memory of the detective handling the case. The disposition of each case is recorded on the investigating officer's report, but these reports are not indexed or arranged for purposes of reference.

[29] Kan. Gen. Stat. Ann. §§21-554 to 21-559 (1949). The punishment provisions were modified in 1959 and are now contained in Kan. Stat. Ann. §21-555 (1964); Mich. Stat. Ann. §§28.326 to 28.329 (1954); Wis. Stat. Ann §943.24 (1958).

amounts to a generalized decision not to charge if restitution is obtained. In Wisconsin and Kansas, the prosecutor's office actively participates in the attempt to get the offender to make restitution.[30] Offenders who are not charged are usually those who have written insufficient funds checks, rather than forgers or those who have written a check on a bank in which they had no account — a so-called no-account check. But in Kansas, the abatement provision of the statute,[31] which was clearly applicable only to insufficient funds checks, was often applied in practice to no-account checks as well. In all three states, some effort is made to determine if the offender is a professional or an habitual bad check passer; if he is, he is more likely to be charged than allowed to make restitution.

Because of the similarity of the general procedures used, except for these differences referred to above, a generalized description of the handling of a bad check case is sufficient to illustrate the procedures used. The prosecutor may be notified that a person is suspected of issuing a bad check either by the police or by a private citizen. If the police are notified first, no investigation is undertaken and the case is forwarded directly to the prosecutor. Typically, the facts are not in dispute and the whereabouts of check writers is usually known. After getting the necessary details from the complainant, the prosecutor suggests to him that he attempt to gain restitution from the check writer. If that has already been done, the prosecutor will then write the offender a letter informing him that, if restitution is not made within several days, prosecution will be commenced against him. He must appear at the prosecutor's office to redeem the check. When the offender responds to the letter, the prosecutor collects the amount shown on the face of the check. A receipt for the amount of money paid is given to the check writer along with the check itself. The complainant is then notified to come to the prosecutor's office to pick up his money. The offender may be permitted to make installment payments to the prosecutor if he is unable to pay the full amount. No charge is made for services rendered in bad check cases.

Reliance on the informal alternative of restitution in bad

30 In Milwaukee, the attempts to get restitution are made by an investigator assigned to the prosecutor's office.

31 Law of Mar. 11, 1915, c. 92, §3, [1915] Kan. Laws 115-116 (repealed 1963) allowed abatement as a matter of right when defendant could show that he had an account in the bank for thirty days prior to the date the check was issued and that he had no intent to defraud. In such cases, the action was abated if defendant paid the amount of the check and costs.

check cases is not specifically recognized in the formal law of any of the three states, except to the extent the abatement provisions in the Kansas statute used to permit it. But even in Kansas, the practice went well beyond what was apparently contemplated by the formal law. Although the practice is not as highly regularized in other "white collar crime" areas, it is clear that, in cases such as borderline business fraud, embezzlement, misuse or sale of mortgaged property, the primary object of the complainant is restitution for his financial loss just as it is in bad check cases. There, too, restitution is a common informal alternative to charging.

D. Censorship of Obscene Materials or Performances

A massive effort is made by Detroit police to protect the citizenry — and particularly children — against the dangers of exposure to obscene books or performances. Violations of obscenity laws brought about by the sale or possession of "hard-core" pornographic materials result in prosecutions of the laws violated.[32] Of greater significance, however, is the Detroit Police Censor Bureau, which the city of Detroit has established by ordinance.[33] That ordinance authorized the police to censor motion pictures, stage plays, burlesque shows, and nightclub entertainment. Though not expressly authorized by the ordinance, the police, acting on the basis of authority they believe exists under state statutes relating to obscenity,[34] also censor paperbacks and magazines. Because the most important objective of the program is protection of the morals of children, no regular effort is made to censor hardcover books, although they will be investigated on complaint.

All film to be shown to the public in the city of Detroit for which an admission charge is to be made must be viewed by the police department prior to showing. Distributors of films provide viewing facilities and absorb the costs. When the viewing policeman decides that particular footage, or the entire film, is questionable, the film is viewed by his superiors who make the final

[32] See, e.g., Kan. Stat. Ann. §§21-1102 to 21-1102(c), 21-1105 to 21-1106 (1964); Mich. Stat. Ann. §§28.575(1) to 28.575(5), 28.576 to 28.578 (Supp. 1968); Wis. Stat. Ann. §§944.21 to 944.22 (1958).

[33] Compiled Ordinances, c. 114, §8 (1954). Revised as Municipal Code, City of Detroit §5-12-12 (1966).

[34] Mich. Stat. Ann. §§28.575(1) to 28.575(5), 28.576 to 28.578 (Supp. 1968)

decision. In some cases, when a film has already acquired some reputation as borderline, those in charge of the bureau will view the film initially. They often call in leaders from groups who might be especially interested, such as clergymen or other community leaders who serve in an advisory capacity. The criteria that are used in reaching a decision are not reduced to writing, but the most commonly applied test is whether the film is "fit" to be viewed by children. This procedure, which generally takes place about two months before the scheduled public showing, resulted in cutting 15,000 feet in 1956 and 45,000 in 1955.[35]

Stage plays, burlesque shows, and nightclub entertainment are not subject to review prior to public showing. Instead, a detail of police spot-checks the entertainment while it is in progress, making no effort to conceal their identity. Indeed, they feel that it is more desirable to make known their presence because of the added deterrent effect when owners know they are subject to frequent but sporadic checking. If anything in the entertainment is viewed as being obscene, informal arrangement is made with the entertainer and management to remove that part of the act or to render it innocuous. There is no generalized verbalization of the standard that is applied in these cases.

By informal arrangement with the major distributors in the Detroit area, the censor bureau officers review every paperback book and magazine well in advance of its intended release date. If the publication is deemed undesirable, the distributor — who may or may not concur in the judgment — usually cancels the shipment to Detroit.[36] The bureau manifests an intention to charge both the distributor and the retailers if the bureau's judgment is ignored and the material distributed.

Because those persons directly concerned derive substantial benefit from the police stamp of approval on their products, approval which is given in the vast majority of cases, they are usually willing to forego serious objections to the operation of this bureau.[37] In this special sense that the operation of the bureau

[35] Fifteen thousand feet of film amounts to viewing time of approximately 6¼ hours. The viewing time of the film cut in Detroit in 1955 was 18¾ hours.

[36] Censorship practices of the bureau resulted in nondistribution of the paperback edition of *From Here to Eternity,* with an estimated loss of 60,000 sales in that area.

[37] The procedure, for example, allows the distributor to inform those who object to the distribution or sale of certain books or magazines that the publications have received the approval of the Detroit Police Department. In the same way, approval of the publication assures retailers that they will not be prosecuted or unduly affected in sales because of inclusion of the publication in such "banned" lists as the one promulgated by the National Organization for Decent Literature.

may be viewed as an alternative to charging, for the procedure followed obviates for the most part any need for a charging decision. By obtaining the cooperation and support of those who might otherwise be violators, violations are at a minimum. If it proves necessary in order to obtain compliance with a police censorship decision, the threat of prosecution is used.

Judged solely in terms of its effectiveness in eliminating from normal distribution channels literature believed by the police to be harmful to the morals of the community and particularly its children, the program is successful. The bureau has accomplished this purpose with a minimum of actual prosecutions.[38]

Although the system of informal censorship was being fully utilized when the survey of Detroit practices was made, this is no longer true. In *New American Library of World Literature, Inc. v. Allen*[39] and *Bantam Books, Inc. v. Melko*,[40] the courts held that such an activity on the part of the police department or the prosecuting attorney, respectively, was beyond the scope of their statutory authority and so unconstitutional.[41] Injunctions against threats of future prosecution or police harassment were granted in both cases. In January 1957, Random House, Inc., and

38 Because of the uncertain standards in the area of obscenity regulation however, it seems inevitable that a great amount of *legal* conduct is also regulated by the censor bureau. See Slough and McAnany, Obscenity and Constitutional Freedom — Part I, 8 St. L.U.L.J. 279, 302-303 n.84 (1964), for some specific evidence on the effectiveness of these censorship practices.

39 114 F. Supp. 823 (N.D. Ohio 1953).

40 25 N.J. Super. 292, 96 A.2d 47 (1953), *modified*, 14 N.J. 524, 103 A.2d 256 (1954).

41 See American Mercury, Inc. v. Chase, 13 F.2d 224 (D. Mass. 1926), in which an injunction was granted a book publisher against the New England Watch and Ward Society, an unofficial organization that compiled its own list of undesirable magazines and books and threatened publishers and distributors with prosecution if sales continued. The language of the court applies equally well to official self-appointed "censors."

"The injury to the persons affected does not flow from any judgment of a court or public body; it is caused by the defendants' notice, which rests on the defendants' judgment. The result on the other person is the same, whether that judgment be right or wrong; i.e., the sale of his magazine or book is seriously interfered with. Few dealers in any trade will buy goods after notice that they will be prosecuted if they resell them. Reputable dealers do not care to take such a risk, even when they believe that prosecution would prove unfounded. The defendants know this, and trade upon it. They secure their influence, not by voluntary acquiescence in their opinions by the trade in question, but by the coercion and intimidation of that trade, through the fear of prosecution if the defendants' views are disregarded. . . .

"[T]his is clearly illegal. The defendants have the right of every citizen to come to the courts with complaints of crime; but they have no right to impose their opinions on the book and magazine trade by threats of prosecution if their views are not accepted." Id. at 225.

Bantam Books, Inc., instituted suit in equity for an injunction against the city of Detroit, its Police Commissioner, and the Police Censor Bureau to lift the ban against sale in Detroit of copies of John O'Hara's *Ten North Frederick.* A temporary restraining order was granted on March 29, 1957.[42] The commissioner subsequently promised in a general press release that the Bureau would "do nothing which might be interpreted as a ban, threat of a ban, or threat of any kind."[43] A permanent injunction was granted in June 1958.[44] So, apparently, the informal alternative to charging — i.e., use of the police censor bureau — is no longer available to the Detroit prosecutor, but he must make a charging decision in cases involving allegedly obscene books or magazines.[45] There is no evidence that police censorship of motion pictures, stage plays, burlesque shows, or other nightclub entertainment under the Detroit ordinance has been affected in any way.

E. The "Court of No Record"

It is quite clear that prosecutors are fully aware of the particularly harmful effects of a criminal record on a youthful violator[46] and make special efforts to avoid inflicting such harm. This

42 2 American Book Publishers Council, Censorship Bulletin No. 2, p. 3 (June 1957). This "decision made clear that police officials do not have the legal power to ban the sale of a book on the ground of obscenity in the absence of a court determination of its illegality. When such officials believe a book to be obscene . . . their authority is limited to making an arrest so that the matter of obscenity can be determined after a trial in accordance with legal requirements." Ibid.

43 Id. at 3-4. See Slough and McAnany, Obscenity and Constitutional Freedom — Part I, 8 St. L.U.L.J. 279, 500 n.455 (1964).

44 3 American Book Publishers Council, Censorship Bull. No. 1, pp. 4-5 (August 1958).

45 The Michigan statute in force when the survey was conducted, Mich. Stat. Ann. §28.575 (1954), was held to be unconstitutional in Butler v. Michigan, 352 U.S. 380 (1957). Mr. Justice Frankfurter, speaking for a unanimous court, reversed the conviction of a publisher-distributor, relying on his contention that the state statute violated the Fourteenth Amendment because it prohibited the sale to an adult of a book unsuitable for minors. See Slough and McAnany, Obscenity and Constitutional Freedom — Part I, 8 St. L.U.L.J. 279, 303-304 (1964). The statute currently in force was thereupon passed in response to Butler. Mich. Stat. Ann. §§28.575(1) to 28.575(5) (Supp. 1968).

46 This attitude is shared to an extent at least by federal authorities. A United States Attorney indicated that, when an offender under eighteen years of age is turned over to him by state authorities for violation of the Dyer Act (transporting a stolen motor vehicle across a state line) (18 U.S.C. §§2311-13 [1964]), he makes use of the Burkland Plan. This consists simply of having the offender sign a statement that he will in the future not violate the law. A record of the violation is retained in the District Attorney's office. He was careful to point out, however, that it is not a public record and, indeed, that the Burkland Plan is used to avoid giving a young offender a criminal record.

attitude, of course, has received explicit legislative concurrence in juvenile court acts.[47]

Illustration No. 1: An eighteen-year-old boy was apprehended for petty auto stripping and taken to the prosecutor's office. It was decided not to charge the youth, but he and his parents were subjected to the "court of no record" in the prosecutor's office.

Illustration No. 2: Two twenty-one-year-old youths were apprehended stealing auto hubcaps. Police detectives brought them and the owner of the auto into the prosecutor's office where it was learned that both suspects would be discharged from military service in eight days. The assistant prosecutor refused to issue a warrant.

In Illustration No. 1, the maximum offense would have been simple larceny. It is virtually certain that the defendant would have been placed on probation after conviction. The assistant prosecutor expressed concern over the effect of a larceny conviction on the suspect's ability to enter the military service or to obtain employment. It is not clear why the boy was not sent to the juvenile authorities since proceedings in juvenile court would not create a criminal record.[48] The assistant prosecutor decided not to charge the boy, but to use the court of no record as an alternative to prosecution. The court of no record is simply an informal hearing in the prosecutor's office in which an assistant prosecutor talks with the suspect and his parents in an effort to avoid a recurrence of the offense without resorting to prosecution. Even though the court of no record is used, the police still retain records of the suspect's apprehension and the disposition of the case. Use of the device is limited primarily to male juvenile offenders who are about to enter military service or who are presently serving a tour of duty.

The maximum offense in Illustration No. 2 would have been simple larceny. Since the suspects had no prior record, probation would be the probable punishment. Each was above the age for

47 See, for example, Mich. Stat. Ann. §27.3178 (598.1) (1962) in which it is provided that "[p]roceedings under this chapter shall not be deemed to be criminal proceedings." See also, Kan. Stat. Ann. §38-801 (1964); Lueptow v. Schraeder, 226 Wis. 437, 444, 277 N.W. 124, 127 (1938). The collateral harm of publicity created by prosecution has also received legislative advertance with regard to juveniles: "Restriction of publicity has been widely achieved in America with respect to certain categories of proceedings, among them juvenile court proceedings, criminal-sexual psychopath proceedings, and others of similar nature." Mueller, Problems Posed by Publicity to Crime and Criminal Proceedings, 110 U. Pa. L. Rev. 1, 10 (1961).

48 See note 46 *supra*.

juvenile court jurisdiction.[49] The assistant prosecutor remarked that the suspects had a clean record in the service and were apparently due for an honorable discharge. Thus, he was concerned with giving the suspects a criminal record, a situation which would not be helped materially by charging a less serious offense. The assistant prosecutor persuaded the complainant to sign a form indicating his desire not to prosecute. The assistant prosecutor indicated that the suspects had already spent two days in jail, which, he thought, would be sufficient to prevent a recurrence. As an alternative to further proceedings, he told the police officer in charge of the case to give the suspects a stern lecture before releasing them. The assistant prosecutor said he is frequently faced with problems of this nature and that he finds them quite difficult to solve.

F. The "Thirty-Day List"

Illustration No. 3: A twenty-year-old Negro youth was brought into the prosecutor's office. The police officer said he wanted a warrant for disorderly conduct because he had apprehended the youth driving without a standard muffler. The suspect was put on the thirty-day list and no warrant was issued.

Illustration No. 4: Upon leaving a grocery store, a woman saw a young man exhibit himself from his automobile. He was arrested and brought to the prosecutor's office. The young man was from an extremely wealthy family, was single, and living with his parents. He had been seeing a psychiatrist about his problem. The assistant prosecutor decided not to charge but put the suspect on the thirty-day list.

Illustration No. 5: A forty-four-year-old physician was apprehended when he accosted a police detective with an offer to engage in a homosexual act. The suspect was single and lived with his parents, whom he supported. He had been homosexual for about ten years and was only occasionally unable to control himself. He had no prior record. The assistant prosecutor decided not to charge the suspect but put him on the thirty-day list.

In Illustration No. 3, the maximum offense would have been

49 In Michigan, the maximum age of juvenile court jurisdiction is 19. See Mich. Stat. Ann. §27.3178 (598.5) (1962). This maximum is 16 for boys and 18 for girls in Kansas, and 18 in Wisconsin. Kan. Stat. Ann. §38-802 (1964); Wis Stat. Ann. §§48.02 to 48.12 (1957).

disorderly conduct, and it was that charge that the police officer sought from the assistant prosecutor. Punishment for that offense probably would have been a relatively small fine. The assistant prosecutor informed the suspect that it would cost him more to defend the case and pay the fine than it would cost to correct the muffler to make it conform to proper standards. An offense less serious than disorderly conduct would be unlikely to be charged, since the maximum offense itself is relatively minor. The assistant prosecutor ascertained that the suspect had a good paying job but had not yet received his first wages. He characterized the suspect as a "substantial citizen," who had no record. Thus, it is not unlikely that unnecessary collateral harm was the principal consideration in the decision not to charge. As an alternative procedure, the assistant prosecutor put the suspect on the "thirty-day list," a device used extensively in cases of this type in Michigan and Wisconsin. This, he explained to the suspect, meant that a warrant for disorderly conduct would be held in abeyance for thirty days and would then be issued unless the muffler condition was corrected during that time.

Another factor present in many charging decisions is the economic and social standing of the suspect. In many such cases, the administrative officials apparently believe they should be more lenient because prosecution would be particularly harmful to the suspect's reputation and the suspect's awareness of and concern for his own standing makes a recurrence of the offense more unlikely. It is a regular practice in the Detroit's prosecutor's office not to charge well-to-do persons accused of offenses such as exhibitionism and homosexual acts. The result of a conviction is uncertain, but it probably would include state-financed psychiatric treatment. Clearly, a conviction would be quite harmful to the suspect's reputation, and charging a less serious offense would be of little aid in that regard, nor would it contribute anything to the solution of the basic psychiatric problem. The assistant prosecutor who denied the warrant in Illustration No. 4 noted that, if his decision were made public, he would be subjected to extensive criticism by the press for behaving in a lenient fashion toward the wealthy. He quickly added that the suspect's wealth was only indirectly the cause of the decision; the reason for denying the warrant was that the suspect could afford his own psychiatrist and, hence, would save the state a great deal of money in his treatment. Regularly, the thirty-day list is used in such cases as an alternative to prosecution. In effect, this is a decision not to charge on the condition that the suspect sees a psychiatrist and the prosecutor's office receives a letter from him on the suspect's progress once a month. The attempt is to prevent further occurrences of the offense without the necessity of formally prosecuting the suspect with the accompanying expense for the state and injury to the suspect's reputation.

G. Counseling Marriage of Pregnant Statutory Rape Victim

> *Illustration No. 6:* A high school boy and girl were in the prosecutor's office with their parents. The girl was pregnant and the boy admitted he was responsible. The girl's father wanted the prosecutor to charge the boy with statutory rape and threatened to bring physical harm to the prosecutor if he did not. Finally, after a long discussion, the prosecutor persuaded all the parties that prosecution would not be to anybody's gain and that the couple should get married.

The maximum offense in Illustration No. 6 would have been statutory rape. An evidence-sufficiency problem exists in the case because one of the two "victims" — the girl — did not want to prosecute. On the other hand, the other "victim" — the girl's father — definitely did want prosecution. Even assuming the evidence-sufficiency problem was solvable and the girl's testimony would have been sufficient to convict the suspect, the girl's attitude was a factor that the assistant prosecutor must have considered. The punishment upon conviction was not certain, but it was clear that the record of a statutory rape conviction would be a serious blot on the suspect's reputation. Another consequence of prosecution adverted to by the assistant prosecutor was that the girl's family would have to support the illegitimate child when it was born. It was clear that from the beginning the assistant prosecutor did not want to charge the suspect, but he found it necessary to persuade the girl's father of the desirability of not charging. The alternative to prosecution suggested by the assistant prosecutor was that the couple get married, a suggestion that apparently met with the approval of all the parties. This would avoid the difficulties created by prosecution and would relieve the girl's father of some of the burden of supporting the child. Prosecutors in Kansas and Michigan indicated that almost all illegitimacies of this type are settled in that manner.

CHAPTER 19

Full Enforcement in Charging

Preceding chapters have been devoted to isolating the factors causing discretion to be exercised at the charging stage. In this chapter, situations are examined in which regular exercise of discretion is departed from in favor of full, or at least comparatively more complete, enforcement of the criminal laws. The purpose of this chapter might be abstracted in this fashion: when factors A, B, and C are present in a case, officials will exercise discretion and charge a less serious offense, but when factor D is added to the first three, officials will charge a more serious offense.

It is the purpose of this chapter to examine D-factors and their effect on the exercise of discretion in charging.

A. To Reflect Press and Public Pressures

Illustration No. 1: Several inmates of the House of Corrections in Detroit had escaped and were apprehended. In recent months there had been a comparatively large number of escapes. An assistant prosecutor approved warrants charging a felony against each of this latest group of escapees.

Normally, escapees from the House of Corrections would be charged under a misdemeanor statute. Only escapees from state prisons and reformatories are prosecuted under the felony statute. Because of the recent "rash" of escapes from the House of Corrections, accompanied by increasing publicity, the prosecutor's office and the Michigan Division of Corrections decided to charge these suspects with felonies.

Illustration No. 2: The suspect had committed several armed robberies in Milwaukee. Newspapers gave the case more than the usual amount of publicity. An assistant prose-

> cutor approved the police recommendation for three warrants, each charging one of the robberies.

Typically, only two warrants are issued in Milwaukee against the multiple offender, no matter how many offenses the officials may be able to prove he committed. Officials feel that issuing more than two warrants is a waste of resources because it does not materially increase the sentence.[1] In cases similar to Illustration No. 2, however, more than two warrants may be issued in order to relieve public pressure for full enforcement, even though officials believe that charging the additional offenses will not materially increase the sentence.

> *Illustration No. 3:* The Detroit press began a campaign to "clean up the bums." Since it was common knowledge that all bums have long vagrancy and drunk records, the police were subjected to severe criticism for their failure to charge them with misdemeanor repeater violations. About 150 of them were charged as repeaters.

Normally, the Michigan misdemeanor repeater provisions are not used in Detroit except in accosting and soliciting cases. Police and prosecutors believe that using the statutes does not materially increase the sentence.[2] Of the 150 bums charged as repeaters in response to the newspaper criticism, only about twenty were sentenced as repeaters. All the sentences, including the twenty, were no more severe than they would have been without the repeater charge, but this effort apparently satisfied the press because their criticism of the police stopped.

In each of the three illustrations, the normal charging decision is to exercise discretion to refrain from fully enforcing the criminal laws against the guilty. In each instance, officials believed they had valid reasons for exercising discretion. When unusually strong publicity is directed against any suspect or group of suspects, however, official response may be to depart from the normal charging practices in favor of full enforcement designed to satisfy the public demands. Although this may entail charging the suspect with a greater offense than usual, with more than the usual number of offenses, or with a violation of the habitual criminal statute,[3] there is no reason to believe that the

1 See Chapter 17.

2 See Chapter 17.

3 It may also involve charging suspects who ordinarily would not be charged. The rackets squad of the Michigan State Police does not usually charge participants

decision to enforce the criminal laws fully against the suspect results in a more severe sentence. Full enforcement at the charging stage satisfies the public demands even though there was no intent to increase the sentence and no increase in fact results. Full enforcement under these circumstances should properly be termed "simulated full enforcement."

B. To Perform a Social Service for the Victim or Suspect

Illustration No. 4: The prosecutor in a rural Michigan county received a phone call from the justice of the peace about a man whose wife had left him and their six children and had run away to Wisconsin with another man. The prosecutor authorized issuance of a warrant charging the wife with abandonment.

Illustration No. 5: One fall morning in Detroit six men walked into the police station and requested that a warrant be issued against them. They were charged with drunkenness, convicted, and sentenced to a period of incarceration in the local jail.

Sometimes suspects are charged who normally would not be because charging is necessary to perform some badly needed social service for the benefit of either the victim or the suspect himself. The prosecutor in Illustration No. 4 said he doubted that the fleeing wife committed any criminal offense at all by her acts. But, he continued, he must frequently charge such a person with the commission of a crime in order to get that person back into the jurisdiction for a purpose other than prosecution. In this case his purpose was to reunite the woman with her husband and children in the hope that she would reconsider the consequences of her action and reassume her marital responsibilities. Normally, no warrant would be approved for acts of the type done by the wife because of the doubtful assistance of the husband in the prosecution;[4] this is especially true when prosecution involves returning the suspect from a sister state.[5] In this case, however, the warrant necessary for extradition was issued to per-

in social gambling with violation of the Michigan gambling laws. Charges may be brought, however, if the social games become too obvious to the public.

4 See Chapter 9.

5 See Chapter 10.

form a family assistance social service function and without commitment or desire to carry through with prosecution.

Illustration No. 5 is representative of an annual event in Detroit and other large cities. When cold weather approaches, habitual drunks who have no homes, no work, and no one to turn to are forced either to request a period of confinement in the local jail or freeze to death. Official response has been to charge these persons with drunkenness because a criminal charge is necessary to confine them in jail, thus providing them with warm quarters and food for the duration of the cold weather. Even the misdemeanor repeater provisions applicable to drunkenness may be invoked if the "suspect" needs a longer period of confinement than is permissible for his present offense alone.[6]

C. To Permit Investigation of Another Offense: Vagrancy and Disorderly Persons Charges

Illustration No. 6: A 34-year-old man was walking down a sidewalk in an intoxicated condition. A married couple who happened to be passing by saw the suspect apparently attempting to entice two small girls into a parked car. They detained the suspect and called the police. The two small girls were so badly disturbed by the incident that they could not identify the suspect. He was charged with public drunkenness under the disorderly persons statute on the basis of the observations of the married couple.

Under most circumstances, no charges would be lodged for relatively peaceful public intoxication even though that itself is an offense under most disorderly persons laws. In Illustration No. 6, and in many other cases, vagrancy and disorderly persons laws are used as a device to detain a suspect for investigation of another offense. In Detroit, this practice termed the "ten-day vag check" involves charging the suspect with vagrancy or disorderly conduct. The convicted suspect is regularly sentenced, after a guilty plea or, at most, a summary trial, to a ten-day term in the local jail. The ten-day sentence permits ample time for in-custody interrogation, for checking the suspect's record, and for permitting the victims to recover from the experience with the probable consequence of being able to identify the suspect.

[6] In Milwaukee this was the only use observed being made of the habitual criminal statute.

D. To Anticipate Possible Developments in the Proof: Multiple Charges for a Single Offense

Illustration No. 7: A store was burglarized between the closing hour of 6:00 P.M. and the opening hour of 8:00 A.M. The police had gathered sufficient evidence to prove the suspect committed the burglary, but they were unable to determine exactly when it occurred. An assistant prosecutor approved issuance of a warrant against the suspect charging him with "breaking and entering in the nighttime" in one count and "breaking and entering in the daytime" in another.

Illustration No. 8: The complainant reported to the police department that he had been held up at the point of a knife. The suspect was apprehended the same day and a knife was found in his possession. The complainant identified the suspect as the robber, but he admitted that he did not actually see the knife. An assistant prosecutor approved issuance of a warrant against the suspect charging him with "robbery armed with a knife" in one count and "robbery not armed" in another.

Frequently, officials have no doubt the suspect committed the act complained of, and that the act was criminal, but they are not certain which of several possible statutes was violated. Resolution of the problem created by this evidentiary doubt may involve charging more than the usual number of offenses.[7] Under Michigan law, burglary is separated into the offenses of breaking and entering in the nighttime and breaking and entering in the daytime. The former is considerably more serious than the latter. When there is no doubt about the time the offense was committed, officials charge one offense or the other, depending upon whether it was literally daytime or nighttime when the offense occurred.[8] Frequently, as in Illustration No. 7, the exact time the offense occurred is not known. In that event, the prosecutor's office in Detroit charges violations of both statutes to permit a conviction consonant with the way the evidence finally develops. Although the Michigan statutes do not require the victim of an

[7] See Chapter 12 for a discussion of the usual multiple offense charging practices.

[8] Even when the time the offense was committed is known, violations of both statutes are sometimes charged for evidentiary reasons. This was done on one occasion when the evidence showed the offense occurred at about 5:45 A.M. — dawn on the day in question.

armed robbery to see the weapon, such an evidentiary limitation is in practice imposed by the Detroit prosecutor's office Thus, if, as in Illustration No. 8, the victim had reason to believe that the suspect had a weapon but he did not see it, two charges are lodged — armed robbery and robbery unarmed — to permit conviction either way the evidence develops.[9]

E. To Promote Suspect Cooperation with Enforcement Agencies

Illustration No. 9: During the several months since he had been released from prison, the suspect had committed six major burglaries. In exchange for being charged with only one of the six offenses, he had agreed to plead guilty and to testify against two of his accomplices and their fence. After being charged, the suspect refused to perform his part of the bargain. Two more burglary charges were brought against him.

Illustration No. 10: The suspect, currently charged with passing a bad check over twenty dollars in value, had a prior felony conviction. The prosecutor offered not to invoke the habitual criminal statute if the suspect would plead guilty to the present offense. The offer was refused. After the suspect was tried and convicted, the prosecutor invoked the habitual criminal statute against him.

If officials offer the suspect a charging concession in exchange for "cooperation" from him of one sort or another, and the suspect refuses the deal, full enforcement charging might be the consequence. Multiple offenders typically are not charged with all the offenses of which officials have sufficient proof for conviction.[10] In some jurisdictions, this practice is accompanied by an agreement not to charge the other offenses if the suspect performs some service for officials. If the suspect refuses to enter into such an agreement, or having agreed, refuses to perform his promises, he might be charged with the other offenses.

In a similar manner, when noninvocation of the habitual criminal statute is coupled with a threat to use it if the suspect does not cooperate, typically by pleading guilty to the present

[9] In other situations, evidentiary doubt may force multiple charging to anticipate possible variances in the development of the proof. Frequently, felonious assault and ordinary assault are charged for the same act, as are manslaughter and negligent homicide.

[10] See Chapter 12.

offense,[11] the statute may be invoked if the suspect refuses to cooperate. By executing his threat to use the statute unless the defendant pleads guilty, the prosecutor apparently believes that he is reinforcing the bargaining leverage of the statute in subsequent negotiations with the defendant and with others.

F. To Rid Society of Particular Offenders

The most important full enforcement category is based on a strong desire by officials to separate the offender from the community. Of course, if the circumstances of the offense are particularly heinous, such as a combination murder-rape, full enforcement is likely, especially in view of the accompanying publicity. But even when the offense is not particularly heinous, a number of factors in the suspect's personal history may make officials especially anxious to "put him away" for a long time. Among them are his criminal record, noncriminal conduct bearing on his "character," official suspicion of the commission of offenses which they cannot prove, or connection of the suspect with a professional criminal or with syndicated criminalism.

1. *The offender who has been a nuisance to enforcement agencies and the community.*

> *Illustration No. 11:* A young lady complained to the police that a dentist slapped her across the face when she told him he was hurting her while extracting a tooth. He failed to respond to the letter routinely sent to professional men about complaints of that nature. In a phone conversation as a follow-up to the letter, he told the police sergeant to go to hell. He failed to appear at the police felony detail at the requested time for a discussion of the matter. A warrant was then issued charging the dentist with assault and battery.

In the Detroit prosecutor's office it is the practice not to charge a professional man, particularly a doctor or dentist, with an offense allegedly committed by him against a patient. Experience has taught that many such complaints are groundless and, in any event, that the patient is usually satisfied by a monetary settlement.[12] If the professional man has proved particularly bothersome to officials and to others, he may be charged despite the usual practice not to charge such men. The dentist in Illustration No. 11 was a member of a firm that had demonstrated for

[11] Ibid.
[12] See Chapter 11.

several years that it had no intention of complying with the rules and regulations of the dental society. False advertising and fraud complaints had been lodged a number of times, but there never was enough evidence to bring charges against them. Within the past week, the firm had hired an unlicensed dentist. The inspector for the dental society had been thrown out of the suspect's office when he called on him to discuss the complaints.

Officials decided that the suspect had made such a nuisance of himself to them and the community generally that an exception should be made to the practice of negotiation with professional men.

> *Illustration No. 12:* A number of complaints had been received against the defendant for nonsupport. Investigation of the latest complaint convinced officials that the suspect had no intention of cooperating with authorities in their nonsupport program and would probably never support his family. A warrant was issued charging him with felonious nonsupport.

In Detroit, nonsupport cases normally are not prosecuted.[13] Under Michigan law, nonsupport can be prosecuted either as a misdemeanor or as a felony. When prosecution is sought, usually a misdemeanor is charged because the prosecutor's office has a strong policy not to incarcerate nonsupport offenders for a very long time. Incarceration prevents support of the family and causes problems at the penal institution, because nonsupport violators are regarded with disdain by the other prisoners. The felony statute is used only when the defendant has a very bad record, and after investigation of the case it appears that he will never support his family and needs to be taught a lesson.

> *Illustration No. 13:* The suspect, aged 66, had been bothering the prosecutor's office and the courts with his frequent misconduct as a beggar. Recently, he was arrested for begging and $199 in cash was found on him. He also had in his possession two bank books showing a total balance of $5700. He had been arrested thirty-five times and convicted twenty times, all on charges of begging or some related offense. It was felt by the prosecutor's office that it was time to teach the old man a lesson. He was charged with begging as a third offender.

The Michigan misdemeanor repeater provisions are used only

[13] See Chapter 18.

rarely.[14] One occasion for their use is presented by the suspect who has proved himself to be a nuisance to the community by committing minor offenses again and again and a nuisance to enforcement authorities by constantly being arrested and charged with minor offenses.

2. *The professional petty thief.*

> *Illustration No. 14:* The victim, a white man, reported to the police that he had been "murphied" by a male Negro. Since the suspect was a parolee and had a number of prior arrests for operating the "murphy game," a warrant was issued charging him with larceny by trick.

Typically, no warrant will be approved when the case simply amounts to a "murphy game" operation — when the victim gave the suspect money for a prostitute and the suspect absconded with it and never produced the girl — because the victim frequently changes his mind about prosecution later, and, even if he does not, officials might not want to prosecute because they often regard the victim as sufficiently culpable to deserve the loss of his prostitution money without official efforts to recover it for him.[15] When, however, as in Illustration No. 14, the suspect has a particularly long record, he may be charged with larceny by trick, particularly if the victim seems determined to carry through with prosecution.

> *Illustration No. 15:* The suspect was apprehended in the act of shoplifting a pair of gloves from a counter in a department store. Since he had a long record of arrests and convictions for shoplifting, he was charged with larceny from a building.

The usual shoplifting committed in Detroit is a violation of two Michigan statutes: simple larceny under fifty dollars — a misdemeanor, and larceny of any amount from a building — a felony. If the offender has no record, or a short record, he is charged with simple larceny.[16] If, however, he has a long record, or if the police suspect he has committed several crimes they cannot prove, then he is charged with larceny from a building.

> *Illustration No. 16:* Eight suspects had been arrested for larceny from an automobile. After in-custody interrogation, police determined that the group was responsible for 345

[14] See Chapter 12.
[15] See Chapter 9.
[16] See Chapter 13.

separate offenses of larceny from automobiles. Through the statements of various of the eight, it was established that they had all worked in concert to commit many of the offenses. Only one warrant was requested in the case, listing all eight defendants. The charge was conspiracy to commit larceny from automobiles.

Normally, multiple offenders are charged only with the most serious offense, the others being brought to the court's attention in the presentence report.[17] When the multiple criminality involves, as in Illustration No. 16, a gang of petty thieves who commit a large number of minor offenses, the charge might be conspiracy to commit larceny. The police simply prove the commission of some of the offenses and use the statements of the suspects to connect each of them to the offenses.

3. *The professional petty vice offender.* The Michigan gambling laws are differentially enforced depending upon whether the offender is believed to be a professional. Although the laws are broad enough to include social gambling, they are enforced only against professional gamblers. The Michigan misdemeanor repeater provisions, except those applying to accosting and soliciting, are rarely used.[18] The Detroit Police Department has a systematic procedure for checking the records of all prostitutes arrested and prosecuted for accosting and soliciting in order to determine whether they should be charged as second or third offenders. After the prostitute is arrested, a form is completed and forwarded to the vice bureau, where it is brought to the attention of an officer assigned to this particular task. The decision to charge the prostitute as a second or third offender rests with this police officer. His decision is usually accepted by both the assistant prosecutor and the judges of Recorder's Court. An offense which occurs within six months of the previous conviction would definitely result in bringing a charge as a second offender. If a year's period has elapsed since the last conviction, the officer would review the defendant's entire record and, unless he found that it contained an arrest for a similar offense within the year's period, the defendant would probably not be charged as a second offender. When a defendant who has been convicted as a second offender commits another offense, a charge as a third offender is automatically brought unless an exceptionally long period of time has elapsed since the previous conviction.

17 See Chapter 12.

18 See Chapter 12.

4. *The syndicate leader.*

Illustration No. 17: A woman was caught with a large quantity of heroin in her possession when the Detroit narcotics bureau raided her home. Wishing to secure convictions against the three persons who were the top men in the narcotics racket in Detroit, officials made arrangements with her and her two carriers to testify against the defendants in exchange for being charged only with narcotics possession instead of sale. The three syndicate leaders were charged with conspiracy to violate the narcotics laws.

The prosecutor's office in Detroit frequently utilizes the common law offense of conspiracy, a felony that carries a maximum term of imprisonment of five years, when a group of defendants habitually act in concert to commit relatively minor vice offenses or when it is extremely difficult, if not impossible, to detect certain members of a group participating in a well-planned and systematic scheme to violate the vice laws. The class of criminal activity most frequently used as a basis for the charge of conspiracy is violation of the gambling laws. Organizations operating numbers rackets are composed of many individuals. It is extremely difficult for police agencies to detect and secure evidence sufficient to prosecute successfully those members of the organization who are on the top level. Extensive observations are made by the police department — sometimes covering a period of several months — to connect all those individuals participating in the illegal activity of the syndicate. The only other evidence necessary, therefore, to prove the act of conspiracy to violate the gambling laws is the connection and close association between the more obvious participants — the "runners" — and the parties at the top level of the organization. The testimony of the runners ordinarily accomplishes this connection.[19] The penalty for the conspiracy conviction is considerably more severe than would be permissible for violating the gambling laws themselves. Even when, as in Illustration No. 17, the offense itself, such as sale of narcotics, carries a more severe penalty than the conspiracy charge, the conspiracy may be selected because it would be extremely risky to assume the burden of proving the

19 Prior to a gambling raid, Detroit police officers are told to take statements from all arrestees immediately, before they are allowed to talk with each other. A judge of Recorder's Court said one advantage of charging conspiracy is that "everything goes." A defendant on the bottom rung of the ladder, for example, a runner in the numbers racket, can testify to what was said, seen or heard by him concerning any other member of the syndicate.

sale itself. In the illustration, evidence of acceptable quality was obtained against only two of the three syndicate leaders with regard to actual narcotics sales, so a conspiracy was charged to permit conviction of all three members.

G. To Compensate for an Acquittal or an Inadequate Sentence

Illustration No. 18: A young man was apprehended for breaking and entering. During clean-up he admitted thirteen other breaking and entering offenses. He was charged with one of the offenses, tried, and acquitted by the jury. Another charge was lodged and again he was acquitted. There was a third charge and a third acquittal. Finally, on the fourth trial, he was convicted of breaking and entering.

Illustration No. 19: The defendant had been negligently operating his motor boat on Lake St. Claire when he rammed it into another craft, killing one of its occupants. He was charged with, and tried for manslaughter, but the jury found him guilty only of simple assault. The state prosecutor and a United States Attorney then decided that the defendant should be tried for his violation of federal law. He was charged with the same crime for which he had been prosecuted in the state court. This time the defendant was convicted of manslaughter.

Despite frequent opportunities, prosecutors do not usually institute a second prosecution against a defendant.[20] Occasionally, however, a subsequent prosecution will be instituted when the prosecutor considers the disposition of the first case a miscarriage of justice. Usually the first case was tried before a jury and the prosecutor considers the jury verdict to be completely without justification. In Illustration No. 18, the three acquittals were explained by the fact that "the lad was rather innocent looking" and had convinced the juries of his innocence for that reason.

20 See Chapter 12.

C H A P T E R 2 0

Control of Prosecutor Discretion

Several charging practices reflecting a desire on the part of the prosecutor to effect less than full enforcement clearly stand out in any survey of modern criminal administration, although full enforcement occurs in some circumstances discussed in the preceding chapter. These practices include charging less than the maximum number of offenses, the use of both formal and informal procedures which may not involve prosecution, and even outright release with no strings attached.

Decisions not to charge — or not to charge as fully as the evidence would technically permit — are made for two quite different kinds of reasons. In some instances, a negative charging decision is made because prosecutors believe that conviction is unlikely even though there is probable cause for charging. In others, the negative decision reflects, instead, a judgment that full enforcement would not be in the overall community interest. Although the term discretion is commonly associated with a negative decision made for both kinds of reasons,[1] the term is used here only in connection with decisions made for the latter kind; the nonevidence-sufficiency factors which impel these decisions have formed the subject matter of this part of the volume.

We have also defined discretion to exclude the raw power to act corruptly, or to make of one's job a sinecure. It is inevitably true that some prosecutors, as some clergymen and some gamblers, are corrupt or grossly incompetent, or unusually indolent and, consequently some charging decisions reflect no more than corruption, gross incompetency, or unusual indolence. Despite

[1] Judicial opinions and commentaries commonly include evidence screening in their discussions of prosecutor discretion, e.g., Howell v. Brown, 85 F. Supp. 537, 540 (D. Neb. 1949); Kaplan, The Prosecutorial Discretion — A Comment, 60 Nw. U.L. Rev. 174 (1965). For further examples, see Chapter 8, note 4, and accompanying text; note 157 *infra*.

the concentration or — indeed preoccupation with — serious improprieties of that nature which characterized the early crime surveys,[2] this volume examined the problems which confront a reasonably competent, clearly honest prosecutor, since these problems are far-ranging, complex, and important enough to merit attention without diversion.

This definition does present problems in analyzing controls over prosecutor discretion without considering instances of corruption, gross incompetence, or unusual indolence. These difficulties arise because judicial attention has tended to focus on these instances, thereby providing few guidelines for the exercise of discretion as it is here defined,[3] and because practically no attention has been paid to the matter by legislatures.[4] Nevertheless, it remains important to understand which legal remedies exist and when they are available, even though they relate only partly to discretion control, because to the extent that prosecutor discretion is subject to legal controls at all, it is through those remedies.

Professor Davis has asserted that there is an "assumption . . . that we can do no better than to repose confidence" in the public prosecutor.[5] One factor behind that judgment is that no one else

2 See, e.g., Bettman and Burns, Prosecution, in Reports of the Cleveland Foundation Survey of the Administration of Criminal Justice in Cleveland, Ohio 192 (1922); Burgess, Summary and Recommendations, in Illinois Crime Survey 1091 (1929); 1 National Comm. of Law Observance and Enforcement, Rep. on the Causes of Crime 123-131 (1931).

3 See notes 12 and 34 *infra*.

4 The states have statutes pertaining in general language to the office of prosecutor which are intended, among other things, to clarify which law enforcement functions are to be allocated to that office. See generally Baker and DeLong, The Prosecuting Attorney, 24 J. Crim. L. 1025 (1934). Special statutes designed to preclude lax enforcement of certain criminal laws also exist. E.g., Wis. Stat. Ann. §26.18 (1957), discussed *infra* note 18; see State v. Coubal, 248 Wis. 247, 21 N.W.2d 381 (1946). And see the discussion in Chapter 8, notes 48-52 and accompanying text. General and special statutes reveal at most a legislative desire that the prosecutor will remain active, that is, that he will exercise his discretion in considering matters called to his attention. Legislatures simply do not attempt to codify what factors he should consider. The distinction between forcing the prosecutor to exercise his discretion and directing him in detail how to exercise it is discussed in note 12 *infra*. See Breitel, Controls in Criminal Law Enforcement, 27 U Chi. L. Rev. 427 (1960); cf. Goldstein, Police Discretion Not to Invoke the Criminal Process: Low Visibility Decisions in the Administration of Justice, 69 Yale L.J. 543 (1960).

Many of the remedies discussed in this chapter are statutory. The legislature usually stops at this point and leaves actual administration of the remedies to others, e.g., trial judges or attorneys general. One case holds that the legislature cannot constitutionally assume an active role in controlling a prosecutor's enforcement policy. McGinley v. Scott, 401 Pa. 310, 164 A.2d 424 (1960) (legislative committee was investigating the prosecutor's activities).

5 1 Davis, Administrative Law 257 (1958).

is in a better position to make charging decisions which reflect community values as accurately and effectively as the prosecutor. Many courts have recognized that the public prosecutor was established as a distinctively American institution, just because Americans believed that an officer in a position of public trust could make decisions more impartially than could the victims of crimes or other private complainants, the persons who made the charging decisions under the older English system of administering criminal justice.[6] Numerous judicial opinions also reflect the corollary to that judgment: ordinarily private citizens should not be allowed to substitute their judgments, by invoking mandamus or similarly-purposed remedies, for those of the official who is responsible to the entire public.[7]

This same confidence in the judgment of public prosecutors is also reflected in a policy of deference to prosecutorial decisions by the trial and appellate judiciary,[8] as well as by high-ranking executive and administrative officials.[9] The prosecutor's general dominance of the initial charging decision insofar as it relates to

[6] The avoidance of prosecution by persons who might be overzealous because of a personal interest was given as a reason for the institution of public prosecution in the three states under consideration. State v. Wilson, 24 Kan. 189 (1880); Meister v. People, 31 Mich. 99 (1875); Biemel v. State, 71 Wis. 444, 37 N.W. 244 (1888); *accord,* State v. Kent, 4 N.D. 577, 62 N.W. 631 (1895); see La Shay v. People, 74 Colo. 503, 223 Pac. 59 (1924); Oglesby v. State, 83 Fla. 132, 90 So. 825 (1922); Jackson v. State, 156 Ga. 842, 120 S.E. 535 (1923); Hayner v. People, 213 Ill. 142, 72 N.E. 792 (1904); Flege v. State, 93 Neb. 610, 142 N.W. 276 (1913); Baca v. Padilla, 26 N.M. 223, 190 Pac. 730 (1920); Perry v. State, 84 Okla. Crim. 211, 181 P.2d 230 (1947); Commonwealth v. Dawson, 3 Pa. Dist. 603 (1894); see Note, 34 Ind. L.J. 477, 480 (1959). This does not mean that the public prosecutor is not allowed any of the advocate's zeal, Di Carlo v. United States, 6 F.2d 364 (2d Cir. 1925) (L. Hand, J.); Keyes v. State, 122 Ind. 527, 23 N.E. 1097 (1890); State v. Kent, *supra.* But the rationale appears to be that the public prosecutor is expected to enter a case dispassionately and his vigorous efforts to secure conviction follow only upon an objective decision that conviction would be in the community interest. See Berger v. United States, 295 U.S. 78, 88, 55 Sup. Ct. 629, 792 Ed. 1314 (1935); Adams v. State, 202 Miss. 68, 30 So. 2d 593 (1947); State v. McIntosh, 333 S.W.2d 51 (Mo. 1960); State v. Egan, 272 S.W.2d 719 (Mo. Ct. App. 1947); Seymour, Why Prosecutors Act Like Prosecutors, 11 Record of N.Y.C.B.A. 302 (1956).

[7] See, e.g., United States v. Brokaw, 60 F. Supp. 100, 101 (S.D. Ill. 1945); State ex rel. Steers v. Holovachka, 236 Ind. 565, 570, 142 N.E.2d 593, 596 (1957); Hermann v. Morlidge, 298 Ky. 632, 183 S.W.2d 807 (1944); Jumonville v. Hebert, 170 So. 497 (La. Ct. App. 1936); Hassan v. Magistrate's Court, 20 Misc. 2d 509, 511-512, 191 N.Y.S.2d 238, 241 (Sup. Ct. 1959), *appeal dismissed,* 10 App. Div. 2d 908, 202 N.Y.S.2d 1002, *appeal dismissed,* 8 N.Y.2d 750, 168 N.E.2d 102, 201 N.Y.S.2d 765, *cert. denied,* 364 U.S. 844 (1960).

[8] E.g., Pugach v. Klein, 193 F. Supp. 630, 635 (S.D.N.Y. 1961); Howell v. Brown, 85 F. Supp. 537, 540 (D. Neb. 1949); Commonwealth v. Wheeler, 2 Mass. (2 Tyng) 172, 173 (1806); for further citations, see Chapter 8, note 54 *supra.*

[9] See note 131 *infra* and accompanying text, discussing the reluctance of attorneys general to interfere in local prosecutions.

evidence sufficiency, which is discussed in Chapter 3, is equally applicable to the discretionary branch of that decision, and for much the same reasons. Indeed, it is widely asserted that in performing his screening function — both in its evidence-sufficiency and discretionary aspects — the prosecutor is more aware of the unique facts which characterize particular cases, and that this greater knowledge, coupled with his direct responsiveness to community attitudes, better qualifies him to assess both whether the suspect is probably guilty and convictable as well as whether and in what manner it is in the public interest to proceed against him if he is.[10]

Although remedies for abuse of this confidence are provided by law, they have been frequently criticized as ineffective, largely because they are rarely invoked.[11] They are, nevertheless, available at least in extraordinary circumstances. But it by no means follows that because the prosecutor largely dominates the initial charging decision free from legal controls, he makes the decision in a void, completely free from the influence of others. Legal controls in the form of recognized and readily available legal remedies are not the only possible controls over the exercise of discretion, whether by a public prosecutor, other administrative officials, or even judges. At least two different kinds of informal controls can be identified as well; those which are self-imposed and those which reflect responses to the wishes — sometimes insistences — of other officials whose actions normally precede or follow the charging decision, as well as other members of the community who have general or special interests in the disposition of particular cases. The suggestions of a trial judge, even when expressed informally, are rarely ignored; the attitude of the victim of a crime is not considered irrelevant in current criminal justice administration.

10 E.g., Whiskey Cases, 99 U.S. (9 Otto.) 594, 603 (1878); State v. Boasberg, 124 La. 289, 50 So. 162 (1909); State ex rel. Griffin v. Smith, 363 Mo. 1235, 1241, 258 S.W.2d 590, 594 (1953); Kosicki, The Function of Nolle Prosequi and Motion to Dismiss in Connecticut, 36 Conn. B.J. 159, 160-161 (1962); see State v. Tufts, 56 N.H. 137, 138-139 (1875); Note, 30 Ind. L.J. 74, 80, 85 (1954). A related contention is that in order to maintain its impartial adjudicatory role, the court should not participate actively in the screening aspect of the charging decision. See Smith v. Gallagher, 408 Pa. 551, 578, 185 A.2d 135, 152 (1962); Note, 48 J. Crim. L.C. & P.S. 531, 540 (1958).

11 Ferguson, Formulation of Enforcement Policy: An Anatomy of the Prosecutor's Discretion Prior to Accusation, 11 Rutg. L. Rev. 507 (1957); Note, 103 U. Pa. L. Rev. 1057, 1075-1081 (1955); Note, 65 Yale L.J. 209-215 (1955).

A. Legal Controls

Some legal controls over charging discretion are direct, and some are indirect. Direct controls are those applied to force the reversal of charging decisions in a particular instance: indirect controls are those which permit the application of sanctions to prosecutors who persistently demonstrate unwillingness to enforce the law in expectable fashion. An action of mandamus to compel prosecution would be an example of the former; ouster from office an example of the latter. One principle runs consistently through the judicial opinions which discuss the administration of both kinds of legal controls: the prosecutor is selected to exercise his personal judgment unimpaired by personal interest or bias, and as long as he does just that and his decisions fall into a pattern that could be called *expectable* in light of available resources and other factors which shape and limit law enforcement practices in accord with community notions of propriety, his exercise of judgment will not be interfered with.[12]

[12] Various kinds of complaints are made about the manner in which prosecutors conduct themselves in office. The criteria used by the prosecutor in selecting particular individuals for prosecution are discussed separately in the subsection on judicial control over positive charging decisions. Affirmative acts of corruption in office are generally disregarded. This leaves those cases in which the complaint is that the prosecutor is achieving less than full enforcement. When actionable, this laxness is characterized as bad faith. Although in some of the cases there are implications that inaction might be related to corruption in office, e.g., State v. Langley, 214 Ore. 445, 323 P.2d 301, *cert. denied,* 358 U.S. 826 (1958), and, in others, separate counts of corruption are contained in the complaint, e.g., Attorney General v. Tufts, 239 Mass. 458, 132 N.E. 322 (1921), these cases join the body of relevant case law when they indicate that bad faith is sufficient justification for taking legal action.

It is important to discern in the cases whether the complaint alleges an ineffective enforcement policy against crime in general, or whether it stresses failure to prosecute particular individuals. The general enforcement issue is typically broadened to such an extent by concern over administrative problems that it cannot be resolved solely in terms of the model of prosecutor charging discretion developed throughout Part IV. For example, there is the issue of the extent of the prosecutor's responsibility for assuring that police detection practices call enough violations to his attention to facilitate effective enforcement. E.g., State v. Winne, 12 N.J. 152, 96 A.2d 63 (1953). Investigation of crime is reserved for treatment in the first volume of this series. Cases involving a complaint of generally lax enforcement are relevant here for only three reasons: (1) some of them amplify the distinction between corruption and bad faith, see notes 19-21 *infra* and accompanying text, (2) they sometimes structure the bad faith issue around discussion of the discretionary factors emphasized in the preceding chapters of this part, e.g., State ex rel. Bourg v. Marrero, 132 La. 109, 61 So. 136 (1913) (resource allocation and community sentiment),

1. *Indirect controls.* The principal possibilities for using legal remedies to control prosecutor discretion indirectly are those which lead ultimately to his displacement from office. They may take the form of disbarment or disenrollment from the practice of law.[13] Criminal prosecution for nonfeasance, misfeasance, or

---

and (3) they often enumerate specific negative charging decisions to exemplify the general enforcement pattern, e.g., Attorney General v. Tufts, *supra.*

When the complaint against the prosecutor isolates particular individuals who could be prosecuted without further investigation if he were willing, the issue is narrowed to one in which the concept of charging discretion is directly relevant, and great care must be exercised to ascertain how successfully the concept is worked into the judicial resolution of the issue. In State v. Moreland, 168 Tenn. 145, 76 S.W.2d 319 (1934) the opinion indicates that displacement of the prosecutor was justifiable because the prosecutor was "wilfully" refusing to prosecute certain persons against whom there was ample evidence. This language presents a conceptual difficulty, because the situation in which the prosecutor fails to prosecute isolated probably guilty persons for nonevidence sufficiency reasons is the very prototype for the model of charging discretion observed in this volume. Close analysis reveals, however, that factors in addition to the mere failure to prosecute are probably universally required to justify legal action against the prosecutor. The "tip-off" to the existence of such plus-factors in the cases lies in the recurrent appearance of terms like "wilfullness," which has been equated with "bad faith," Ferguson, Formulation of Enforcement Policy: An Anatomy of the Prosecutor's Discretion Prior to Accusation, 11 Rutg. L. Rev. 507, 516 (1957). The general rationale appears to be that, when the prosecutor is credibly informed that certain persons can reasonably be suspected of crime, he must exercise his discretion in deciding whether to charge, that is, he must consider the types of nonevidence factors emphasized throughout Part IV to determine whether prosecution would be in the community interest. See State ex rel. McKittrick v. Wymore, 343 Mo. 98, 110, 132 S.W.2d 979, 988 (1939). When he "wilfully" refuses to charge without making these considerations he is not exercising his discretion at all, and this constitutes actionable bad faith. When he considers the community interest factors, however, he is regarded as acting in good faith, and legal action will not lie to direct him in detail how to decide. See notes 28-34 *infra* and accompanying text. But see note 51 *infra* and accompanying text.

[13] It is suggested by Dash, Cracks in the Foundations of Criminal Justice, 46 Ill. L. Rev. 385, 405 (1951) that the solution to the problems of corruption and lax enforcement which he observed in Chicago lies in greater housekeeping activity by the bar. Disbarment of a prosecutor might work an automatic forfeiture of office, Commonwealth ex rel. Pike County Bar Ass'n. v. Stump, 247 Ky. 589, 57 S.W.2d 524 (1933), or at least might indirectly result in his ouster from office, Note, 103 U. Pa. L. Rev. 1057, 1077 (1955). Less drastic sanctions include the reprimand, In re Dreiband, 273 App. Div. 413, 77 N.Y.S.2d 585 (Sup. Ct. 1948), and the suspension from the practice of law for a period, In re Voss, 11 N.D. 540, 90 N.W. 15 (1902). In one case a prosecutor was removed from the roll of attorneys qualified to practice law before a federal court because of laxness in enforcing state gambling laws. Wilbur v. Howard, 70 F. Supp. 930 (E.D. Ky. 1947), *moot on appeal,* 166 F.2d 884 (6th Cir. 1948). Most of the cases are not relevant for present purposes because they involve outright corruption in office or other specific misdeeds having nothing to do with charging practices. E.g., In re Norris, 60 Kan. 659, 57 Pac. 528 (1899). One court has refused to disbar a prosecutor for mere bad faith falling short of corruption. In re Graves, 347 Mo. 49, 146 S.W.2d 555 (1941) (court did issue a reprimand). In at least two cases, however, disciplinary action was predicated on

malfeasance in office — with the expectation that conviction will carry automatic ouster as a sanction or will provide a basis for initiating a separate ouster suit — is everywhere a possible remedy.[14] Finally, an ouster suit or quo warranto action may be brought directly without preliminary use of other remedies.[15]

Public officials — including public prosecutors — are occasionally charged with a crime commonly referred to as breach of public trust, a rubric that embraces the offenses of nonfeasance, misfeasance, and malfeasance in office.[16] Prosecutions of public prosecutors are scarce; indeed no case has been found in Kansas, Michigan, or Wisconsin,[17] although in each state statutes applying to public officers in general are certainly broad enough in their language to cover public prosecutors.[18]

It is sometimes assumed that proof of corruption is necessary — that the public official must have reaped a personal financial

---

lax enforcement of gambling or liquor laws for which the prosecutor could offer no satisfactory excuse. Wilbur v. Howard, *supra*, In re Voss, *supra*. These cases can be lined up with those involving the other indirect controls that are invoked because of bad faith. See generally Note, 57 Yale L.J. 125 (1947).

14 See Note, 103 U. Pa. L. Rev. 1057, 1076 (1955).

15 Methods for removing a prosecutor from office might be provided for in state constitutions or statutes, or both. See Commonwealth ex rel. Attorney General v. Howard, 297 Ky. 488, 180 S.W.2d 415 (1944) (prosecutor is a constitutional officer subject to removal only by methods specified in constitution); Attorney General v. Tufts, 239 Mass. 458, 132 N.E. 322 (1921) (statutory removal); State ex rel. Prince v. Rogers, 57 N.M. 686, 262 P.2d 779 (1953) (impeachment of prosecutor provided for in constitution). Another possibility is the common law action of quo warranto. State ex rel. McKittrick v. Wymore, 343 Mo. 98, 119 S.W.2d 941 (1939).

16 See Perkins, Criminal Law 409 (1957); 3 Wharton, Criminal Law and Procedure §§1401 to 1410 (12th ed. 1957); Comment, 102 U. Pa. L. Rev. 547 (1954).

17 A few cases from other jurisdictions have been located: Speer v. State, 130 Ark. 457, 198 S.W. 113 (1917); Commonwealth v. Rowe, 112 Ky. 482, 66 S.W. 29 (1902); State v. Winne, 12 N.J. 152, 96 A.2d 63 (1953); State v. Bolitho, 103 N.J.L. 246, 136 Atl. 164 (1937); State v. Jefferson, 88 N.J.L. 447, 97 Atl. 162 (Sup. Ct.), *aff'd*, 90 N.J.L. 507, 101 Atl. 569 (1916); State v. Langley, 214 Ore. 445, 323 P.2d 301, *cert. denied*, 358 U.S. 826 (1958).

18 These provisions, without referring specifically to the prosecutor, provide criminal sanctions against public officers in general. Kan. Stat. Ann. §21.807 (1964) ("willful and malicious oppression, partiality, misconduct or abuse of authority . . . ."); Kan. Stat. Ann. §21-812 (1964) (neglect of any duty enjoined by law); Mich. Stat. Ann. §28-746 (1954) (willful neglect of duty); Wis. Stat. Ann. §946.12 (1957) (applies to an officer who "exercises a discretionary power in a manner inconsistent with the duties of his office . . . or the rights of others and with intent to obtain a dishonest advantage"). There is another kind of statute, however, which does refer specifically to the prosecutor. Wis. Stat. Ann. §26.18 (1957), providing for criminal sanctions when a prosecutor fails to enforce the laws protecting forest lands, is representative of this form of special legislation. For further discussion of special legislation see Baker and DeLong, The Prosecuting Attorney, 24 J. Crim. L. 1025 (1934); Note, 30 Ind. L.J. 74, 80-81 (1954); and see the discussion in Chapter 5, notes 48-52 and accompanying text.

or political gain at the expense of the public.[19] But some of the few opinions which speak to the point show that a lesser requirement than outright corruption is sufficient for conviction.[20] General though it may be, perhaps the most expressive phrase is "bad faith." "Bad faith" and its counterpart "good faith" are rarely explicitly defined in judicial opinions. Their meanings emerge only from an analysis and assessment of both the facts of and results of two classes of cases; those discussed above in which a prosecutor is himself a defendant in a prosecution for some form of breach of public trust,[21] and, more commonly, those in which an attempt is made to show that a prosecutor has shown himself to be disqualified to continue in office.[22]

19 E.g., Note, 103 U. Pa. L. Rev. 1057, 1076 (1955). Indeed, there is considerable authority in cases involving criminal actions against officers other than prosecutors that to sustain a conviction the alleged misconduct associated with discretionary functions (as opposed to ministerial duties specifically enjoined by law) must be accompanied by corrupt or evil intent. E.g., People v. Ward, 85 Cal. 585, 24 Pac. 785 (1890); Commonwealth v. Wood, 116 Ky. 748, 76 S.W. 842 (1903); State v. Wheatley, 192 Md. 44, 63 A.2d 644 (Md. Ct. App. 1949); Commonwealth v. Hubbs, 137 Pa. Super. 244, 8 A.2d 618 (1939). The Superior Court of New Jersey in State v. Winne, 21 N.J. Super. 180, 91 A.2d 65 (Law. Div. 1952), *rev'd*, 12 N.J. 152, 96 A.2d 63 (1953), was convinced that these authorities had established the need for the element of corruption to support an action for criminal nonfeasance against a prosecutor and dismissed the indictment for its failure to allege this element. Ferguson, Formulation of Enforcement Policy: An Anatomy of the Prosecutor's Discretion Prior to Accusation, 11 Rutg. L. Rev. 507 (1957) makes the common assumption that in reversing this dismissal the Supreme Court of New Jersey broke new ground in regard to punishment for noncorrupt inaction. The assumption is based in part on Ferguson's assessment of the strength of a theory of "absolute immunity of the prosecutor to accountability for the noncorrupt exercise of the powers of initiation and compromise." Id. at 510; see United States v. Brokaw, 60 F. Supp. 100 (S.D. Ill. 1945); People ex rel Schreiner v. Courtney, 380 Ill. 171, 43 N.E.2d 982 (1942).

20 In Speer v. State, 130 Ark. 457, 198 S.W. 113 (1917) and State v. Winne, note 19 *supra*, indictments specifying neglect of duty but not corruption were held to be sufficient. In State v. Langley, 214 Ore. 445, 323 P.2d 301, *cert. denied*, 358 U.S. 826 (1958) the court noted that corruption is a necessary element of the offense of malfeasance, but not the offense of nonfeasance of which this prosecutor was convicted. See In re Voss, 11 N.D. 540, 90 N.W. 15 (1902). Whether corruption is a necessary element did not arise in the three cases cited in note 17 *supra* involving criminal actions against prosecutors.

21 See note 12 *supra*.

22 As discussed in note 12 *supra*, the assessment of prosecutorial enforcement policies in terms of good and bad faith is common to cases concerning both direct and indirect controls. The present discussion is confined primarily to treatment of the indirect control cases, with citation to the others which are specially relevant. The "bad faith" rationale is discernible in cases involving all the indirect controls. Most of the leading cases reflecting it are removal cases, as indicated in note 30 *infra*. Disbarment cases, on the other hand, as indicated in note 13 *supra*, rarely turn on the meaning of good and bad faith and more often involve outright corruption which has been proved convincingly enough that there is no need to discuss the less serious aspects of undesirable enforcement, i.e., bad faith.

Some remedies are used as both indirect and direct controls. Judicial appoint-

Provisions for removal from public office are found in all three states, although they vary in form. Both Michigan and Wisconsin have statutory or constitutional provisions for removal by the governor. The Wisconsin provisions refer specifically to the prosecutor, the Michigan provision does not.[23] The absence of appellate cases[24] in which efforts have been made to remove prosecutors in these two states casts doubt on the legal efficacy of the remedy or on its political desirability, or it may simply attest to the honesty and efficiency of public prosecutors in those jurisdictions. In Kansas may be found three of the leading cases on removal of public officials, including prosecutors. The remedy there is a civil suit brought on behalf of the state by the attorney general.[25] Still, only four cases have been found in which an effort has been made to remove a Kansas prosecutor and only three of them have been successful.[26]

---

ment of a substitute prosecutor is treated in this chapter primarily as a direct control. Some cases hold, however, that appointment of a substitute prosecutor to conduct a campaign against crime in general or against particular illegal operations prior to the filing of charges against particular suspects is tantamount to the indirect control of full removal of the regular prosecutor from office, and that, therefore, the constitutionally and statutorily prescribed procedures and judicial determinations of grounds for full removal must be observed. State ex rel. Ilvedson v. District Court, 70 N.D. 17, 291 N.W. 620 (1940); Smith v. Gallagher, 408 Pa. 551, 185 A.2d 135 (1962). The attorney general might also intervene for purposes more general than the prosecution of particular cases. E.g., State ex rel. Dalton v. Moody, 325 S.W.2d 21 (Mo. 1959) (intervention to assist in a grand jury investigation of election frauds). These cases are cited along with other indirect control cases when they are helpful in explaining the bad faith rationale.

[23] Mich. Const. art. 5, §10, provides that the governor may remove public officers "for gross neglect of duty or for corrupt conduct in office, or for any other misfeasance or malfeasance therein. . . ." Wis. Const. art. 6, §4, lists the prosecutor among the officers removable by the governor after a hearing. The statutes are more explicit. Wis. Stat. Ann. §17.11 (1957) provides that the governor can suspend the prosecutor from office pending an investigation that may lead to removal; the governor can do so when he is informed that the district attorney (or sheriff) "wilfully neglects or refuses to perform his duties. . . ." Wis. Stat. Ann. §176.90 (1957) provides that "any district attorney who shall without proper excuse neglect or refuse to perform the duties required of him herein [in the chapter pertaining to liquor offenses] . . ." can be removed by the governor under section 17.11 *supra*. Section 176.90 *supra* is another example of special legislation (discussed in note 18 *supra*) which seeks to avoid lax enforcement of certain laws by providing sanctions against prosecutors for failure to enforce those laws.

[24] There is, however, an opinion of the state attorney general advising the governor that he could legally initiate a removal action against a prosecutor. 14 Ops. Wis. Att'y Gen. 351 (1925).

[25] The remedy of removal is in the form of quo warranto, and it may be obtained when an officer "wilfully misconducts himself" or "wilfully neglects to perform any duty enjoined on him by law." Kan. Stat. Ann. §§60-1201 to 60-1205 (1964).

[26] Three Kansas cases are relevant to the current discussion of good or bad faith revealed in charging decisions. State ex rel. Griffith v. Carl, 120 Kan. 570, 245

Typically, both in Kansas and in other jurisdictions, the moving party, who is often the attorney general of the state,[27] charges that a pattern of unjustifiable laxity in enforcement is revealed by a series of negative charging decisions. If the defendant is able to explain or justify the pattern by showing, as an example, that vigorous enforcement of only selected laws, or of enforcement against properly selected offenders, would represent a sound allocation of his limited time and resources, he will uniformly be vindicated.[28] Prosecutor decisions which reflect the kind of factors discussed in this Part are apparently expectable and thus considered to have been made in "good faith."[29]

When the prosecutor cannot justify or explain a proven pattern of nonenforcement, he will lose.[30] The net effect of the cases

---

Pac. 150 (1926); State ex rel. Coleman v. Trinkle, 70 Kan. 396, 78 Pac. 854 (1904); State ex rel. Johnston v. Foster, 32 Kan. 14, 3 Pac. 534 (1884). A Kansas prosecutor was removed in a fourth case, but this was for his failure to assure that judgments of conviction were executed and fines were collected. State ex rel. Griffith v. Baird, 117 Kan. 385, 231 Pac. 1021 (1925).

27 Removal actions for example are usually initiated by the attorney general. E.g., Kan. Stat. Ann. §§60-1202 to 60-1206 (1964); Commonwealth ex rel. Attorney General v. Howard, 297 Ky. 488, 180 S.W.2d 415 (1944); Attorney General v. Flynn, 331 Mass. 413, 120 N.E.2d 296 (1954); State ex rel. McKittrick v. Graves, 346 Mo. 970, 144 S.W.2d 91 (1940). Sometimes, however, the action is begun by the signing of a petition by a specified number of private citizens, e.g., In re Perez, 194 La. 763, 194 So. 774 (1940); State v. Purchase, 57 N.D. 511, 222 N.W. 652 (1928); Graham v. Stein, 18 Ohio Cir. Ct. 770 (Erie Cty. 1894), or by action of the grand jury, State ex rel. Prince v. Rogers, 57 N.M. 686, 262 P.2d 779 (1953).

28 State ex rel. Bourg v. Marrero, 132 La. 109, 61 So. 136 (1913); State ex rel. McKittrick v. Wallach, 353 Mo. 312, 182 S.W.2d 313 (1944). In both cases prosecutors avoided removal from office through their defenses of good faith based on resource considerations.

29 State ex rel. Gebrink v. Hospers, 147 Iowa 712, 126 N.W. 818 (1910) (prosecutor delayed prosecution until constitutionality of governing statute could be tested); State ex rel. Coleman v. Trinkle, 70 Kan. 396, 78 Pac. 854 (1904) (prosecutor's leniency motivated by consideration of undue harm to suspect); see Jones v. Eighth Judicial District Court, 67 Nev. 404, 409, 219 P.2d 1055, 1058-1059 (1950); Chenault v. McLean, 48 Ohio App. 284, 193 N.E. 352 (1933); Note, 103 U. Pa. L. Rev. 1057, 1058 (1955). All of the above cases involved attempts to remove prosecutors from office. See also a case involving attorney general intervention. State ex rel. Dalton v. Moody, 325 S.W.2d 21 (Mo. 1959) (prosecutor suspected that indictments against reputable citizens had been politically inspired). One writer makes a somewhat unguarded interpretation of New Jersey law that would allow the prosecutor to consider only one of the discretionary factors, resource allocation. Ferguson, Formulation of Enforcement Policy: An Anatomy of the Prosecutor's Discretion Prior to Accusation, 11 Rutg. L. Rev. 507, 514-516 (1957). He fails to assess the implications, for example, of forcing prosecution for every minor or technical violation regardless of undue harm to the suspect.

30 Not particularly relevant to the present discussion are cases such as In re Norris, 60 Kan. 659, 57 Pac. 528 (1899) (disbarment); Commonwealth v. Rowe, 112 Ky. 482, 66 S.W. 29 (1902) (criminal action); In re Mason, 147 Minn. 383, 181

seems to be that, once the state has established a pattern of nonenforcement, the defendant-prosecutor must assume some of the burden of explaining his actions,[31] but an explanation in terms

---

N.W. 570 (1920) (removal), in which sanctions have been applied against prosecutors for corrupt activities and in which the courts have not had to face the issue of whether less than corruption is actionable. The cases that would suggest a less remote restraint on the charging discretion of the basically honest prosecutor are those in which sanctions are based on inaction which is characterized as bad faith when no satisfactory excuse of it is given. E.g., Wilbur v. Howard, 70 F. Supp. 930 (E.D. Ky. 1947) (moot on appeal), 166 F.2d 884 (6th Cir. 1948) (disenrollment); Speer v. State, 130 Ark. 457, 198 S.W. 113 (1917) (criminal action); State ex rel. Hardee v. Allen, 126 Fla. 878, 172 So. 222 (1937) (suspension by governor); State ex rel. Griffin v. Carl, 120 Kan. 570, 245 Pac. 150 (1926) (quo warranto); State ex rel. Johnson v. Foster, 32 Kan. 14, 3 Pac. 534 (1884) (quo warranto); Attorney General v. Pelletier, 240 Mass. 264, 134 N.E. 407 (1922) (removal); Attorney General v. Tufts, 239 Mass. 458, 132 N.E. 322 (1921) (removal); State ex rel. Kinsella v. Eberhart, 116 Minn. 313, 133 N.W. 857 (1911) (removal by governor); State ex rel. McKittrick v. Graves, 346 Mo. 990, 144 S.W.2d 91 (1940) (quo warranto); State ex rel. McKittrick v. Wymore, 345 Mo. 169, 132 S.W.2d 979 (1939) (quo warranto); State v. Winne, 12 N.J. 152, 96 A.2d 63 (1953) (criminal action); State v. Purchase, 57 N.D. 511, 222 N.W. 652 (1928) (removal); In re Voss, 11 N.D. 540, 90 N.W. 15 (1902) (suspension from practice of law); State v. Langley, 214 Ore. 445, 323 P.2d 301, *cert. denied,* 358 U.S. 826 (1958). But see State v. Patterson, 181 Ind. 660, 105 N.E. 228 (1914) (cannot be removed for "mere neglect" of duty). A qualifying observation must be made even about these cases insofar as their constraint on the honest prosecutor is concerned. They sometimes emphasize certain indiscreet activities accompanying prosecutor inaction, e.g., In re Voss, *supra* (prosecutor patronized gambling establishments), and sometimes indicate that the prosecutor was suspected of corruption. E.g., State v. Eberhart, *supra*; State v. Langley, *supra*. Consideration of these forms of affirmative misconduct may have had an influence on the results of the cases. Nevertheless, what emerges from the basic judicial preoccupation with unexplained inaction is a doctrine of prosecutor accountability for bad faith.

[31] It would ordinarily make a difference in the allocation of the burden of explanation whether the moving party purported to establish refusal to prosecute certain specified instances of criminal behavior or whether he proposed to show a general lack of effort to curb widespread lawlessness. See note 12 *supra*. In the former situation it has been held that a taxpayer's petition seeking removal of a prosecutor was insufficient in alleging merely that certain indictments had been nolled on recommendation of the prosecutor, because it is his normal prerogative to recommend nolle prosequi. The complainants were required to plead — and by implication to accept the burden of proving — facts that would overcome the presumption that these particular recommendations were made in good faith. Chenault v. McLean, 48 Ohio App. 284, 193 N.E. 352 (1933). On the other hand, an indictment charging the prosecutor with general laxness, with specification of certain examples of unavailed opportunities to prosecute, has been held sufficient. State v. Winne, 12 N.J. 152, 96 A.2d 63 (1953). In other cases moving parties have prevailed, apparently because their evidence of widespread and notorious lawlessness established a prima facie case, thereby shifting a burden of explanation which he could not meet to the prosecutor. E.g., State ex rel. McKittrick v. Wymore, 345 Mo. 169, 132 S.W.2d 979 (1939).

However, this distinction between general laxness and specified inaction must be qualified when special legislation literally directs the prosecutor to prosecute every instance of known violation of certain specified laws. E.g., Wis. Stat. Ann. §25.18

of resource limitations or other factors which regularly impel prosecutors not to enforce fully is all that is needed.[32] Furthermore, "good faith" decisions need not necessarily be wise ones; an honest effort is enough.[33]

Though these indirect sanctions are rarely invoked, they are at least theoretically available. Thus they have a potential for deterring corruption and for influencing the prosecutor to work at his job. To that extent, they may influence charging patterns by motivating a prosecutor to, at a minimum, exercise his discre-

---

(1957), discussed in note 18 *supra*. As discussed in Chapter 8, note 51 *supra* and accompanying text, the courts have not interpreted this legislation so literally as to preclude all negative charging decisions when the evidence shows probable guilt. They have, however, gone so far as to shift to the prosecutor the initial burden of showing that each such decision was made in good faith. In other words, the moving party is relieved of the initial burden of overcoming the presumption that individual negative charging decisions were made in good faith. See State ex rel. Coleman v. Trinkle, 70 Kan. 396, 78 Pac. 854 (1904); State v. Langley, 214 Ore. 445, 323 P.2d 301, *cert. denied*, 358 U.S. 826 (1958). These cases construed special legislation pertaining to liquor and gambling respectively. Compare In re Voss, 11 N.D. 540, 90 N.W. 15 (1902).

The famous Massachusetts cases of Attorney General v. Pelletier, 240 Mass. 264, 134 N.E. 407 (1922) and Attorney General v. Tufts, 239 Mass. 458, 132 N.E. 322 (1921) indicate that allocation of the burden of explanation can be the determining factor in the disposition of certain charges. In reviewing some of the charges brought against these two prosecutors, the court placed the burden of proving improper motives on the attorney general, and the finding of "not guilty" was voiced in terms of his failure to meet this burden. For other charges the court, without any articulated rationale, shifted the burden to the defending prosecutor; when his excuses for inaction were found unsatisfactory he was found "guilty." A possible explanation is that the burden was shifted to the prosecutor when he was charged with failure to prosecute singularly outrageous crimes. See Attorney General v. Pelletier, *supra* at 342, 134 N.E. at 434; but see Attorney General v. Tufts, *supra* at 532-533, 132 N.E. at 345.

[32] Compare cases cited note 28 *supra*, with cases cited note 30 *supra*.

[33] See State ex rel. Kinsella v. Eberhart, 116 Minn. 313, 319-320, 133 N.W. 857, 860 (1911) (ignorance of law does not constitute grounds for removal from office). The cases cited in note 34 *infra* indicate that courts refuse to regard charging decisions as grounds for legal action against the prosecutor merely because they are unwise.

Cases concerning direct control remedies add a dimension to the conceptual assessment of enforcement practices in terms of good and bad faith. See State ex rel. Williams v. Ellis, 184 Ind. 307, 112 N.E. 98 (1916); State ex rel. Ilvedson v. District Court, 70 N.D. 17, 291 N.W. 620 (1940); Mahaffey v. Territory, 11 Okla. 213, 66 Pac. 342 (1901); Frederick v. Douglas County, 96 Wis. 411, 71 N.W. 798 (1897). Collectively, these cases suggest that when the public selects a prosecutor it bargains for impartial and honest exercise of personal judgment on his part. When he is doing just this to the best of his ability — that is, when he is exercising discretion — the public is getting all it bargained for and legal action is not available. When he is not exercising his discretion to the best of his ability, either because he is absent or unwilling to consider the community interest, a substitute prosecutor can be appointed. This can also be done of course when his personal judgment is impaired by corruption or other forms of personal interest.

tion by making decisions based on criteria that are not clearly illegal. But not much can be gleaned from these decisions about specific criteria or guidelines for the exercise of that discretion on a day-to-day, decision-by-decision level. First of all, they may reflect toleration of some practices rather than approval of them.[34] Second, the number of cases, and so the number of times a particular practice comes to the attention of the appellate judiciary, is too small to permit conclusions to be drawn confidently. In short, unless lawlessness is rampant, enforcement at a low level and public indignation at a high one, the prosecutor is relatively immune from sanctions that might influence routine decision-making. When to lack of specific guideposts for the exercise of discretion is added the fact that actions are rarely instituted,[35]

[34] The courts are primarily concerned with comparing the defending prosecutor's acts with those of the ordinary honest prosecutor. Thus courts review certain decisions in situations which fall into patterns regularly encountered by the ordinary prosecutor. In evaluating the prosecutor's reasons for deciding as he did, the courts make statements that can be treated as judicial recognition of factors commonly considered by prosecutors in making negative charging decisions. For example, in Attorney General v. Tufts, 239 Mass. 458, 132 N.E. 322 (1921) (removal action) the court found the prosecutor not guilty of bad faith on some of the counts which cited instances of less than full enforcement, accepting his excuses that (1) dockets were congested and resources were inadequate, id. at 507, 132 N.E. at 334, (2) the suspect had given evidence against his accomplices, id. at 517, 132 N.E. at 338, (3) undue harm to suspects was considered, id. at 517-522, 132 N.E. at 338-340. At one point, however, the court characterized a decision as an unwise one but nevertheless held that it did not constitute grounds for removal. Id. at 503, 132 N.E. at 334; *accord,* State ex rel. Dalton v. Moody, 325 S.W.2d 21, 32 (1959). The Massachusetts court, in another removal case, stated that the wisdom of the prosecutor's decisions is not at issue in the search for bad faith. Attorney General v. Pelletier, 240 Mass. 264, 343-346, 134 N.E. 407, 435-436 (1922). Thus there are two degrees of judicial recognition of the discretionary factors: (1) what the prosecutor may consider, and (2) the wisdom of his decision. Sanctions may be imposed on the prosecutor for considering inappropriate factors but not for making honest but unwise decisions. Most cases simply do not indicate recognition of this distinction.

The courts appear to be circumscribing the scope of discretion, that is, marking out lines beyond which the prosecutor cannot go without being called to account, and nothing more. In fact a judicial policy has been articulated to the effect that the courts only assure that the prosecutor does exercise his discretion, but once he is doing so and his decisions fall within the boundaries conceived he will not be directed in detail how to exercise that discretion. E.g., Leone v. Fanelli, 194 Misc. 826, 87 N.Y.S.2d 850 (Sup. Ct. 1949) and see the discussion in note 12 *supra.* Thus it becomes preferable, as a general rule, to repose confidence in the prosecutor and presume that his decisions will be in the community interest rather than to formulate a cogent body of administrative law that might offer definitive guidelines for decision-making in recurring situations. See 1 Davis, Administrative Law 257 (1958), quoted in text accompanying note 5 *supra.*

[35] In the three states under consideration only four cases involving removal from office were located, and only three of these evaluated the prosecutors' charging practices. These are cited in note 27 *supra.* One case of disbarment was located, but it turned on corruption rather than charging practices. In re Norris, 60 Kan. 659, 57 Pac. 528 (1899). No cases of criminal action against a prosecutor were

the efficacy of these indirect sanctions as controls over prosecutor discretion becomes highly attenuated.[36]

2. *Direct controls.* Direct controls over prosecution are defined as those which may be used to cause a particular suspect to be prosecuted despite a prior decision by the regular prosecutor that he should not, and those which prevent prosecution when the basis for selection is an improper one. They reflect intervention on the part of private citizens, the trial judiciary, or the attorney general. The private citizen acting as a complainant may seek to compel the regular prosecutor to proceed by an action known as mandamus.[37] He may instead, seek to assume a sort of double-role of complainant-prosecutor, employing a private attorney to conduct the actual prosecution.[38] The trial judge may have statutory authority to compel continuance of prosecution. In some jurisdictions a decision by a prosecutor not to file an information after a bindover is ineffective without judicial concurrence.[39] In many states, a prosecutor may not discontinue a prosecution after an information has been filed or an indictment returned without the approval of the trial judge.[40] The judge may simply issue a direct order to proceed, or, if necessary, use the contempt power for that purpose. Or he may appoint a substitute prosecutor, either a private attorney,[41] or even the state's attorney general in some jurisdictions.[42] With great variations in power from jurisdiction to jurisdiction, the attorney general may decide to intervene on his own motion when he disagrees with negative charging decisions made by the regular prosecutor. In some jurisdictions he may do so only if requested by the trial judge, by the governor of the state, or the state legislature.[43]

Conversely, the defendant may, himself, challenge a prosecutorial decision on the ground that he was improperly selected for prosecution while others similarly situated were not.[44] To do

---

located. Only six criminal cases from other jurisdictions were found (cited note 17 *supra*), and only three of these evaluate charging, the others being concerned with corruption.

36 See authorities cited note 11 *supra*.

37 See Ferguson, Formulation of Enforcement Policy: An Anatomy of the Prosecutor's Discretion Prior to Accusation, 11 Rutg. L. Rev. 507, 517-521 (1957).

38 See generally Note, 65 Yale L.J. 209 (1956).

39 Note 103 U. Pa. L. Rev. 1057, 1065 (1955).

40 Id. at 1067.

41 State ex rel. Clyde v. Lauder, 11 N.D. 136, 90 N.W. 564 (1902).

42 See, e.g., O'Reardon v. Wilson, 4 N.J Misc. 1008, 135 Atl. 230 (1926).

43 Note, 103 U. Pa. L. Rev. 1057, 1078 n.143 (1955).

44 See generally Comment, 61 Colum. L. Rev. 1103 (1961).

so, he may move to dismiss the information,[45] or, under some circumstances, seek to enjoin the prosecutor or prohibit the judge from proceeding in actions known respectively as injunction and prohibition.[46]

All of these means of seeking to cause or prevent charging as well as the remedies invoked to effectuate them represent potential controls over prosecutor discretion. Analysis of current practices reinforces the conclusion reached from a study of the decided cases that they are not often attempted and when attempted are not often successful. Their potential as controls, however, is of sufficient significance to demand careful consideration of them here. It is also possible that in some jurisdictions the preliminary examination, or the grand jury, or both, might serve as regular or occasional barriers to affirmative initial charging decisions made on bases which are either constitutionally forbidden or not in accord with prevailing community sentiment. Because grand juries are not used in the jurisdictions under intensive study here, no basis exists for assessing the usefulness of that body as a check.[47] Although the preliminary examination is available for all serious offenses in Kansas, Michigan, and Wisconsin, there is no indication of its use as a check on positive initial charging decisions other than to test the technical sufficiency of the evidence to sustain them.[48] This is not to assert that a preliminary examination never serves this purpose in the three states: it is an assertion that no preliminary was observed which could be identified as one in which this function was performed or even explicitly considered.

a. *Judicial control over prosecution.* A problem of central and continuing concern in the administration of criminal justice is the extent to which the prosecutor should be forced to share with the trial judge his traditional power to discontinue prosecu-

45 See Kosicki, The Function of Nolle Prosequi and Motion to Dismiss in Connecticut, 36 Conn. B.J. 159, 168 (1962); Comment, 61 Colum. L. Rev. 1103, 1131, (1961).

46 See Traux v. Raich, 239 U.S. 33 (1915) (injunction); Chaires v. City of Atlanta, 164 Ga. 775, 139 S.E. 559 (1927) (injunction); Fenster v. Criminal Court, 46 Misc.2d 179, 259 N.Y.S.2d 67 (Sup. Ct.) *aff'd,* 24 App. Div. 2d 840, 263 N.Y.S.2d 1010 (1965), *aff'd,* 17 N.Y.2d 641, 216 N.E.2d 342, 269 N.Y.S.2d 139 (1966) (prohibition); Powell v. Criminal Court, 44 Misc. 2d 838, 255 N.Y.S.2d 1 (Sup. Ct 1964) (prohibition).

47 Its efficacy as a check has, however, been widely questioned. E.g., Baker and DeLong, The Prosecuting Attorney, 24 J. Crim. L. 1025, 1058 (1934); Lashly, Preparation and Presentation of the State's Case, in Missouri Crime Survey 119-120 (1926); Note, 65 Yale L.J. 209, 212 (1955).

48 The preliminary hearing in current administration in these three states is discussed in Part III. Note, 103 U. Pa L. Rev. 1057, 1062-1064 (1955) concludes that the preliminary affords only minimal checks on prosecutor discretion.

tions.[49] In the absence of a statute establishing a contrary rule, it has been the historically established prerogative of the prosecutor in most jurisdictions to discontinue, *nolle prosequi,* a criminal prosecution without judicial approval at least after the formal charge embodied in an information or indictment is lodged against a suspect.[50] Early concern over this unbridled discretion in the prosecutor resulted in legislation in many states which,

49 It must be remembered that the law reveals less than the whole picture of the locus of decision-making in regard to discontinuance of prosecution. Attitudes expressed in appellate opinions — for example, the idea that active participation in charging decisions is incompatible with the judicial role (see note 10 *supra*) — do not necessarily reflect the policies actually followed by judges at the magisterial and trial levels; the judge can influence in detail the exercise of prosecutor discretion through informal arrangements that these two officials have worked out between them. It is only when they cannot reach an informal agreement about the desirability of continuing a prosecution that the formal law must be consulted to determine whether the judge can enforce his wishes against those of the prosecutor. The present concern is over the situation in which the prosecutor wishes to discontinue and the judge does not. The reverse situation in which the question is whether the judge can unilaterally discontinue a prosecution is reserved for treatment in the subsection on judicial control over positive charging.

50 In the absence of a statute allocating the authority to discontinue, recourse has been to the common law to determine who should prevail when the prosecutor and judge disagree on the desirability of continuing a prosecution. See generally 2 Wharton, Criminal Law and Procedure §1310 (12th ed. 1957); the term "nolle prosequi," which denotes a discontinuance, derives from the prosecutor's ancient practice of writing on the back of the indictment that he did not wish to prosecute the defendant further, United States v Brokaw, 60 F. Supp. 100, 102 (S.D. Ill. 1945). The majority of American courts have interpreted the common law to mean that the prosecutor's wish to dismiss the charge prevails regardless of the wishes of the judge. E.g., Confiscation Cases, 74 U.S. (7 Wall.) 454, 457 (1868); Gray v. District Court, 42 Colo. 298, 94 Pac. 287 (1908); Commonwealth v. Tuck, 37 Mass. (20 Pick.) 356, 364-365 (1838); Commonwealth v. Wheeler, 2 Mass. (2 Tyng) 172 (1806); State ex rel. Griffin v. Smith, 363 Mo. 1235, 258 S.W.2d 590 (1953); State v. Tufts, 56 N.H. 137, 138-139 (1875). A qualification to the majority position is that the judge can prevent the entry of nolle when the prosecutor's action is corrupt, United States v. Brokaw, *supra,* and even perhaps when it is in bad faith, see People ex rel. Hoyne v. Newcomer, 284 Ill. 315, 120 N.E. 244 (1918).

The authorities discussing the nolle prosequi usually associate it with the discontinuance of prosecutions of serious crimes that have reached the level of general trial jurisdiction after the filing of an indictment or information. E.g., Wharton, op. cit. *supra.* These authorities and the leading cases typically do not indicate whether the same common law rule obtains at the magisterial level, either in prosecutions for crimes minor enough to be tried in the lower courts, or during preliminary proceedings in serious offense prosecutions. Dicta in United States v. Brokaw, *supra,* does suggest that it obtains there, but case law expressly directed to the point is not uniform. Kansas and Michigan have taken opposing positions on the authority to discontinue at the magisterial level, and Wisconsin appears to lean in the Michigan direction (notes 56-64 *infra* and accompanying text). One possible interpretation of People ex rel. Hoyne v. Newcomer, *supra,* in which a judge was allowed to prevent the dismissal of charges, is that the usual common law rule was modified because the dispute arose in a minor offense prosecution in the lower courts. Compare People ex rel. Kunstman v. Shinsaku Nagano, 389 Ill. 231, 249-250, 59 N.E.2d 96, 104 (1945).

at a minimum, forced the prosecutor to explain his reasons for doing so in writing, thus assuring greater visibility of the manner in which the prosecutor acted; at a maximum it required that he receive judicial approval to make his decision effective.[51] So strong was the concern that the American Law Institute's Code of Criminal Procedure,[52] promulgated in 1930 largely in response to the findings and recommendations of the early crime surveys, forbade discontinuance without judicial approval either after a bindover order and prior to the placement of a formal charge or after a charge in the form of an information or indictment had been placed.

1. Judicial control prior to bindover order. In both Kansas and Wisconsin, warrants may be issued by magistrates without prosecutor approval, and so the criminal prosecution may be begun without the prosecutor's knowledge or against his wishes.[53] Except in limited circumstances, Michigan statutes require prosecutorial approval for warrant issuance, but if security for costs is posted by the private complainant, approval is not necessary.[54]

51 The majority American interpretation of the common law of nolle prosequi coincides with the policy of the indirect controls: the courts can take action to correct corruption or even perhaps bad faith; that is, they can assure that the prosecutor does exercise his discretion, but they cannot direct him in detail how to exercise this discretion or dictate what decisions he will reach. See notes 12 and 34 *supra*. Some statutes changing the common law, however, permit the judge to veto the prosecutor's discontinuance decision simply because he disagrees with the decision. See generally Baker and DeLong, The Prosecuting Attorney, 24 J. Crim. L. 1025, 1060 (1934); Note, 103 U. Pa. L. Rev. 1057, 1066-1067 (1955). Moreover, the judge can enforce his desire to continue by various means, including the appointment of an attorney to prosecute in substitution for the reluctant prosecutor. And he can do all of this without invoking any special grounds such as bad faith or misconduct on the part of the prosecutor. State ex rel. Clyde v. Lauder, 11 N.D. 136, 90 N.W. 564 (1902). The judge, in some instances, not only directs in detail how discretion is to be exercised but also shares discretion with the prosecutor as a matter of routine.

52 ALI, Code of Criminal Procedure §295 (1930); the comment at 895 exhaustively catalogues the statutes found in the institute's survey which in one way or another sought to provide greater judicial control over the nolle prosequi.

53 Kan. Stat. Ann. §§62-601, 62-602, 63-201 (1964); Wis. Stat. Ann. §§954.01 to 954.02 (1957).

54 Mich. Stat. Ann. §§28.860, 28.1195 (1954). At the time the survey was conducted, the issuance of a warrant at the instance of a private complainant with neither prosecutor approval nor posting of security for costs although not in strict compliance with the statute, gave the magistrate jurisdiction of a criminal action. People v. Griswold, 64 Mich. 722, 31 N.W. 809 (1887). However, this case has recently been overruled by People v. Holbrook, 373 Mich. 94, 128 N.W.2d 484 (1964) which thus blocks what had been allowed to exist by Griswold as one more potential avenue for the initiation of prosecutions without prosecutor approval. And the court apparently set out to do just this, as indicated by the following language: "The policy behind the statute would appear to be to insure orderly procedure by, in the main, funnelling all law enforcement through the prosecuting

Although in ordinary circumstances it is uniform practice to defer to prosecutor wishes at this stage,[55] the potentiality for proceeding at least initially against his wishes is present. Leading Kansas cases make it abundantly clear, however, that Kansas prosecutors may without judicial approval prevent further steps from being taken by appearing at a preliminary examination and dismissing a felony case,[56] by directing the return of a warrant without service,[57] or by directing the dismissal of misdemeanor cases.[58] An early Michigan case, on the other hand, denied to the prosecutor the right to order return of a warrant unserved,[59] and other early cases asserted the inability of the prosecutor to prevent the holding of a preliminary examination[60] or to discontinue misdemeanor prosecutions[61] against the wishes of the magistrate. Thus, though the Michigan court urged magistrates to respect the wishes of the prosecutor in the matter of warrant issuance as well as the dismissing of cases at the preliminary examination,[62] it did not go so far as to deny the power of the magistrate to proceed without prosecutor concurrence if he wished.[63] Wisconsin law bearing directly on this point is lacking.[64]

---

attorney . . . ." Id. at 97, 128 N.W.2d at 486. The judges of the court were divided on the jurisdictional point in this case and have remained divided on it although the majority position remains substantially the same. See People v. Carter, 379 Mich. 24, 148 N.W.2d 860 (1967). Thus, Michigan law expressly seeks to assure regular prosecutor participation in the decision to issue a warrant, an assurance that is not written into the law of Kansas or Michigan.

55 Prosecutor domination of the warrant decision is discussed in Chapter 3 *supra.*

56 Foley v. Ham, 102 Kan. 66, 169 Pac. 183 (1917). The court held that the prosecutor could not be prevented from appearing and taking control of the prosecution, and that the magistrate had to abide by his decision to dismiss.

57 Ex parte Broadhead, 74 Kan. 401, 86 Pac. 458 (1906). Here the sheriff returned an unexecuted warrant on the instructions of the prosecutor. The court held that it was the prosecutor's prerogative to terminate the prosecution in this manner.

58 State v. Zier, 138 Kan. 235, 25 P.2d 583 (1933); State ex rel. Mitchell v. Court of Coffeyville, 123 Kan. 774, 256 Pac. 804 (1927).

59 Beecher v. Anderson, 45 Mich. 543, 8 N.W. 539 (1881).

60 Ibid.; Meister v. People, 31 Mich. 99, 104 (1875). Contrary to the Kansas position discussed in note 56 *supra* the court held that the prosecutor could not appear and assume control of the prosecution unless requested to do so by the magistrate.

61 Jaminet v. Board of Supervisors, 77 Mich. 245, 43 N.W. 910 (1889).

62 Beecher v. Anderson, 45 Mich. 543, 548, 8 N.W. 539, 541 (1881).

63 In this connection, see the discussion in note 50 *supra* of the majority American position establishing the authority of the prosecutor to control criminal prosecutions. The Michigan position could be said to contravene the majority except that the authorities establishing that view do not typically indicate whether it applies to proceedings before magistrates.

64 There is, however, a case involving a city ordinance prosecution which may have been made relevant to the present discussion by the court's denial that the proceeding was civil in nature — the court stated that, like state criminal prosecutions, this action was primarily concerned with the preservation of law and order.

2. Judicial control after bindover but prior to formal charge. If a preliminary examination has been held in either Michigan or Wisconsin, and the magistrate has issued a bindover order, the prosecutor is required either to file an information or to state his reasons in writing for not doing so and secure judicial approval of those reasons. If the trial judge disapproves, the prosecutor is obliged to file the information.[65]

Although the Kansas statute requires the same statement of reasons, it does not authorize effective judicial disapproval of a prosecutorial decision not to file an information in ordinary circumstances.[66] A separate section of the Kansas statutes permits a trial judge to compel prosecution, but it confines the exercise of the power to "extreme cases,"[67] and Kansas cases make it clear

---

Guinther v. City of Milwaukee, 217 Wis. 334, 258 N.W. 865 (1935). In Guinther the city attorney wished to discontinue the prosecution contrary to the wishes of the trial court, and the latter appointed a substitute prosecutor to conduct the proceedings. This trial court's action was upheld in an opinion stating that judges, not prosecutors, are vested with ultimate authority for deciding whether a prosecution is in the community interest. This result was reached without the aid of a statute modifying the common law, and it would appear to conflict with the majority position discussed in note 50 *supra*, with one caveat: the authorities establishing the majority position are typically silent on the allocation of the authority to discontinue minor offense prosecutions.

[65] Mich. Stat. Ann. §28.981 (1954); Wis. Stat. Ann. §955.17 (1957). The Michigan provision has been regarded as rendering perfunctory the function of the prosecutor in filing the information. In re Elliott, 315 Mich. 662, 675, 24 N.W.2d 528, 533 (1946). Because the statute contemplated that the filing of an information would ordinarily follow the return of a bindover order as a matter of course, the court held that jurisdiction was conferred on the trial court by the return of the bindover order, not by the filing of the information.

Both statutes provide that the statement of reasons is to be filed with the court to which the defendant was bound over for trial, and both provide that, if the court is dissatisfied with those reasons, the prosecutor must file an information. Conversely, if the court is satisfied with those reasons, the Michigan provision does not expressly require the court to make any notation or entry on the record to that effect, and presumably the mere filing of the reasons without further judicial action would effectively terminate the prosecution. Certainly, it has been held that when the court did go ahead and make an entry of satisfaction with the reasons this constituted a final order terminating the prosecution. Spalding v. Lowe, 56 Mich. 366, 23 N.W. 46 (1885). The Wisconsin provision expressly requires the trial court to examine the reasons and endorse his approval on them. Although there are no cases construing the Wisconsin provision, it appears to proceed hand-in-hand with the language of the court in Guinther v. City of Milwaukee, 217 Wis. 334, 258 N.W. 865 (1935), discussed note 64 *supra*.

[66] Kan. Stat. Ann. §62-804 (1964). The provision simply requires the statement of reasons and says nothing about judicial approval.

[67] Kan. Stat. Ann. §62-807 (1964). Like the Michigan and Wisconsin provisions, the statute gives the court of general trial jurisdiction the authority to order the filing of an information. Unlike the other provisions, however, it does not expressly predicate an exercise of this authority upon the court's unilateral dissatisfaction with the statement of reasons offered by the prosecutor for not informing. In terms,

beyond cavil that except under extraordinary circumstances, the decision of the prosecutor is to be respected.[68] Apparently, a trial court decision to invoke the extreme cases section is subject to full appellate review.[69] In summary, the power of the Kansas prosecutor to dismiss prosecutions is regarded as part and parcel of his general power to control the prosecution of criminal cases. On the other hand, the Wisconsin and Michigan statutes make it quite clear that discontinuance after a bindover and prior to filing of an information is permissible only when the prosecutor and the judge concur.

3. The nolle prosequi. In both Kansas and Michigan, statutes limit the power of prosecutors to discontinue prosecution after an information or indictment has been lodged.[70] Both statutes appear to require judicial approval and have since before the middle of the last century.[71] No Michigan case has been found interpreting its statute, but the same leading Kansas cases which establish the general power of the prosecutor to control prosecutions, without referring to the apparently controlling Kansas statute, find power in the prosecutor to dismiss without judicial approval at any stage in the proceedings.[72] Apparently a belief

---

it restricts the authority to instances when someone else (presumably a citizen or another official) has filed affidavits in the court stating the commission of a crime.

68 In Foley v. Ham, 102 Kan. 66, 69, 169 Pac. 183, 184 (1917), the court derived a negative inference from the statute. Since the statute authorized the district court to order an information only in extreme cases, it must have been contemplated that the prosecutor would make the effective decision in routine cases. Compare State ex rel. Pitchford v. District Court, 323 P.2d 993 (Okla. Crim. 1958).

69 The implication of the discussion of the statute in Foley v. Ham, *supra* note 68, is that the trial court's exercise of the power to order an information is subject to review to ascertain whether the facts of the case were such as to take it out of the class of ordinary cases, in which the prosecutor's charging decisions are final, and place it in the extraordinary class in which the authority to make the dispositive decision passes to the court. In other words, there would be a legal issue whether a court had overstepped its authority and infringed the domain of the prosecutor, a question which would merit appellate review.

70 Kan. Stat. Ann. §62-1437 (1964); Mich. Stat. Ann. §28.969 (1954).

71 The Kansas provision currently provides that no "indictment or information shall be dismissed, except by order of the court, on motion." It appears to be derived from Kan. Terr. Laws, c. 27, §205 (1859). A provision similar to the present one was contained in Mich. Rev. Stat., c. 164, §23 (1846). The current Michigan provision specifies that no prosecutor shall dismiss an indictment without first obtaining "leave of court." (By virtue of Mich. Stat. Ann. §28.942 (1954), the provision also applies to dismissal of informations.)

72 Williams v. Cave, 138 Kan. 586, 27 P.2d 272 (1933) (general statements applicable to all stages); State v. Zier, 138 Kan. 235, 25 P.2d 583 (1933) (dismissal of misdemeanor charges pending before justice of peace); State v. Finch, 128 Kan. 665, 280 Pac. 910 (1929) (does not indicate what stage was at issue or whether the charges were misdemeanor or felony); Foley v. Ham, 102 Kan. 66, 169 Pac. 183

in the importance of leaving individual charging decisions in the hands of the public prosecutor on a theory that any other allocation would unduly interfere with the orderly performance of his duties explains the apparent deviation from the statute.[73]

The absence of a statute in Wisconsin, leaves the law there uncertain. The *Guinter*[74] case permits alternative inferences. Arguably the failure to legislate in the true nolle prosequi situation in Wisconsin, accompanied by specific legislation in the pre-information situation, leads to an inference that the traditional common law power of the prosecutor remains there.[75] Conversely, it could be argued on an a fortiori kind of reasoning that, if the prosecutor needs judicial approval to dismiss even before an information is filed, surely he needs that approval when the case is in a more advanced stage.[76] What is merely a possible

(1917) (dismissal of felony charges at preliminary hearing). Since the statute refers in terms to dismissal of indictments and informations, it arguably applies only to serious offense prosecutions that have reached the court of general trial jurisdiction. This would explain the result reached in at least two of the earlier cases. In Cave, however, all three of the earlier cases were cited as support for the general authority of the prosecutor. Another possible explanation is that, without making its position explicit, the court regarded the statute as merely changing the common law rule stated in United States v. Brokaw, 60 F. Supp. 100 (S.D. Ill. 1945) that allowed the prosecutor effectively to terminate a prosecution without applying for a judicial order of dismissal. The language of the statute — "No indictment or information shall be dismissed except by order of the court, on motion" — does not expressly grant to the court the authority to refuse the motion. Compare the discussion of another state's law in Kosicki, The Function of Nolle Prosequi and Motion to Dismiss in Connecticut, 36 Conn. B.J. 159, 169 (1962).

[73] See Foley v. Ham, *supra* note 72.

[74] Guinther v. City of Milwaukee, 217 Wis. 334, 258 N.W. 865 (1935). The court held that the trial court, in a prosecution for city ordinance violation, could refuse the prosecutor's request for dismissal.

[75] Although Wisconsin does have a statute (cited and discussed in note 65 *supra* and accompanying text) requiring judicial approval of the prosecutor's reasons for not filing an information, the statutes are silent on where the authority to dismiss rests once an information (or indictment) is outstanding. The majority American position, discussed note 50 *supra,* is that this authority is in the prosecutor by virtue of common law when the statutes are silent. The fact that the Wisconsin legislature gave attention to the authority to refuse to file informations could be said to support an inference that it also considered the closely related question of dismissal of informations, decided that the majority common law position was acceptable, presumed that this position would be adopted if any test case arose in the state, and therefore declined to take the step of expressly adopting the majority position. This chain of inferences, however, appears weak in light of the Guinther case. It is true that the case involved a prosecution for a minor offense and thus may not be persuasive with regard to the authority to dismiss formal charges in prosecutions for more serious crimes. However, strong language in the opinion appears to make it applicable to prosecutions for criminal offenses in general, and there is a possibility that it stands as a rejection for Wisconsin of the majority American position.

[76] See Ferguson, Formulation of Enforcement Policy: An Anatomy of the Prose-

inference in Michigan has been made explicit in Wisconsin by the statutory requirement of judicial approval.[77] The only hesitation one has in asserting the conclusion categorically is that the same kind of statute in Kansas has been so severely limited by that state's court.[78]

4. Judicial control in current administration. In current administration,[79] trial judges rarely decline to accept the prosecutor's statement of reasons for discontinuing prosecution, whether before or after an information is filed.[80] In Kansas, where guilty

---

cutor's Discretion Prior to Accusation, 11 Rutg. L. Rev. 507, 511 and n.20 (1957). As he has it, the entire administration of criminal justice is "court oriented." This could be said to become increasingly true as a prosecution nears adjudication, a peculiarly judicial function. It is arguable that the nearer a case comes to adjudication, the greater should be the authority of the court to control all decisions that vitally affect guilt determinations.

77 Mich. Stat. Ann. §28.969 (1954), discussed notes 70-71 *supra* and accompanying text.

78 It is possible, as discussed in note 72 *supra*, that the Kansas court interpreted the statute as granting no authority to the court to refuse a motion to dismiss made by the prosecutor. The statute does not literally preclude this interpretation. The Michigan statute, however, does appear to preclude such an interpretation, and it would be more difficult for a court to so interpret it. It states that the prosecutor cannot dismiss an indictment (or information) without first obtaining "leave of court," a phrase that certainly implies judicial discretion to refuse.

79 It is necessary at this point to distinguish two parallel processes in administration. The first of these screens certain persons out of the criminal machinery, terminating prosecutions against them entirely. Discussion of this process is the peculiar province of this volume. The second process, by contrast, concerns persons against whom it is clear that a prosecution will be carried to adjudication and it involves selection of the particular charge or charges that will be adjudicated. One of the principal components of this process is the bargain for a plea of guilty. Certain charges might be "reduced" — the original ones would be discontinued and lesser charges substituted — or some of the original charges might be dropped, leaving the others outstanding, in exchange for a plea of guilty. The bargaining aspects of the charge-selection process fall within the coverage of the volume on conviction (Newman, Conviction, 1966) but mention must be made of it here because it involves the same questions about allocation of authority to discontinue charges as the process of terminating prosecutions completely. Moreover, as discussed in the volume on adjudication, the discontinuance of particular charges may reflect some of the same sort of discretionary considerations that might lead to an outright termination of prosecution. (For example, the prosecutor might be moved by considerations of undue harm to the accused in addition to his desire to obtain a guilty plea.) To the extent that judges control the selection of the particular charges that are to be adjudicated, they are controlling one aspect of prosecutor discretion, and this chapter on control of discretion would be incomplete without mention of this.

80 It is widely assumed that judicial acquiescence is given perfunctorily. E.g., Note, 65 Yale L.J. 209, 214 and n.14 (1955) and authorities cited. In Detroit the post-information nolle prosequi is most often requested by the prosecutor because the complaining witness has become reluctant to testify against the accused. The judge usually allows this without question, but only after the prosecutor has brought the witness into court — as he customarily does — and has had the witness

plea bargaining occurs between the time the warrant is issued and the information is filed, the information itself reflects the results of the bargain in the form of a charge reduction.[81] This is done because the trial judge lacks extensive sentencing discretion.[82] Because he agrees with the results of the bargains, or believes that the judgment properly belongs to the prosecutor, the trial judge routinely approves the reduction though his approval is not even technically required at this stage.[83] Indeed, one Kansas judge participates in the bargaining process, itself, in open court.

Because the Wisconsin trial judge has extensive sentencing discretion, charge bargains are not common.[84] When they do occur,

---

state his reluctance to the judge. This is not necessarily a perfunctory approval since it is likely that informal working arrangements exist between prosecutor and judge through which each is informed just what can be expected of the other and which tend to prevent disagreements from arising at the crucial moment when a request for nolle is made. See Kaplan, The Prosecutorial Discretion — A Comment, 60 Nw. U.L. Rev. 174, 178 (1965). Perhaps the judge defers to the prosecutor's assessment of the factual developments causing him to reconsider the charging decision in a particular case because the judge is assured that the prosecutor will reciprocally defer to general policy expectations which the judge has informally communicated to him. In Milwaukee both the municipal and district court judges require that reasons be given by the prosecutor for a "reduction" in charges. Memoranda from the prosecutor to his staff indicate that respect is maintained for the judges' desire that the reasons be substantial ones.

Another possibility is that opportunities may be presented to work out informally any disagreement between prosecutor and judge about the desirability of dismissing charges in a particular case in advance of the formal request made by the prosecutor. The judges of the Court of Common Pleas in Wichita were observed on occasion participating actively in plea bargaining negotiations between defense and prosecution, and their suggestions often were followed. Instances were observed when these judges even attempted to persuade prosecutors to move to dismiss prosecutions entirely, and, in case a prosecutor complied, the judge's subsequent approval of the motion could hardly be called perfunctory. See Chapter 14 for a discussion of other instances in which charges might be dismissed and alternative procedures invoked at the behest of the judge. In short, the relationship between prosecutor and judge is considerably too complex to allow the hypothesis of judicial passivity to be predicated upon the exposed part of an iceberg appearing as acquiescence at the crucial moment of request for dismissal of charges.

[81] The Kansas practice is discussed in detail in Newman, Conviction 83-87 (1966).

[82] District court judges are not allowed, for example, to set the maximum term of imprisonment; instead the statutory maximum for each offense is applied. Kan. Stat. Ann. §62-2239 (1964). Since the Kansas judge does not have enough discretion to allow sentencing concessions to be the primary inducement for an accused to plead guilty, the inducement must exist in charging concessions.

[83] The Kansas statute, discussed in note 66 and accompanying text, does not require judicial approval when the prosecutor declines to file an information.

[84] Wisconsin judges, for example, have authority to set maximum terms of imprisonment less than the statutory maximums prescribed for each offense. Wis. Stat. Ann. §959.05 (1957). Newman, Conviction 61, 87 (1966) discusses the Wisconsin bargaining practices that have emerged under this sentencing structure and contrasts them with the practices found in Kansas.

the action usually reflects a desire to avoid the stigmatic effect of convictions of crimes with sexual overtones, and trial judges normally give the necessary approval. Indeed, discontinuance of an action after bindover but prior to the filing of the information is extremely rare. In Milwaukee for instance, a judge of the municipal court indicated that a prosecutor has failed to file an information after a bindover order not more than ten times in the preceding twenty years.[85] Instead, when the Milwaukee prosecutor wishes to discontinue prosecution entirely, he seeks judicial approval of a nolle prosequi filed after the information has been filed.[86] Although the ground for discontinuance most commonly asserted is insufficient evidence — perhaps because of the existence of a previously unknown defense — frequently dismissals reflect a judgment that a defendant who has suffered some penalty for an offense arising out of the same transaction or has spent some time in a mental institution under a pretrial commitment would undergo undue punishment harm if the process were continued. Routinely, the prosecutor's wishes are acceded to.[87]

The limits on sentencing discretion in Michigan also lead to charge reductions,[88] sometimes the result of a bargain, sometimes

85 As discussed note 65 *supra* and accompanying text, the prosecutor is required to file an information unless he can get judicial approval of his reasons for not filing.

86 As discussed notes 74-76 *supra* and accompanying text, there is no unequivocal requirement in Wisconsin law that the prosecutor request judicial approval before dismissing an information (or indictment). Nevertheless, prosecutors were observed making such motions. And the judges appear to assume more than a passive role in regard to these motions. For example, in one case involving a charge of assault with intent to do great bodily harm, the assistant prosecutor informed the court that he had conferred with the assistant prosecutor who had issued the original warrant. He stated that they had agreed that, if the case were tried, an acquittal would result since the defendant's version of the incident indicating self-defense was corroborated by two witnesses whereas the state could produce only one witness who would negate self-defense. He stated further that the state had recently lost an assault case at trial because of a self-defense argument. The assistant requested a dismissal and the judge asked if the other assistant concurred in the dismissal decision. This was answered in the affirmative and the judge then asked "Is this a valid self-defense situation?" After another affirmative answer the court dismissed the case without prejudice and without costs and told the defendant that he was discharged. It is of interest that the assistant during this colloquy also informed the judge that a warrant charging the lesser offense of aggravated assault would be issued after dismissal and that the accused would plead guilty to this charge.

87 See note 80 *supra* for a discussion of whether this fact supports the hypothesis that judicial approval is given perfunctorily.

88 The statutes provide a relatively elaborate scheme in which the judge is directed as to the length of sentence according to whether the defendant has previously been convicted of a felony. Mich. Stat. Ann. §§28.1080 to 28.1085 (1954). The judge thus has less discretion than in Wisconsin to offer concessions in the form of sentencing leniency as inducements to plead guilty. Thus, concessions must be offered in the form of charge reductions. See Newman, Conviction 54, 61 (1966).

not. Unlike the Kansas practice, the bargaining in Michigan occurs after an information containing an "on-the-nose" charge has been filed.[89] The nolle prosequi is most often used in Detroit to effectuate the bargained-for charge reduction, although it is sometimes used without bargaining when either the prosecutor or the trial judge himself believes that a plea to the maximum charge would require the latter to impose a sentence out of keeping with the circumstances under which the offense was committed or with the past record of the defendant. Obviously when the judge suggests the reduction himself, and in fact when it is initiated by the prosecutor, judicial concurrence in the nolle prosequi is nearly automatic.[90] In practice the result is accomplished by adding to the information the lesser charge to and nolle prossing the original charge.[91]

Some other uses are made of the nolle prosequi. Obviously, the discovery of facts which, had they been known earlier, would have resulted in refusal of a warrant request — or the issuance of a warrant charging a less serious offense — will lead to a charge dismissal or reduction as seems appropriate. Less obviously in the case of informants who agree to perform some service in return for nonprosecution or some lesser charge, the nolle prosequi is used to dismiss charges originally filed to insure that the defendant will carry through on his commitment.[92] Occasionally facts will become known that suggest that a sex-psychopath or a mental illness commitment would be more appropriate than a criminal prosecution. When these facts are discovered after the initial charge has been filed, the case is nolle prossed.[93] Once again the facts may be discovered by the judge, who may then suggest the dismissal of the criminal charges and the use of the indicated alternative.[94] However discovered, judicial approval of the use of the alternative is nearly automatic and when it must be reflected in the approval of a nolle prosequi, that approval is forthcoming.[95]

89 It will be recalled — see note 81 *supra* and accompanying text — that bargaining occurs in Kansas before the information is filed and that the charge embodied in the information has already been reduced to whatever extent the parties have agreed during bargaining.

90 This fact does not, however, necessarily mean that the judicial function is exercised perfunctorily. See note 80 *supra*.

91 The practice in Detroit is discussed in detail in Newman, Conviction 79-83 (1966).

92 This practice is discussed extensively in Chapter 15.

93 The use of alternatives to prosecution is discussed in Chapter 14.

94 See Chapter 14, section A, discussing civil commitment for insanity as an alternative to prosecution; see particularly Illustration No. 8.

95 See note 80 *supra* for a general discussion of informal working arrangements

5. Remedies available. Although no instances were observed of prosecutors persisting in their positions when a trial judge has refused to concur with them — indeed trial judges rarely deny a motion — a scattering of appellate cases in several jurisdictions make it clear that occasionally the protaganists remain steadfast.[96] The simplest remedy[97] when that situation exists is an order by the trial judge directing the prosecutor to proceed.[98] Although the use of such drastic measures must certainly be rare, the Kansas statute authorizes a trial judge to compel compliance by attachment, fine or imprisonment as well.[99] Presumably courts in other jurisdictions would find an inherent contempt power as a basis for attachment to compel performance.[100] But a trial judge might well be reluctant to compel a truly unwilling prosecutor to act against his own wishes and judgment. While he might suggest to the attorney general that he assume control of the case either directly or, where required by statute, through the governor or legislature,[101] that action might seem unduly unwieldy from an administrative point of view. In any event, trial judges have appointed substitute prosecutors — usually private attorneys — to handle a particular case.[102]

---

between prosecutor and judge that probably enable them, in routine cases, to reach an agreement on the desirability of dismissal — regardless of which of them made the first suggestion in this direction — by the time this is formally requested by the prosecutor.

96 E.g., Gray v. District Court, 42 Colo. 298, 94 Pac. 287 (1908); People ex rel. Hoyne v. Newcomer, 284 Ill. 315, 120 N.E. 244 (1918); State ex rel. Griffin v. Smith, 363 Mo. 1235, 258 S.W.2d 590 (1953); State ex rel. Clyde v. Lauder, 11 N.D. 136, 90 N.W. 564 (1902). A case handed down before the survey was conducted indicates that this has also happened in a lower court in one of the three states under consideration, Guinther v. City of Milwaukee, 217 Wis. 334, 258 N.W. 865 (1935), discussed note 64 *supra*.

97 Cf. Switz v. Township of Middleton, 40 N.J. Super. 217, 230, 122 A.2d 649, 656 (App. Div. 1956).

98 The Kansas and Michigan provisions authorizing the court to force prosecutors to file informations contemplate this device, although they do not use the term "order." Kan. Stat. Ann. §62-807 (1964) ("require"); Mich. Stat. Ann. §28-981 (1954) ("direct").

99 Kan. Stat. Ann. §62-807 (1964).

100 See Territory v. Harding, 6 Mont. 323, 325, 12 Pac. 750, 753 (1887); Appeal of Levine, 372 Pa. 612, 95 A.2d 222, *cert. denied,* 346 U.S. 858 (1953).

101 See Note, 103 U. Pa. L. Rev. 1057, 1078 and n.143 (1955).

102 An extensive survey of state constitutional, statutory, and case law concerning the judicial appointment of substitutes is contained in Note, 65 Yale L.J. 209, 215-218 (1955). As discussed in note 22 *supra,* substitutes are sometimes appointed pursuant to a complaint that the regular prosecutor is failing to effectively combat crime in general. In this situation appointment would be classified as an indirect control. The present discussion is concerned with appointment of a substitute to conduct proceedings against persons who have either already been charged or who have otherwise been isolated from the class of criminals in general as suspects in such a way that charging is an imminent possibility.

Any discussion of the appointment of a substitute prosecutor must begin with an important distinction. If the decision not to proceed, at whatever stage the case has reached, requires judicial approval, and the regular prosecutor insists that he will not prosecute, the power to appoint a substitute seems clear.[103] If, on the other hand, the prosecutor retains the common law nolle prosequi power in general, or if he may decline to file an information without judicial approval of his non-action, or if he may recall warrants, the appointment of a substitute to do the very thing the law permits the regular prosecutor to refrain from doing would obviously create an unusual situation requiring resolution at the appellate level.[104] It is not surprising therefore that, when the trial judge's appointment of a substitute merely reflects his authorized insistence on continuation or initiation of prosecution, appellate courts have uniformly upheld his underlying decision not to concur with the prosecutor.[105]

Substitute prosecutors may sometimes be appointed even when in law judicial approval of negative charging decisions is not normally required. Two basic situations present themselves. In the first the appointment of a substitute is based on one of the usual statutory grounds; absence, partiality, bias, or inability to proceed.[106] In the second, the trial judge invokes what he con-

103 Spaulding v. State, 61 Neb. 287, 85 N.W. 80 (1901); State ex rel. Clyde v. Lauder, 11 N.D. 136, 90 N.W. 564 (1902); see Guinther v. City of Milwaukee, 217 Wis. 334, 258 N.W. 865 (1935), discussed note 64 *supra*. But see State v. Heaton, 21 Wash. 59, 56 Pac. 843 (1899).

104 The appellate court disapproved an appointment on the basis of this reasoning in Gray v. District Court, 42 Colo. 298, 94 Pac. 287 (1908).

105 Cases cited note 103 *supra*.

106 The statutory provisions for appointment in the three states under special consideration are typical grants of authority to judges. Kan. Stat. Ann. §19-711 (1964) (sickness, absence, or disability); Kan. Stat. Ann. §19-715 (1964) (vacancy of office because of death, resignation, or otherwise); Mich. Stat. Ann. §5.758 (1954) (vacancy of office, absence, inability to attend to duties); Wis. Stat. Ann. §17.11 (1957) (disqualification and absence). There are also authorizations for officials other than judges to appoint substitutes. Mich. Stat. Ann. §28.1275 (1954) (prosecutor himself if disabled can appoint substitute); Wis. Stat. Ann. §17.11 (1957) (governor can appoint if prosecutor is credibly accused of a criminal offense or if prosecutor "wilfully neglects or refuses to perform his duties"). Other states have similar provisions for judicial appointment. Ind. Stat. Ann. §49-2505 (1964) (failure to attend court); N.D. Code §11-16-06 (1960) (vacancy of office, absence, inability to attend duties, or refusal or neglect to perform prescribed statutory duties); Ore. Rev. Stat. §148.110 (1953) ("when the criminal laws are not being faithfully . . . enforced and the circumstances justify the appointment. . . ."). Utah Const. art. 8, §10 ("fails or refuses to attend and prosecute according to law").

There is implicit authority in some of these provisions for appointment of substitutes to take over the regular prosecutor's general enforcement functions. See Oglesby v. State, 83 Fla. 132, 90 So. 825 (1922) (substitute appointed for entire term). The primary concern in the present discussion is over appointment of substitutes to take over particular prosecutions.

ceives to be an inherent power[107] to supplant a corrupt prosecutor or one whose refusal to prosecute is based on "bad faith" reasons. In either of those situations, appellate courts are ob-

---

Appointment on some of these statutory grounds implies no misconduct or bad faith on the part of the regular prosecutor. E.g., Glavino v. People, 75 Colo. 94, 224 Pac. 225 (1924) (absence from the court); King v. State, 43 Fla. 211, 31 So. 254 (1901) (sickness and absence from the court); State v. Jones, 306 Mo. 437, 268 S.W. 83 (1924) (prosecutor personally interested because his car had been involved in the collision in question); Korth v. State, 46 Neb. 631, 65 N.W. 792 (1896) (prosecutor had previously been private attorney for defendant); State v. Gauthier, 113 Ore. 297, 231 Pac. 141 (1924) (sickness); Ziedler v. State, 189 Wis. 44, 206 N.W. 872 (1926) (prosecutor himself testified at trial about certain statements made to him by defendant). On the other hand, the personal interest that disqualifies a regular prosecutor and justifies appointment of a substitute may arise because the regular prosecutor is himself implicated in matters under investigation by a grand jury, or at least guilty of bad faith in not effectively combatting those matters himself. See State ex rel. Spencer v. Criminal Court, 214 Ind. 551, 15 N.E.2d 1020 (1938) (there must, however, be a proper judicial determination of personal interest); Northcutt v. Howard, 279 Ky. 219, 130 S.W.2d 70 (1939) (dictum); State v. Borgstrom, 70 Minn. 20, 72 N.W. 799 (1897).

107 It has been held that when appointment is made in the indirect control situation — when the regular prosecutor's enforcement policy has been undesirable and the substitute is expected to conduct a general campaign on crime — the authority to do this must be expressly granted to the judge by statute or constitution. State ex rel. Ilvedson v. District Court, 70 N.D. 17, 291 N.W. 620 (1940); Smith v. Gallagher, 408 Pa. 551, 185 A.2d 135 (1962).

When, however, suspicions of crime have begun to center around certain individuals who have thus been isolated from the mass of criminals in general, the possibility for a countervailing argument supporting judicial authority to summarily appoint a substitute for the inactive prosecutor begins to emerge. A leading case has held that the court possesses inherent authority to take action to assure that its adjudicatory function will not lapse for failure of anyone to bring matters before the court. Territory v. Harding, 6 Mont. 323, 12 Pac. 750 (1887) (appointment of substitute when regular prosecutor was absent held proper even in the absence of statutory authority). This reasoning becomes especially cogent when the grand jury is considering indicting certain individuals, since the court is facilitating a routine judicial function, the administration of the regular grand jury system. See Taylor v. State, 49 Fla. 69, 38 So. 380 (1905).

In State ex rel. Ilvedson v. District Court *supra,* the appellate court denied any inherent authority in the trial court to appoint a substitute to initiate action against a group of persons who had not yet been charged. It was said in dictum that the situation changes drastically when charges are pending before the appointing judge. He then acquires an *inherent authority* to do what is necessary in aid of his adjudicatory function. He can appoint because the regular prosecutor is disqualified because of a personal interest, in order to maintain the impartiality of adjudication (accord, State v. Jones, 306 Mo. 437, 268 S.W. 83 [1924]), and also because the prosecutor's unwillingness to prosecute demonstrates bad faith.

The Michigan position discussed in note 110 *infra* denies the inherent authority to appoint at any stage, since it requires strict adherence to enumerated statutory grounds even after charges are pending in the appointing court. Of course the issue might become moot if the enumerated grounds include bad faith or its equivalent expressed in other terms like "wilful neglect" (see note 12 *supra*), but not all statutes do include this, and the Michigan provision is one that does not (see note 106 *supra*). The issue also retains importance because of the implication that, if inherent authority exists, it may be exercised summarily.

viously concerned that the decision to supplant is appropriate, and the decision is indeed subject to judicial review. It must be shown that either the statutory grounds exist, or that the negative charging decision violated the good faith principle.[108]

In current administration, substitute prosecutors are appointed only if the regular prosecutor requests their appointment, perhaps because he recognizes a possible conflict of interest or other basis for impaired impartiality, or perhaps because he is aware of limitations on his own resources.[109] Even when the regular prosecutor agrees to or even urges appointment of a substitute, that does not necessarily end the matter. The Michigan court among others has insisted that unless grounds, statutory or otherwise, exist the prosecution is not a valid one and may be challenged by the defendant.[110]

[108] In one situation appointment can be made merely because the judge disagrees with the prosecutor's personal judgment that prosecution is not in the community interest: when the judge has authority, discussed note 103 *supra* and accompanying text, to prevent discontinuance of prosecution. No case was located which expressly states that appointment can be made in other situations unless at least bad faith of the regular prosecutor is shown; and some cases expressly deny that this can be done. Mahaffey v. Territory, 11 Okla. 213, 66 Pac. 342 (1901); State v. Flavin, 35 S.D. 530, 153 N.W. 296 (1915); State v. Heaton, 21 Wash. 59, 56 Pac. 843 (1899). Gray v. District Court, 42 Colo. 298, 94 Pac. 287 (1908), discussed note 104 *supra*, holds that not even bad faith will suffice; there must be a showing of corruption.

In Quinton v. State, 112 Neb. 684, 200 N.W. 881 (1924), appointment on the grounds that the prosecutor was "incompetent" was upheld. This probably connotes more than a lack of professional skill, however, which was held to be insufficient in Mahaffey v. Territory *supra*. More likely there was ineffectiveness in enforcement, too extreme to be explained by lack of skill, which supported an inference instead that the prosecutor had made a sinecure of his office. This constitutes bad faith. See notes 12, 30 to 33 *supra* and accompanying text. Moreland v. State, 168 Tenn. 145, 76 S.W.2d 319 (1934) upheld an appointment made when the prosecutor was "wilfully" refusing to prosecute persons reasonably suspected of crime. As discussed in note 12 *supra*, the term "wilfulness" indicates a finding of bad faith.

[109] The only instances of substitution reported in the field survey occurred in Wisconsin. In one case — to the knowledge of the officials interviewed the only substitution in Ashland County in recent years — the prosecutor asked the judge to appoint a substitute because the prosecutor had looked into the subject matter of the criminal action on behalf of the defendants prior to his election. In another criminal action in Milwaukee the regular prosecutor disqualified himself, because the action was against an assistant prosecutor, and a substitute was appointed. In a third case in Eau Claire County, the prosecutor and county court judge refused to issue a warrant because it was their feeling that the complainant had provoked the violence that had occurred. The complainant then secured a warrant from a justice of the peace, whereupon the prosecutor requested appointment of a substitute to conduct the prosecution he was willing to undertake.

[110] The statutes pertaining to substitution in the three states under consideration are set out in note 106 *supra*. Michigan is the only one with a significant body of case law on the subject, and the position recurrently expressed is that the prosecutor's duties can be delegated to someone else only when there is strict compliance

b. *Attorney general intervention.* One of the principal recommendations of some of the early crime surveys was that law enforcement generally be centralized at the state level.[111] Partly the suggestion reflects a desire for increased efficiency in enforcement, partly a desire to prevent corruption.[112] Certainly it stems from dissatisfaction with nearly exclusive local control of prosecution. Its asserted advantages would include a standardized system of record-keeping, thus assuring greater visibility as well as greater uniformity.[113] The system, of course, is not unknown. It exists in a few eastern states as well as in the federal jurisdiction today.[114] Indeed, Judge Breitel has recently suggested increased

with the statute. See Engle v. Chipman, 51 Mich. 524, 16 N.W. 886 (1883). In Sayles v. Genesee Circuit Judge, 82 Mich. 84, 46 N.W. 29 (1890), the statute was construed as restricting the authority of the circuit judge to appoint to instances when the case to be prosecuted by the substitute is pending before that judge. Moreover the court has restricted appointment to situations in which the enumerated statutory grounds (absence and inability to attend to duties) are present, Meister v. People, 31 Mich. 99, 102 (1875) (dictum), and this restriction applies to the appointing judge even when the case to be prosecuted is pending before him, People v. Johnston, 326 Mich. 213, 40 N.W.2d 124 (1949). In Johnston, the regular prosecutor requested the appointment of a substitute to prosecute a pending case which the regular prosecutor said he lacked the experience to handle. The appellate court overturned the appointment because he was not unable to attend to his duties but was merely reluctant to try. *Accord,* State v. Boasberg, 124 La. 289, 50 So. 162 (1909) (prosecutor's consent cannot validate appointment in absence of statutory grounds); Mahaffey v. Territory, 11 Okla. 213, 66 Pac. 342 (1901) (inexperience of prosecutor insufficient to support appointment); Smith v. Gallagher, 408 Pa. 551, 185 A.2d 135, 153 (1962) (prosecutor's consent irrelevant).

One case, People v. Auerbach, 176 Mich. 23, 141 N.W. 869 (1913) allowed substitution because of a personal interest disqualifying the prosecutor The court did not mention that that disqualification is not among the enumerated statutory grounds. Other courts inclined toward strict adherence to enumerated grounds have occasionally permitted appointment because of disqualification, even when the ground is not enumerated. Northcutt v. Howard, 279 Ky. 219, 130 S.W.2d 70, 71 (1939); Lattimore v. Vernor, 142 Okla. 105, 288 Pac. 463, 465 (1930). Perhaps the Michigan court, if faced with the issue, would likewise provide an exception to its strict rule and allow appointment to be based on bad faith, which is not enumerated. This would, however, necessitate serious reconsideration of the Johnston case, which is the latest case in point.

111 E.g., National Comm. on Law Observance and Enforcement, Rep. No. 4 on Prosecution, 9-16 (1931); Pound, Criminal Justice in the American City — A Summary, in Reports of the Cleveland Foundation Survey of the Administration of Criminal Justice in Cleveland, Ohio, 599, 607 (1922); see generally DeLong, Powers and Duties of the State Attorney-General in Criminal Prosecution, 25 J. Crim. L. 358, 380-385 (1934); Fairlie and Simpson, Law Officers in Illinois, 8 John Marshall L.Q. 65 (1942); Note, 65 Yale L.J. 209, 212 and nn.14-15 (1955).

112 See Note, Prosecutor Indiscretion: A Result of Political Influence, 34 Ind. L.J. 477, 491 (1959).

113 See, e.g., Boggs and Jamison, Record Systems, in Missouri Crime Survey 377 (1926); Burgess, Summary and Recommendations, in Illinois Crime Survey 1091, 1096 (1929).

114 The systems of a few eastern states, as well as proposals for similar systems

centralization of enforcement, supervision of local prosecutors, and publicized standards for selection of cases to be prosecuted.[115]

Although other methods could be worked out, for example, the establishment of administrative boards to direct prosecutions,[116] the attorney general would be the logical focal point for any increased centralization, at least at the charging level.[117] To the extent that centralization can be said to exist at all today, it exists in the office of the attorney general.[118] Provisions for attorney general intervention in local prosecutions are not uncommon, although they are far from uniform. In Kansas the attorney general is required by statute to appear in and conduct criminal prosecutions whenever the governor or either branch of the legislature directs him to do so.[119] There is strong indication in the case law that he may also appear on his own initiative without any such gubernatorial or legislative direction.[120] Whether he intervenes under direction or on his own, the attorney general can dismiss the prosecution without gubernatorial, legislative, and apparently even judicial approval.[121]

---

in other states, are discussed in Note, 103 U. Pa. L. Rev. 1057, 1079-1080 (1955). For dicussions of statutory creations of state departments of justice, modeled upon but considerably less cohesive than the federal system, see DeLong, Powers and Duties of the State Attorney-General in Criminal Prosecution, 25 J. Crim. L. 358, 380-385 (1934); Note, 48 J. Crim. L.C. & P.S. 531, 536 (1958).

115 Breitel, Controls in Criminal Law Enforcement, 27 U. Chi. L. Rev. 427, 433-435 (1960). Compare Caldwell, How to Make Prosecuting Effectual, 16 J. Am. Jud. Soc. 73, 77 (1932) (suggests chain-of-command arrangement with ultimate responsibility for law enforcement in governor).

116 Note, 30 Ind. L.J. 74, 82 (1954).

117 DeLong, Powers and Duties of the State Attorney-General in Criminal Prosecution, 25 J. Crim. L. 358-359 (1934).

118 See generally Note, 48 J. Crim. L.C. & P.S. 531 (1958).

119 Kan. Stat. Ann. §75-702 (1964). Kansas cases hold that the attorney general has no discretion to refuse to comply with the request. See State ex rel. Stubbs v. Dawson, 86 Kan. 180, 119 Pac. 360 (1911).

120 See State v. Finch, 128 Kan. 665, 280 Pac. 910 (1929). The court held that the authority to intervene had been established at common law, and that no constitutional or statutory provision had modified this authority. Two other cases hold that the attorney general could intervene on his own initiative, but this was predicated on provisions of the now repealed Prohibitory Law. In re Gilson, 34 Kan. 641, 9 Pac. 763 (1886); State v. Nield, 4 Kan. App. 626, 45 Pac. 623 (1896).

121 See State v. Finch, 128 Kan. 665, 280 Pac. 910 (1929), cf. State v. City of Kansas City, 186 Kan. 190, 350 P.2d 37, *cert. denied*, 363 U.S. 881 (1960). Much controversy has centered around the interpretation of common law made by the courts of Kansas and other states which would allow the attorney general to intervene on his own initiative. The Pennsylvania position is similar to that of Kansas. See Commonwealth ex rel. Minerd v. Margiotti, 325 Pa. 17, 188 Atl. 524 (1936). More recently the justices of the court have divided sharply in their separate opinions in Commonwealth v. Fudeman, 396 Pa. 236, 152 A.2d 428, *cert. denied*, 361 U.S. 902 (1959).

The attempt is made to equate the modern prosecuting officials' authority and

In Wisconsin the governor, or either branch of the legislature, may direct the attorney general to intervene in and prosecute a criminal case,[122] and when he does so, he assumes complete control of the matter.[123] The Michigan attorney general is authorized to appear on his own motion,[124] and the statute which authorizes him to do so has been liberally construed to cover a variety of situations.[125] A statement in one Michigan case suggests that the

functions with those of the Attorney General of England under the common law. One difficulty is that the states not ony have single attorneys general as claimants for the inherited authority from England, but local prosecutors as well. Compare Westover v. State, 66 Ariz. 145, 185 P.2d 315 (1947), with Capitol Stages, Inc. v. Hewitt, 157 Miss. 576, 128 So. 759 (1930). See generally People ex rel. Elliott v. Covelli, 415 Ill. 79, 112 N.E.2d 156 (1953); State v. Winne, 12 N.J. 152, 96 A.2d 63 (1953), *rev'g* 21 N.J. Super. 180, 91 A.2d 65 (Law Div., 1952); DeLong, Powers and Duties of the State Attorney-General in Criminal Prosecution, 25 J. Crim. L. 358 (1934); Note, 48 J. Crim. L.C. & P.S. 531, 532-534 (1958); Note, 60 Yale L.J. 559 (1951).

122 The governor or a branch of the legislature may request him to prosecute criminal actions, Wis. Stat. Ann. §14.53(1) (1957), and he has no discretion to refuse the request, Emery v. State, 101 Wis. 627, 646, 78 N.W. 145, 150-151 (1899). Moreover, lacking any common law authority, he cannot intervene unless requested to do so. See State v. Industrial Comm., 172 Wis. 415, 179 N.W. 579 (1920). Wis. Stat. Ann. §14.53(3) (1957) states that he is to consult with and advise local prosecutors, but only at their request. His general lack of supervisory capacity is inferred from State ex rel. Arthur v. Superior Court, 257 Wis. 430, 43 N.W.2d 484 (1950), in which his authority to supervise and take action on his own to assure that lobbying offenses were prosecuted was predicated on special legislation conferring this authority. This intervention statute cited above in terms refers only to his intervention in particular cases, and it appears that a direct control is contemplated. Another statute, however, is associated with an indirect control. Wis. Stat. Ann. §17.11(1) (1957) provides that when the prosecutor is suspended because of bad faith by the governor, the attorney general may be appointed to act as prosecutor during the period of suspension.

123 Wis. Stat. Ann. §14.53(1) (1957); see State ex rel. Jackson v. Coffey, 18 Wis. 2d 529, 118 N.W.2d 939 (1963); Wis. Stat. Ann. §17.11(3) (1957).

124 Mich. Stat. Ann. §3.181 (1961). This section also requires that the attorney general appear for the people in prosecutions when requested by the governor or a branch of the legislature. This provision and Mich. Stat. Ann. §3.211 (1961) go beyond the Wisconsin law and expressly authorize intervention on his own initiative. Both of these provisions speak in terms of intervention in particular cases and thus of direct controls. Another provision, however, appears to authorize what is in the nature of an indirect control. Mich. Stat. Ann. §3.183 (1961) places him in a generally supervisory capacity over local prosecutors. Three cases dispel any doubt that he can, on his own initiative, intervene and take over general campaigns against local crime. Mundy v. McDonald, 216 Mich. 444, 450-451, 185 N.W. 877, 880 (1921), states that he has common law authority in addition to that conferred by statute. In the other cases nothing improper was found in his activities, and it is clear that his staff was participating at the investigative level in general campaigns on crime. In re Watson, 293 Mich. 263, 291 N.W. 652 (1940); People v. O'Hara, 278 Mich. 281, 270 N.W. 298 (1936). Compare Winne v. County of Bergen, 21 N.J. 311, 121 A.2d 733 (1956) (attorney general replaced local prosecutor during unexpired term of the latter).

125 People v. Johnston, 326 Mich. 213, 40 N.W.2d 124 (1949) (allowed to inter-

trial judge also has inherent power to appoint the attorney-general as a substitute prosecutor.[126]

Despite the statutory provisions reflecting efforts to establish some measure of centralized control over local prosecutors, and despite the generally liberal interpretation of them by appellate courts,[127] it remains true that the remedy is rarely used in current administration, and then almost always at the request, or at least with the concurrence, of the local prosecutor.[128] The principal reason seems to be that prosecution is regarded by front-line administrators as well as higher ranking officials as essentially a local matter.[129] In some of the few instances of intervention,

---

vene when local prosecutor unwilling to prosecute because of inexperienced staff); In re Watson, 293 Mich. 263, 291 N.W. 652 (1940) (made motion to compel testimony during one-man grand jury investigation of gambling); People v. O'Hara, 278 Mich. 81, 270 N.W. 298 (1936) (conducted investigation and resulting prosecutions for election frauds in a county).

126 People v. O'Hara, 278 Mich. 281, 295, 270 N.W. 298, 303 (1936).

127 Some cases allow attorney general intervention without a showing of special grounds, like bad faith on the part of the local prosecutor, which restrict use of most of the other controls. State v. Finch, 128 Kan. 665, 280 Pac. 910 (1929); State v. Nield, 4 Kan. App. 626, 45 Pac. 623 (1896); State v. Major, 181 La. 822, 160 So. 425 (1935). Perhaps other controls are confined to categorically defined "extraordinary circumstances" whenever they involve giving to private movants, or attorneys commissioned as substitutes, some say in law enforcement, because this would be incompatible with the theory of public prosecution if allowed on a routine basis. See Engle v. Chipman, 51 Mich. 524, 16 N.W. 886 (1883); Meister v. People, 31 Mich. 99 (1875); State v. Peterson, 195 Wis. 351, 218 N.W. 367 (1928). The attorney general is, on the other hand, a duly selected public official himself, and a prosecution can remain a public one if he takes it over. See State v. Becker, 3 S.D. 29, 33-35, 51 N.W. 1018, 1019-1020 (1892). There appears to be a general preference for giving control of prosecutions to the attorney general rather than private citizens or attorneys. See People v. Johnston, 326 Mich. 213, 40 N.W.2d 124 (1949); Smith v. Gallagher, 408 Pa. 551, 565-566, 185 A.2d 135, 142 (1962); Emery v. State, 101 Wis. 627, 646-647, 78 N.W. 145, 150-151 (1899). Compare State ex rel. Steers v. Holovachka, 236 Ind. 565, 142 N.E.2d 593 (1957), with Lake County Property Owners' Ass'n. v. Holovachka, 233 Ind. 509, 120 N.E.2d 263, *petition to reinstate appeal denied,* 233 Ind. 509, 121 N.E.2d 721 (1954).

128 It is probable that the bulk of routine business passing through the local prosecutor's office is never called to the attention of the attorney general, and although further field research is called for to verify these statements, it is moreover probable that most matters pertaining to local law enforcement considered by the attorney general are called to his attention by local prosecutors requesting assistance. Interviews with prosecutors in Kansas indicate that attorney general intervention against their wishes is rare. One, however, stated that he felt free to call on the attorney general for assistance in an unusual prosecution, or one beyond his personal experience. It can be hypothesized that informal working arrangements exist between prosecutor and attorney general that not only determine what matters are extraordinary enough to be called to the attention of the latter, but also avoid policy disagreements that would lead to intervention in the first place as well as disagreements over charging that might arise when the attorney general does decide to participate actively at the local level. In fact, most of the adjudication giving rise to the case law on the subject has been raised by the objection of

the results have been unsatisfactory, and this experience has apparently caused a marked reluctance on the part of the Michigan attorney general to interfere.[130] The same reluctance was noted in Kansas and Wisconsin.[131] In the latter state it is routine practice to respond to complaints about lax local law enforcement by sending the local prosecutor a form letter in the following

---

someone other than the local prosecutor to attorney general intervention. E.g., State v. Nield, 4 Kan. App. 626, 45 Pac. 623 (1896) (defendant objected to being prosecuted by attorney general).

An assistant in the office of the Wisconsin attorney general stated in interview that much of his time is spent giving informal opinions over the telephone as well as writing official opinions at the request of local prosecutors. In his sixteen years experience in this office, he recalled no cases in which the attorney general has had to formally intercede and force prosecutors to do their duty. This official indicated that, in the year previous to the interview, his only activity in local prosecution was assisting the local prosecutor in the trial of an arson case. He indicated that attorney general participation in arson trials was required by statute for some reason, and that the requirement is bothersome. He said that assistants usually do not participate actively at these trials even though their presence is required. In the current year he said he had assisted in the trial of one murder case pursuant to the request of the local prosecutor.

129 See authorities cited note 10 *supra*. In Winne v. County of Bergen, 21 N.J. 311, 322-323, 121 A.2d 733, 739-740 (1956), the court indicated that routine business should be handled by the local prosecutor, and that only in extraordinary circumstances, when local law enforcement breaks down, is active attorney general participation at the local level contemplated in law. It is true, as discussed in note 127 *supra*, that the formal law is not structured in such a way as to preclude attorney general intervention categorically in all but the exceptional situations, but the New Jersey court clearly thought it undesirable to confer unlimited authority to intervene on the attorney general. Like the court in People v. Johnston, 326 Mich. 213, 40 N.W.2d 124 (1949), the New Jersey court was satisfied that the lower courts have discretion and would exercise it to disallow intervention when it reflected purely political motivations or would be detrimental to local law enforcement. Although they are not as well articulated as they are in connection with the other remedies, limits on the use of the remedy to change the patterns of local law enforcement do appear to exist. See State ex rel. Dalton v. Moody, 325 S.W.2d 21 (Mo. 1959).

130 An assistant prosecutor in Detroit, Michigan stated that in 1941 an assistant attorney general was sent into Wayne County to investigate and prosecute prostitution and narcotics violations, which appeared to be flourishing at the time. The assistant spent several months in Detroit and hired a great many Negro informants, most of them with criminal records, to aid in investigation. Practically every charge brought by the assistant was dismissed for insufficient evidence because of poor cooperation from the hired informants. Since that time the attorney general has not attempted to interfere with Wayne County prosecutions. A municipal court judge in another Michigan city recalled a prosecution that had been handled somewhat ineptly by an assistant attorney general.

131 See note 128 *supra*. A further example is that the managing director of the Wichita Crime Commission wrote to the state attorney general urging that action be taken to correct the local prosecutor's failure to declare bail bonds forfeited when defendants failed to appear at their preliminary hearings or trials. The attorney general refused to act, stating that a random sampling of bond forfeiture cases had indicated no official misconduct.

gentle, if cryptic, language: "I have been notified of violations coming to your attention within your jurisdiction. We present the following information for your decision as to whether action should be taken."[132] There is no basis for judging the effect of such letters. The principal reason for this reluctance to use his full powers reflects a conclusion that the "man on the scene" has better and more detailed information about what is happening and is thus better able to allocate his resources most effectively. To repeat, "prosecution is a local problem."[133]

c. *Power of the private citizen to insist on prosecution.* At various times and at various places the law has recognized at least three ways in which a private citizen — usually the aggrieved party — can influence charging discretion: (1) by initiating and carrying out prosecution through a private attorney employed for that purpose; (2) by employing a private attorney to assist and aid the regular prosecutor; and (3) by seeking a writ of mandamus — a judicial order directing the reluctant regular prosecutor to take action.

1. Private prosecution. Although the American states have almost completely replaced the ancient system of prosecutions conducted by private attorneys employed by private citizen complainants, some vestiges remain.[134] To the extent that private citizens may participate actively in the prosecution — certainly if they can displace the regular prosecutor — there is at least in theory another form of legal control over prosecutor discretion.

In Kansas, Michigan, and Wisconsin, a combination of statutes and judicial decisions has made it clear that private prosecution has, with minor exceptions, been supplanted by a system of public prosecution.[135] In Kansas, the prosecutor need not share

132 This information was obtained in the interview with the assistant attorney general which is discussed in note 128 *supra.*

133 See Note, 48 J. Crim. L.C. & P.S. 531, 537-538 (1958). One local official in Milwaukee stated that "prosecution is a local problem. The attorney general is not located in Milwaukee and therefore does not have a true picture of what is going on. To have him control the operations or be able to supersede the district attorney would throw the entire system into chaos."

134 See generally Note, Private Prosecution: A Remedy for District Attorneys' Unwarranted Inaction, 65 Yale L.J. 209 (1955). This author favors an expansion of private prosecution, but would restrict its use to extraordinary circumstances in which the regular prosecutor's enforcement policy is an undesirable one or has broken down. No authorities have been located favoring a full-blown return to the type of private prosecution that existed at common law.

135 See, e.g., Foley v. Ham, 102 Kan. 66, 169 Pac. 183 (1917); State v. Wilson, 24 Kan. 189 (1880); People v. Holbrook, 373 Mich. 94, 128 N.W.2d 484 (1964); People v. Hillhouse, 80 Mich. 580, 45 N.W. 484 (1890); Engle v. Chipman, 51 Mich. 524, 16 N.W. 886 (1883); Meister v. People, 31 Mich. 99 (1875); State v. Peterson, 195

this power even with the trial judiciary except under extraordinary circumstances.[136] In Michigan and Wisconsin, the prosecutor must indeed share his power with the trial judge,[137] but the important point is that private prosecution is effectively precluded in those states beyond the stage of the preliminary examination. This is because of the limitation that only prosecutors may file informations.[138] Again, although the trial judge may compel the prosecutor to do so,[139] or appoint a substitute,[140] if he disagrees with the prosecutor, the prosecution from this point forward must be public and not private.[141]

Three general exceptions may be found to the public prosecutor's exclusive control over prosecution in normal circumstances. Conservation offenses may be prosecuted in Michigan by conservation officers without prosecutor approval.[142] Similarly state police officers are generally authorized to prosecute for traffic

---

Wis. 351, 218 N.W. 367 (1928); Biemel v. State, 71 Wis. 444, 37 N.W. 244 (1888); citations to cases from other states are contained in note 6 *supra*.

136 The private complainant, acting without prosecutor approval, can take two steps: (1) he can secure judicial approval of a warrant, and (2) he can secure a judicial mandate forcing the prosecutor to file an information, at least in extraordinary circumstances. However, the prosecutor can block either of these efforts by exercising his authority to discontinue prosecutions at either the magisterial or trial court level. See notes 53-58, 66-69, 70-73 *supra* and accompanying text. Compare Perry v. State, 84 Okla. Crim. 211, 181 P.2d 280 (1947) (role of complainant in special scheme for prosecution of adultery).

137 As discussed in notes 53-54 *supra* and accompanying text, it is possible for the private complainant to secure the issuance of a warrant without prosecutor approval in both states, but somewhat more difficult in Michigan. Once the warrant is outstanding, Michigan law is clear and Wisconsin law is in accord by implication (notes 59-64 *supra* and accompanying text) that the prosecutor cannot discontinue a prosecution at the magisterial level if the private complainant has convinced the magistrate of the desirability of continuing. Also, in Michigan the prosecutor cannot even appear at the magisterial level unless requested to do so by the magistrate, and presumably the proceedings would be conducted by counsel for the complainant. It must be understood that these are hypothetical possibilities inferred from older case law that has been left outstanding, probably because in practice prosecutors conduct the proceedings as a matter of course. Occasions for reevaluating the earlier case law probably do not arise.

138 Mich. Stat. Ann. §28.980 (Supp. 1965); Wis. Stat. Ann. §955.13 (1958).

139 Note 65 *supra* and accompanying text.

140 Authorities cited note 103 *supra*.

141 The Michigan policy was made explicit in Meister v. People, 31 Mich. 99 (1875): although some opportunity for active participation by complainants and their counsel might be presented at the magisterial level, once the proceeding in serious cases comes to the vital phase in which the formal charges will be adjudicated, it must be conducted solely by a duly constituted public official.

142 Mich. Stat. Ann. §13.1222 (1967); see People v. Holbrook, 373 Mich. 94, 128 N.W.2d 484 (1964); People v. Black, 156 Misc. 516, 282 N.Y.S. 197 (Otsego County Ct. 1935).

offenses.[143] In both of these classes of cases, the shift of prerogative is to another public official rather than to the private citizen.[144] The third instance may represent, at least in theory, a limited revival of the power of private prosecution. A Wisconsin statute expressly relieves the district attorney from any general duty to prosecute assault and battery cases.[145] But even here a study of current administration does not show any pattern of private prosecution.[146] At least in Milwaukee the police — to whose attention these matters first come — refer routine assault and battery cases to the city attorney for prosecution as municipal ordinance violations. If the assault results in serious injury, or the assailant is discovered to have a lengthy police record, the case is referred to the district attorney who conducts the prosecution in the usual fashion. In short, private prosecution is at most a theoretical possibility — certainly, in current administration it is not a practical reality — and thus is not an effective control over prosecutor charging discretion.

2. Privately employed assistants. A vestige of the older institution of private prosecution which remains in some states is

143 See Mich. Stat. Ann. §28.860 (1954).

144 The inference from the cases is that there is a general preference for passing the prerogatives of law enforcement from the regular prosecutor to other duly constituted officials, rather than to interested private parties. The preference for attorney general intervention is discussed in note 127 *supra*. Although the appointment of substitute prosecutors must be supported by special grounds and is a more restricted remedy than attorney general intervention (notes 106-110 *supra* and accompanying text), nevertheless the fact that the attorney has been officially appointed, albeit temporarily, should place him in a more favorable posture to satisfy the demands of the theory of public prosecution than would the attorney retained by the private complainant. See State v. Becker, 3 S.D. 29, 51 N.W. 1018 (1892) (permissible for temporary assistant appointed by attorney general to prosecute liquor offense); Biemel v. State, 71 Wis. 444, 37 N.W. 244 (1888). The private complainant or his counsel appears to be in the least favorable light as a possible recipient of law enforcement prerogatives. See Oglesby v. State, 83 Fla. 132, 90 So. 825 (1922); compare People v. Auerbach, 176 Mich. 23, 141 N.W. 869 (1913) with Meister v. People, 31 Mich. 99 (1875).

145 Wis. Stat. Ann. §59.47(2) (1957). Note, 1953 Wis. L. Rev. 170 argues that exempting this from the realm of public prosecution revives the common law of prosecutions and therefore raises the possibility that a common assault and battery case might be conducted entirely by retained counsel for the complainant, at least at the magisterial level. Note, 65 Yale L.J. 209, 221-223 (1955) documents the results of a questionnaire and formal law survey indicating that private prosecution remains not only a hypothetical possibility but a reality in the lesser courts of some jurisdictions.

146 Note, 1953 Wis. L. Rev. 170, 175-176 offers one possible reason for this: the private complainant, upon discovering that he cannot persuade the prosecutor to act, is usually unwilling to go to the trouble of hiring counsel and conducting the prosecution, preferring instead to drop the matter altogether.

found in Kansas, although it is not permitted in Michigan or Wisconsin.[147] Two sections of the Kansas statutes authorize the use of private attorneys as trial assistants. One of them is only peripherally relevant to this discussion, since it merely authorizes judicial appointment of an assistant upon application of a private complainant. The trial judge exercises his discretion in deciding whether to make an appointment and in selecting the assistant.[148]

The other section, however, directly authorizes the employment of an attorney by the prosecuting witness at his own expense.[149] There is no requirement that he obtain prosecutor or judicial consent to do so. The Kansas cases have approved the procedure, but have carefully noted that the regular prosecutor "was in full control of the prosecution at all times."[150] The ques-

147 See note 150 *infra*.

148 Kan. Stat. Ann. §19-718 (1964) (applies only to counties with population less than 10,000); State v. Ellis, 192 Kan. 315, 387 P.2d 198 (1963).

149 Kan. Stat. Ann. §19-717 (1964).

150 State v. Atwood, 187 Kan. 548, 558, 358 P.2d 726, 734 (1961); see State v. Wilson, 24 Kan. 189 (1880). Other cases hold it to be within the discretion of the trial court to allow the practice. State v. Rue, 72 Minn. 296, 75 N.W. 235 (1898); State v. O'Brien, 35 Mont. 482, 90 Pac. 514 (1907); State v. Hale, 85 N.H. 403, 160 Atl. 95 (1932); State v. Carden, 209 N.C. 404, 183 S.E. 898, *cert. denied*, 298 U.S. 682 (1936); People v. Tidwell, 4 Utah 506, 12 Pac. 61 (1886); State v. Hoshor, 26 Wash. 643, 67 Pac. 386 (1901); see Polin v. State, 14 Neb. 540, 16 N.W. 898 (1883). One court denied the trial court any discretion to prevent the practice as long as the prosecutor approves. Gardiner v. State, 55 N.J.L. 17, 26 Atl. 30 (Sup. Ct. 1892), *aff'd per curiam*, 55 N.J.L. 652, 30 Atl. 429 (Ct. Errors & App. 1893). Some cases appear to allow the assistant to control the prosecution, or at least to take the most active role in the trial. State v. Matthews, 341 Mo. 1121, 111 S.W.2d 62 (1937); State v. Ward, 61 Vt. 153, 17 Atl. 483 (1889); Jackson v. Commonwealth, 96 Va. 107, 30 S.E. 452 (1898).

Other cases, like those of Kansas, find the practice compatible with the theory of public prosecution only when the regular prosecutor remains in control. Oglesby v. State, 83 Fla. 132, 90 So. 825 (1922); Jackson v. State, 156 Ga. 842, 120 S.E. 535 (1923); State v. Petrich, 122 La. 127, 47 So. 438 (1908); State v. Lucero, 20 N.M. 55, 146 Pac. 407 (1915); State v. Kent, 4 N.D. 557, 62 N.W. 631 (1895); State v. Stafford, 89 W. Va. 301, 109 S.E. 326 (1921); see Perry v. State, 84 Okla. Crim. 211, 181 P.2d 280 (1947). Other reservations have been voiced. The assistant cannot be paid on a contingent fee basis. Price v. Caperton, 62 Ky. 207 (1864) (dictum); Baca v. Padilla, 26 N.M. 223, 190 Pac. 730 (1920); see Benningfield v. Commonwealth, 13 Ky. L. Rep. 446, 17 S.W. 271 (1891). The Illinois courts have placed limits on the permissible number of assistants in order to avoid legal talent being heavily arrayed on one side. People v. Blevins, 251 Ill. 381, 96 N.E. 214 (1911); Hayner v. People, 213 Ill. 142, 72 N.E. 792 (1904); see Flege v. State, 93 Neb. 610, 142 N.W. 276 (1913) (assistant hired by person himself suspected of the crime).

At the far end of the spectrum is a small minority that do not allow privately employed assistants to assist at trials. Meister v. People, 31 Mich. 99 (1875); Biemel v. State, 71 Wis. 444, 37 N.W. 244 (1888); see La Shar v. People, 74 Colo. 503, 223 Pac. 59 (1924) (personal opinion of judge writing for majority); Commonwealth v. Williams, 56 Mass. (2 Cush.) 582 (1849) (prosecutor can employ assistant only if the

tion of the extent of the prosecutor's power to dismiss a case under those circumstances has not had the benefit of judicial discussion. The statute itself provides that the regular prosecutor may not dismiss over the objection of the privately retained associate ". . . until the reason of the county attorney for such dismissal, together with the objections thereto of such associate counsel, shall have been filed in writing, argued by counsel and fully considered by the court."[151]

The practice in Wichita does not always conform to the case-law reservation that the regular prosecutor retain control at all stages. The private attorneys are employed by complaining witnesses, they are permitted complete freedom in handling the cases, even to the extent of dismissing them if they believe that action should be taken. Ultimate control is retained by the regular prosecutor, however, and if the evidence is obviously too weak to support a conviction, he will insist on a dismissal despite objection by the private attorney.[152]

3. Mandamus. Private citizens sometimes attempt to force

---

attorney employed is not paid by interested parties). Note, 65 Yale L.J. 209, 219 and n.51 (1955) discusses this minority and some of the qualifications that have been made to it by later cases.

[151] A district judge in Wichita was interviewed concerning the practice under this statute. He recalled one case in which a rape complainant had hired a special assistant. The judge regarded the evidence as being insufficient to warrant further prosecution, and he convinced the prosecutor that the case should be dismissed. The assistant refused to acquiesce in the dismissal. Pursuant to the statute the judge arranged to have the assistant and the prosecutor present arguments in open court. He indicated that he would ordinarily have held the arguments in chambers, but in this case there had been considerable publicity, and the complainant, a schoolteacher, was bent on protecting her reputation. Therefore he decided that in order to avoid any distorted publicity he would have the arguments presented openly. Each side was permitted to examine witnesses in an informal manner. The complainant was present, as well as members of her family, a number of friends, and newspaper representatives. The judge was convinced that the evidence was insufficient and so he granted the prosecutor's motion to dismiss.

[152] The district judge who recalled the instance recounted in note 151 *supra* also indicated that the prosecutor usually allowed the privately employed assistant to take over complete control of the case, and it even became his decision whether to dismiss. The instance given in note 151 *supra* was exceptional.

A private attorney interviewed in Wichita indicated that he had considerable experience as a special assistant in prosecutions. He had often been retained by the victim or his family who wished to ensure that the offender would be convicted. The usual practice was that, once retained, the private attorney would appear at the preliminary and trial. When the prosecutor had confidence in his professional ability, the assistant would take over active control of the case. The prosecutor was usually content to take a backseat, except when he had less confidence in the particular assisting attorney, in which case he would conduct the hearing or trial. After concluding his questioning of witnesses he would ask the assisting attorney if he had any questions to ask.

reluctant prosecutors to initiate prosecutions by asking a court to issue a writ of mandamus — an order directing the prosecutor to take action.[153] It is standard doctrine that this remedy is available only to compel a public official to perform a clear-cut "ministerial" duty required of him by law.[154] A duty is conceived as "ministerial" if the person whose duty it is has no discretion whether to perform it — has no right to exercise his judgment about the advisability of proceeding.[155] Accordingly, many courts hold that the remedy is never available against a public prosecutor because whether prosecution should be initiated is the very prototype of the discretionary or judgmental decision.[156] A second position is that mandamus is available to force a prosecutor to exercise his discretion, but not to interfere when he is exer-

153 The extent to which standing requirements or prior exhaustion of non-extraordinary remedies is a prerequisite to a mandamus action by a private citizen is discussed in Ferguson, Formulation of Enforcement Policy: An Anatomy of the Prosecutor's Discretion Prior to Accusation, 11 Rutg. L. Rev. 507, 518-520 (1957).

154 17 McQuillin, Municipal Corporations §51.19 (3d rev. ed. 1968).

155 Martin v. Ingham, 38 Kan. 641, 651, 17 Pac. 162, 168 (1888).

156 E.g., Pugach v. Klein, 193 F. Supp. 630 (S.D.N.Y. 1961); Howell v. Brown, 85 F. Supp. 537 (D. Neb. 1949); Taliaferro v. Locke, 182 Cal. App. 2d 752, 6 Cal. Rptr. 813 (1960); Hassan v. Magistrate's Court, 20 Misc. 2d 509, 191 N.Y.S.2d 238 (Supt. Ct. 1959), *appeal dismissed,* 10 App. Div. 2d 908, 202 N.Y.S.2d 1002, *appeal dismissed,* 8 N.Y.2d 750, 168 N.E.2d 102, 201 N.Y.S.2d 765, *cert. denied,* 364 U.S. 844 (1960). See United States v. Cox, 342 F.2d 167, *cert. denied,* 381 U.S. 935 (1965); United States v. Woody, 2 F.2d 262 (D. Mont. 1924). In several of these cases the denial of mandamus is buttressed by separation of powers doctrine. Another consideration is that the granting of mandamus would substitute the private citizen's judgment for that of the duly constituted official. See Hermann v. Morlidge, 298 Ky. 632, 634, 183 S.W.2d 807, 809 (1944).

There are some cases making mandamus available to force prosecutors or attorneys general to initiate various civil actions, typically quo warranto actions, to oust usurpers of public office. These cases do not employ the model of discretion observed in this volume. Instead, the courts take "discretion" to mean that when facts indicating a possible violation of law calling for a civil remedy are presented to the prosecutor, he must exercise his judgment in determining whether the facts actually make out a violation. Once he has decided that they do, or the evidence is strong enough to convince a reasonable man that a violation has occurred, "discretion" is at an end, the duty to act becomes ministerial, and mandamus will lie. Vanhoose v. Yingling, 172 Ark. 1009, 291 S.W. 420 (1927) (dictum); Blankenship v. Michalski, 155 Cal. App. 2d 672, 318 P.2d 727 (1957) (dictum); see People ex rel. Miller v. Fullenwider, 329 Ill. 65, 160 N.E. 175 (1928); Pound v. Oren, 119 Mich. 528, 78 N.W. 541 (1899); Cain v. Brown, 111 Mich. 657, 70 N.W. 337 (1897); Lamoreaux v. Ellis, 89 Mich. 146, 50 N.W. 812 (1891). In contrast the California courts have allowed the prosecutor discretion to refuse to act even though the facts clearly show a violation. This view recognizes the realities of prosecutorial discretion as actually practiced in current administration. City of Campbell v. Mosk, 197 Cal. App. 2d 640, 647, 17 Cal. Rptr. 584, 588 (1961); Taliaferro v. Locke, *supra;* see Wilson v. Sharp, 42 Cal. 2d 675, 268 P.2d 1062 (1954). The California courts denied mandamus against prosecutors exercising this form of discretion.

cising it, nor to direct him to exercise it in a particular way.[157]

An apparent exception has developed in some jurisdictions. This exception turns on a catch-phrase which, like "bad faith," demonstrates the principle that prosecutorial judgment may be interfered with if it reflects an unjustified departure from expectable patterns of decision-making. That catch-phrase is "abuse of discretion," and the rule in jurisdictions using it is that the prosecutor may be forced to act only if his non-action may be characterized as an "abuse of discretion."[158] The similarity between the two concepts — "bad faith" and "abuse of discretion" is confined neither to their "catchiness" nor to their vagueness. In general, "bad faith" and "abuse of discretion" are merely different phrases used to express about the same combination of factors in about the same sets of circumstances.[159] Whether variations in the rules are more than theoretically significant is difficult to determine. No case has been found in Kansas, Michigan, or Wisconsin in which an effort has been made to compel criminal prosecution by mandamus.[160] This absence of cases is not

157 17 McQuillin, Municipal Corporations §51.16 (3d rev. ed. 1958); McLaughlin v. Burroughs, 90 Mich. 311, 51 N.W. 283 (1892); see City of Atlanta v. Wright, 119 Ga. 207, 45 S.E. 994 (1903). This formulation dovetails with the rationale behind restrictions on the use of some of the other controls. See note 12 *supra*.

158 Ackerman v. Houston, 45 Ariz. 293, 43 P.2d 194 (1935); Brack v. Wells, 184 Md. 86, 40 A.2d 319 (1944); see generally Comment, 10 Okla. L. Rev. 197 (1957). Neither of the above cases found an abuse in the prosecutor's failure to initiate criminal action.

159 State ex rel. Cook v. Richards, 61 S.D. 28, 245 N.W. 901 (1932) is a rare example of a court employing a model of discretion similar to that observed in this volume and granting mandamus because of the prosecutor's abuse. He was compelled to take action of a noncriminal nature, but the court indicated that he had discretion not to act even though the facts would warrant it if, in his judgment, the county interest would not be served. The court indicated that, if when presented with the facts he refused to consider the county interest in reaching a decision not to act, this would constitute abuse. This is analogous to the proposition that bad faith is shown when the prosecutor fails to prosecute a criminal complaint without considering discretionary factors, indeed, when he refuses to exercise his discretion at all. See note 12 *supra*. The case continues to parallel the bad faith cases in the court's denial that unwise judgment in assessing the factual merits of situations is abuse of discretion. See note 33 *supra* and accompanying text. The case becomes unique, however, when the court states that the prosecutor entertained no culpable attitude toward his job (such as unexplained inaction supporting an inference of laziness), but nevertheless finds an abuse because his reasons for inaction constituted an erroneous interpretation of the law pertaining to his right to take the action in the given circumstances. Unlike an unwise assessment of the factual merits, error of law was regarded as an insufficient excuse for inaction. Accord, State ex rel. Smith v. Thues, 114 La. 1097, 38 So. 870 (1905); Commonwealth v. Hipple, 69 Pa. 9 (1871) (mandamus issued in both cases). But see State ex rel. Kinsella v. Eberhart, 116 Minn. 313, 321, 133 N.W. 857, 860 (1911) (ignorance of law does not constitute actionable bad faith).

160 The availability of mandamus to compel a city prosecutor to prosecute an

attributable to any general reluctance of Kansas, Michigan, or Wisconsin courts to make use of mandamus. This fact is demonstrated by cases in which these courts have followed the practice of other states in using mandamus against public officers other than prosecutors and even to compel prosecutors to bring civil actions.[161] There is a clear inference from the total absence of appellate decisions in the three states — an inference supported by the lack of any suggestion in the field studies of even occasional use of the remedy — that mandamus is not a practically effective remedy, even if it proved to be legally available under limited circumstances, to compel prosecution against the wishes of a public prosecutor.

d. *Judicial power to override a decision to prosecute.* To this point we have been concerned with control of prosecutor discretion when it takes the form of negative charging decisions. Sometimes prosecutors choose to charge individuals who would not normally be charged, or to charge with more or more serious offenses persons who, under normal circumstances, would be treated less severely. The circumstances under which fuller enforcement occurs are discussed in detail in Chapter 19. The question here is whether there are controls which insure the proper operation of the selection process and the appropriateness of the criteria used in operating it.

In a number of jurisdictions, trial judges are given statutory authority to dismiss cases, without the consent of the prosecutor, when it would be "in furtherance of justice" to do so. Cases in-

action characterized as "quasi-criminal" for violation of city ordinance arose as an issue in Guinther v. City of Milwaukee, 217 Wis. 334, 258 N.W. 865 (1935), discussed note 64 *supra*. The action of the lower court appointing a substitute to carry out a prosecution which the regular prosecutor desired to discontinue was upheld. The court rejected a contention that the only permissible action would have been to compel the regular prosecutor to continue by mandamus, but it implied that this was a possible alternative. This situation differs, however, from the issue of availability of the remedy to compel the initiation of a prosecution, because there was already in progress a prosecution which could not be discontinued without the consent of the court. The court's order to carry out the prosecution would, in other words, be mandatory on the prosecutor, and this could be called a ministerial duty. See note 103 *supra* and accompanying text.

161 See, e.g., Lauber v. Fireman's Relief Assn., 195 Kan. 126, 402 P.2d 817 (1965) (mandamus available only to compel performance of clearly defined and specifically enjoined duty of an officer); McLaughlin v. Burroughs, 90 Mich. 311, 51 N.W. 283 (1892) (mandamus will lie to force prosecutor to exercise his discretion in regard to a civil action, but not to direct him what decision to reach); State ex rel. Adams County State Bank v. Kurth, 233 Wis. 60, 288 N.W. 810 (1939) (mandamus unavailable when the officer's performance requires the exercise of judgment and discretion).

terpreting those statutes have, on the whole, given them liberal treatment and have made it clear that they confer on the trial judiciary the same kind of discretion to prevent prosecution even on sufficient evidence normally held and exercised by prosecutors.[162] Currently, the American Law Institute's Proposed Model Penal Code contains a section authorizing judicial acquittal of what are described as "de minimis" violations.[163]

Clearly such statutes provide a control over prosecutor discretion. In addition, in the jurisdictions studied here, this kind of control is reflected in judicial acquittals of the obviously guilty, as well as in their conviction of lesser offenses.[164] No statutory or common law authorization for the exercise of this power is found in any of the three states. The leading Wisconsin case, *State v. Evjue*,[165] disapproved of the practice, but concluded that, if a judge chose to acquit improperly, the double jeopardy clause prevented a re-trial. In short, the Wisconsin court recognized the power of the judge to take this action at the same time it denied his right to exercise that power.[166]

162 E.g., Idaho Code Ann. §19-3504 (1948); Iowa Code Ann. §795.5 (1950); Minn. Stat. Ann. §631.21 (1947); N.Y. Code Crim. Proc. §671 (1958); Utah Code Ann. §77-51-4 (1953); State ex rel. Anderson v. Gile, 119 Mont. 182, 186-187, 172 P.2d 583, 585 (1946); People v. Quill, 11 Misc. 2d 512, 177 N.Y.S.2d 380 (King's County Ct. 1958). The American Law Institute's survey of statutes in its Code of Criminal Procedure 895 (1930) revealed that fourteen states had statutes of this kind.

163 Model Penal Code §2.12 (Proposed Official Draft 1962).

164 This subject is discussed extensively in Part IV of Newman, Conviction (1966).

165 254 Wis. 581, 37 N.W.2d 50 (1949).

166 It will be recalled from the discussion in notes 50-51 *supra* and accompanying text that, in the absence of a statute changing the common law, the majority American position is that the prosecutor can nolle prosequi charges because of his consideration of the discretionary factors and the judge cannot prevent this. When the situation is reversed, and it is the judge who wishes to dismiss against the wishes of the prosecutor, the majority again rules against the judge. This is true even if a statute is outstanding requiring judicial approval of the nolle prosequi. Although the judge can veto the prosecutor's decision, under the terms of the typical statute he lacks authority to dismiss on his own motion, and both prosecutor and judge must concur in the decision to dismiss. E.g., Commonwealth v. Cundiff, 149 Ky. 37, 147 S.W. 767 (1912). The court noted a well-established qualification: if on demurrer the judge found that the indictment failed to state an offense known to law he could dismiss without prosecutor concurrence. Of course, a judge can dismiss for lack of jurisdiction or when statutory time limits on prosecution have expired. Kosicki, The Function of Nolle Prosequi and Motion to Dismiss in Connecticut, 36 Conn. B.J. 159, 168-169 (1962). To these examples can be added the authority of the judge as guardian of constitutional provisions to dismiss, for example, because the prosecution denies the equal protection of the laws. State v. Pirkey, 203 Ore. 697, 281 P.2d 698 (1955). What is denied to the courts by the cases, however, is a formal recognition of the authority to discontinue unilaterally because of consideration of the discretion factors, in the absence of statutes like those cited in note 162 *supra* expressly granting this authority. E.g., Goldberg

Although the discussion in the *Conviction* volume of this series makes it abundantly clear that the practice occurs with some frequency in all three states, it also demonstrates that not every exercise of judicial discretion at the adjudication stage is in fact against the wishes of the prosecutor.[167] There is some indication that, although willing to abide by the judge's decision, the prosecutor may believe that the onus of dismissals which are likely to result in unfavorable publicity can more easily be borne by a judge who is less directly — or at least frequently — accountable to the electorate. In short, it is not clear in current administration whether acquittal of the guilty acts as a control on prosecutor charging discretion.

It will be recalled from earlier discussion[168] that the argument sometimes made by defendants, that other similarly circumstanced persons have been treated differently, does not in itself enable them to avoid prosecution or secure gentler treatment. When, in addition to asserting that others have been treated more leniently than he, the defendant claims that the selective enforcement policy denies him the equal protection of the laws and, therefore, violates his constitutional rights, he is in a quite different legal posture.[169] Dismissals by trial judges on that ground which have been upheld by appellate courts are rare,[170] probably because to date the courts have placed a very heavy burden on defendants to establish a deliberate and unjustifiably discriminatory enforcement policy.[171]

In addition to dismissing cases on the ground that the selective enforcement policy of the prosecutor was unconstitutionally discriminatory, some courts have issued injunctions to force discon-

---

v. Hoffman, 225 F.2d 463 (7th Cir. 1955); State ex rel. Ronan v. Stevens, 93 Ariz. 375, 381 P.2d 100 (1963); State v. Anderson, 119 Tex. 110, 26 S.W.2d 174 (1930); see State ex rel. Dowd v. Nangle, 365 Mo. 184, 276 S.W.2d 135 (1955); see generally Annot., 69 A.L.R. 240.

167 See also the discussion in note 80 *supra* of the hypothesis that judges and prosecutors are able to reach informal agreements about the desirability of discontinuance.

168 Chapter 8, notes 65-68 *supra* and accompanying text.

169 See generally Comment, 61 Colum. L. Rev. 1103 (1961).

170 The only case located upholding a dismissal is State v. Pirkey, 203 Ore. 697, 281 P.2d 698 (1955). A New York Court's dismissal of an indictment on equal protection grounds was reversed on appeal. People v. Paine Drug Co., 39 Misc. 2d 824, 241 N.Y.S.2d 946 (Monroe County Ct. 1963), *rev'd,* 22 App. Div. 2d 156, 254 N.Y.S.2d 492 (1964), *aff'd,* 16 N.Y.2d 503, 208 N.E.2d 176, 260 N.Y.S.2d 444, *cert. denied,* 382 U.S. 838 (1965). An exhaustive case survey added no other cases. Comment, 61 Colum. L. Rev. 1103, 1131-1132 (1961).

171 See, e.g., State v. Jourdain, 225 La. 1030, 74 So. 2d 203 (1954); People v. Utica Daw's Drug Co., 16 App. Div. 2d 12, 225 N.Y.S.2d 128 (1962).

tinuance of prosecution on the same ground.[172] In addition to the heavy burden of proof which the defendant must sustain when he seeks dismissal on equal protection grounds in the criminal proceeding itself, invoking the power of a court of equity to issue an injunction gives him further problems. The usual rule that equity will not interfere to prevent prosecutions is subject to an exception when irreparable damage to personal or property rights is threatened.[173] But one seeking to bring himself within the terms of the exception must show that he has no adequate legal remedy and that his damages would be significant.[174] Because that burden is also not easily met, the injunction is not at present a very effective way of preventing prosecutors from enforcing some laws in an unconstitutionally discriminatory manner. Habeas corpus directed to the custodian[175] and prohibition directed to the trial judge[176] who has refused to dismiss in a proper case would also seem to be possible methods of raising the issue, but they too — because of their classification as extraordinary legal remedies — present difficulties.[177] In any event the paucity of decided cases makes discussion of these remedies speculative in the extreme.

B. Informal Controls

Whether the prosecutor is the "pivotal figure" in current criminal justice administration is a matter of some dispute; no doubt the response to that kind of evaluative inquiry depends on which system objective is under consideration. Thus, the trial judge rather than the prosecutor may have the primary responsibility for overseeing the activities of other front-line officials — particularly the police — to assure that appellate court mandates declaring constitutional standards are regularly followed. The

172 See generally Comment, 61 Colum. L. Rev. 1103, 1135-1140 (1961).

173 Truax v. Raich, 239 U.S. 33 (1915); State ex rel. Thomas v. Snelling, 71 Kan. 499, 80 Pac. 966 (1905) (dictum); Kenyon v. City of Chicopee, 320 Mass. 528, 70 N.E.2d 241 (1946); see generally Comment, 33 Cornell L.Q. 579 (1948).

174 Comment, 61 Colum. L. Rev. 1103, 1134-1139 (1961).

175 This was the remedy used in the leading case of Yick Wo v. Hopkins, 118 U.S. 356 (1886).

176 E.g., Fenster v. Criminal Court, 46 Misc. 2d 179, 259 N.Y.S.2d 67 (Sup. Ct.), *aff'd*, 24 App. Div. 2d 840, 263 N.Y.S.2d 1010 (1965), *aff'd*, 17 N.Y.2d 641, 216 N.E.2d 342, 269 N.Y.S.2d 139 (1966).

177 See Powell v. Criminal Court, 44 Misc. 2d 838, 255 N.Y.S.2d 1 (Sup. Ct. 1964) (prohibition not available to petitioner whose rights can be protected adequately on appeal); Amsterdam, Search, Seizure, and Section 2255: A Comment, 112 U. Pa. L. Rev. 378 (1964) (more difficult to raise constitutional issues on collateral attack in habeas corpus than on direct attack).

police, on the other hand, seem to bear primary responsibility for deciding how best to allocate limited enforcement resources, and thus, by controlling the system at the intake level, set the outer limits of enforcement. Of one thing there can be no doubt: in states which no longer use grand juries, the choice to charge is fundamentally the prosecutor's. And this is true both in law and in current administration.

But public prosecutors operate as part of a system which begins to affect citizens earlier than at the charging level and continues to affect some of them long after the prosecutor's role has been played out. Clearly decisions made by officials who function earlier in the process, as well as the anticipated responses of those who participate later, affect the charging decision itself. And in some instances, the influence of persons who are not officials is strong. Of particular current interest, and of overriding long range importance, is the question of what impact recent decisions of the Supreme Court of the United States requiring earlier participation of counsel will have on day-to-day administration of the criminal justice system.

1. *Influence of the police.* The police may affect the charging decision both negatively and positively. Most simply, if the police do not think that prosecution is warranted despite adequate evidence, they release suspects without calling them to the attention of the prosecutor at all.[178] Less simply, they may request a warrant, but may make obvious to the prosecutor that they do not believe that prosecution is desirable. In many cases prosecutors agree with the police assessment, but in others they simply defer to it.[179] Sometimes this reflects recognition of particular expertise

178 The field survey revealed that, in 1956, out of a total of 67,175 persons arrested in Detroit, Michigan, the police sought to have only 28,732 of these prosecuted.

179 Police influence on charging is especially prominent in Milwaukee, Wisconsin. As discussed in the text, the personnel in the prosecutor's office rely almost exclusively on the charging recommendation contained in the police report in the majority of cases. It is not unusual in serious cases for the prosecutor or his assistants to hold an informal conference with the police present before issuing a warrant, but typically an informal agreement is readily reached on charging. In one instance a police officer came into the prosecutor's office with two young male suspects and two girls. The officer stated "I've got a burglary here I want a warrant for." The assistant prosecutor read the complaint prepared by police, and then asked the girls which one was Mary. Mary identified herself and the assistant asked "Did you see this man go into the store to get this beer?" Mary replied that she did. The assistant asked the officer if statements had been taken, and he replied that they had. Then the assistant asked, "Is there any reason why I should take a statement here from these witnesses?" The answer was "No." Then he asked "Do you have a statement from the defendant?" The officer replied, "Yes we have

in some classes of cases. In Detroit, for example, the decision whether to invoke the repeater statute in an accosting and soliciting case is made by a police officer in the vice bureau.[180] In other instances, a negative charging decision reflects awareness of the need for cooperation to permit police to carry out enforcement objectives. The decision not to charge informants or to charge offenses less serious than possible is a response to perceived police needs to maintain an active surveillance of vice activity.[181] In one dramatic instance, a young police officer was found to be involved with a group of homosexuals. The prosecutor indicated complete willingness to drop the matter so that there would be no reflection on the police department which might impair its general effectiveness. Frequently, the issue is not whether to charge at all, but which charge to select. Here too, the prosecutor frequently cooperates with the police.[182]

---

all the statements that are necessary, just issue me the warrant." The assistant authorized issuance of a warrant.

Various forms of pressure from the police might also cause the prosecutor to defer to their assessment when he might otherwise be inclined to disagree with the police. Since the police reports submitted with recommendations for charging are retained on file, the police keep track of the charging decisions made, and they influence charging by making their displeasure known when their recommendations are not followed. See the memorandum from the prosecutor to his staff quoted in text following note 197 *infra.*

180 When warrants are requested by other specialized police units, such as the women's division, the prosecutor or his assistants usually recommend issuance of a warrant, because of their feeling that these units are familiar enough with the kinds of crimes they investigate to know in particular instances whether prosecution is desirable.

181 The handling of informants is discussed in Chapter 17.

182 The following example occurred in Milwaukee, Wisconsin. A police officer asked an assistant prosecutor for warrants. He said, "The inspector feels three warrants against Jones and one warrant against Smith will be satisfactory. We already have two on Smith and if you will make out three against Jones and another one against Smith that will make three each and I am sure the inspector will be satisfied. These guys will probably plead anyway, probably get concurrent sentences, so I think this will hold it O.K." The officer added, "I have taken statements from Jones and I have statements from Jones in the presence of Smith so everything is all right." The assistant thereupon filled out the warrant authorization as requested.

There is some indication that the prosecutorial personnel in Detroit, Michigan take more initiative with regard to charge selection. It was found that they often regarded facts submitted in the police report as establishing the elements of a more serious crime than that recommended in the report; for example, in one case the assistant prosecutor informed the detectives that the facts of a case made out a case of "assault with intent to do great bodily harm" rather than the recommended "felonious assault." When the facts will support a charge graded higher than the recommended one, the prosecutorial personnel usually insist on bringing the more serious one. Although the initiative in charging is shared more, there is no indication that this impedes the ability of police and prosecutorial personnel to accom-

Police requests for undercharging to avoid extra court appearances are sometimes treated sympathetically by prosecutors.

The influence on charge selection is perhaps greatest when the police report which accompanies a warrant request also contains a recommended charge. In Milwaukee, personnel in the prosecutor's office were estimated to have placed almost total reliance on those reports in about 75 per cent of the cases. When, in addition, the police officer is permitted to "shop around" for an assistant prosecutor whom he believes will be more receptive to police suggestions than would other assistants, police influence on the charging decisions increases. This practice is widespread in Wichita; it exists subject to a system of final review in Detroit; it has been effectively eliminated in Milwaukee.[183]

2. *Judicial influences.* In addition to the formal legal controls discussed earlier in this chapter, trial judges influence the charging decision in a variety of informal ways. One indirect but important influence exists because prosecutors consider what dispositions are likely to be made by judges in response to particular charges. For example, warrants might be issued for less than all of the offenses that the evidence would justify if, based on past experience with the sentencing judge, it is anticipated that only concurrent sentences would be imposed. Lesser offenses might be charged if it is expected that no greater sentence would be imposed on conviction of serious charges. Especially is this true when the lesser charge is likely to result in a guilty plea, while the greater is likely to result in trial. But even if no more is accomplished than a trial less demanding in terms of resources and time, the same result might follow. The Detroit practice discussed earlier of charging "engaging in an illegal occupation" rather than "gambling" reflects a considerable saving in police and prosecutor time without significantly affecting the disposition of the case.[184] In a different context, the known antipathy of certain Recorder's Court judges in Detroit to accosting and soliciting cases has resulted in fewer charges when those particular judges have trial responsibility in that area.[185]

---

modate informally any differences between them and reach an agreement on the charge that will ultimately be brought.

183 This is discussed in connection with self-imposed evidence-sufficiency controls in Chapter 1 *supra*.

184 This practice is discussed in Chapter 12, along with other anticipatory factors taken into account in the charging decision.

185 Administration of the laws regarding prostitution is discussed in LaFave, Arrest 450-465 (1965).

More directly influencing the charging decision is the specific "request" or "suggestion" of the trial judge. In Milwaukee, for instance, a judicial "request" that a single warrant be used in certain multiple offense situations, with the other offenses simply stipulated by prosecutor and defense counsel as pending and thus brought to the judge's attention so that he can consider them in determining sentence, was honored without question. Similarly in Detroit, two instances reflect this same policy of deference to the wishes of the trial judiciary. First, the judges of Recorder's Court have asked that prosecutors screen all accosting and soliciting cases, even though the statute does not require him to do so. This was acceded to without question. Second, the same judges have instructed the prosecutor not to invoke the habitual criminal statute without a request from the trial judge to do so, and the prosecutor has again agreed.[186] The reasons are relatively complex, but they ultimately come down to a combination of two factors: (1) general awareness of the need for accommodation by each official to meet the needs of other officials in the system; and (2) a realization that with judicial power — though not authority — to dismiss in appropriate cases as well as sentencing discretion, it would be futile to refuse to meet these requests. Furthermore, it is clear that in many instances the prosecutor, though less often the police, agrees with the trial judge.

3. *Other officials.* Apart from the specialized police agencies, other specialized groups effectively control the charging decision in particular classes of cases. In Detroit, for example, probation officers assigned to nonsupport cases sometimes recommend prosecution when less formal means of exacting support payments from fathers have been ineffective. The Detroit prosecutor almost invariably issues a warrant when it is requested by probation officers in that class of cases.[187] Perhaps even more automatic is the issuance of warrants for nonsupport when recommended by the Milwaukee Welfare Department. And in Milwaukee, the findings of the medical examiner in homicide cases as well as his warrant recommendations are almost always followed by the prosecutor's office.

4. *The private complainant.* The discussion in Chapter 9 made clear that the wishes of the victim of a crime are accorded considerable weight. Clearly the reluctance of the victim to prose-

[186] Administration of the habitual criminal law is discussed in Chapter 12 *supra.*

[187] Administration of the Michigan nonsupport laws is discussed in Chapter 18 *supra.*

cute accounts for a substantial number of negative charging decisions. Sometimes an insistent victim may cause a positive charging decision to be made when it would not otherwise occur. The usual cases are those in which the father of a statutory rape victim, or of a child who has suffered relatively minor molestation, insists on prosecution. If the prosecutor's efforts to change the father's mind fail, he will often — though reluctantly — issue a warrant.[188] In other classes of cases, police and prosecutor insist on a victim's promise, sometimes backed by security for costs, that they will carry through prosecution if it is initiated.[189]

5. *Public opinion.* Prosecutors, like other public officials, are sensitive to public opinion.[190] Usually elected for short terms, they face the electorate more often than judges and under circumstances which make their continuance in office less certain than either judges or the police. Although it is commonly asserted that this subjects him to improper pressures,[191] certainly public accountability is never totally disadvantageous.[192]

Although the field studies themselves do not directly support the oft-heard hypothesis that the prosecution decision is greatly influenced by a desire to maintain a good conviction record,[193]

188 See Chapter 9 *supra.*

189 This insistence occurs especially in nonsupport cases, in which experience with complainants has revealed the likelihood that a woman will have a change of heart after the county has spent much money, for example, in securing return of the husband via extradition, and that she will refuse to cooperate further in the prosecution. See Chapter 18 *supra.*

190 See Snyder, The District Attorney's Hardest Task, 30 J. Crim. L.C. & P.S. 167 (1940).

191 E.g., National Comm. on Law Observance and Enforcement, Rep. No. 4 on Prosecution 11 (1931) (elective nature of office involves it too deeply in politics); Note, Prosecutor Indiscretion: A Result of Political Influence, 34 Ind. L.J. 477 (1959); Note, 48 J. Crim. L.C. & P.S. 526, 531 (1958) (in order to placate press, prosecutor unduly focuses efforts on certain sensational matters). Dean Pound has maintained that public opinion is not the effective check that it was in pioneer America when communities were small and everyone kept track in detail of official activities. Now politics is a hindrance. The prosecutor must take advantage of possibilities of publicity, and he will tend to compromise routine cases in order to concentrate his efforts on sensational crimes. The record he makes may appear glamorous to the lay public, but it does not necessarily indicate effective law enforcement. Pound, Criminal Justice in America 185-187 (1930). See Cates, Can We Ignore Laws? — Discretion Not to Prosecute, 14 Ala. L. Rev. 1, 7 (1961-62); Note, 65 Yale L.J. 209, 210 and n.7 (1955).

192 See Note, 48 J. Crim. L.C. & P.S. 531, 538 (1958) (elective official has more initiative than appointed one); but see Baker and DeLong, The Prosecuting Attorney and His Office, 25 J. Crim. L. 884 (1935); Caldwell, How to Make Prosecuting Effectual, 16 J. Am. Jud. Soc. 73, 74-75 (1932); Kosicki, The Function of Nolle Prosequi and Motion to Dismiss in Connecticut, 36 Conn. B.J. 159 (1962).

193 See, e.g., Polstein, How to "Settle" a Criminal Case, 8 Prac. Law. 35 (Jan. 1962).

two factors point in that direction: (1) the charging standard is a conviction standard in practice though not in law; (2) prosecutors and former prosecutors regularly assert the conviction-record hypothesis.[194] The assertions of former prosecutors must be subjected to carefuly scrutiny. An assertion of what one would do in a hypothetical situation and an after-the-event explanation of the motivating factors for a past course of conduct are two of the most undependable means of gathering facts. So the conviction-record hypothesis must remain uncertain. It is possible to explain a conviction standard for charging in terms other than the prosecutor's record. For one thing, it may reflect a desire to lean over backward in an effort not to convict the innocent — indeed to mitigate the harshness of the law if it were applied with computer accuracy.[195] For another, it may reflect resource limitations. Too few men and too little money may mean that both must be saved for the best cases.[196]

It is clear that greater visibility and more immediate accountability make prosecutors very aware of public reaction and criticism. One of the ways in which interested persons, whether they be private citizens, judges, or police officials, sometimes influence charging practices is to enlist the aid of publicity media.[197]

Dissatisfaction with negative charging decisions in certain assault cases led to the following memorandum from the prosecutor to his staff:

> In all cases where there has been a criminal violation, issue a warrant regardless of the fact that the complainant is reluctant to testify. This memorandum is prompted by a statement by the Chief of Police that it has been our practice not to issue warrants in cutting cases. I know of no such instance and if you have failed to issue warrants in such cases please be more careful about it in the future.

What may or may not have been an instance of a judge using publicity media to put pressure on a prosecutor in negligent homicide cases is reflected in the following memorandum:

> In failure to yield the right of way cases ascertain whether the

194 See Kaplan, The Prosecutorial Discretion — A Comment, 60 Nw. U.L. Rev. 174, 180 (1965); Seymour, Why Prosecutors Act Like Prosecutors, 11 Record of N.Y.C.B.A. 302, 304 (1956); Worgan and Paulsen, The Position of a Prosecutor in a Criminal Case — A Conversation with a Prosecuting Attorney, 7 Prac. Law. 44 at 51 (Nov. 1961).

195 See Worgan and Paulsen, note 194 *supra*, at 51.

196 See Kaplan, note 194 *supra*, at 180.

197 See Pound, Criminal Justice in America 185-187 (1930).

> injured party, if any, is in a critical condition. If he is, adjourn the case until you see whether he recovers or dies. In the event of death, reevaluate the facts to see if there is a basis for a negligent homicide prosecution. I am trying to avoid adverse publicity which was wrongfully received in connection with a misrepresentation by Judge __ when he was quoted as saying that if the defendant had been charged with negligent homicide he would have been found guilty. Upon investigation I found the circumstances of the case did not justify a negligent homicide warrant. I also found that Judge __ claims that he was misquoted.

And it will be recalled that, in Detroit, all cases which might raise "sticky" public relations problems are referred to the chief prosecutor.[198]

6. *Other controls.* Much of what was said in Chapter 1 regarding self-imposed evidence sufficiency controls could be repeated here. To give but one example, the Detroit practice of providing that warrant decisions made initially by younger assistants be reviewed by one of two experienced review assistants is as much designed to insure fairness and uniformity in the exercise of discretion as it is to insure that adequate evidence is available.[199]

C. Summary

The problem of the extent of prosecutor discretion has been separated from the problem of controls over the exercise of that discretion. In a sense the separation is artificial, for the existence and use of control devices — whether they be legal or informal — marks the boundaries of discretion. Yet, in addition to convenience in describing and analyzing prosecutor discretion in current administration, the separation serves another purpose. It also reflects the important distinction between the routine day-by-day decision-making process and the occasional controversial, not-so-easy-to-resolve problem. In the former situation, the prosecutor makes his decision relatively free from control, although informal accommodation between him and other officials is important. In the latter situation, the legal controls assume some importance, but there can be no doubt that the informal accommodation process remains as the most significant means of assuring responsible exercise of charging discretion in current administration.

198 The System of intra-office review is discussed in Chapter 1.

199 See also Klein, District Attorney's Discretion Not to Prosecute, 32 L.A.B. Bull. 323 (1957) (discussing intra-office controls in Los Angeles.)

Whether the present system of controls over prosecutor discretion should be changed is, of course, a matter of great importance and of considerable current concern. The question whether administrative decision-making, characterized as it is by ready adaptability to different sets of circumstances, is an adequate substitute for — or necessary supplement to — clearly promulgated and strictly enforced judicial controls is no easier to answer in the field of criminal justice administration than in other areas. It is not the purpose of this volume to offer judgments of that nature. It is its purpose to analyze as carefully as possible the ways in which charging discretion is exercised and controlled in current criminal justice administration.

CONCLUSION

Governmental processes are ultimately a series of decisions made by human beings. The charging decision is one step in the criminal justice administration system. It may occur relatively early in that process, immediately after identification of a suspect and preceding arrest. It may be the ultimate decision in that process; that is, the decision may be not to charge. Most commonly the charging decision is intermediate; it follows arrest and leads to further action, sometimes formal, sometimes informal.

The institutional structure of the criminal justice system not only provides the setting within which decisions are made but also sets limits on the alternatives available to the decision-makers. It is not obvious that the system works equally well when charging occurs at one time as when it occurs at another; when the decision is positive as when it is negative; when an informal alternative is selected as when a conventional formal one is used. Nevertheless, some institutional pattern is administratively essential, even if some loss of flexibility results. The practices analyzed highlight two aspects of the charging decision: (1) how to assure that there is enough evidence to support the decision to charge; (2) how to assure that socially desirable decisions are made.

Assurance that charges are made only when there is adequate evidence seems easier to achieve in practice than it is in theory. The traditional fear that an innocent person will be carried too far in the process seems rarely to be realized.

Two observations should be made, however. First, the primary reason why innocent persons are rarely prosecuted may be found in the nature of the institutions involved. The central figure in charging is the prosecutor, and for a variety of reasons prosecutors do not charge people they believe to be innocent. Prosecutors seem fully aware of their traditional obligation to protect the innocent, especially in the early stages of the criminal justice process before they have made a decision which represents a commitment of their resources.

Second, the very presence of other officials who could (and occasionally do) step in — the magistrate at the preliminary examination, for example — doubtlessly reinforces the generally cautious attitude of the prosecutor faced with a charging decision. The combination, then, of a desire to protect the innocent, a marked limitation on available resources, and the presence — if often in the background — of personnel such as magistrates and trial judges and juries explains why the truly innocent person is rarely prosecuted.

This is reflected most clearly in the elaborate controls that prosecutors in large offices impose on their assistants. But there is another aspect to the problem. It is more common to see a "guilty" person charged — that is, one who clearly did the forbidden act with the requisite state of mind — when that person may, in a practical sense, be immune to conviction because of conduct by police or even the prosecutor that is of doubtful legality or of clear illegality. That situation occurs primarily because of the "timing" or "sequence" in which various steps in the process occur. Prosecutors are understandably reluctant to forego convictions of obviously guilty persons — persons who may be extremely dangerous and on whose apprehension much time and money has been expended. In general the legality of the official conduct can be determined only after charging occurs. The motion to suppress illegally seized evidence occurs after the indictment or information is filed; the hearing on the voluntariness of a confession, or whether it was given without adequate notice of the defendant's rights to silence and to counsel, takes place after the trial has begun. When the defendant wins because the evidence necessary to convict him was obtained by an unconstitutional search and seizure, it is ordinarily clear that a guilty man will go free. And very frequently a confession is ruled inadmissable despite overwhelming indications of its truthfulness. I have not in this volume and I do not propose to argue here the merits of these Constitution-based rules: I do offer them as explanations of why some unconvictable persons are charged.

Since it is doubtful that unconvictable persons should be charged, proposals to restructure the system to permit early resolution of questions of admissibility of evidence are entitled to careful attention. It is clear that the problem is complex. I believe it to be one of the most significant problems disclosed by this study, worthy of major research efforts as well as some hard thinking by judges, lawyers, and legal scholars.

The second problem of general importance emphasized in this

study is the one commonly referred to as prosecutor discretion. It is no surprise to learn that discretion is an essential ingredient in a system as complex as the criminal justice system. And certainly it has long been recognized as proper that charging discretion should rest in the prosecutor. What is perhaps less widely known are (1) the range of alternatives available and (2) the lack of effective controls over that discretion.

The most striking characteristic of the range of alternatives is that so many of them are informal. They are, in effect, alternatives to charging in some instances, to conviction in others. But they have in common characteristics which, for a variety of reasons, often make them more attractive methods of disposition than carrying the criminal justice process further. Some, indeed many, alternatives illustrate partial use of the criminal process to accomplish social objectives regarded as desirable but for which society has failed to provide resources. Their variety in a system whose controls over exercise of discretion are rudimentary in fact, if more complex in theory, gives rise to concern over whether dispositions of persons who come into the system are selected on a fair and objective basis. Inequality of treatment is abhorrent when it is the result of deliberate malice or even lack of concern. It is, though to a lesser degree, also undesirable when the selection is dictated by fortuitous circumstances, or randomly. This danger then is the second major problem disclosed by this study. Like that of finding means for eliminating unconvictable persons from the system as soon as possible, it also needs a major research effort and some hard thinking

At least two approaches deserve consideration. Perhaps the most obvious is to extend the role of the defendant's counsel in the *charging* decision beyond his now recognized duty to guard the defendant's right to remain silent and to force the state to supply its own evidence. By presenting to the prosecutor all the alternatives available, by using his skills as an advocate, the defense counsel could contribute to a more rational and uniform basis for selecting charging alternatives as well as alternatives to charging. A second approach is to involve social work personnel in the charging process. Pre-charge social histories could be prepared.

With both proposals, however, it must be recognized that time once again plays a critical role. If the charging decision must be made quickly because of requirements imposed by the appellate judiciary or the legislature, the time for investigation by either lawyer or social worker may be too short to be of help. Still, charging can and does occur in stages. Perhaps the interval between the initial appearance and the preliminary examination, between the initial charge and the final charge, could be utilized. It is certain that some system which would insure uniformity of treatment in the charging process should be devised.

EPILOGUE TO THE SURVEY OF THE ADMINISTRATION OF CRIMINAL JUSTICE

Prosecution is the last volume to appear in the American Bar Foundation's Survey of the Administration of Criminal Justice in the United States. This volume and its four companions[1] are based on a field study that was originally conceived as a pilot inquiry to be followed by a more general investigation.[2] The "pilot" project has proven to be substantial in cost and long in duration. The cost of the field work and the writing cannot be accurately calculated, owing to large amounts of indirectly compensated labor in the enterprise and to changes in accounting practice over its life. However, the cost is certainly in excess of a million dollars. The duration of the project is a simple fact: twelve years from conception to completion. It has been a major undertaking.

Like Columbus's voyage, it was not planned quite that way. The miscalculation lay in underestimating the difficulty of describing and analyzing processes that were regarded as common legal knowledge, and the impossibility of doing so in a "definite" way. This miscalculation implied underestimation of the complexity of criminal law administration and a misapprehension of the function of research. These mistakes were made, it should be remembered, by a group of authorities preeminent in the field. Those who today think they have simple answers to our crime control problems might ponder that, for if the difficulties in studying the criminal law are great, those in reforming it are much greater still. Be that as it may, the Survey discovered how hard it is to make accurate straightforward statements about criminal law administration.

[1] Tiffany, McIntyre and Rotenberg, Detection of Crime: Stopping and Questioning, Search and Seizure, Encouragement and Entrapment (1967); LaFave, Arrest: The Decision to Take a Suspect into Custody (1965); Newman, Conviction: The Determination of Guilt or Innocence Without Trial (1966); Dawson, Sentencing (1969).

[2] See Foreword to McIntyre, ed., Law Enforcement in the Metropolis, American Bar Foundation (1967).

This discovery may well be the most important single finding of the Survey.[3] We now recognize that the goals of criminal law in the United States are ambivalent and its processes diffuse. We know that the system cannot be comprehended in a formula — "law and order" or otherwise — nor reconstituted in a stroke. We thus can infer, for example, that a fresh "war on crime" will be a failure: a campaign to control crime conceived on the model of a war effort will lack the durability, subtlety, and pervasiveness required to do the job. This is a truth that we are reluctant to acknowledge in these days of extremity, but one which we must face.

The difficulty with undertaking a "definitive" study of the administration of criminal justice is less apparent. There are at least three reasons why the goal is unachievable. First, to grasp the whole in sufficient detail in a short time would require a research team larger than can effectively be managed by conventional legal research institutions. The time allowed for such a study is relatively short because — and this is the second reason — the dynamics of social change are now so rapid that the phenomena of crime control change before they can be completely observed.[4] The third reason is more philosophical and more elusive: a study is "definitive" not simply because it is intrinsically persuasive but because it is accorded general acceptance in the community as being such. A study of a major legal problem is unlikely in its time to be accorded such acceptance precisely because a major legal problem represents an unresolved social or political problem, where little agreement can be expected.

Nevertheless, the study is "definitive" in the sense that it identified factors which other research confirms to be determinative or highly influential in the functioning of the criminal law system. These include:

The relatively wide discretion that officials have in enforcing the criminal law, which invites questions about the viewpoint and training of the officials;

The impossibly ambitious goals of our criminal law (public security and private civil liberty, uniformity and individualiza-

3 Anyone who doubts that it was a discovery should compare the technical literature on criminal law administration before the Survey and since.

4 The time dimension in science, in contrast, is glacial: for purposes of the science of physics, the universe is still as it was in the time of Newton, or of Cain. The same is true in biology. Such a time dimension may be the critical component of a "hard science."

tion, bodily safety and purity of morals), which invites questions about community purpose;

The rampant autonomy of law enforcement agencies, which invites questions about who the "authority" is that the public is supposed to have respect for;

The fact that achieving a high *conviction* rate is not necessarily the central aim of criminal law administration, which invites questions as to what its other purposes are. These findings and others suggest there are certain constants in American criminal law administration, for they correspond to findings made in studies before (e.g., the Wickersham Commission) and since (e.g., President Johnson's Crime Commission).

It is also the case, however, that many of the Survey's *findings* are now dated — notably those concerning the relationship between the police and the black communities. This obsolescence reflects a rapid social change — here in black self-consciousness — of the kind earlier referred to. The increasing speed of social change is itself a phenomenon of profound importance to criminal law, and for legal institutions generally.

The traditional legal and political procedures for controlling and reforming legal institutions require substantial time to operate. These procedures include: discussion and debate concerning what the law shall be; marshalling substantial popular and parliamentary majorities in favor of specific reform proposals; educating the responsible agencies in their new responsibilities; giving the agencies time to work out implementation by trial and error; making sporadic review of performance; and reopening discussion and debate over again. Under contemporary conditions by the time this cycle has run, the underlying situation has changed: the drug problem has moved from the inner city to the suburb; violence in the inner city has become a form of insurrection with corresponding political overtones; police training and recruitment has become a major problem of municipal administration and finance.

We have already seen this phenomenon in other domestic contexts. For example, new highways are overcrowded soon after completion, because while they were being built people made anticipatory adaptations of their transportation habits; the same is true of the schools. That this now appears true of criminal law administration may indicate critical shortcomings in the procedures for monitoring and modifying our laws and legal procedures generally. Many of the reforms suggested by the Survey will be inadequate because by the time the public accepts the need for them, the problems of criminal justice administration will have changed again.

Paradoxically, the rapid obsolescence of knowledge concerning legal procedures and institutions is the most compelling reason why research generating new knowledge is essential on a continuing basis. It would be nice if we could have complete and up-to-date comprehension of how our legal institutions work, were it possible. It is better to have incomplete or obsolescent knowledge, however, than to rely either on tradition (which consists of very obsolescent knowledge) or surmise. Put more emphatically, if our perception of how legal institutions actually work is not constantly corrected by fresh inquiry, the law as we have experienced it will go the way of the Bourbon constitution. Moreover, legal institutions are now constituted of so many parts and so obscured from public view that organized research is the only way to put them in general perspective. The method of "informed public opinion" and amateur parliamentary surveillance on which we have so long relied are passing into the legal reliquary along with the hue and cry.

The Survey generated still other products as well. It permitted us to see the machinery of criminal justice as a system. However disjointed, the various institutions that were the subject of the Survey have system-like attributes. Common to all of them is the offender, the man and his file who get moved through the maze. Common also is a recognition by the official participants that their activities are interrelated. Every operative in the system — policeman, prosecutor, judge, correction officer — one way or another takes into account the probable response of others in the system to whatever action or decision he undertakes.

Recognizing that the agencies of criminal law are a system is one thing; putting the lesson into practice is something else. The agencies of criminal justice are still balkanized, sealed off from each other by boundaries of legal jurisdiction, political allegiance and budgetary responsibility. There is almost complete lack of over-all management or coordination.[5] At the same time, performance specifications are pursued or imposed in one part of the system without reference to their impact on other parts of the system. The Due Process explosion emanating from the Supreme Court is a much-debated illustration, in which the police are required to increase the procedural quality of their performance

[5] In a few localities, specifically Los Angeles, some real advances have been made toward remedying this situation, but such efforts are exceptional.

without being provided the resources to do so. But the police insistence that the "clearance rate" is the relevant measure of their performance reflects a similarly incomplete analysis: the public is not served by a high solution rate simply on crimes that the police *know* about.

In broader perspective, the efforts to deal with the problem of crime are hampered by the tendency of each agency to pursue its own ends oblivious of the interests of other agencies and of the aggregate effect on criminal law administration. Now that Congress has at last interested itself seriously in the problem of criminal law administration, we see it continuing to make the same kind of mistake. The Omnibus Crime Control and Safe Streets Act of 1968[6] contemplates massive augmentation of police resources without corresponding increases in the capacity of prosecutorial offices, criminal courts, and correction agencies to handle the new "business" that increased police forces presumably will generate. These kinks sooner or later may be ironed out, but there will be a good deal of distress and confusion before that goal is realized.

The study also permits us to see that the administration of criminal justice is a "system" from the point of view of its "customers" — the criminal offender, the potential criminal offender, and the public-at-large. The aim of the criminal law is to protect society from serious domestic evils. This goal is achieved in part by the moral condemnation implicit in criminal prohibitions and in part by punishing those who violate the prohibitions. But there is an educational and demonstrative function of the criminal law system beyond these measures. Law enforcement officials are models — and in this sense teachers — of what proper behavior ought to be. This is the simple, but profoundly important, basis for responsible concern about "police brutality" each unnecessary use of the billy-club, each racial slur, each instance of officiousness, is a lesson of some kind to someone The lesson to be learned from such official miscreancy is surely not one that we want taught.

At the time of the Survey, there seemed to be little overt official brutality in the communities that were studied, testimony to the efforts of the agencies to do a professional job. That was probably true in most parts of the country at the time and, again with some important qualifications, appears to be substantially true today. However, the incidence of what might be called

6 82 Stat. 197 (1968).

"psychic" brutality is widespread. A good deal of this is attributable to the personal and cultural characteristics of people who are drawn into law enforcement work, and some of the callousness is no doubt the consequence of the abrasions they suffer while performing very tough and exasperating jobs. But the Survey indicated something else for which society has to take responsibility: at dozens of points, with a repetitiveness that settled into monotony, the system was ignorant, indifferent, or abrupt with the people with whom it was dealing simply because there were too many cases, involving too many people, being handled by two few officials with too little time to do a decent job.

It is not merely that the police, the prosecutors, and the magistrates have to make rapid decisions on the basis of inadequate information and insufficient reflection. *Even where the objective circumstances would have permitted some kind of pause, the resources were not available to make use of it.* It is now notorious that the policeman's arrest decision is a complicated choice made on the spur of the moment. But the phenomenon repeats itself in the prosecutor's office, where the files whiz by the hasty perusal of a junior deputy, and go past a senior deputy at even faster rate. It repeats itself again in court where the cases are served up to an overworked magistrate for drumhead treatment. What kind of a system of justice is it where the aggregate professional involvement in the average case, including police, prosecutor, magistrate, and probation officer, is probably less than five hours and where the final judgment that society makes — the hearing in court — takes less than five minutes? And what shall we say of anti-riot procedures that pit police against crowds too large for them to handle with non-forcible techniques? In light of these facts, the "breakdown of law and order" is not so much anarchistic conspiracy as an accumulation of public neglect. As soon as we can abandon the search for scapegoat — whether the police, the Supreme Court, youth unrest or the black man — we may get down to the serious business of organizing a system for the prevention of violence that will really work over the long pull.

Another contribution of the Survey may be used to close this epilogue. The study has helped the legal profession become more aware of the weaknesses in criminal justice, the law's central institution. The criminal law is the pillar of the administration of justice, representing at the same time the most serious of society's legal concerns and the most sensitive of its legal processes.

The legal profession has always claimed a special responsibility for it. What the Survey has told the legal profession is no doubt what Justice Jackson, who inspired the study, had suspected it would: that the real significance of the criminal law is not so much its doctrinal refinement but its "delivered value" — its practical reality, day-on-day, year-on-year, at the level of enforcement.[7] In this perspective, the processes of statutory reform and appellate judicial law-making appear as guidelines for social action rather than action itself. The question thus implied is whether, having propounded a criminal law which we say we are committed to, we are prepared to take the public action that will make it a reality. It is pleasant for us to moralize through the medium of the criminal law. It may be more appropriate, however, for us to ask what kind of social protection is really worth having. Let us hope the legal profession can help our society confront that question.

7 See Jackson, Criminal Justice: The Vital Problem of the Future, 39 A.B.A.J. 743 (1953).

Index